GET READY! GET SET! GO!

GET READY!

GET SET!

GO!

*A European Travel Guide
for Young People*

STAN RAIFF

Illustrated by William Accorsi

DOUBLEDAY & COMPANY, INC., GARDEN CITY, NEW YORK   1970

71108

CONTENTS

THANK YOU

My sincere appreciation to the twenty-one nations of the European Travel Commission which sparked my interest in travel and, in particular, those people and offices that assisted in the writing of this guide: Rudolf Mattesich, Christine Bergthaller (Austrian National Tourist Office, New York); Dr. Johanna Kral (Fremdenverkehrstelle der Stadt Wien, Vienna); Axel Dessau, Ilma Brummé, Per Arman (Danish National Travel Office, New York); Jeanne Steinmetz (Danish Tourist Board, Copenhagen); Jørn Erik Schreiner (Odense Turistforening, Odense); Myron Clement, Adela Lindeman (French Government Tourist Office, New York); Nicole Garnier, Christiane Mulot (Commissariat General au Tourisme, Paris); Ruth Aldendorff, Karl Kumrow (German National Tourist Office, New York), and their public relations counselor John Fanelli (Stephan Goerl Associates, New York); Otto Hiebl (Fremdenverkehrsamt, Munich); Ed Antrobus, Helen Newman, Jennifer Ogilvie (British Travel, New York); Sean White (Irish Tourist Board, New York); Alan Glynn, Stíofán Hilliard (Dublin Regional Tourism Organization, Ltd., Dublin); Josephine Inzerillo (Italian Government Travel Office, New York); Franco Tancredi (Ente Provincial Per il Tourismo, Florence); Eveline Boon (Netherlands National Tourist Office, New York);

Thank You

Max Lehmann (Swiss National Tourist Office, New York); Walter Rösli (Official Tourist Office, Berne). A special thanks to Catalina Sodero's thoughtful interest, Patricia Greenler's observations of Vienna, Claudia White's and Shelley Davidson's valuable help, Lucille Hoshabjian's knowledgeable research, and to my editor, Maria Polushkin, whose encouragement made this book a reality.

This or any other guidebook directing visitors to places to see, things to buy, food to eat, etc. is subject to changes relating to hours, prices, and other such matters. All information was accurate at the time this book was written but it may be a good idea to check when you arrive in each city.

INTRODUCTION

GET READY for your European adventure, something you will long remember. At least eight weeks before your departure date read the chapters that apply to the cities you'll be visiting. Although each chapter is complete in itself, you may want more background information beforehand. The local tourist offices are a good source of material, including city maps. The names and addresses are listed on page 489. Some of the activities suggested in the guide require that you write in advance to take advantage of them. Many places not normally open to travelers can be visited by readers of *Get Ready! Get Set! Go!* and their companions. When you write to make your arrangements be sure to mention that you read about them in this guide. Allow at least six to eight weeks for a reply. If you have not

received an answer before you go, upon arrival you can telephone or ask your hotel for
assistance. Preplanning is half the fun and
ensures you'll get the most out of the limited
time you have in each city.

GET SET   by putting yourself in a European frame of
mind. The hotels listed are selected for their
European atmosphere or their closeness to
museums, parks, or other places not requiring
adult supervision. The restaurants chosen give
you a feeling for the types of places and
different foods eaten in each country. Euro-
peans enjoy long, leisurely meals; share the
experience with them and also try the different
dishes no matter how unusual they look. The
shops and price ranges listed will assist you
in planning how much you can spend in each
city. Once the budget has been agreed upon
by everyone, stick to it. Try not to cram too
much into each day. The best part of traveling
is taking time to allow things to happen, a walk
in the park, a picnic lunch, or a chance soccer
game.

GO   and get to know a different way of life. (You'll
also find many similarities to America.) Euro-
peans, whether young or old, tend to be a
little formal. They are not likely to tell you
everything about themselves in one meeting.
Slowly, as you get acquainted, the friendship
will grow and with it mutual understanding
and knowledge about your host and his coun-

try. And in a short while you'll find you're getting to know the European's Europe, the real reason this guide was written.

"Bon voyage" (French)
"Buon viaggio" (Italian)
"Gute Reise" (German)
"Goede Reis" (Dutch)
"Happy journey," or as the Irish say—
"Go n eíri an bóthar leat"
"May the road rise with you."
And when you return, let me know the highlights of your trip so that we may pass them on to other young travelers.

1. AMSTERDAM

A Little Dutch Treat

"Welkom" to Amsterdam, a city old and new, built on one hundred islands with six hundred bridges over one hundred canals and the capital of an amazing country below sea level, the Netherlands (lowlands). Most nations boast about their bigness—the widest highways, the tallest buildings, the longest bridges, the largest hotels. The Dutch take pride in what they have accomplished with their neat, tiny "homeland by the sea." Half the people live less than 25 miles from the sea and no place is more than 130 miles inland. You can drive the entire length of the country, 180 miles, in less than four hours.

Yet the Netherlands would be even smaller had it been left to nature. The Dutch have won nearly half the area from the water. The reclaimed parts are now pumped dry, but are still below sea level. The work of draining land started in the thirteenth century and continues today. The excess water is pumped into canals and eventually sent to the rivers and the sea. Some of the power used in pumping is provided by windmills, which were first used about 450 years ago. Today, however, most of the power comes from modern plants.

Many people refer to the entire country as Holland, the name of the two most heavily populated provinces, which include the cities of Amsterdam, Rotterdam, and The Hague. Holland means "hollow land" or a place without solid soil. Part of the original coastline was indeed so "hollow" that medieval travelers said they couldn't see where the sea ended and the land began. The proud citizens point out that "God made the world, but the Dutch made the Netherlands."

Constantly fighting the sea has taught the Dutch to work well together, overcoming all disasters and hardships. They take pride in a job well done, in being thrifty, in keeping their houses clean, and in making their cities, towns, and countryside attractive. For visitors, Holland's diminutive size becomes an endless source of pleasant surprises. Among your many discoveries in Amsterdam will be the narrowest house, the skinniest restaurant, and the smallest coin.

A BEGINNING THAT STARTED SMALL

About a thousand years ago some fishermen put their boats on a sandbank where the Amstel River flowed into the Y River, then an arm of the Zuiderzee. These fishermen prospered, were joined by others, and built a dam across the Amstel as part of a sea wall that protected their village. The original houses of Amsterdam stood on the Dam Square, where the Royal Palace now stands. Three centuries later, the village became a trading center. In 1482 it was walled. Then, due in part to the decline of the port of Antwerp (Belgium), Amsteldam (Dam on the Amstel), later known as Amsterdam, grew in power. By the seventeenth century its ships were seen in every major city in the world, its flags flew over trading companies on every continent.

Water was one of the reasons for the city's development. The first canal was mainly a moat. As the city expanded, a second, third, and fourth ring of canals was built until it was possible for cargo from the Indies to unload from the ship right into the heart of the city. Many of the houses' upper stories were used for storing tea, spices, silks, and furs. Some of these storerooms can still be seen. The heavy beams jutting out from the top gables of these houses need only a rope and men to pull it to create the atmosphere of the past. Imagine these patrician mansions populated by the silver-buckled burghers (businessmen) whose portraits you can see in the museums as painted by the great Rembrandt and Frans Hals.

Besides being a source of transportation, the canals have served as a means of fortification. Twice during the seventeenth century the city's locks were opened and the surrounding countryside flooded to defend Amsterdam from the attacks of Prince William II and Louis XIV. But in 1795 the flooding strategy failed, the temperature fell, the water froze, and Napoleon's cavalry was able to ride across the ice and capture the city for France.

Amsterdam today, lively with barrel organs and flower-brightened streets, busy with shipping and commerce, is a bustling city for you to enjoy.

THE DUTCH BY WATER

Get acquainted with the city by taking a glass-roofed sightseeing boat on a tour of the canals—a trip lasting one hour and a quarter. Glide past old houses with their gabled roofs and building façades designed like stairs, a neck, an upright triangle, or a bell. Since the buildings were originally unnumbered, the distinctive façades in front of the roofs were used as a means of identifying where you lived. By the seventeenth century numbers were introduced as a better method of knowing who lived where. Unlike other European cities Amsterdam was built by merchants and businessmen rather than royalty. There is only one royal palace in all of Amsterdam. Often the merchant's warehouse was on the top floor and his family lived below. You're not getting woozy if you think the buildings appear to be leaning forward slightly; they were so constructed to prevent cargo from smashing against the houses when hoisted to the storerooms. The houses are narrow by design. Taxes were calculated by the width of the building. By law, none of the exteriors can be changed from their seventeenth-century appearance. Today many of the buildings are occupied by business firms.

Farther along on your ride you'll see the fifteenth-century Schreierstoren (Tower of Tears), where wives of Dutch sailors said their tearful goodbyes. Hendrik Hudson set sail from here in his ship the *Half Moon* on April 4, 1609. His explorations led him to what is now New York and to the river that bears his name. Be sure to spot the Ropemakers' Ditch, considered the tiniest canal, and the Magere Brug (Skinny Bridge), very much like the ones you'll see in paintings of the artist Van Gogh.

Finally, you're out in the huge harbor of Amsterdam, going past freighters with faraway names, past tremendous ships lifted from the sea for cleaning, and past the merchant school boats where young boys learn to become seasoned sailors. The canal and harbor tours leave from Damrak daily every ten minutes, the cost 2.50 guilders (70 cents). In summer there are nighttime tours when the seventeenth-century canals are aglow with little lights from the over one thousand moored houseboats. Due to the housing shortage some people choose to live in these attractive floating homes, many permanently attached to the pier.

THE DUTCH BY LAND

One of the best ways of "going Dutch" into the heart of Amsterdam is on a bicycle. You can rent one from the shops at the Central Station, and you're off. The cost is as little as 2 guilders (56 cents). This is a city of bicycles with high steering bars, which allow the rider to sit tall in his seat. You'll see nuns and priests, tiny babies (not alone, of course), men reading newspapers, and smartly dressed ladies in high heels energetically peddling along. Everywhere you look there are bicycles in all sizes and colors, parked in front of homes or by shops, on trains or crammed into restaurant cloakrooms. There is no doubt about it, the bicycle is *the* most popular way of getting around. There are half as many bicycles as there are people, there are special bicycle traffic signs and separate bike paths running along major highways. A popular Dutch saying is "Only people under two or over ninety do not ride bicycles."

But if cycling is not one of your favorite activities, Amsterdam is also great for walking or for riding in modern streetcars. Don't be surprised if you see an Amsterdammer chasing after the streetcar waving something in his hand. He is trying to mail a letter in the red mailbox attached to the back of the car. The mail is emptied when it arrives at the railroad station. The fare for your streetcar ride is 50 Dutch cents (14 cents), but less expensive if you buy a seven-trip ticket, 3 guilder 25 (91 cents). The same ticket can be used twice within forty-five minutes for no extra charge.

Now let's be on our way.

The city was carefully laid out almost like a delicately woven spider's web. It all began where the river Amstel flowed into the Y River, almost like the capital letter "T." Where the stem and the crossbar meet was the central port, where ships tied up and people would stroll directly to the boats. In the late 1800s the city built a narrow island by sinking thousands of wood piles into the water, and then placed the railroad station atop the piles. The square in front of the station was named Damrak. Many of your excursions will begin here.

By the seventeenth century the old city was suffering severe growing pains and could not hold any more people. So the enterprising burghers started their spider's web by mapping out a system of broad, sweeping canals that form a series of semi-circles around the "old city" and eventually empty into the open sea. The innermost ring is called the SINGEL; the outside one, the SINGELGRACHT ("gracht" means canal). Between the two farthest rings are the HERENGRACHT (Lords' Canal), the KEIZERSGRACHT (Emperor's Canal), the PRINSENGRACHT (Princes' Canal) and the LIJNBAANSGRACHT (Ropewalk Canal). Like the spider's web or spokes of a wheel the streets ("straat" or "weg") begin from the "old city." Acquaint yourself with the names of the spokes, learn the order of the rings, and you'll be pretty sure of not losing your way.

The Barrel Organ's here. Strike up the band!

Listen for a joyful sound perhaps in the Dam Square or on another street in Amsterdam. It comes from an overgrown music box eight to fifteen feet long, decorated with brightly painted mechanical figures. The dainty nymphlike doll strikes a tinkling bell, the Harlequin clangs the bass drum. The strange but delightful music makes people dance in the streets and throw coins from windows.

The barrel organ is part of the Dutch scene. People are anxious to keep it alive. Today there are only about eighty but they have been given new leases on life by one man and his family. His name is Gijsbert Perlee. The Perlees themselves can rarely be found standing on the street enjoying the lively melodies from the organs. They are busy in their crowded workshops keeping all parts of the organs in top performing condition (carving pipes, puttying angelic wings, repainting faded scenery, replacing old dolls and puppets). And they do thousands of other jobs so that the barrel organs will not fall into disrepair, as have the scores of others that once performed throughout Europe.

Mr. Perlee spends most of his working time, about sixty hours a week, cutting new and old favorite melodies on paper "signed" by one of the four people in Holland capable of writing in this musical form. The best composer is a judge who punctures holes in long rolls of paper in his free time because he wants to keep the art alive.

The barrel organs are rolled out for their husky men to rent. Round every corner they go, turning the wheel-sized crank that makes this gigantic music box pour forth a mixture of drums, pipes, and cymbals that play a waltz, jazz, a round dance, and sometimes a popular song.

Those who are especially curious about this brand of music-making can visit the **Perlee workshop** at 119 Westerstraat. But when you see these masterpieces, please don't call them by the ordinary street variety name of "hurdy-gurdies."

A visit to **Anne Frank's Home** at 263 Prinsengracht will be a sad but memorable experience. In this building a young Jewish girl of fourteen spent two years hiding from the Nazis during World War II. Along with her parents, her older sister, and family friends she crowded into the secret hiding place protected by a Dutch family. Finally the Gestapo broke in and sent them to die in the gas chamber. Only Otto Frank, Anne's father, succeeded in escaping. After he returned to Amsterdam he discovered the diary she had written during the time of their self-imprisonment. The book was published and young and old people alike still read this brave girl's moving story.

The building is open weekdays 9 A.M. to 4 P.M. You'll walk behind the bookcase hiding a staircase to the upper apartment, then into empty rooms where the family stayed. On the walls you'll see aging photographs of Anne's favorite movie stars and world personalities. Downstairs don't miss some of the inspiring work of the Anne Frank Foundation, which has built a meeting center for youth from all nations.

Canal mansions do not have a spare inch wasted, but don't be mislead by the narrow fronts. The buildings are usually quite deep. Wooden stairways with rope banisters lead to cozy but very small rooms. The stairs are so steep and narrow that furniture has to be moved through the windows. The windows are first taken out and the furniture is lifted up on strong ropes suspended from the beams.

Rooms are spotlessly clean. The colored tile fireplaces are sometimes covered in gray- or brown-streaked porcelain squares so that the smoke will not ruin them. Rugs are carefully placed on the table for guests to enjoy the intricate woven patterns. The bedrooms are normally tiny but compact. Washbasins are carefully placed under or over a piece of furniture to keep them out of the way.

Delicate lace curtains at the windows are always pulled to the side. When asked, the Dutch say this is because a governor long ago had threatened to levy a tax on all houses that had lace curtains. The ladies were determined to have their dainty curtains in the windows, so to spite the authorities they hung them but kept them parted. Today the curtains are never closed, but to display the immaculate cleanliness of the homes, not to defy local authorities.

There are two canal houses you should visit and one you should admire from the outside.

The Toneelmuseum (Theater Museum), 168 Herengracht, is open daily 10 A.M. to 5 P.M. except Sunday, when it opens at 1 P.M. Fee: 50 Dutch cents (14 cents).

Besides lots of stage items, old props, costumes, scene models, posters, and sketches to look at, there is the typical Dutch interior decor. Marble floors and walls, frescoes, and little plaster figures are all reminders of another century.

The Willet-Holthuysen Museum, 605 Herengracht, is open daily 9:30 A.M. to 5 P.M. except Sunday, when it opens at 1 P.M. Fee: 50 Dutch cents (14 cents).

This is an elegant old Amsterdam house with examples of glassware, china, gold, ivory, and an old sea chest. What precious treasure could the strongbox have once contained?

The house of Mr. Tripp's coachman, the narrowest in Amsterdam, is at 26 Kloveniersburgwal. It was built for the coachman by a wealthy seventeenth-century merchant named Tripp who lived in a broad mansion on the other side of the canal. The coachman had been overheard saying, "I'd be happy if I had a house as wide as Mr. Tripp's front door." So Mr. Tripp made his wish come true. Rumor has it that the coachman's sheep dog had to learn to wag his tail up and down instead of sideways because of the size of the building.

Gapers are for gaping. It's an odd name for equally odd-looking statues. These are the brightly painted oversized carvings that hang above "apothekers" (pharmacists). Each figure's wide-open mouth, almost as if it were yelling, is in that position for a reason. Long before most people in the Netherlands could read, back in the Middle Ages, walking advertisers paraded the streets to encourage the sale of spices used to cure illnesses. The herb doctor and salesmen would wander through the market places with Moors or boys dressed as jesters to attract attention for their exotic products. The gaudily dressed boys would ring bells to gather large crowds. Then they would stick out their tongues to prove their good health, which they enjoyed thanks to the excellence of the herb products. When the herb merchants decided to move into permanent shops the boys were replaced by the wooden-headed figures hanging near the door. A particularly interesting gaper is located at 4 Wijde Heisteeg, off the Singel.

Windmills do speak. Do you doubt it? In the early days, the positions of the arms were used to send messages. Their whirling was an important source of power for producing products and keeping the country safe. Windmills ground wheat, sawed lumber, made flour, and dredged the land to keep it safe and dry.

When the country changed to electricity, the windmills lost their importance. In fact, these days there are windmills which are better talkers than workers. Here's a key to their language. It is important to understand that the sails of a mill always turn from right to left, the opposite of a clock. If the upper sail stops before it reaches the highest point it is expressing joy, perhaps the announcement of an engagement, marriage, or birth of a new baby. When the sail passes the highest point and stops it means sad news. The miller's family is ill or unhappy. Arms in a cross-like position signifies all is calm but arms at a 45-degree angle means closed, not working.

Windmill sails are decorated at times with Cupids, arrows, banners, and bows to enhance a happy occasion such as a wedding. These sturdy wooden workers also served the Dutch during World War II. The setting of the sails formed a code which warned of the enemy's approach.

Throughout the country there are 991 windmills left from the original 9000. In Amsterdam there is one working windmill, named **De Bloem** (The Flower), at 465 Haarlemmerweg. You can tour it during the summer months. As you enter you don a flour apron. The miller and his family personally greet you. You then climb narrow wooden steps up to the ledge of the windmill, underneath its gigantic vanes and sails. You'll see firsthand all the inner workings of the mill. As you leave, you're presented with your own bag of flour, almost as if you have earned it yourself.

After your visit, you can dazzle your friends back home. Tell them you've learned to speak "windmill," the one language that's definitely not taught in school. For more information about other windmills throughout the Netherlands write to De Hol-

landsche Molen (The Dutch Windmill Association), 9 Regu-
liersgracht, Amsterdam, or telephone 020-38703.

DUTCH EXPLORATIONS

By 1600 the Dutch were anxious to expand their borders.
Two firms were formed to carry on trade and establish colonies
on far-flung continents. The Dutch West India Company went
to Africa and the Americas. In 1623 the directors planned the
founding of Nieuw Amsterdam on the tip of an island called
"Manhattes." A few years later the first group of people settled
there and purchased most of the island from the native Indians
for the value of 60 guilders ($16). Later the colony was taken
by the English and named New York, after the Duke of York.
A marker at 75 Haarlemmerstraat near the train station shows
you where it all began. The building is now an orphanage.
The Dutch East India Company reached the high point of its
success during the seventeenth century as it developed the island
of Java into one of the wealthiest of all colonial possessions. The
Company extended its trade into China and Japan and other
places in the Far East.

The Tropenmuseum (Tropical Museum), 2 Linnaeusstraat,
is open weekdays 10 A.M. to 5 P.M., (4 P.M. in winter), Saturday and Sunday from 1 P.M. Fee: 50 Dutch cents (14 cents)
for adults and half price for children.

Here is an explorer's dream come true, an entire museum devoted to life in the tropical areas of the world. One room is
furnished with the desks, chairs, and paintings of the Dutch
East India Company. Other rooms have push-button cases to
show costumes, dwelling places, puppets, canoes, totems, priceless native jewelry, and practically every aspect of tropical life.
Another section displays a collection of exotic musical instru-

ments. Sundays at 3 P.M. songs and dances of the tropics are performed at no extra admission charge.

The Maritime Museum, 57 Corn. Schuytstraat, is open weekdays 10 A.M. to 4 P.M., Sunday from 1 P.M. Fee: 50 Dutch cents (14 cents), half price for children.

This museum presents another chance to satisfy those who have a severe case of "sea fever."

THE GOLDEN AGE—DUTCH ART

The seventeenth century saw Holland dominate the seas and become one of the powerful nations of Europe. Trading brought great sums of money to the merchants, who were anxious for neighboring countries to realize the beauty of the Dutch landscape and the prosperity of its city life. Civic pride was strong and the working guilds effective. All these factors influenced the artists' paintings. They created portraits of men and places, citizens' habits, squares, the countryside, and the sea and sky. The artists had to keep in mind the wishes of their patrons, who, having acquired wealth and position, wanted small, realistic paintings to hang on the walls of their compact houses as a permanent record of their prosperity. What the artists finally painted sometimes represented a compromise between art and commerce. But out of this "Golden Age" come some of the greatest masterpieces ever put on canvas.

The Rijksmuseum (National Museum), 42 Stadhouderskade, is open 10 A.M. to 5 P.M. Monday to Saturday, Sunday from 1 P.M. Fee: 50 Dutch cents (14 cents).

FRANS HALS (1580–1666) has been called the first modern painter and is best remembered for his portraits. He knew how to capture on canvas the quick and often jovial expressions of his subjects. Fantastically adept, he could turn out a portrait in an hour, everyone from a civil guard to a town drunkard. On the second floor there's a room with several superb portraits by Hals. "The Merry Toper" is one of his best-known pieces. With a few quick strokes of his brush he fashions lace, velvet, satin, and metal. The hands and face tell a whole story by themselves.

REMBRANDT VAN RIJN (1606–1669) had a totally different way of using paint than did Hals; he also refused to go along with the ideas of the Dutch burghers, who failed to understand his imagination. He left the story of his life in a series of self-portraits (sixty pictures) ranging from a happy youth to the tragic old man painted before he died. For eleven years Rembrandt was the most popular painter in Amsterdam and could command huge sums for his work. He was financially careless, lavishing jewels on his wife, buying paintings and antiques irresponsibly. In addition, he lost interest in painting the exact-likeness portraits which his solid Dutch patrons were seeking.

The four rooms leading to Rembrandt's great painting, "The Night Watch," contain pictures done by the master's best pupils. Then, at last, the famous painting. This is its story. In 1639 Rembrandt was asked to paint "The Company of Captain Frans Banning Cocq" on the occasion of the visit of Maria de Medici, widowed queen of France, to Amsterdam, when the civic guard acted as her escort. The captain and each of the sixteen men had given money to Rembrandt so that he would show them as exemplary men of military bearing. But when Rembrandt delivered the painting, the men discovered that they were depicted in a disorderly fashion leaving the armory in the middle of the day. Rembrandt's use of light clearly showed those who were setting out, but those in the doorway were left in darkness. And worst of all, a dwarf girl and ten reservists who had not paid for their portraits were included in the picture. Angered guards sawed off both ends of the picture and placed it in an anteroom which was warmed by an open fire. By the eighteenth century soot had grown so thick on the painting that everyone believed it was a night scene, and it came to be called "The Night Watch."

Glowing light and shadow are Rembrandt's special talent. The light is so unusually warm that it seems to shine with an inner radiance and has come to be known as "Rembrandt's light." Besides the outstanding paintings, don't miss the famous trophies of explorers and naval heroes and a delightful doll's house.

The Rembrandthuis (The House of Rembrandt), 4 Joden-breestraat, is open 10 A.M. to 5 P.M. weekdays, 1 to 4 P.M. Sunday. Fee: 75 Dutch cents (21 cents), half price for children.

The interior of the house is refurnished in the furniture style of Rembrandt's time. At the age of twenty-six he married a stout, attractive blonde, Saskia van Uijlenburgh, the daughter of a wealthy man. Her dowry amounted to 40,000 guilders $11,200. Eight years of lavish living followed, climaxed by the purchase of this very expensive house. He had to buy it on credit, incurring heavy debts which he never succeeded in paying.

Refusing to compromise with the burghers' ideals, Rembrandt had to move to a poorer section of town. Soon his wife died of tuberculosis, leaving a sickly son, Titus. Rembrandt hired a housekeeper to take care of his family. At the age of fifty the artist was declared bankrupt, his house was sold, and all his paintings were auctioned. The housekeeper and Titus set up an art shop for him. When his housekeeper died Rembrandt became completely dependent upon his son, who unhappily died before him. At the end of his life Rembrandt went to his grave in poverty, almost unknown.

In the Rembrandthuis are displayed more than 250 of Rembrandt's etchings (the largest single collection of them in the world), many sketches, his etching press, and some of his actual copper plates.

Etching is a unique process of printing pictures or designs. The word is from the Dutch "etsen," to eat, and that is exactly what happens. A copper plate is first covered with wax or varnish. Using several different needles the etcher cuts his design freely, exposing the metal below but not cutting into the surface. An acid is poured onto the plate and this etches, or bites, the exposed parts of the metal for a short time. Ink is then thoroughly worked into the bitten furrows. A sheet of moist paper is passed over the plate, and together the two are put through a press. Just the ink from the furrows appears in the drawing, making it look like a pencil or crayon sketch. Only a limited number of good prints can be pulled from each plate so some etchers destroy the plates after carefully numbering the prints they have made. Rembrandt was one of the greatest of etchers.

THE DUTCH AT WORK

Diamond cutting is an important industry. **A. Van Moppes and Zoon,** 2 Albert Cuypstraat, conducts free tours from 9 A.M. to noon and 1 to 5 P.M. weekdays, and from 9 A.M. to noon Saturday.

It's like magic! A plain-looking, misshapen lump of stone arrives, is carefully cut and polished and turned into a sparkling gem. The finishing actually determines the price of the stone more than the stone itself. First, the diamond is closely scrutinized, sometimes for as long as six months, before a single mark is made. The cutter has nerves of steel, for his decision can make the difference between a precious jewel or a mass of glass splinters. Then, after it is cut, a long time is spent polishing even the smallest stone so that all sides are of equal size and luster. This means that a "brilliant cut" (a diamond with fifty-eight sides) or a "single cut" (a stone with sixteen sides) might be placed on the polishing wheel over one hundred times before the desired shine is achieved.

The history of the famous diamonds cut or polished in Amsterdam reads almost like a mystery story. The Cullinan, believed to be the world's largest stone, was sent to King Edward VII as a gift. It arrived as a dull-looking lump because it was much less expensive to purchase this stone in the rough than to buy it polished. It took Amsterdamer Josef Asscher to bring out the beauty of this stone and to reveal its over 3000 carats (units of weight), which were more than fit for a king. The stone was split into various shapes and sizes and all are part of the British crown jewels today. The Koh-i-noor, at 106 carats, is supposed to be the third largest diamond in the world. It was refashioned for Queen Victoria by two Amsterdam cutters who were sent to London to serve Her Majesty.

As you tour a diamond-cutting factory you'll see a little museum which contains paste copies of the Cullinan and the Koh-i-noor and smaller stones, including those which have to be examined under a microscope. You don't need to be a millionaire to enjoy your visit. All you really need is some time and you'll have one of the richest experiences of your life.

School voor Banketbakkers (Confectioners' School), 220–222 Webautstraat, is open 2 to 4 P.M. Wednesday and by special appointment other weekdays. The hours are limited because this museum-library is used to train young people for the baker's trade.

Can a cookie mold become a sweetheart's valentine, a membership card, or a news photograph? It could if it were a Dutch antique "koekplank." That is the name of the old-fashioned wooden cookie molds which today are used for wall decoration instead of baking.

Membership in the Dutch bakers' guild used to require applicants to hand-carve the koekplank. With this mold spicy cookies called "speculaas" are prepared for the Feast of St. Nikolaas (Santa Claus). Since "speculaas" comes from words meaning mirror and St. Nikolaas, many early bakers shaped their cookies to look like the saint, people from the Bible like Adam and Eve, or Christmas figures. Among the other popular subjects were figures of ordinary people which sweethearts exchanged as tokens of their love. Some cookies were designed to depict news events of the day. All of these curious molds are carefully arranged in this rare museum.

Along with the large collection of koekplanks are other interesting items. There is an eighteenth-century pressure cooker that will show you where the modern Dutch oven began. Also an oven light that is thought to date from the twelfth century and looks exactly like Aladdin's lamp, and a huge collection of over one hundred thousand menus, the earliest dating from Napoleon's time.

See a floating flower market. Walk along the Spui to the Singel, where you will find streets crowded with colorful flowers of all kinds. You can climb aboard the barges moored to the cobbled quay and join the Dutch as they shop for flowers and shrubs. Being close to flowers is a Dutch way of life. Almost every house has its cheerful garden, even if it is only a two-by-four plot, or pots and vases filled with tastefully arranged blossoms. In the spring the Dutch will bicycle for hours to see the tulip and hyacinth fields in bloom, and return home laden with garlands and bouquets. Perhaps this great love of flowers is a way of dressing up the flatness of the land and giving it a bright look.

To see really elaborate floral arrangements visit the shop called **Aziatische Bloemsierkunst** along the quay at 506 Singel.

FUN—YOUNG DUTCH STYLE

Elleboog Circus at 169 Egelantierstraat is a pint-sized showcase for performers seven to fifteen who do everything in staging and operating a three-ring show, even to taking the parts of the animals. It started in 1948 as an idea to keep young people in poor neighborhoods from being bored and getting into trouble. In an old workshop, simple tightrope walking and acrobatics were taught to children who were climbing roofs. Soon everyone was excited about the fledgling big top and it was recognized by the government. The official clubhouse was rebuilt from an abandoned sugar factory. The members knocked down walls, moved staircases, painted, sewed, and created a comfortable place of their own. Even the name "Elleboog" came from the members of the troupe. They thought that since the big-time national Swiss circus was called "Knie," meaning knee, then this smaller-sized version should be named for a smaller joint, the elbow.

At the performance, you'll be amazed to see very young people, six years old, balancing on high-rising unicycles, and you'll marvel at the grace of the donkeys, kangaroos, penguins, giraffes, bears, lions, and worms. Boys juggle flagpoles on their chins, walk on their hands, handle stilts, and perform other feats that surprise everyone. The company performs in various places throughout the Netherlands and all Europe. It is best to call 020-65822 ahead of time to find out their schedule.

Children's Theater. Free puppet shows are set up in the middle of Dam Square Wednesday and Saturday afternoons and are presented throughout the afternoon. Although the show is in Dutch, you'll see young people of all nationalities enjoying the antics of the comic puppets.

The Rialto Theater on the Ceintuuerbaan (telephone 72-34-88) has a special Wednesday afternoon children's movie.

The Artis Zoo is located on the Plantage Kerklaan and can be reached by trains 7, 9, and 10 and by bus 11. It is open from 9 A.M. until dusk.

The "World of Darkness" building is the first "nocturnal house" especially constructed for animals who usually sleep all day and are active at night. It is light enough for you to see the animals in full action—monkeys, flying bats, flying squirrels, anteaters, owls, and Nieuw Guinea cuscuses (similar to kangaroos).

The rest of the zoo has many all-time favorites and some rare animals. Murugam, an elephant presented by former Prime Minister of India Nehru remains the most popular. Barbar, a twelve-year-old gorilla, is a close second. Sam, an orangutan, is frequently sought for his "lovely face," while "Auntie," a Mississippi alligator, is looked upon as the old lady. She was old when she arrived in 1919.

Some animals are not to be seen in captivity anywhere else in the world. Such a rarity is a female Bawean deer, from an island near Java. The zoo people say there is no other animal like it alive today. On the rare list too are three owl-faced monkeys, three Przhevalski's horses, seven white-tailed gnu, two hedgehog tenrecs, two snow leopards, and three pygmy hippopotamuses.

Near the zoo is an equally famous **Aquarium,** where the electric eels are stimulated into lighting up a string of bulbs. It is at 53 Plantage Middenlaan and is open 9 A.M. to 6 P.M.

TINY TOURS FROM AMSTERDAM

Each of these side trips can be completed in one day, allowing enough time to return to your hotel by evening. Each had been chosen to put you closer "in touch with the Dutch."

Alkmaar and Schagen. Cheese has been of major importance to the Netherlands since the Middle Ages. Today the Netherlands is the largest cheese-exporting country in the world. The chief market place is located in the city of **Alkmaar,** less than one hour from Amsterdam. Here for over three hundred years cheese has been sold in exactly the same manner. Every Friday at 9:30 A.M. the Edam cheese, red and ball-shaped (the only cheese shaped in a perfect sphere), is brought in front of a splendid old weigh-house to be sold. It arrives by barge and is unloaded by means of a sort of juggling act conducted by the porters. They pitch the cheeses onto barrows, which resemble stretchers. From there, twenty-eight carriers take the cheese to the market place in front of the weigh-house. The men are divided into four groups, all dressed alike in white shirts and pants but distinguished by blue, green, red, or yellow ribbons around their hats, indicating the company they work for. Each team has three pairs of runners with the leader wearing a silver badge. He sees that his men are spotlessly clean, on time, and well behaved.

The cheeses are placed in separate sections. The factory-made cheeses are in big, long piles; the smaller piles come from dairy farms. Then the actual selling begins. The buyer makes one fast scoop with his knife and bores out a round piece of cheese. A taste, a whiff, and a little crumbling of the cheese to test for moisture, and he makes up his mind about his bid. Then fierce bargaining begins, only to end in a quiet handshake, as binding as a signed contract. The cannonball-sized cheese is then whisked away by the porters to their own company scale. The weighmaster shouts the total value and notes the amount on the blackboard. From there a pair of carriers, the older man in back and the younger in front, begin their careful bobbing gait out to the waiting trucks and barges that will carry these wheel-shaped gems to the storehouses. Eventually they will be sent all over the world. Then at last the cheese will arrive at your table as a yummy sandwich, a tasty snack, or part of a delicious casserole.

By the end of the morning the jogging porters build up their tally for the day. The members of the group receiving the highest score are made chief guildsmen for the next week. At the close of the market the porters retire to their own quarters and drink a specially brewed beer from centuries-old pewter mugs that have been part of their tradition. Over the fireplace in their quarters is a "shame board," which states who was late for work or used curse words during the past week.

When each hour strikes don't forget to look up at the weigh-house clock tower and see the "Knights' Tournament." The clock's moving figurines enact a glorious scene, a trumpeter blows his horn, the doors burst open, and the horsemen charge forward with their lances held high to depict a royal battle.

Do climb the weigh-house tower for a view of the town. The tower dates back three hundred years and more. From the top you'll see windmills turning in the face of sea-scented breezes. Every once in a while you'll spot a bit of color, a precious garden, springing up among the many canals.

Schagen, one hour from Amsterdam, has another bustling cheese auction. It has its market on Thursdays in July and August. Farmers and their wives come from miles around dressed in their regional costumes to make their purchases and enjoy some lively folk dancing. The market goes on all day, but at 11:30 A.M. an exhibition of folk dancing takes place by the church. At 2:45 P.M. oldtime folk games begin in the same spot. The day is topped off by a concert and dancing in the music garden at 8 P.M. By the way, don't forget to notice the village ladies busily engaged in spinning and lacemaking.

Aalsmeer and Lisse. Flowers are everywhere in Holland. Of the 13,500 miles of land, 90 acres near Amsterdam are devoted solely to the growing of a dazzling variety of sunny daffodils, yellow-centered narcissuses, delicate lilies, and hundreds of other types of plants.

At **Aalsmeer,** about twenty minutes from Amsterdam, is the most important all-year-round flower auction hall in all of Europe.

The five rooms, two for potted plants, two for cut flowers, and one for bulbs, are partly over a canal allowing the flowers to be delivered on barges. In one year as many as 36 million carnations, 5 million chrysanthemums, 50 million roses, 9 million sprays of lilacs, and hundreds of millions of other floral varieties are bought and sold on these premises.

The action begins around 7 A.M. and lasts until everything is sold, about 11:30 that morning. A simple picking up of a sample flower from a larger lot begins the excitement. The auctioneer turns on a vast clocklike instrument with two sets of numbers, in the middle and on the outer rim. The numbers in the center refer to the buyers' seats, each of which has an electric buzzer. The outside numerals refer to prices for the entire bunch of the flowers or plants being bid on from the sample held up. A huge hand begins to circle the clock, but instead of beginning at the least expensive price it starts at the highest bids. Ever so slowly the big hand makes its way around. The moment an eager buyer decides on the right price he presses his button and his seat number lights up on the clock face. About six hundred different lots of flowers are sold each day in this manner with a great deal of rushing from room to room to make sure that people buying cut flowers are not getting lower prices than those purchasing plants.

When the sale is completed, the flowers are taken to the packing and delivery sheds. Those being sent out of the country are carefully wrapped and rushed to the nearby airport, and are admired in Stockholm, Paris, Rome, and London just hours after they were sold. Many other loads are delivered by truck to local shops and markets in every corner of the Netherlands.

The town of **Lisse** is the "shopwindow" of the bulb industry. As many as 5 million bulbs blossom here in a world-famous park, Keukenhof, either in hothouses where they can grow as high as three feet or in flower beds nestling beside calm lakes and streams. In the glass pavilion you can watch an amazing show of how to arrange flowers in special ways. And, of course, a calm windmill carefully watches the entire rainbow-colored scene.

The true bulb is like a large bud that grows underground with roots at its base. It is almost like an onion with a number of thick coverings that can be pulled off. The Dutch have specialized in bulb growing for over four hundred years, since the first tulip was brought from Turkey. The debut was a sensation. Buyers bid outrageous sums to own the most unusual shape or color. It was like a wild day at the stock market and everyone was certain that this particular moment would be the beginning or ending of a fortune. In 1625 two bulbs were sold for 3000 florins ($831.40). They were then painted in a tulip book to be admired and studied for years to come.

The park is open from the end of March to mid-May daily from 8 A.M. to a half hour after sunset. The fee is 2.50 guilders (70 cents) for adults and 1 guilder (28 cents) for children under ten. On May 1 the children have a special holiday and take over the entire town. It becomes one fantastic blossom as the young people parade in a long, winding path of flower-covered floats, each more splendid than the next. It is really the song of spring.

Volendam, Marken, and Spakenburg-Bunschoten. Regional costumes are still worn in various parts of the country. Men and women in Volendam and Marken, twin cities just twelve miles from Amsterdam, wear the traditional clothes as a way of showing visitors what life was like in ancient times. In **Volendam** the women have blue-gray-striped or black-pleated skirts and jackets. A high-pointed white lace hat tops off the outfit, while colorful aprons and red coral necklaces give it the final touch. The men wear large baggy trousers and on Sundays fancy jackets pinched at the waist and loaded down with a silver button and chain. You can even dress yourself up in a costume and have your picture taken.

Marken, the other town, used to be a fishing island. Here the women wear a long-sleeved "shirt" under a waistcoat with red and white striped sleeves. Over this goes an embroidered bodice and a woolen yoke of flowered cotton. On each head is a bonnet with a cardboard form inside to keep the shape. Men dress in baggy pants, bright red sash, a blue smock with white collar, a neckerchief and a gold button placed at their throats. Don't be confused when you see the boys and girls dressed alike in checkered bibs, bonnets, and aprons. The boys are in white bibs and blue skirts.

Spakenburg-Bunschoten are two other twin fishing towns about thirty miles from Amsterdam. The women's costumes are unusual because of what appear to be shoulder boards, yokes of brightly flowered cotton standing out so stiffly from the neck that a slim girl looks like a knight in armor while a chubby one looks like a football tackle. A tight-fitting cap dons the head while klompen (wooden shoes) protect the feet. These clogs are not worn by city people but mainly by fishermen, dairymen, and farmers. They keep the dampness out better than any other kind of footwear and are very safe to wear around boats, where it is apt to be wet and slippery. When entering a house, each person removes his wooden shoes. But they are worn for certain kinds of country dancing. When pounded on a wooden floor during these dances, they make a racket the likes of which you've never heard before, even if you've attended a concert of the Beatles, the Monkees, the Animals, or any other rock music group.

During the week there are many activities going on in the villages. Monday is washing day and the harbor is festooned with multicolored garments. Wednesday and Friday mornings the fishing fleet comes into port to sell its catch, putting out to sea in the afternoon at 4 P.M. Saturday and Sunday all the ships are in and you can go aboard to see the eels that were caught. Saturday, starting at 3 P.M., is also market day.

The Hague and Scheveningen. The Hague is Holland's parliamentary city and is less than thirty-three miles from Amsterdam. It has many different names. The French call it La Haye, some prefer Den Haag, and the Dutch name is Gravenhage, which means "Counts' Hedge." The city's beach area is called Scheveningen.

You can call The Hague by any of its names, but one phrase will describe it—"a delightful place to visit." Here are some of the splendid places you can enjoy.

Madurodam is the smallest town in the world. It covers four and a half acres and is a composite of Holland in miniature but in perfect scale 1 to 25. You'll feel like Gulliver among the Lilliputians. None of the details of daily living have been over- looked. The chimes in the vest-pocket-high towers ring, the ships move slowly into port, and the traffic is as busy as any you'll find on real highways and streets. You will see medieval streets and modern buildings, and the re-enactment of tradi- tional ceremonies such as the pageantry of the arrival of the Golden Coach in the inner courtyard of the Parliament for the opening session. Music is in the air when the barrel organ and brass band play, and a gay fun fair is in full swing. This is a spectacle by day and even more so by night when Madurodam's 46,000 lights are a sea of magic. What an enchanting sight it is to witness the Golden Coach and other carriages, and the Guard of Honor and the Royal Military Band as they draw up into their place of honor. The park is open March 23 to October 1 daily from 9:30 A.M. to 10 P.M. (11 P.M. some summer months). Fee: 1.50 guilders (46 cents) for adults, 60 Dutch cents (17 cents) for children under fifteen.

The Panorama Mesdag on Zeestraat (Sea Street) will give you a firsthand impression of what a nineteenth-century sea- port looked like. You enter through dark paneled passages under man-made dunes and emerge into a huge tentlike area. The scaffolding "boardwalk" permits a stroll around the inside of one of the world's largest paintings—over one mile of canvas mounted in a circle. The picture-in-the-round, 375 feet long and 48 feet high, records the view of the nearby coastal beach of Scheveningen as it was in 1881. To add to its realism, the artificial dunes have bits of glass and nets, parts of shipwrecked boats, wooden shoes, and even bottles of the period. The seascape is so real that you may hear some local person say "you could catch fish in it." The exhibit is open 10 A.M. to 4 P.M. weekdays and 1 to 4 P.M. Sundays. Fee: 10 Dutch cents (2½ cents).

Three other museums to visit are: (1) **The Mauritshuis** behind the Ridderzaal (Knights' Hall) at 29 Plein. Open from 10 A.M. to 5 P.M. weekdays, from 1 P.M. Sunday. Fee: 1 guilder (28 cents), half price for children. The building itself is a work of art. It was built as a palace, and the paintings, by such geniuses as Rembrandt, Frans Hals, Vermeer, and the Brueghel brothers, seem to go with the setting. Find the wonderful seventeenth-century skating scene painted by Hendrik Avercamp. (2) **The Torture Museum,** 33 Buitenhof, is open 10 A.M. to 4 P.M. daily, from 1 P.M. Sunday. Fee: 50 Dutch cents (14 cents). Once part of an old palace gate, this museum is chilling. It shows how prisoners were housed and tortured during the seventeenth century and afterward. After seeing the stone where the victims stood while drops of icy water fell on their shaven skulls, you won't be surprised to learn they went mad within a day and died three days later. The cells directly opposite the kitchen housed prisoners who were kept without food. The smell of cooking would make them confess to anything. (3) **The Netherlands Costume Museum,** 14 Lange Vijverberg, is open 10 A.M. to 5 P.M. daily, from 11 A.M. Sunday. Fee: 25 cents (7 cents). The mannequins are dressed in the typical clothing worn by the wealthier people during the last two centuries. Their hair styles, jewelry, and make-up are complete to the last detail, and the room settings match the period.

VERBLIJVEN: TO STAY

Hotel de l'Europe, 2 Nieuwe Doelenstraat, nestles on the back of one of Amsterdam's busiest and most colorful canals. It is just one block from Muntplein (Mint Square), the heart of the city. From the glass-enclosed dining room you can watch the passing boats. Most of the rooms have small balconies where you can enjoy splendid views. Two other specialties are terry-cloth robes and magnetic closet doors that quietly shut themselves. Price for most double rooms with bath is 70 guilders ($19.60) including breakfast.

The Parkhotel, 1 Hobbemastraat, is just a few steps from the Rijkmuseum (with the famous "Night Watch" painting) and the lovely Vondelpark. The surprise here is the big, busy glass-roofed billiard room with sixteen tables. Double rooms with bath average 45 guilders ($12.60) including breakfast.

The Port van Cleve, 178 Nieuwe Zijds Voorburgwal, occupies five floors above a world-famous restaurant of the same name. Most rooms have good views of the area through garret-type windows. It has real Dutch-style charm. Double rooms with bath are about 52 guilders ($14.56).

ETEN: TO EAT

Snacks are yummy! You'll shortchange yourself if you don't sample some of the treats in markets, at snack bars, and from street vendors. Herring is almost a national food. You can eat herring fillet on toast in restaurants, but the best way is the Dutch way. Buy your herring from a street vendor and gobble it down right there. "Young herring," called maatjesharing, is caught in May and June and considered the finest of all. In fact, the first catch of this delicacy goes to the Queen as soon as it is fished from the sea. The charge for this delicious morsel is 50 Dutch cents (14 cents). Barend van Berkum owns a clean glass-fronted stall on Raadhuistraat. At 9:30 A.M. he arrives and usually finds a line of people waiting.

"Broodjeswinkels are spotless sandwich shops and are located everywhere. The "broodjes" are do-it-yourself sandwiches where you choose your own combination of meats, cheeses, fish, and other delicacies displayed before your eyes. If it sounds dull, you haven't tried a Dutch sandwich. One favorite is the "uitsmijter." This is an open-faced sandwich consisting of two fried eggs, sunny side up, placed on ham or roast beef slices on buttered bread. These masterpieces of sandwichry can be eaten on the spot, or on the run. Particularly good shops are: **Broodje van Kootje,** 12 Rembrandtsplein, and **28 Spui** at 20 Leidseplein. The broodjes cost about 1 guilder (28 cents).

"Poffertjes" (pronounced poh-furt-yoys) are Dutch pancake shops and are named for little fried cakes which the Dutch say "taste like angels skimming the tongue." You won't argue with them. Or you can eat waffles with heavy whipped cream at these shops. Another dessert is a "pannekoek" (pancake). One variety, "spekpannekoek," is a meal in itself. It's about a foot long and a half inch thick, filled with lots of bacon, and served with apple syrup or molasses.

Serving time for regular meals is about the same throughout the country. Breakfast is served in your room or the hotel dining room. It usually consists of rolls, bread or Dutch rusk (a sweet muffin), thin slices of Dutch cheese, prepared meats and sausages, butter and jam, and steaming tea or hot chocolate (sometimes a soft-cooked egg). Lunch, from 12 to 2, is called "Koffietafel" (Dutch coffee table). Sandwiches of cold cuts and cheese on raisin or dark barley bread and warm side dishes like an omelet or a small cottage pie are finished off with fruits and beverage. The evening meal is what you've been waiting for. It is a full-course meal and is often eaten as early as 6 P.M. Dutch portions are often king-sized, so don't order too many dishes at one time. The traditional dishes are enjoyed today by Hollanders as if they were eating them for the first time. To start with soup, there are two typically Dutch ones. "Erwtensoep" is a thick split pea soup afloat with pieces of smoked sausage and served with slices of dark bread. The other is "Groentensoep," a clear broth loaded with vegetables and tiny meatballs. Some main dishes are: "Rolpens met Rodekool"— thin slices of pickled minced sausages, sautéed in butter, topped with a slice of fried apple, and served with red cabbage; "Boerenkool met rookworst"—a hodgepodge of crisp kale and potatoes mashed together and served with smoked boiled sausage; "Stokvis"—whitefish cooked in milk, drained, and served with potatoes, rice, fried onions, melted butter, and mustard sauce; and "Kapucijners"—peas served with boiled potatoes, chunky pieces of stewed beef, fried onions, bacon cakes, melted butter, molasses, and a green salad—which, believe it or not, all fits together in a delicious blend. Try it. Seafood is especially good. Try "Gebakken zeetong" (fried fish) and "Lekkerbekjes" (specially prepared whiting). Desserts are mainly ice cream or fruit with toppings of whipped cream.

Restaurants are plentiful and of many different types, but do not miss the chance to sample a meal from far-off Indonesia.

De Groene Lanteerne (The Green Lantern), 43 Haarlemmerstraat, is known as the skinniest restaurant in the world (six feet wide, three stories high). It opened in 1602 and has tried to keep the atmosphere of those days, with wooden benches, porcelain fireplace, and antique clocks. The waitresses wear costumes similar to the clothes worn by Rembrandt's housekeeper. The food is delicious but inexpensive, about 11 guilders ($3) for a three- or four-course meal per person.

Swarte Schaep (Black Sheep), 24 Korte Leidsedwarsstraat, is on the second and third floors of a typical seventeenth-century building. The stairways have oiled rope banisters, and the candlelit rooms have casement windows with stained glass, dark paneled walls, and copper pans on the walls. It all adds up to a pleasant Dutch dinner for about 18 guilders ($5) each.

Bali, 95 Leidsestraat, is the ultimate in Indonesian food, which is a bit spicy but splendid. You shouldn't pass through the city without trying "Rijsttafel" (rice table). The Dutch discovered this meal during the days of their empire in the East Indies (now Indonesia). It is made up of one large dish of rice surrounded by as many as twenty to forty-six smaller dishes (roast pork on sticks, liver, pork in soy sauce, mixed vegetables). One by one you sample each small dish, which you add to the rice. Try each dish slowly, and you shouldn't run into difficulty. Iced tea, lemonade, or mineral water is served with your meal. The dinner is served by real Indonesian waiters, wearing brilliantly colored turbans and authentic clothes. An average portion of Rijsttafel is enough for two people and costs about 12.50 guilders ($3.50). As the Dutch usually say, "Eet smakelijk" (Enjoy your meal).

GELD: GUILDERS AND WHAT THEY WILL BUY

The basic unit of money is the guilder, also known as the florin. For this reason the letters "F" or "Fl" are written next to the price. Each guilder is worth about 28 cents, enough to buy at least one filling broodje at the sandwich shop. The guilder is made up of 100 Dutch cents, so that 50 Dutch cents are equal to about 14 American cents, which is about all you need for a "dropje" (salty licorice), "a stroopwafel" (thin cookie with syrup), or a "gevulde koek" (large cookie filled with almond paste). There are several different coins—1, 5, 10, and 25 cents. The 10-cent piece is nicknamed the "dubbeltje" and is said to be one of the tiniest coins in the world. Although it is worth only 2.8 U.S. cents, three of them can get you a barrel organ concert.

WINKELEN: TO SHOP

TOYS

De Bijenkorf (The Beehive), 90 Damrak, is the largest department store in Amsterdam and has a fine toy section. The good dolls start at about 18 guilders ($5). **Merkelback & Co.**, 30 Kalverstraat, has lots of mechanical toys as well as regional dolls. **Tesselschade**, 33 Leidsestraat, has a great collection of inexpensive kites.

HANDICRAFTS

Ina Broerse, 57 Nieuwe Spiegelstraat, is a pleasant little shop with handmade dolls and wooden gift items. Priced from about 11 guilders ($3).

CHOCOLATES, COOKIES, AND OTHER DELECTABLES

Try **W. Berkhoff**, 46 Leidsestraat, or **Dikker en Thijs**, 82 Leidsestraat (specialty goods). **De Franse Kaasmaker**, 192 Marnixstraat, will give you a chance to smell the aroma of more than sixty-five different varieties of cheeses.

SPECIAL GIFTS

Carel G. H. van Pampus, 56 Kalverstraat, has Dutch-style silver spoons, boxes, dishes. Gold charms (windmills, "wooden" shoes) start at 7 guilders ($2).

IN TOUCH WITH A VRIEND: A DUTCH FRIEND

Upon introducing yourself and politely saying "How do you do?" don't be surprised if you are greeted with a hearty handshake, a slight bow, and the announcement "Jansen" or whatever the name might be. The handshake is one brisk movement. This is not meant to be cold. Overfriendliness is regarded as rude.

Dutch parents are great believers in education, and the standards are very high. Young people have to go to school from the age of six to fourteen. Most schools start at 9 A.M. and finish at 4 P.M. with lunchtime between noon and 2 P.M. Wednesday and Saturday are half days. Students who have not satisfactorily finished their term assignments have to repeat a whole year's work. Often there are students of different ages in the same class. For that reason, some slower students never get beyond the sixth grade. Because the country is small and almost in the center of Europe, it is necessary to learn several foreign languages. English is one of the key languages but starting in the "Gymnasium," the grammar school, Latin and Greek are taught as well. After completing examinations, young people have a choice of six universities or five other institutes of higher education. They reside at home or in rented lodgings since there are no places on campus to stay in.

Many Dutch families live on barges, carrying products up and down the rivers and canals. Being constantly on the move, these young people have to attend schools in the main towns they visit. They are given exhaustive homework, which is handed in and discussed at the school in the next port of call.

Because there are so many lakes, rivers, and canals, water sports are very popular. Ice skating in the winter is a favorite. Schools always let out for one or two extra half days during the coldest months so that everyone can participate in the national pastime. No one would think of going out without a few coins to tip the "baanveger" (ice sweeper), who clears away the powdery ice caused by excessive skating.

To get to meet the young Dutch at home, just tell the government tourist office (called VVV there) what type of family you would like to visit, and everything will be arranged. The Dutch are so enthusiastic about this program, called "Get in Touch with the Dutch," that families of almost every background have volunteered for it: lawyers, acrobats, teachers, etc. You can even get acquainted with a canal boat skipper's family on their boat home. The VVV Tourist Office in Amsterdam is at 5 Rokin. The phone number is 66-444.

Often happy friendships develop from these meetings. So when you get home, you'll want to keep a supply of airmail stamps on hand. You'll probably be staying in touch with the Dutch via the mails long after your visit is past.

TOT ZIENS: SO LONG, FOR NOW!

Practically everyone speaks English in Amsterdam, much to your delight and ease. But that is not surprising, since many popular words in the English language are Dutch in origin.

To name a few: "golf" comes from "kolf," an ancient Dutch game which was played on ice in Holland long before that game was exported to Scotland. "Skate" is another Dutch word. It comes from "schaats."

The compact-size country on the North Sea also gave America many terms associated with sailing: "skipper," "marline," and "yacht," to name a few. Northerners or "Yankees" were supposedly named after a Dutchman, Jan Kees (the "J" in Dutch is pronounced as a "Y" in English). The word "baas" is now

"boss" to Americans. Hungry? Have a "krul"—cruller to you;
or a cookie—"koekje" to the Dutch.

At the end of your stay in Amsterdam, you'll realize that
physical size is not the only thing that makes giants. It certainly
hasn't kept the Netherlands from being crammed full of wonders enough to fill a couple of places twice as big. By the time
you must say goodbye you certainly will know one Dutch word,
"gezellig," which, loosely, means "cozy."

SPREKEN: TO SPEAK

ENGLISH	DUTCH	PRONUNCIATION
My name is	Ik heet	Ikh hate
Good morning	Goede morgen	Hoo-dun mor-hen
Good day	Goeden dag	Hoo-dun dahk
How are you?	Hoe gaat het met U?	Hoo haht ut met oo
Very well	Uitstekend	Out stayk-end
Thank you	Dank U	Dahnk ew
Please	Alstublieft	Ah-stoo-bleeft
Excuse me	Pardon	Par-dawn
Where is the hotel?	Waar is de hotel?	Vahr iz duh ho-tel
the restaurant?	de restaurant?	duh res-to-rahng
To the right	Rechstaf	Rekhts-af
To the left	Linksaf	Leenks-af
Straight ahead	Rechtdoor	Rekht-dour
How much is it?	Hoeveel kost het?	Hoo-fayl kawst het
When?	Wanneer?	Vah-neer
Yesterday	Gisteren	His-ter-en
Today	Vandaag	Van-dahkh
Tomorrow	Morgen	Mor-hen
Breakfast	Ontbijt	Ohnt-bayt
Lunch	Lunch	Lunch
Dinner	Diner	Dee-nay

ENGLISH	DUTCH	PRONUNCIATION
Dutch coffee table	(Hollandse) koffietafel	Cof-fee taf-fel
Please write it out	Wilt U het opschrijven?	Vilt ew het op-sray-ven
Men	Heren	Heh-ren
Women	Dames	Dah-mes
1	een	ayn
2	twee	tway
3	drie	dree
4	vier	veer
5	vijf	vayf
6	zes	zes
7	zeven	zay-vun
8	acht	akht
9	negen	nay-hen
10	tien	teen
11	elf	elf
12	twaalf	tvalf
13	dertien	dare-teen
14	veertien	vare-teen
15	vyftien	vayf-teen
20	twintig	twen-tih
50	vijftig	vayf-tih
100	honderd	hon-durt

DATA: DATES

January 1 — **New Year's Day.** Visiting friends and feasting on special pastries ("duivekater") and drinking of hot, refreshing "slemp" (milk and delicious spices).

January 6 — **Three Kings' Eve.** Young people dressed in fantastic costumes carry paper-star lanterns mounted on tall poles. Songs tell how young people represent the wise men of the East following the Star of Bethlehem.

Special cake baked with one bean. Owner crowned king in mock ceremony.

February–Mid-March **Ice hockey matches,** figure skating demonstrations and contests (long-distance skating).

February-March (Shrove Tuesday) **Fast Eve.** Any foolishness is permitted for three days prior to Lent. Outlandish costumes, dancing in the streets, and masquerade balls.

Sunday before Easter **Palm Sunday.** Boys and girls dressed in best clothes parade with curiously decorated huge stick (boxwood prop covered with paper flags, eggshells, sugar rings, oranges, etc.). Nonsense songs accompany begging for eggs.

End of March–Mid-May **Bulb fields** in full bloom.

Saturday before Whitsun **Lazy Bones Market.** Starts at 4 A.M. Young people begin whistling, beating pots, kettles, and pans, ringing doorbells, and making such a racket it is impossible to sleep. Dates back to legend of Pret Lak, the watchman, who was caught napping during French invasion. Herring stalls, ice cream wagons, and booths filled with gingerbread furnish refreshments for merrymakers.

April 30 **Queen's Birthday Celebrations.** Parades and floral tributes.

May 5 **Liberation Day.** Many colorful celebrations.

Mid-May **Flag Day.** Marks opening of herring season.

Mid-June–Mid-July **Holland Festival of Music and Drama.** Concerts, opera, ballet, and exhibitions.

End of July–1st of August **International Rowing Regatta.**

Early September **Floral Parade**—decorated floats also in Aalsmeer.

Third Tuesday in September **Opening of Parliament.** The Queen in the Golden Coach rides in procession to the Hall of Knights, The Hague.

November 11 **St. Martin's Day.** Boys and girls serenade, begging for firewood and goodies "for St. Martin's feast." Harvest festival with bonfires and homemade lanterns of scooped-out turnips, carrots, or beets.

December 5 and 6	**St. Nikolaas or Sinter Klaas Eve and Day.** Gift bringer for over six hundred years. Long-bearded bishop in white robe and red cassock arrives with "Zwarte Piet," Black Peter, his Moorish servant. The saint trots over house rooftops on a white horse. Zwarte Piet climbs down chimney to make deliveries to young people who have been good and gives the bad ones a spanking with switches. The saint's official arrival is aboard steamship *Spanje* (Spain), followed by retinue on ship *Madrid*. Booming bells, shouts, cheers, and long, brilliant processions through city or town. Followed by songs, enacting of quaint customs, delicious special foods, and small gift giving.
December 25 and 26	**Two Days of Christmas.** Quiet visiting and eating holiday foods—"Kerstkrans" (Christmas Wreath) pastry decorated with white icing and candied fruits.

2. BERNE

Bear City

"Willkommen!" Welcome to a city in Switzerland that looks like a picture from an old-fashioned storybook set in the Middle Ages. It has low, snug, red-roofed houses; tall, turreted buildings; ancient towers; long networks of arcaded shops; bright legendary statues on flower-laden fountains; cobbled stone streets; and most of all bears, the symbol of the city. The sacred beast is the trademark of the streetcars, a biscuit manufacturer, an insurance company, restaurants, publishers, and grocers. You'll see the shaggy animal in wood, stone, or bronze on coins, seals, and flags. You can even enjoy the taste when his shape is converted into cakes, ginger cookies, and delicious chocolates. Best of all, feed the real bears in their own special pits. They'll respond by dancing a jig, rolling over, or clapping their paws. The people of Berne are so enamored of their mascot that they claim to have taken on some of his personality traits—"a little slow, a little lazy, and a little hardheaded." When did the lovable, clumsy mammal become the center of the town's attention? What does it feel like to live in a city that looks exactly as it did in medieval times? Let's find out.

THE CITY IS BORN

Like a blue ribbon the river Aare twists around the old city, seemingly to fulfill its original purpose of protecting the town. When in the twelfth century Berchtold V, Duke of Zähringen, first found the peninsula formed by the river, he decided it would be an excellent location for a strong fortification. Here he could ward off the raids carried out by those barons living to the east and west. The Duke summoned his nobleman Kuno of Bubenberg and gave him the task of developing a city around the mighty Nydegg castle, already built at the end of the peninsula about a hundred years earlier. The oak forest was chopped down and the wood used for the houses. The city wall was constructed at a natural hollow in the ground which acted as a moat. The great Clock Tower was made to adorn the main gate, which was the entrance to and from the countryside beyond.

The Duke was said to be very fond of hunting in the woods around Berne. He decreed that the first animal to be killed would give its name to the new town. A bear (in German "Bär") fell prey to the hunter, and the city was named Berne. But even in earlier times, the bear had been specially honored in this part of the country; in Muri near Berne six small bronze statues from ancient times were found. The one representing the Dea Artio, the bear goddess, can be seen in the Historical Museum. The oldest town seal, dating back to 1224, already shows a bear as a symbol; and the banners as well as the coat of arms have since early times shown the bear rampant on a golden stripe against a red field.

A town brook also dating back to the foundation of the city flowed through the main streets down to the river. This open creek served to get rid of garbage. Even in the Middle Ages,

Berne had the reputation for being the cleanest city in Europe. As traffic increased, the town brook was covered over with stone slabs.

By the thirteenth century the city's frontier was extended westward and a new city wall with the Käfigturm (Prison Tower) as its main gateway was erected. One hundred years later a third wall reached to where the train station stands now. It was built in a year and a half, remarkably fast for those days, but was torn down in 1864 as a result of an election decided by four votes. It was a superb gate called the Christoffelturm and had a tremendous head of St. Christopher sculptured in painted wood saluting from his niche visitors leaving the city.

In 1405 the greater part of the town was destroyed by fire. The houses were rebuilt on the old foundations; instead of wood, sandstone from nearby quarries was used as building material. And so the heart of Berne has remained intact. Only the two oldest gates survived of all the original structures. They had guarded the city and it seems only right that the city should have preserved them.

But the city is no mere museum; it is very much alive as the capital of the country, with the seat of the Swiss Parliament and government and the residence of the diplomatic corps of sixty embassies. It is a city of 160,000 people who live mainly in the lovely modern suburbs around the old town. Berne has succeeded in keeping its old-world charm and yet is very much a part of modern times.

THE ARCADES

Berne is the only city that has entire main and side streets completely covered by arcades, for a total of about eight miles. Chronicles do not state when they appeared but they are known to have been part of the original city. It is said that the pillars of the oldest arcades were actually stems of former trees whose roots had grown right into the primeval rock. Early arcades were built in front of the houses jutting out into the street and were used as forerooms where customers could watch the craftsmen work and at the same time select an item on display.

In the beginning the arcades were made of wood. Then after several fires, they were reconstructed in stone. You can identify the oldest shops by their large archways that open onto the arcades. A wooden shutter covers the entire front at night. During the day it divides into two parts; the upper half fastens to a hook in the arcade ceiling and the lower half is a serving counter. Buyers needn't enter the shop but can make their purchases right from the arcade.

Although the arcades preserve the medieval character of the city, the shops inside have the latest merchandise shown in attractive, up-to-date displays. The stone benches tucked away along the columns provide a nice meeting place for the women of Berne, who sit and chat while their children play under the archways safe from the dangerous traffic. The cellar doors opening onto the street lead to huge basement rooms, some changed into shops, night clubs, and small theaters for folk-singing concerts, musical revues, and serious plays.

MEDIEVAL STATUES

Glancing down the main streets, you may notice how the buildings curve inward on either side of the statues in the center of the road. In olden days this allowed the horse-drawn carriages to avoid the crowds gathered around the fountains. Today the traffic, streetcars, and automobiles have greater difficulty in circling the obstacles, but the Bernese would have it no other way. The long-spouted fountains with their gaily colored statues serve as a reminder of the vital part they played in daily medieval life. Up until 1869 they were the sole source of all water for washing, cooking, and drinking, and the most important meeting places in the town. From here the latest gossip was swapped and news from the outside world was heard as the rider, carriage, or runner stopped to quench his thirst and water his horse. It was the setting for the constant coming and going of workers needing water for their trade, servants filling buckets and jugs for their masters, and water carriers who for a small payment toted water to private homes.

The fountains had uses beyond helping with the daily chores. Somebody making himself particularly unpopular found a few sturdy fellows ready to dunk him into the nearest fountain. When fires started to break out, each person seized a container, rushed to the fountain, and formed a chain of people to help drench the flames.

Just as in early times, the fountains still have many everyday functions. Here artisans fill their vessels for use at their trades and in the tiny troughs in front of the large basins small animals and donkeys pulling milk carts stop to rest and refresh themselves. Standing stately above all the events both past and present are the more than thirty-five statues remaining, each a memorial to a famous hero, an important moment in history, or the retelling of a strange incident. The next section will describe the legends behind many of the statues.

A WALK THROUGH TOWN

Ask the hotel clerk for a city map to plan your tour. A suggested route could begin at the Bubenberg Memorial near the train station. The memorial salutes Adrian von Bubenberg (1424–79), a famous war hero and the city's earliest chief magistrate. Begin your walk down the main street, Spitalgasse, through the City Tower arch and continue to the end of the

peninsula, Nydegg or Lower Gate bridge. Cross the bridge for
a visit to the Bear Pits. Return via Junkerngasse, "the noblemen's street," as far as Kreuzgasse, leading to the Rathaus
(Town Hall). The route enables you to see many old fountains,
arcades, towers, the cathedral, and, of course, the Bear Pits.
On the way back you can see the stately homes on Junkerngasse.
One has a mysterious haunted history. Here are some highlights
of the tour:

The Bagpiper Fountain on Spitalgasse was chosen to honor
the musicians' guild, as a symbol that musicians were no longer
looked down upon as poor strolling players. They had been
elevated to citizens. To prevent them from becoming too vain,
there are holes in the bagpiper's shoes and breeches, reminding
musicians of their humble origins!

The Prison Tower marks the limits of the city after it expanded beyond the Clock Tower in 1256. The cells actually
held prisoners. The only light came from the few narrow windows piercing the thick walls.

The Marksman Fountain on Marktgasse is a symbol of the
armed might of the old Bernese Republic. Even the little bear
beneath the statue stands ready with his gun to defend the
honor of the city.

The Ogre Fountain is just around the corner on Kornhausplatz. The ogre carries his victims away in a sack while others
try to escape. This is supposed to be a reminder of those rash
boys who had fallen into the city moat, which used to be at
this place, and a warning to other children to avoid a similar
fate. Figures of this kind to frighten children were very much
in keeping with medieval ideas of education. Another story says
the statue was designed to enable older people to enjoy the romantic beauty of the place undisturbed by noisy children.

The Clock Tower (Zytglogge) is Berne's oldest landmark.
Its clock was the official time after which all other clocks were
set. The distances of the roads were measured starting from

this spot and all the milestones on the highways outside the city refer to it. To the nine-foot-wide wall of the archway all official announcements and laws were and still are affixed so that everyone may study them.

By 1405 the tower bell was cast but had to be struck by hand to announce the hours. It was in 1530 that the clever astronomical clock, showing the position of the sun, moon, stars, and planets as well as the month and day of the week, was completed. Then the delightful mechanical figure-play was also unveiled.

Here's how the "puppet show" works. Three minutes before the hour a rooster to the left of Father Time crows and flaps his wings. One minute later the jester above Father Time wiggles his arms and legs and rings a bell above his head to announce the striking of the hour. The rooster then crows a second time and a parade of bears emerges from the tower; led by a captain on horseback, the bears follow him proudly, carrying on high the Bernese flag. Father Time turns his hourglass to indicate the passing of the hour. Then he slowly moves his mouth, counting the number of strokes issued at the top of the tower by the golden-armored knight's hammer hitting the bell. Father Time moves his scepter as the lion heralds in the hour by nodding his head to the rhythm of the chimes. The rooster crows for a third time and the new hour has begun.

You can arrange for a personal tour of the inside of the tower by writing: Secretary, Official Tourist Office of Berne, Bundesgasse 20, or by telephoning 22-39-51. The tours are conducted Monday to Friday at 11:30 A.M. and assemble at the Tourist Office, very near the tower. You'll get a chance to see the whole puppet show from the outside and then examine it closely inside as the keeper of the clock goes about his task of winding it up.

The Duke Berchtold V Fountain in front of the Clock Tower honors the founder of the city. It shows a standing bear with visor down holding a banner. The severity of the stalwart warrior is softened by the bear cub peacefully enjoying a grape at the feet of his determined-looking father.

The Bernese Cathedral is on the street next to the Clock Tower, Münstergasse. Work on this impressive Gothic building took almost five hundred years to complete (1421–1893). On the site chosen for the cathedral a church already stood and the new church was simply built up around it so the services could continue uninterrupted. The tower is the highest in Switzerland and was formerly used as a lookout for fire and approaching enemies.

THE MAIN DOOR has a remarkable sculptured scene called "Last Judgment." It captures in stone the vitality of the medieval mystery play, portraying a vivid warning of the punishment awaiting the wicked. The artist worked at it for twenty years, creating 42 life-sized figures and over 140 smaller ones. The masterpiece is not without its touches of medieval humor. The Bernese Lord Mayor (just below the archbishop in the pointed hat) is shown in Paradise, while the Lord Mayor of Zurich (in the center above the old lady clasping her hands) has clearly been sent to Hell!

THE GARGOYLES, figures hanging off the sides of the building, also have their funny side. The men with horrible faces appearing to be sick are just that. They are there to remind passers-by what they will look like if they eat or drink too much.

As you look at the cathedral from the front, the left side has an additional humorous touch. When the original portion of the cathedral was finished the townspeople were very critical. The comments were, "just too fancy," "much too modern," and "all that time and look what we have to show for it." The designer was furious. As his final comment to the citizens, he put a sign toward the top of the building which reads MACH'S NO, which means "copy it"—if you can.

THE PLATFORM OR GARDEN on the right of the cathedral has

a story too. This promenade is actually older than the cathedral building by about sixty years. Twenty villages had to provide the materials to get it to its present height. The marker on the wall describes the fantastic event. It seems during the opening day celebrations large groups of students were excitedly singing, dancing, and shouting. A priest from the little village of Teobold Weinzapfli ("cork of a wine bottle") just outside of Berne happened to be riding his horse onto the platform. The noise and confusion so terrified the horse that he jumped over the wall with the priest still on his back. The horse unfortunately died but the priest lived on for forty more years. As you look over the side of the wall and see the tremendously sharp drop, you'll understand why this is such a miraculous tale.

Inside the cathedral there are brilliant stained-glass windows showing scenes from the New Testament. The choir stalls are attractive and amusing. The carvings reveal something of the everyday life in the sixteenth century, since not only religious figures are shown but a dairymaid, a baker, and a tailor. It proves that craftsmanship was held in high esteem in medieval Berne. The pulpit has a very practical item on it, an hourglass. When the sermon begins, the minister turns it upside down. There is no excuse for looking at your watch, for exactly when the sands run out (usually forty-five minutes) the sermon comes to an abrupt conclusion.

The spiral staircase leads to the tower platform, about 170 feet above the ground. A magnificent view over town and countryside rewards you for the strenuous climb of the 254 steps.

The Moses Fountain in the cathedral square should not be overlooked. Moses is holding a tablet of the Ten Commandments and sternly points to the second one. The Bernese interpret this to mean that Moses looks down from his high pillar at the meat market held here twice a week taking note of the people who may be guilty of cheating.

The Justice Fountain on Gerechtigkeitsgasse is on your way to the end of the peninsula. It is considered one of Berne's finest fountains. A charming blindfolded female in ancient costume and jewelry holds the sword of justice in her right hand and a pair of scales in her left. Assembled at her feet are the great of the earth who are her subjects: the Sultan, the Emperor, the Pope, and the Lord Mayor of Berne! You may wonder if there is any reason or justification to portray Justice as a woman, since most women in Switzerland do not have the right to vote.

The Messenger Fountain stands on a small square near the Nydegg bridge. It is said to be named for a Von Lerber, a member of the guild of runners, who used to carry messages to foreign countries. When a French king remarked that it seemed strange that the messenger did not speak French, Von Lerber replied, "It seems stranger that the King of France does not speak the language of my Bernese master [German]." The King must have had a good sense of humor, for he sent Von Lerber back with a letter of recommendation.

The Bear Pit is straight ahead across the Nydegg bridge and to your right. It is not surprising that a permanent home was made for these city favorites. The first record of a bear pit goes back to 1480, when the city council ordered for their feed several bags of acorns. In 1513 the victorious Bernese returning from a battle brought back, among other booty, a live bear. A stable was built for him in the city moat near the central gate. The place is still called Bärenplatz (Bear Square). Since then bears have always been kept in Berne—with one interruption.

When Napoleon's troops plundered the city in 1798, they took the bears off to Paris along with other city treasures. One cub was left dead in its pit; a model of it may be seen in the Historical Museum as the "last bear of Berne."

The present site was established in 1587. The deep pit, twenty-two yards in diameter and four yards deep, is the home of some twenty or more bears from Russia, Hungary, Yugoslavia, and Turkey. They are fed a strictly non-meat diet. Each bear gets approximately four pounds of bread and five to six pounds of bee-root per day. Occasionally they also get milk and fruit. Every winter they receive cod-liver oil, of which they are very fond. Other welcome additions to their diet are biscuits, nuts, figs, and carrots, which you can throw to them in the pit. The tidbits can be purchased at a booth located between the pits for Fr. .50 (12 cents).

A bear at birth weighs only 10 to 12 ounces but reaches 550 pounds fully grown. He can live in captivity thirty or more years without showing signs of old age. At about three to five years the female can give birth to her first young ones, usually about the end of December, in litters of one or two. The cubs remain blind for about thirty days and at eight to nine weeks start to walk. A very special attraction is at the Easter season, when the babies are let out of the nursery for their debut. People come from far and near to watch the small animals making their funny jumps and having their clumsy little quarrels.

Approximately every five years the enormous climbing firs in the pit are replaced, a most difficult task. Extra-strong firs have to be chopped down. In both the felling and replacing of the trees, the greatest care is needed to avoid breaking the branches. The bear delights in climbing and he seems to get a lot of fun out of swinging into the highest branch and taking a look at the neighborhood. There may be bears with interesting backgrounds in zoos or pits elsewhere, but they will certainly not be loved in quite the same way the Bernese love their bears.

The Junkerngasse is the street to your left as you return from the Nydegg bridge. This street leads you past Berne's haunted house. You'll recognize it by the shuttered windows, closed day and night. Recently some courageous students undertook to spend a night in the house. By morning they burst out of the house in a state of terror. Afterward they explained they didn't close their eyes all night, for the noise of footsteps going up and down the stairs kept getting louder and louder. Yet they felt their limbs were more or less paralyzed, so that they could not budge from the spot.

Another ghost, that of a knight, is said to live inside the old walls. Frequently mischievous boys call out his name. Then the majestic figure of the knight emerges from the walls. When he perceives that the person concerned has only been making fun of him, he gives him a good slap in the face which leaves its mark for a long time after.

The houses in this section are some of the oldest in the city. They stand on the sites of the original buildings and belonged to the noblemen who watched the rafts transporting all the town's merchandise on the river Aare below. As the Duke of Savoy in 1255 insisted, all the houses measure 200 feet in width and 120 feet in depth, and the walls up to the first floor are a thickness of 7 feet. The long, narrow entrance of each house was designed as a means of defending the household against any intruders. The small towers belong to spiral staircases which served as lookout points. Each house has its own history, often going back to the thirteenth century. Mansions of old nobility, convents, and even monasteries are among them. Old coats of arms tell of families long gone and of historic happenings. Turning right on Kreuzgasse will take you to the Rathaus (Town Hall) and the next point of interest.

The Venner Fountain in Rathaus Square is named for the man who carried the flag of the city into battle. He played an important role in the history of old Berne. The city was divided into four districts and the flag-bearers of each were considered head of their part of town. They inspected weapons and influenced the choice of members to the city council and in turn the government and law courts. Only four guilds had the right to choose the flag-bearers, who, next to the Lord Mayor, were the most important citizens. The nobility, always anxious to increase their power, were eager to become members of the guilds. It seems quite fitting that a little cub statue behind the Venner should stand ready to assist in any way he can.

The Rathaus (Town Hall) was begun in 1406 and not completed until ten years later: a very large building for a town which then had only five thousand people. Go inside and see the lovely pillared hall on the ground floor with its splendid oak ceiling.

MUSEUMS WITH THE SWISS TOUCH

All of the museums are in one part of the city, located across the Kirchenfeld bridge. They are not overcrowded with exhibits but skillfully selective, and arranged so that you can enjoy your visit at a comfortable pace.

Berne Historical Museum, Helvetiaplatz 1. Open every day 9 A.M. to noon, 2 to 5 P.M. Closed on Monday morning. Free. If you decide you have time for only one museum, this is it. Don't fail to take a careful look at the outside of the building. From the moment you pass the front gates guarded by two all-knowing stone bears you're in a castlelike atmosphere. The colorful mosaic scene over the front door with sorcerers, magicians, knights, and fair maidens sets the mood for your visit.

Inside, the LOWER LEVEL has displays of Bernese handicrafts and re-created old farmhouse rooms complete with wooden cooking utensils, large cupboards, and tile stoves. On the staircase to the second floor is a superb model of Christoffelturm, the third city gate, which was torn down. And on the nearby wall is the actual great wood-carved head of St. Christopher with peculiar glazed staring eyes.

The SECOND FLOOR has two amusing statues depicting William

Tell shooting the apple off his son's head. Also on this floor are wonderful woven carpets from as early as 1200; each one tells a blood and thunder mystery story of how honor and justice won out. Observe the people shown in these carpets; notice the delicate workmanship of the hands and the wild expression in the eyes; even the horses seem to have their own special madness.

One particularly dramatic carpet is "Trajan und Herkinbald-steppich." It was taken from a chieftain's tent in the thirteenth-century. From the size of the wall covering, the tent must have been immense. The story as woven in the carpet is in four parts. The first scene depicts Emperor Trajan on his way to war being stopped by a widow fallen to her knees. Someone from among Trajan's immediate group has killed her son. She pleads that Trajan find the guilty one before he leaves. He forces the murderer to confess. The second part takes place five centuries later. When Trajan's coffin is opened, to everyone's amazement, his tongue, which was known for always speaking the truth, was still in his skull. In the third picture another emperor, Herkinbald, is ill, ready to die. When he finds out that his son has attacked a young girl, he has a fierce rage and chokes the boy to death. The last part shows Herkinbald dying and being refused the last rites of the church because of the murder of his son by his own hands. Mysteriously, the Holy Communion wafer in the bishop's box disappears and winds up in Herkinbald's mouth.

On the TOP FLOOR is a collection of ancient musical instruments, an exhibit of charming folk costumes from different parts of Switzerland, and an old apothecary shop with a stuffed alligator hanging from the ceiling and another one on the druggist counter. Perhaps the fierce-looking creatures were used as a warning to possible thieves.

Swiss Alpine Museum, Helvetiaplatz 4. Open daily 9 A.M. to noon, 2 to 4 P.M., to 5 P.M. in the summer. Closed on

Monday morning. Fee: Fr. .50 (12 cents), children Fr. .20 (5 cents).

Anyone enjoying skiing and mountaineering will find this museum a rare treat. The unique exhibits include models of Alpine shelter huts, souvenirs of famous mountain climbers, very old skis, and an unusual display of rescue equipment. The really outstanding feature is the huge relief map showing every detail of the different parts of the Alps.

The Postal Museum, in the basement of the Alpine Museum, has over one hundred thousand stamps displayed in hinged cases—the largest collection in the world. There is no admission fee.

Natural History Museum, Bernastrasse 15. Open daily 9 A.M. to noon, 2 to 5 P.M. Sunday opens at 10 A.M. Fee: Fr. 1 (23 cents), half price for children.

This museum has a wonderful collection of minerals and rock crystals and shadow boxes with Swiss animals and birds and other animals from all over the world. The most popular exhibit is the preserved figure of Barry, the famous St. Bernard rescue dog. These dogs seem to sense the coming of a storm and show it by restlessness and barking. Their sense of direction makes it possible to send them out all alone. Their intelligence leads them to do all they can for those in distress, guide them to shelter or run and fetch help. Even in new snow they can find their way. When the St. Bernard encounters an avalanche he searches in it for buried persons, and if he senses that someone is lying under the snow he immediately begins to dig away. Then he completes the work of rescue by fetching his master to help the injured traveler.

Barry's exploits—he saved the lives of over forty people by his efforts—have made him the best known of these dogs and won fame for this breed. After twelve years of hard work Barry's strength failed and he was sent to Berne, where he peacefully passed the last years of his life.

A FEW MORE SWISS ATTRACTIONS

Market days are held Tuesday and Saturday on the Bundes-
platz (in front of the Parliament Building). The area is a
rendezvous of town and country. Interesting shoppers' helpers
are the dogs who patiently carry their mistresses' purchases by
toting the straw baskets in their mouth. The meat section is on
Kesslergasse and over toward the cathedral.

The Dählhölzli Tierpark (Zoo) is situated partly in a woods
and partly on the steep slope down to the banks of the Aare.
It is a few minutes from the station by motorbus T. Most of
the animals are European wild species that live in Switzerland
or lived there in former times. Especially popular are the mountain animals: the marmots kept in the open, the chamois in the
enclosure on the riverbank, and the kids that leap from rock to
rock. The domestic animals have many young friends, particularly the "dwarf" donkey (which you can ride), the Hungarian
sheep, the dwarf goats, and the guinea pigs. Finally, the comedians of the park, the capuchin monkey and the rare "woolly
monkey," are an unending source of enjoyment.

Gurten is a mountaintop retreat only twenty minutes from the
center of town by bus or streetcar. A funicular (cable car),
the fastest in Europe, takes you the last part of the way. On
this lovely car-free vantage point you can choose from many
activities—a spectacular view of the Alps, a stroll through the
forest, a ride in a paddle mini auto or on a small locomotive, a
picnic lunch complete with outdoor grills, or, in winter, skiing.
Some people enjoy this ideal spot so much they stay at the
Gurten-Kulm Hotel here and use it as the center for touring
the city. The hotel restaurant is very good and ranges in price
from Fr. 2 (hot dogs) to Fr. 12 for a "Filet à la mode du
chef" (the chef's steak), 46 cents to $2.76. An especially tasty

dish is the "Cordon bleu," breaded veal prepared in a delicious way; and for the finale, a "coupe maison," an ice cream cup crammed with fruit and topped off with whipped cream and a cherry—complete price about Fr. 13 ($3).

The Bellevue-Palace, Kochergasse 5, high on the riverbank, has rooms with balconies that have a splendid view of the Alps. Elegant is the word for the antique furniture and crystal chandeliers. It is delightful to dine on the big, sunny front terrace. All the museums are across the bridge just at the end of the street. Doubles with bath and breakfast start at about Fr. 91 ($21).

Kreuz, Zeughausgasse 41, is more a family hotel. Situated in the center of the old city, it has modern rooms that are comfortable and cozy. Doubles with bath and breakfast start at Fr. 40 ($9.20).

You'll quickly discover that Berne is a treat not only to the eye but also to the palate. Here is a guide to some of the specialties and the restaurants that serve them.

Taverne Valaisanne, in the Hotel Hirschen, Neuengasse 40 (near the station), is one of the cheese kings. Try a fondue in the Swiss chaletlike atmosphere of the room upstairs. Fondue is a blend of different cheeses mixed in white wine with a few extra ingredients tossed in. The dish is cooked and served in a chafing dish right at your table. To eat it, you fork pieces of bread and dip them into the boiling cheese. Ask the waitress

what the penalty is for dropping the bread. Price about Fr. 4
($1) per serving.

Kornhauskeller, Kornhausplatz 18 (by the Ogre fountain),
is called the "Great Cellar." That's exactly what it is, complete
with oom-pah-pah band (some not too good pop tunes), oversized beer barrels, and seats for more than one thousand people.
It has become such a curiosity that school children are invited
to come here. "Berner Platte" is the suggested dish, a selection
of pork, boiled beef, sausage, and either lots of sauerkraut or
green beans cooked with the meat. Cost about Fr. 12 ($2. 76).
Closed Mondays.

The Simmental Stube of the Hotel Schweizerhof, Bahnhof-
platz 11, is a dining room from an old house dismantled and
reassembled to the last splinter. Ask for "Zürcher Leberspiessli
mit grünen Bohnen and Rösti," pieces of calf's liver and bacon
on a skewer, spiced with sage leaves and served with string
beans and hashed brown potatoes. The Rösti (potato dish)
was created by a Bernese chef. Cost about Fr. 17 ($3.91).

Tea rooms specialize in glace (ice cream), milk shakes, tea,
and snacks. **The Tea Room Capri,** Kramgasse 70, in one of
the main shopping plazas, is a favorite with young people at
around 4 P.M.

The Mövenpick chain is for a quick lunch at inexpensive
prices. The one near the City-Garni Hotel on Bubenbergplatz
is the best.

GELD: MONEY AND WHAT IT WILL BUY

The basic unit is the franc (Fr.), which is divided into 100
centimes. Presently a franc is worth 23 cents. For quick reckon-
ing figure 50 centimes as 10 cents and 1 franc as a quarter.
A 10-franc note worth $2.30 will buy a wood-carved bear hold-

ing the Bernese flag in its hand; a 5-franc coin converts to $1.15 and will get you a trip up to Mount Guten by cable car, plus lunch at its hotel; and a 20-centime coin, 5 cents, is enough for a Swiss chocolate bar.

EINKAUFEN: TO SHOP

Store hours are usually 8 A.M. to 6:30 P.M. weekdays. Closing time Saturday 5 P.M.

CANDY, SWEETS

Abegglen, Spitalgasse 36; **Tschirren**, Kramgasse 73. Ideal for confectionery bears of gingerbread or hazelnut and chocolate, all neatly packed to take home as gifts. Prices range from Fr. 5 to 10 ($1.15 to $2.30).

CLOCKS, WATCHES

Papeterie Raeber, Kramgasse 83 (near Clock Tower). Small clocks with carved scenes begin at Fr. 12 ($2.76); more elaborate musical cuckoos up to Fr. 200 ($46).

Uhren—Boutique Brändlin, Kramgasse 76. For miniature clocks, Fr. 32 ($7.36); musical clocks from Fr. 48 ($11.04); and mod watches, Fr. 38 ($8.74).

HANDICRAFTS

The Old People's Home, Nydegghof 9, (near the Bear Pit) sells beautiful handmade dolls and figures of familiar animals, along with other handmade items, a genuine bargain from Fr. 4 to 15 (92 cents to $3.45). While you are here, have a look at the imposing statue of Duke Berchtold V, the city founder. The statue (a bear is holding the Duke's helmet) is right outside the Home.

SKIING, CAMPING CLOTHES, AND EQUIPMENT

Kaiser, Amthausgasse 22 (near Parliament Square). Rucksacks, Fr. 35 to 80 ($8.05 to $18.48); Bally hiking shoes, Fr. 50 ($11.50); after-ski wool socks with leather soles, Fr. 15 ($3.45).

Vaucher, Hotelgasse 6 (near Clock Tower). Beginner's skis with bindings, Fr. 30 ($6.90); regular skis with bindings, Fr. 250 and up ($57.50); ski boots, Fr. 70 ($16.10); sleeping bags, Fr. 30 ($6.90); climbing picks, Fr. 40 ($9.20); and special ski sunglasses, Fr. 4 (92 cents).

TOYS

Toys designed by **Peter Husler** of Berne are in many small shops. They consist frequently of ingenious and colorful arrangements of wood. Separate pieces of wood looking like arrows when apart become a funny-looking man when stacked together; clever arrangements of pegs result in a bright fish. Most of the toys cost Fr. 10 to 20 ($2.30 to $4.60).

Bilboquet, Gerechtigkeitsgasse 22 (near the cathedral), has unusual puppets and marionettes. Prices begin at Fr. 5 ($1.15).

Oberländer Heimatwerk, Kramgasse 61, has delightful wooden toys of all kinds (puzzles, animals, and doll furniture). Prices start at about Fr. 3 to 15 (69 cents to $3.45).

FREUNDE TREFFEN: FRIENDS TO MEET

The Berne Tourist Office could not be more friendly or helpful. The people there will do all they can to put you in touch with someone of your own age and similar interest, but be sure to give them plenty of time, at least four to six weeks, particularly in the summer. The address to write to: Secretary, Official Tourist Office of Berne, Bundesgass 20, Berne, Switzerland. Or you can telephone 22-39-51.

WIE GEHT'S? HOW GOES IT?

This might seem like a peculiar farewell to the city, but not really. The slang phrase is used among friends who've gotten to feel at home with each other. What other city could you get acquainted with in less than thirty minutes, the time it takes to walk from one end to the other. Where else would you find warm, friendly people who immediately make jokes comparing themselves to their city mascot, the bear? They claim there is a common physical resemblance: thickset, bull-necked, broad-chested, with dangling long arms and a nonchalant walk—or is it the bear that imitates the gait of his human brother? In character too, the Bernese say there is a similarity: Awkward and somewhat grumpy, they dislike their toes being trodden on but are easily appeased by friendly treatment. The Bernese are right. The whole city is like a bear, warm and cozy—like a hug. If you return (you're sure to want to) you'll once again feel immediately comfortable, almost like coming home and find yourself saying "Wie geht's?"—How goes it?

SPRECHEN: TO SPEAK

Switzerland is a multilingual country. In Berne the language is German; in other parts of the country it is French or Italian or, especially in country sections, a peculiar Swiss combination called Romansch.

ENGLISH	GERMAN	PRONUNCIATION
Good morning	Guten Morgen	Goo-ten more-gen
Good day	Guten Tag	Goo-ten tahg
Good evening	Guten Abend	Goo-ten ah-bend
What is your name?	Wie heissen Sie?	Vee hi-sen zee

ENGLISH	GERMAN	PRONUNCIATION
My name is	Ich heisse	Isch hi-sah
How are you?	Wie geht es Ihnen?	Vee gate s ee-nen
I am fine	Es geht mir gut	S gate meer goot
Thank you very much	Danke sehr	Dunka sehr
Speak slowly, please	Sprechen Sie bitte langsam	Sprech-ken zee bit-a lahng-sam
You speak too fast	Sie sprechen zu schnell	Zee sprech-ken tsoo schnell
You're welcome	Bitte sehr	Bit-a zehr
Please	Bitte	Bit-a
Goodbye	Auf Wiedersehen	Off vee-dehr-zehn
Pardon me, please	Verzeihen Sie, bitte	Fehr-tsi-en zee, bit-a
What is that?	Was ist das?	Vas ist das
Where is	Wo ist	Vo ist
How do I get to	Wie komme ich zu	Vee kom-a isch tsoo
Right	Rechts	Reschts
Left	Links	Links
Right around the corner	Gleich um die Ecke	Gleisch uhm dee ek-ka
Straight ahead	Geradeaus	Ger-ad-a-aus
Can you tell me where	Konnen Sie mir sagen wo	Kur-nen zee meer sahgen vo
I can't speak German	Ich kann kein Deutsch sprechen	Isch kan kein Deutsch sprech-ken
Do you speak English?	Sprechen Sie Englisch?	Sprech-ken zee Ehng-lish?
Will you help me, please?	Wollen Sie mir helfen, bitte?	Vol-len zee meer hel-fen, bit-a
I am looking for the hotel	Ich suche das Hotel	Isch soo-ka das ho-tel
Excuse me, please	Entschuldigen Sie, bitte	Ehn-schul-dee-gen zee, bit-a
How do you say	Wie sagt man	Vee sockt mahn

ENGLISH	GERMAN	PRONUNCIATION
How much does it cost?	Wieviel kostet das?	Vee-feel cost-a das
What time is it?	Wieviel Uhr ist es?	Vee-feel oohr ist
Men/Women	Männer/Frauen	Men-ner/Fraw-en
Entrance	Eingang	Eyn-gahng
Exit	Ausgang	Aus-gahng
Drugstore	Drogerie	Drug-erie
Barbershop	Coiffeur (Herren)	Cwof-fwur
Toilet	Toiletten	Toil-let-ten
1	eins	eynz
2	zwei	tswhy
3	drei	dry
4	vier	fear
5	fünf	fuhnf
6	sechs	sex
7	sieben	seeben
8	acht	acht
9	neun	nawyn
10	zehn	tschn
11	elf	elf
12	zwölf	tswolf
13	dreizehn	dry-tsehn
14	vierzehn	fear-tsehn
15	fünfzehn	fuhnf-tsehn
20	zwanzig	tswan-such
50	fünfzig	fuhnf-sich
100	hundert	hoon-derd

WICHTIGE DATEN: DATES TO REMEMBER

January 1	**Neujahrstag** (New Year's Day). General merrymaking. Housewives cook goose, special bread, and "Birewegge" (pear pie). Young people start rounds

of friends singing "Good day and good cheer" and are invited for treats. Folklore states day predicts outcome of year. Red sky means storm or fire. To encounter a woman first brings bad luck: man or child, good sign.

January 2   **Berchtold's Tag** (Berchtold's Day). From early autumn young people horde for this "nut feast." Nut eating and nut games followed by singing and folk dancing. Favorite stunt making "Hocks"—trying to place five nuts one on top of the other.

February-
March   **Fastnacht** (Carnival). Various celebrations and festivities.

March-April   **Ostern** (Easter). Church service with magnificent music. Small gifts given by parents and friends—chocolate and marzipan rabbits, sugar eggs, and chocolate eggs. Egg competitions, egg throwing into flat basket, and racing on horseback.

April-May   **Fronleichnamsfest** (Corpus Christi Feast). Processions with handsome church vestments and soldiers in uniform.

August 1   **National Independence Day.** Bonfires and general dancing in the streets.

November,
late   **Zybelemärit** (Onion Market). Picturesque market filled with all varieties, sizes, and shapes of onions. Farmers come to town to celebrate. Young people surge through arcades throwing bright-colored confetti. Singing and dancing into the night.

December 6   **Samichlaus Abend** (Santa Claus Night). Samichlaus, with a sack of nuts, apples, and cookies slung over his shoulder, parades in the street, rewarding good children and switching bad ones. The many lights and noise are a holdover from primitive times and are thought to frighten midwinter's demons and devils.

December 24   **Heiliger Abend** (Christmas Eve). Gift giving of practical items—knitted mittens, caps, warm jackets and frocks—and, as a little extra, hand-carved toys or homemade dolls. Bell ringing and carol singing. Folk superstition says animals are given power of speech at midnight since they were present at the Infant's birth. Special foods are left for them. Young people make a wish drinking from nine fountains and then go to church.

December 25   **Weihnachten** (Christmas). Beginning of winter sports —skating, skiing, sledding, and tobogganing.

December 31   **Silvesterabend** (New Year's Eve). There is a tradition that Silvester, spirit of darkness, walks about on this night. Bells and grotesque costumes are used to frighten him away. Young people rise early, for whoever is last becomes Silvester. Both at home and school latecomers are greeted with shouts of "Silvester." New Year's is ushered in with dancing in the streets and fond embraces.

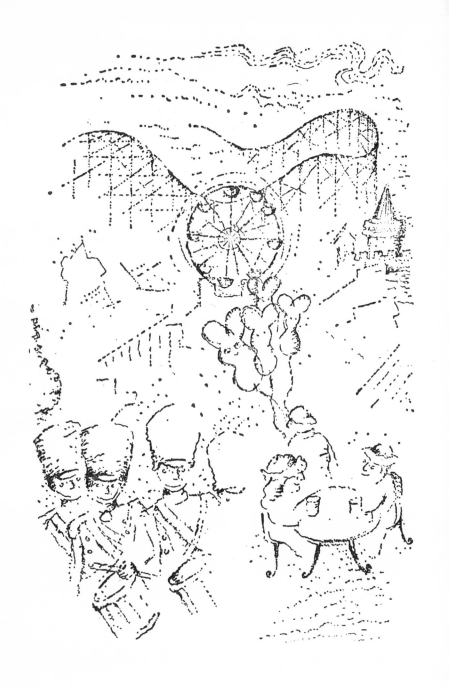

3. COPENHAGEN

"Once Upon a Time There Was . . ."

"Velkommen!" Welcome to the city of smiles. To the Danes visitors are the second best thing in the world. They do not think of themselves as the first. Traveling is that. The next best is for the world to walk in and say "hello!"

The call "welcome" is everywhere—in the green canals, the red and green copper roofs and emerald green spires, the honey-colored brewery horses, the wiggle of the duck family on the street, and the flashing metal of speeding bikes. Half of all the people go briskly through the streets riding bicycles. They all seem to be rushing to meet a friend. Join them at the Royal Danish Ballet. Eat a meal-in-itself "smørrebrød" (open-faced sandwich) or a real Danish pastry at a downtown "konditori." Try a seafood restaurant. Fish will never taste the same.

How about the early Danes? Were they as fierce as legends say? See for yourself at the National Museum. Look at, but don't touch, the crown jewels at Rosenborg Castle. (If you touch the showcase, it sinks into the floor, bells ring, and all the doors close.) Sight-see by boat through Copenhagen's canals past "Den Lille Havefrue" (The Little Mermaid) in the harbor.

Take a trip to Elsinore Castle where Shakespeare's Prince Hamlet was thought to have lived. (The Danes call it Kronborg Castle.) And most of all, get to know the sad story of the magic storyteller Hans Christian Andersen both in Copenhagen and his childhood home of Odense. Your visit can't help but be "once upon a time" because of the food, fun, and fairy tales.

A GOLDEN GODDESS

Long, long ago (about the first-century A.D.) the Norsemen, the early inhabitants, came from barren lands of ice and snow and believed in rugged gods. They sought war, adventure, and a hero's death, believing fallen warriors went to Asgard, home of the gods. There in the finest hall, Valhalla, the gods celebrated and feasted. Every morning they went joyfully to battle and killed each other. By evening, they returned to life, dining together in blissful friendship.

Four chief gods gave English names to the days of the week: Tiw or Tyr (Tuesday), Woden or Odin (Wednesday), Thor (Thursday), and Freya (Friday). Tiw, the war god, was very brave. To save the other gods, he put his hand into the mouth of the enormous wolf Fenir and had it bitten off. Odin, the king of the gods, had only one eye. The other he gave in exchange for a drink from the spring of wisdom.

The golden goddess Gefion was responsible for establishing Denmark. She did not like the idea of growing up in her father's house and country, Sweden, and demanded land of her own. Her father believed he could trick her by offering all the land Gefion could fence in with the hide of a bull and have plowed by oxen in one day. Gefion cunningly cut the bull's hide into very thin strips and marked the largest area possible. With a crack of her whip she turned her four sons into oxen and drove them till sundown. Triumphantly, she carved out much of what became Denmark and claimed it as her own.

Gefion's statue stands at the entrance to the promenade along the Langelinie (Long Line), near the gray English church of St. Alban's. The godly amazon has her whip in hand over the heads of water-spouting oxen who are trying to pull her through the foaming water.

THE MIGHTY VIKING

"Save us, O God, from the violence of the Norsemen." So ran the church service throughout Western Europe during the ninth century. The terrified people were praying that fierce Vikings such as Harold Bluetooth and Sven Forkbeard would not swoop down in their man-oared, dragon-headed "lanskibe" (long ships) to loot and raid their villages. The strongest boys and the most attractive girls would be dragged off to become "tralls" (slaves), the best kept and the rest traded. Although the Vikings are recalled in sagas (written stories), little thought is given to the reasons for their warlike behavior, or to their gentler side.

The hearty blond, blue-eyed stalwarts got their name, Vikings, from their original home in the "viks" or fjords (the long, narrow bays with high banks) of Norway, southern Sweden, and Denmark. (The dark-haired and black-eyed men are said to have come from Denmark.) The women are described as very beautiful with long golden hair, clear eyes, and lovely skin. Even the most unfriendly sources agree the Vikings were brave and fearless, always honoring their word, and at times overly generous.

The Vikings farmed on meadowlands cleared from a countryside covered by mountains and forests reaching to the sea. Tracks through the forest were fit only for horsemen traveling single file and were neither easy nor safe. The sea became the only roadway and was called "Ship's Path," "Swan Road," or "Whale's Bath." Living by the shores and seas which are the roughest, most broken and dangerous in the world, the Vikings were forced to learn about the elements. They became the best shipbuilders and sailors of their time. But ships were not only efficient, they were also beautiful, painted in bright hues of orange and purple. Shields hung over the sides and were displayed in alternate colors of black and yellow or blue and red. On special occasions, a spare set of dress sails made of a velvet-like material lined with fur or silk would be flown. What a show!—the vividly decorated ship plunging through the foaming green water with the chieftain's banner flying from the mast, emblazoned with his personal emblem—perhaps a raven.

At first the Vikings' exploratory trips to Russia, France, Spain, and the Mediterranean were largely peaceful trading voyages. The Norsemen loaded their vessels with fish, amber, furs, whale oil, walrus teeth and ivory, falcons and hawks (of which they had plenty), and traded for silk, dyes, honey, silver, gold ornaments and jewelry, luxury items of the countries visited. Soon after A.D. 800, Charlemagne, who had been keeping Europe in order, died, and weak rulers allowed the continent to fall into a state of defenseless confusion. The Vikings quickly took advantage and decided it was cheaper to seize things than to trade for them.

Many voyages, however, were not for looting or trading. After A.D. 900 Harold Fairhair became what amounted to the first real king. He made and imposed laws applying to everybody, levied taxes, and declared that certain crimes were punishable by exile. Moreover, the Vikings' own land was beginning to be overpopulated. By law, the eldest son ordinarily inherited his father's property, and as time went on, the younger children had difficulty finding suitable land to settle. The Vikings began to look overseas for new homes, and a string of colonies spread to

England, Scotland, and Ireland, then farther to Iceland and Greenland.

In A.D. 982 Eric the Red of Iceland killed a man in a brawl and was banished for three years. To pass the time, he explored the coast between Newfoundland and Cape Cod and spent a winter in what is now southern New England. Whether Christopher Columbus and Spain and Italy or Eric the Red and Scandinavia can claim the discovery of America is still a topic of heated concern to partisans of each explorer.

Constant moving and seafaring conditioned the Viking family life. As land was sighted, the Viking leader had his high seat pillars, or throne-poles, brought from storage and tossed overboard. The frame of the thronelike chair was for the head of the family. The spot where it washed ashore was the site of the new colony. This was more than superstition, for where the chair landed, there would also be other driftwood necessary for building and for fuel. Shipbuilding influenced the shape of their houses. Since the earliest shelters consisted of boats drawn up and overturned on the shore, the wooden walls of the later, permanent houses were often curved like the sides of ships. The shape seemed to withstand the gales of the northern winters.

As active people in a cold climate, the Vikings had to give a great deal of thought to food. They ate two enormous meals a day, in the morning and evening. In the more northern areas, they hunted for whales, bears, and seals. A great deal of milk, buttermilk, and whey (the watery portion left after cheese is removed) was drunk, as well as ale and mead—a drink made by fermenting honey and water. Needing large amounts of supplies on their long voyages, the Vikings learned a lot about preserving food, drying, smoking, or salting fish and meat or pickling it in vinegar, whey, or brine. Other people concealed the taste of tainted foods by using pepper and other spices. The Vikings used ice to keep foods from spoiling. Good food was important.

So was clothing. Sea-working clothes were sometimes made of oiled skin or heavy wool. A hip-length coat of hide with fur inside for added warmth was worn. If a fight seemed likely, a shirt of chain armor was put on under the jerkin or coat for protection against spears and arrows. Long capes with a hood were used both in winter and summer and often served as a blanket. Cloth socks were sewn into the trousers like today's baby pajamas and leather boots pulled over them. Heads were protected by woolen caps or, in combat, helmets of iron and leather. Fighting or not, shields were always present. Evidently the Vikings felt undressed without them and used them in many ways other than against arrows—as umbrellas in heavy rainstorms and as baskets to gather grapes.

While sea clothes were plain, the Vikings' dress for special occasions was entirely different. They wore flamboyant clothes such as skintight trousers or wide knickers of rich material. Embroidered jackets sometimes had a sort of trailing gown which laced up the side and had sleeves ten feet long. Men not only wore gold bracelets but gold anklets and gold bands around their forehead. Eventually, the men became more fashion-conscious than the women. Throughout all the crazes, including kilts, the men stuck to beards, moustaches, and shoulder-length hair. The heavy hair proved excellent protection against the biting winds and burning suns of the open North Atlantic.

Women's work clothes were sensible, long-belted wool dresses over petticoats of linen. Their heads were covered by linen kerchiefs and an apron protected their dresses from soiling. The only jewelry was a large brooch from which dangled several fine chains. Fastened to these were things a housewife might need in a hurry—scissors, keys, a small knife, and cases with needle and thread. Unmarried women and widows wore their hair loose down their backs. While working, they tucked it into their belts. Married women braided their hair and pinned it up. All in all, Viking women looked very businesslike.

Dress-up times made up for the drab periods. Ladies wore silks, brocades, and velvets trimmed with gold and silver threads and adorned themselves with rings and bracelets of gold and silver, strings of pearls or vivid glass beads. Heads of animals were the favorite pattern in the jewelry, followed by leaves, vines, and flowers. Women were particularly proud of their smooth white arms and shoulders and designed their best dresses with no sleeves, low necks, and short trains. Their golden hair was pinned high on their heads and held by glittering pins and diadems. Ladies at a party were radiant.

Courage, endurance, and athletic ability were valued very highly and both boys and girls were trained to develop these qualities. Sickly or crippled babies were sometimes left outdoors to die because the Vikings felt the physically weak could not endure their rugged life. Girls were taught to sew, cook, milk cows, make butter, spin and weave. In addition, they could swim, ride, handle livestock, and even use weapons effectively. Social graces were also taught—ballad singing, playing musical instruments, reading and writing, and being informed on current events. When a girl was ready to marry, her father selected a likely suitor, although if she did not care for him, she was not obliged to wed. This was quite unusual for the time and indicates that the Vikings did respect individual tastes and feelings.

The ideal of the Vikings was to train every boy to become a hero, a little bit larger than life in his thoughts and deeds. As soon as a boy learned to walk, he started to swim and ride, to use weapons and handle a boat, and to hunt and do chores around the farm. He also mastered ballad writing, singing, and harp playing, and became skilled at checkers and chess, falconry, fencing, and wrestling. In order that training be done without interference, parents sent boys away at the age of seven to foster parents who were trusted friends of the family. By the age of eleven or twelve, a boy was capable of dealing with any everyday problem and his sister was a competent housekeeper.

As a boy reached his teens, his fight training was put to the test. If there was a war he joined the army; and if not, he joined the raids. No one could be a coward; but the degree of bravery had to be proven. A champion was always welcome but he had to keep fighting to defend his reputation. The best champions of all were "berserkers." These were a small and special class of fighting men who seem to have gone insane in the heat of battle. The word means "bare shirt" and comes from the berserkers' habit of rushing into a fight without their armor shirts or shields. The word is still used today to describe someone who is so mad he doesn't care what he does.

What became of the Vikings? The answer is not simple. Some people say the other countries organized their own fighting forces according to Viking methods and in time were able to cope with the raiders. Others think the Vikings spread themselves too thin. As they conquered and settled in various countries, the families intermarried and were brought up by different, less rigid standards. Perhaps in a softer kind of life the Vikings felt they did not need the old toughness and fire. So gradually the Vikings were absorbed into the new world around them. But they have not disappeared. Their legacies are in our art, speech, and literature, in some of our laws, customs and ideas. And many people can even trace their family backgrounds to the Vikings. Let us enter the realm of these sturdy individualists and see what remains of their hearty lives.

The Nationalmuseet (National Museum), 12 Frederiksholms Kanal. Open June 16 to September 15 daily 10 A.M. to 4 P.M. (several sections closed on Tuesday). September 16 to June 15, various hours for different sections. Free.

Many intriguing hours can be spent here, for the entire history of Denmark from earliest times is displayed. It is one of the largest museums of its kind in the world. The sections have splendid exhibits and scenes of costumes and cultures of practically every country. You can't possibly see all the sections in one visit.

On your first visit go to the rooms devoted to The Viking Period (A.D. 800–1050), where there is a fine selection of rune stones. As the Vikings traveled, they learned the importance of transferring ideas by means of marks onto paper, wood, or stone. They developed an alphabet of their own called the "runes," based on Greek and Roman letters. The Vikings felt there was magic in the runes, and they engraved runic inscriptions on their belongings. On a sword owned by Tor the sentence might appear "May Tor spare none." These rune stones tell the story of a man or event. There are also objects from the grave of a Viking chieftain. Don't be surprised if you find a pet among the items. The Vikings dearly loved them, and had laws with steep fines for anyone killing a dog. The charge varied. The smallest fine was for a watchdog, more for a hunting or sheep dog, and most of all for a lap dog. Falconry and racing hawks were favorite pastimes, and fancy names were given to each bird that accompanied his master on his travels. Some households kept a peacock for no reason other than its beauty. One owner loved his bird so much that he requested that it be killed and buried with him.

Other things to note are: carefully sculptured battle-axes and a two-edged sword; the models of the Jelling barrow, traditional burial place of Gorm, the first known king of united Denmark; and huge silver arm rings, sometimes used in trading.

After looking through the other rooms of this early Danish period, proceed to the Danish Peasant Life section. Furnished rooms and collections give you a feeling for country life and folk art. Find the carved mangle boards, used for pressing clothes after they are washed. These were given as gifts to a sweetheart to ask for her hand in marriage. One of the mangle boards depicts Adam and Eve and has the inscription "We can walk on roses."

Highlights on your return might include visits to: the Arctic Peoples and American Indians section (strange masks of the

Nunivak Eskimos, an amazing polar Eskimo dog sled, kayaks from West Greenland, and a complete re-creation of the winter house of the polar Greenlanders) and the Asian collection (entire exotic temples of Mongol lamas, fanciful Chinese theater costumes, children's costumes and toys, and Siamese temple statues with weird make-up).

A BISHOP NAMED ABSALON

The year was 1167 and as Victor Borge, the Danish pianist and comedian, describes it: "One day the good Bishop Absalon looked out the window in his apartment in Roskilde, a short distance from Copenhagen, from where he ruled everything in Denmark he possibly could grab hold of, and said to himself, 'I have a small seat. I want a bigger and better one. This would be a good year to start building Copenhagen.'" Actually, Bishop Absalon expanded what was the tiny fishing village of Havn into a walled city, with a fortress, his home. He called the town Købmannehavn, or "Merchants' Harbor," and today the Danes call it København, which means the same thing.

A POINT OF IDENTIFICATION

The Radhus (Town Hall) is in the square in the center of town. Its green-topped tower rises 350 feet. A gilt statue in copper honoring Bishop Absalon stands above the main entrance of the Rådhus. He is guarded on the roof ridge by six bronze statues representing night watchmen from various historical periods. Inside the Rådhus is the astonishing Jens Olsen World Clock. It not only tells time throughout the world, but the position of the stars, the phases of the moon, and about two dozen other nuggets of information; and it's wound up only once a week, on

Thursday evenings at 8 P.M. Outside, standing by the square stone pillar, near the edge of the pavement, you are at the heart of all Denmark, for this is the point from which all distances in the country are measured. Looking up at the Richs Building from a far corner you can see the weather forecast on the giant thermometer. If the weather is fine, the girl with the bicycle comes out of hiding. Letting your eye travel to the east side, you see Strøget, a long, winding thoroughfare with changing names that finally leads to Kongens Nytorv. It is a mile-and-a-half shopper's paradise free from traffic since 1962.

Sculptures are dotted all about the square. Near the Palace Hotel there is a column with two bronze figures ("lur" blowers) on the top. The ancient instruments they are playing are great bronze trumpets. The original instruments were very large—several feet in length, nearly always made in pairs curving in opposite directions like the horns of an ox. There are people today who still play them. The construction of the lur is ingenious. It is made in separate parts joined together by rings and can be taken apart and easily reassembled for convenience of transport. The Danes are so proud of the instrument that it has become the trademark for the dairy industry. **The Dragon Fountain** stands to the right side of the square. Dragons as ornaments were popular with Vikings. Here a ferocious monster battles a bull. Farther to your right is the statue of the creator of enchanting folktales, and here our journey actually begins.

A MAN WHO SEARCHED FOR A PRINCESS, HANS CHRISTIAN ANDERSEN

Hans Christian Andersen was born in 1805 in what was once the sleepy town of Odense. His mother was an illiterate washerwoman, his father a poor cobbler with flights of fantasy. His unfortunate grandfather died insane. The family lived in one tiny room. They had very little except this frail, awkward boy, whom some people thought odd enough to go the way of his grandfather. Yet within Hans Christian Andersen's lifetime, he saw his fairy tales known the world over. Dukes and duchesses, princes and princesses, kings and queens competed to honor him. How did it all begin?

As a small boy he preferred to be alone. At home he had enough toys made by his father, who was excellent at handicraft. He had cutout pictures that changed when you pulled a string, a mill that made the miller dance when it was started, a peep show, and quaint dolls that could nod their heads. Hans Christian loved making clothes for the dolls, pretending they were people in a story. Best of all, he loved just simply to sit in the yard under a makeshift tent and gaze at the leaves of the gooseberry bush, watching them day after day change from little green buds to big yellow, drooping leaves.

Then one day he discovered the theater. All dressed up, he went with his parents to his first performance. And the theater became his favorite haunt. Although he could not afford to attend many performances, he became friendly with the man who distributed the programs. Soon he could go home with only the handbill and imagine the entire play based on the name of the piece and the players in it. Finally he was given a walk-on part. There was no longer any doubt in his mind. His future was on the stage in the capital city. Thousands would cheer "bravo" as he sang to his imagined fair princess, for to Hans Christian it was important that each play feature an ideal woman. His twirling and whirling ballet steps and final leap would leave the audience gasping. (He did not look carefully at his huge feet, which even at his young age were size eleven.) No! He would be an actor and the people would laugh until they cried from just a wiggle of his nose or ears. They would truly sob when he emoted about his illusory kidnapped princess. When his father died after returning from Napoleon's army, Andersen felt the time was right. His mother wanted him apprenticed to a tailor, but he got his own way.

He entered Copenhagen in 1819; fourteen years old, tall and leggy, awkward and almost penniless. He had saved thirteen rigsdalers ($3.64), three of which he spent on the journey. He had attracted attention in his town for his singing, writing, and reading and had found several well-wishers, but all of these told him not to venture any further. But his faith in his own destiny urged him on. Alone in the capital city and the world, he cherished a big dream. Let's follow him and his determination to achieve fame.

Frederiksberg Hill with its splendid gardens and majestic palace is the starting point (twenty minutes north of the city). The pumpkin-shaped mail coach came to a halt at this spot and Andersen alighted. He did not have enough money to reach the city gate; so he stood in the miserable clothes and looked about him. The hill looks today almost as it did the day he arrived. The gateway leading into the gardens has sandstone vases with replicas of human heads on them. Inside there is a hill from where Hans Christian got his first full view of the city, looking over the red-tiled roofs and green spires. Perhaps his reluctant initial glimpse of the city below inspired him later when he wrote "The Ugly Duckling." "To ducks the duckyard is the center of the world, even though wise old ducks know better. 'Oh, what a big world it is!' cried all the tiny ducklings. And of course they did have a lot more room than inside the eggshell. 'Don't think this is all the world!' said their mother. 'It stretches a long way past the other side of the garden, right over to the parson's field! But that's a place I've never been to!' You might wonder what she would have done there, for life in the duckyard presented problems enough."

For centuries people of Copenhagen have come to the hill to celebrate Whitsunday by watching the sunrise. That is why it was originally called "Sun Hill" until King Frederik IV built his palace. The winding canals were used by a later king for state ceremonies as he sailed around them dressed in an admiral's uniform while picnicking subjects waved. Today they are a delightful spot for rowboats. There is also a wading pool and a pond for ducks and miniature sailboats. The King's Chinese tea pavilion lies hidden among old trees and bushes on a little island. It is locked up but you can see the red-lacquered columns and the gilded dragons on the roof. This was Hans Christian's first encounter with the wonderland of the East, which he later wrote about in "The Emperor's Nightingale."

The Zoo and Zoological Gardens are across the way, 32 Roskildevej. Open every day from 9 A.M. to sunset (never later than 8 P.M.). Fee: 6 Kr. (84 cents), children half price.

The PLAY ZOO has animals to pet and ride. The other 2800 inhabitants come from the snowy heights of Greenland and the dark depths of Africa. Don't fail to see the ill-tempered front-horned Sumatran rhinoceros or the rare okapi, an African mammal closely related to the giraffe but lacking the long neck. Time your visit to the feeding schedule posted by the main entrance. The walruses and seals are fed at 11 A.M. Don't miss the ride up the Chinese pagoda version of the Eiffel Tower. In good weather you can just about see the shores of Sweden.

The ZOO RESTAURANT makes a specialty of organizing children's birthday parties. On a blackboard by the entrance you can read the name of the honored guest. If you like surprises you can order the "uspecificeret" (unspecified) smørrebrød (open-faced sandwich) of the day. There is also a section near the restaurant marked "Familiehave" where you may eat the smørrebrød you have brought with you.

ENTERING THE CITY

After exploring the parks Hans Christian picked up his bundle and made his way down the fine avenue of faintly yellowing linden trees (Frederiksberg Allé), then through a half-built-up suburb until he at last stood before the gate of Copenhagen. It was a long way. You may wish to take a bus or cab, but do stop at two side-by-side delightful museums on the way. They will re-create for you the old city exactly as it looked on that misty morning when Hans Christian arrived.

Kobenhavns Bymuseum (Town Museum of Copenhagen), Vesterbrogade 59. Open April through October daily 10 A.M. to 4 P.M.; November through March 1 to 4 P.M. Closed on Monday. Tuesday also 7 to 9 P.M. Fee: 60 øre (8 cents), Wednesday and Friday free.

Meet Copenhagen of bygone days, a charming tour down through nine centuries. The adventure begins in front of the museum building. A miniature model of the city in A.D. 1500 shows the crowded streets and the thick walls and moat that separated the countryside from the inner city. The strongly fortified castle on the little island represents the one erected by Bishop Absalon in 1167.

Inside, stroll down "The Street" as it was in the eighteen hundreds, past toy stores, furniture shops, and the hanging signs announcing the Hatter, the Clockmaker, the Butcher, and others. Peep into peep shows illustrating street lighting in earlier times: train oil lamps from 1853, gaslights after 1853, and electric arc lights in 1890. See models of a windmill which up till 1847 stood close to this very building and a replica of the main guardhouse that protected the harbor until 1874.

Starting in ROOM 8 you can actually walk through Copenhagen of the first half of the nineteenth century by looking at the numerous pictures and exhibits: pictures of fishwives along the canal; Copenhagen scenes depicted in porcelain; and the old Royal Theater just as it looked when Hans Christian was about to storm it. In ROOM 13 you'll find cutouts done by Hans Christian illustrating his fairy tales. Finally, spot the miniature tramcars, the double-decker buses, and the fire brigade in action with their buckets and pumps rushing to rescue entire city streets during the dreadful fire of 1728.

The Post and Telegraph Museum, next door, has a full-size pumpkin-shaped mail coach, perhaps the same design as the one Hans Christian rode for twenty hours from his home in Odense. Antique mailboxes, old postmen's uniforms, and a large stamp display make up this unique collection, which is open Thursday, Sunday, and holidays May to October 10 A.M. to 4 P.M.; November to April, 1 to 3 P.M. Free admission.

BY THE CITY GATE

As you saw in the model outside the museum, the city was contained within its broad, tree-clad ramparts, where windmills turned here and there. The walls were still standing only a little over a hundred years ago. To enter the city you had to go through one of four great gates guarded by customs officers and soldiers whose duty it was to obtain the list of passengers arriving in every mail coach. The King liked to examine the list, so that he could be sure who was visiting the city. Twelve o'clock at night the gates were closed and locked and the keys brought to the King, who was said to put them under his pillow. All of this would seem quite in order to Hans Christian, especially that the King would have been notified of his arrival.

Some of Hans Christian's fellow passengers had mentioned an inn quite close to the gate. It was located at number 18 Vestergade. It was here he lodged his bundle. But with not a minute to rest, out he went to see what he could of the city, especially the goal of his ambition, the Royal Theater at Kongens Nytorv (King's New Market). A flower woman showed him the way to the dignified eighteenth-century building at the end of the open space. Several times he circled the building adoringly. As he paced, a grimy fellow came up to him and asked if he wanted a ticket for the play. Delighted with the friendly gesture, Hans Christian thanked the man heartily and said he would gladly accept a ticket. The man asked him which seat he preferred. "Any you would be kind enough to give me," he replied. The furious ticket-sharper shouted, "Long gawk! You are trying to make a fool of me." Terrified, Hans Christian ran away.

The next day proved equally disappointing. He boldly went to the home of the theater's leading ballerina, Madam Schall. The staircase at Bredgade 19 is still as it was when Hans Christian so hopefully ascended it. Once inside her room he pulled off his boots, took off his big hat (used it as a tambourine), danced a whole scene from a play he knew by name only, made strange, wild gestures and improvised the music and songs as he went along. Madam Schall looked astounded at the tall, gawky boy, but she was touched by his frantic desire to go on the stage. She promised that she would speak to the ballet master to see if there was an opening, but Hans Christian sensed she was merely trying to get rid of him, and went sadly away.

The following day he decided on another plan. In Odense he had seen a newspaper story about a Mr. Giuseppe Siboni, an Italian, being made head of the Royal Theater singing school. He charged out and found Siboni's house. An Italian was a rarity in Copenhagen. Quickly he rang the bell. The housekeeper explained that Mr. Siboni was having a dinner party. Hans Christian immediately told her not only his errand but his entire pathetic life story, told it with all the fire and tears of his desperate mood. Soon the entire dinner party crowded out to the landing and gazed at the half-trembling, half-crying boy. There were artists, composers, and poets who finally drew the forlorn Hans Christian inside to sing. He not only sang and danced, but recited some sad poems which so overwhelmed him that he burst into real tears. The whole company applauded. Among the guests were some of the celebrities of the day, and this strange boy's performance made such a strong impression that they decided to give him their help and support. A composer, Professor Weyse, was one of them. The next day Hans Christian went to see him and was given a small sum of money raised by the guests.

The houses where the boy experienced his first disappointments and joys in the big city still stand as they were in his day. Mr. Siboni's apartment was in Vingaardsstraede and Professor Weyse's in Kronprinsessegade by Kongens Have. It was the quarter around St. Nikolaj Church that Hans Christian came to frequently. Later on he lived awhile in Dybensgade 20 at the corner of Nikolojgade. His first lodging on Holmengade was the oddest place imaginable. The bold women sitting in the windows had long ceased to pay attention to Hans Christian on his way to and from ballet school, when he stood by the wall and practiced standing on his toes. His so-called room with two holes in the door for windows was so small that it held only two chairs on top of each other and barely space for him to dress. Unable to sit, he would go to bed early, at six o'clock, with a candle and his supper on a tray. His time was spent reading or dreaming. Soon he missed his doll theater in Odense and made himself a new one. Now in his sixteenth year, he passed his evenings lying in bed and making costumes for his dolls.

During the day Hans Christian was intensely happy. The real theater was his whole life. He took singing lessons and was a pupil in the ballet school. Let's visit the place where he diligently studied.

Teatermuseet (Theater Museum) is in one of the wings of the Christiansborg Palace, Christiansborg Ridebane 18. Open Wednesday and Sunday 2 to 4 P.M. Fee: 1 Kr. (14 cents).

The museum is housed in the Old Court Theater, complete with antique chairs and oval-shaped balconies. Architect Nicolas Henri Jardin designed the theater so that the floor could be raised to the level of the stage, making it suitable for the masquerades that were popular at court. King Christian VII was so interested in the theater that he chose to play some roles himself, including the part of an "enlightened" sultan who kills himself and his sweetheart out of jealousy. It was here that Hans Christian, the ballet pupil, came and went with a little black-eyed girl, Johanne Louise, who became the theater's prima donna. The great day came when for the first time Hans Christian was given a small role. Though the part was only that of a troll, an anonymous goblin in a corps of goblins, he was overjoyed. He saw his name in print! The day the posters were up, he rushed out from lampposts to walls, from walls to lampposts. Could it indeed be true? At night he took the program to bed with him and stared at the printed page. "Andersen—Troll." Then again and again. "Troll—Andersen." Finally he would become a star of the theater.

Go up on the stage by the little stairs. The dressing rooms on the right have had many noted guests such as Sarah Bernhardt. On the opposite side is the actors' entrance. Up this staircase Hans Christian hurried, anxious to find fame. In the glass case is the rare program for the ballet *Armida* listing "H. Andersen" as a troll and Johanne Louise as a cupid.

Opposite the museum wing is the magnificent old riding school, where you can watch the horses go through their paces. There are other interesting parts of the palace to visit.

Christiansborg Palace. Tours every hour on the hour, April to October 10 A.M. to 4 P.M. daily (closed on Monday); November to March, only Thursday to Sunday. Fee: 2 Kr. (28 cents).

The entrance is from the cobblestoned central courtyard. You'll visit the Folketing, where the laws of the land are made, and the Royal Presence Chambers, where state banquets and receptions are held. In one of the rooms you will even find a portrait of Hans Christian. Most unusual is the separate tour of the basement, which leaves at the same time as the regular tour of the rest of the palace. Below, where the city began over

seven hundred years ago, are the ruins of Bishop Absalon's for-
tress-castle. Be sure to see the Well of Absalon (royal children
were baptized in its waters). If it hadn't been for the fierce,
glorious Absalon, who rode, fought, swam, and was one of the
most intelligent men of his time, Denmark would have been
destroyed by the Wendish pirates.

Tojhusmuseet (Royal Arsenal Museum), also on the palace
grounds, is open May to September 1 to 4 P.M. weekdays,
10 A.M. to 4 P.M. Sunday; October to April 1 to 3 P.M. weekdays, 11 A.M. to 4 P.M. Sunday. Free.

More uniforms, armory, and arms than you would hope to
see in a lifetime. The ARMORY HALL upstairs is stacked with
engraved seventeenth-century armor, rapiers and sabers, ceremonial swords, wheel-lock pistols, and rifles. One of the oldest
displays is a fifteenth-century wrought-iron handgun. But the
most amazing and cruel display is on the TOP FLOOR. These are
the head models (Turks and Moors) used in the 1700s for
carrousel riding and shooting practice. Carrousel riding was
an offshoot of knightly tournaments. Guns and lances were
aimed at the figures. If the dummy was not hit in the center of
the neck, the figure would pivot and strike the horse with its
shield or sword, causing pain to the horse and shame to the
rider.

The Royal Library is adjacent to the palace. Pass through
five low arches and into a marvelously landscaped garden. Long
ago all this land was covered with water and was part of the
naval harbor. You can still see two of the iron rings to which
the ships were tied. Inside, the library is full of books by and
about Hans Christian, diaries, letters, manuscripts, photographs,
clippings, and scrapbooks. The building is open weekdays 9 A.M.
to 6 P.M. Free.

Between rehearsals at the Court Theater, Hans Christian explored the surrounding area with tremendous pleasure, for the odd sizes and shapes of the buildings fed his insatiable fancy. Perhaps he even pictured himself as a guest of King Christian IV (1577–1648). Beyond the King's love of water and ships, spirited horses, sports, lively ladies, and his twenty-two children, he had a passion for buildings. Over twenty of Denmark's finest palaces and churches owe their existence to him. Here are a few of his nearby beguiling creations.

Borsen (Stock Exchange), at Børsgade, has a roof and steeple with sheets of glittering copper that change, chameleonlike, according to the shifting lights of the season and hours of the day. The spire is made of the entwined tails of four copper dragons standing on their heads. The King worked with his own hands on the construction of the unusual spire.

Inside, the red brick, gabled building is still used to conduct business as the world's oldest exchange. You may visit Monday to Saturday 12:30 P.M. to 2:30 P.M. The room on the left side is the scene of many important transactions. On Thursdays the price of Danish butter is fixed there. Don't make a single gesture or you may wind up owning several years' supply of something you wouldn't possibly be able to take home.

Rundetarn (Round Tower), Købmagergade, is another of Christian IV's buildings. It served as an astronomical observatory and rises nine stories high. To reach the summit there is neither elevator nor stairs, only a spiral roadway broad enough to drive a horse and carriage up it. The only person said to have done so was Peter the Great, when he visited Copenhagen in 1716. Some say he went on horseback while his wife rode in a carriage. The superb view from the top is well worth the circling climb. At night you can study the stars through the observatory glass. These lofty heights remained vivid in Hans Christian's mind when he wrote the fairy tale "The Tinder Box." Many of his stories were based on folk tales told to him as a young child. In them the number three plays an important part. In "The Tinder Box" a soldier does the bidding of an old lady and goes underground to seek his fortune. He finds three dogs, each one bigger than the other. The author describes these monsters by the size of their eyes: The first has eyes as big as breakfast cups, the second as big as mill wheels, and as for the third: "Really though, it was horrid! The dog in there actually did have eyes as big as the Round Tower! And they were going round and round in its head like wheels!" Open April to October every day 10 A.M. to 5 P.M. (Sunday from noon); November to March, 10 A.M. to 4 P.M. (Sunday from noon). Fee: 1 Kr. (14 cents), children half price. The Historical Astronomical Collection is separate and is open Sunday noon to 4 P.M. Fee: 25 øre (3 cents).

A NEW CAREER IS LAUNCHED

But Hans Christian's happy days in training at the Court Theater were short-lived. One New Year's Day the management told him, "Neither your appearance nor your voice is fit for the stage." Practically penniless and almost in shock, he wandered about aimlessly. Suddenly he recalled the old Danish superstition which said that what you do on New Year's Day determines the course of the year. All other means to the stage having failed, he decided to try magic. Although the theater was closed he sneaked past the sleeping doorman, fumbled his way past the scenery and curtains and out onto the dimly lighted stage. Falling to his knees, he tried to remember the lines from a play, any play. But none would come. Slowly he started to speak.

He was creating his own play on the spot. After he finished he quietly left the theater, convinced that his luck would change.

Gray, cold months passed and nothing happened. Money had to be obtained. He started to write his own plays and read them to anyone who would listen. He submitted the scripts under the name of William Christian Walter to a newspaper. While Christian stood for himself, it was sandwiched in by William for Shakespeare and Walter for Scott. A critic wrote a little piece about one of his plays, saying "quite remarkable considering his lack of education." Finally he found a sympathetic ear and had one of his dramas reviewed by the directors of the Royal Theater. The beginning of the meeting went badly. "The script could never be produced—but there is a glint of gold in it. If you would attend school and study seriously you might someday be able to present the Danish stage with works worthy of being performed." Both because they thought his manuscripts showed some talent and because Hans Christian seemed unspoiled, the directors had decided to send him away and pay for his education.

Dazed, Hans Christian stammered his gratitude and stumbled out of the room. His new career was born. Soon he would be a theatrical giant, this time as a playwright, putting just the right words into the actors' mouths. He immediately wrote an exultant letter to his mother telling her how his fortune was won. His mother showed the letter to everyone, including Karen, his half sister. The word "theater" dazzled her. Karen thought that she too could do no better than seek fame in Copenhagen. On Hans Christian's last day in the city before leaving for school Karen arrived at his attic door. To his utter consternation as well as her own, she entered the room. Could this dark little hole be her brother's residence? What could he do? He had to leave, somewhat bitter by the unannounced arrival of his sister. Later he was cheered up by the boisterous singing of young students during their journey to school as Hans Christian made his way into a new life.

In 1827 when he returned to Copenhagen his sister had gone her own way and Hans Christian obtained another attic in Vingaardsstraede 6, a fine old building where his room with its sloping walls and dormer window still stands unchanged. Here he spent several happy years writing the first of many important works. A few lesser ones too, among them poems for which he was paid coffee and a roll every Sunday. The dormer window opened onto a view of the red-tiled roofs slanting in different directions, a gleam of canals, and a glimpse of shipping boats, church spires, and castle towers. Only three or four people could stand comfortably in the room at one time, but it had a royal view. Hans Christian leaned out, facing the May sunset, and recalled the miserable years he had just spent gaining an education.

The very fact of having to start at the lowest grade and at seventeen sit in class with boys twelve and thirteen was severe enough. But worse still was the headmaster, Simon Meisling, who enjoyed destroying Hans Christian's dreamy, sensitive nature. Greek and Latin were the headmaster's favorite subjects but Hans Christian's poorest. The headmaster, extremely quick-tempered, seemed to delight in hurling terrible insults at Hans Christian in front of the other students. This destroyed the young boy and he was in constant fear of disgrace. The experience made such a lasting impression that even in old age he would have bad dreams about this particular teacher. In 1826 the headmaster was transferred to Elsinore, the setting for Shakespeare's play *Hamlet*. Hans Christian's sponsors urged him to go along. There things were even more dismal, "the darkest, the bitterest time in all my life." But now it was all past and he would be going to the university in Copenhagen. Soon he would begin the rounds as a regular dinner guest at the best houses in the city. He had received an invitation from one of the men who

sponsored his education, Commander P. F. Wulff. There was
to be a lavish party at Amalienborg Palace, where the commander lived. Let's go along and see the setting for the lavish
ball.

Amalienborg Palace (Amalienborg Slotsplads) is where the
King lives with his family. Amalienborg is really four palaces,
built in the eighteenth century by prominent noblemen. The King
bought them when the palace of Christiansborg had been gutted
by fire in 1794. The present King occupies the far palace on
the left, known as Frederik VIII's Palace. The near one on the
left is Christian VIII's Palace, where the present King's father
lived. The palace on the far right, Christian IX, is the residence
of the heir to the throne, Princess Margrethe, her husband, Prince
Henrik, and their two children. The other two are used for
state functions and as apartments for distinguished guests.
They were probably the buildings where Commander Wulff lived
and where the party was to be held. The rooms cannot be visited
but you can see the colorful changing of the guard at noon every
day. The thirty-six members of the Royal Guard will probably
not be wearing the red full-dress uniform tunics you have seen
on posters and toy guardsmen. The red tunics are worn only
on special occasions; the regular uniform is a smart dark blue
color and is topped off by black bearskin busbies, like those of
the hussars. A thirty-one-piece band precedes the guards and
sets the tempo for their proud steps, brightening the morning
with martial music of trumpet and drum, fife and clarinet. The
colorful parade seems like a picture from one of Hans Christian's
stories as the band assembles under the King's window to give
its brief concert. When the music is over the Danish flag is
brought from the palace. The band then leads the retiring guard
away as the fresh group, with appropriate life-guarding expressions, takes its stations around the square. Ask one of the guards
to show you the special flag which flies when the King is home.

Time for lunch? **Langelinie Pavillionen,** Langelinie, overlooks the famous statue of the Little Mermaid. There is a wonderful view of the harbor from all the tables. Try a tasty "rejemad"— buttered bread and shrimps. Price about 10 Kr. ($1.40).

Now for a closer look at the statue. There sits the pet of Denmark: Hans Christian's Little Mermaid. The life-size figure is the epitome of gentle longing. In the story the little Sea Princess, "skin as clear and fine as a rose leaf and eyes as blue as the deepest sea," had a fishtail instead of legs and longed to come up from the ocean bottom to see the other world of ships and towns, of men and animals. One stormy night she rescued from the sea "the handsomest of all young human Princes with great black eyes."

"If human beings are not drowned can they live forever?" asked the little mermaid of her grandmother.

"They too must die and their life is even shorter than ours," replied the old lady. "We can live to be three hundred years. Then we become only foam on the water. But humans have a soul which lives forever, lives even after the body has turned to earth. It rises through the bright air up to all the shining stars."

"I would gladly give all the hundreds of years to be a human and have an immortal soul," sighed the little mermaid. To make her wish a reality the little mermaid made a pact with the sea witch, who lived in a house of "white bones from shipwrecked men."

"You can become the loveliest daughter of man if you can bear the pain. For each step you take will feel like you're walking upon sharp knives," croaked the ugly witch. "And if your precious Prince marries another, your heart will break and you will become foam on the water."

"Give me the magic potion at once!" said the little mermaid as she thought of her handsome Prince and the immortal soul.

"In exchange, since you have the finest voice here at the bottom of the sea, you will give it to me," roared the witch.

So the little mermaid became a mortal, a foundling, a slave, an outsider. Day by day the Prince grew more fond of her but more as a good child rather than his wife. Then he announced he would marry a princess of a neighboring country, for he was sure she was the mysterious creature that had rescued him from the sea that stormy night. The night before the wedding the little mermaid's sisters arose out of the sea; they were pale, like herself; their long hair no longer fluttered in the wind—it had been cut off.

"We have given it to the witch for this knife. Kill the Prince and come back! Hurry!"

The little mermaid looked at the sharp blade and fixed her eyes on the Prince, who in his sleep murmured his bride's name. She held the knife for a second in her trembling hand. Then she flung it far away into the waves, threw herself into the sea, and felt her body dissolving into foam.

The next morning, "invisible, she kissed the forehead of the bride, smiled to the Prince, and mounted with the other children of the air on the rosy cloud which floated through the sky," for she had earned an immortal soul.

Now the bronze statue of the little mermaid sits out on her rock ever watching the ships that come and go, looking for the mortal Prince who will never return.

The **Langelinie** (Long Line) is a favorite place to promenade. It follows a narrow strip of land with flowering trees and a moated park surrounding an old fort called the Citadel. When winter comes the moat freezes and young people go ice skating. At one end of Langelinie is the church of St. Alban's and the statue of the grasping goddess Gefion, who carved out most of Denmark for herself. Langelinie is as popular now as it was at the turn of the century when King Christian IX would exercise his pet dog here and passers-by would stop to pat it. Nurses push baby carriages and flirt with sailors. Judges and diplomats mix with dock workers and circus performers, as the ships and kayaks ply their way through the water. If you're weary of walking you can take a boat trip that leaves from close beside the Little Mermaid. It takes you to Gammel Strand (near Kongens Nytorv), where the ruddy-faced fishwives are selling their odorous wares. The cost is 2 Kr. (28 cents), children half price. There are several other harbor trips you can take, ranging in price from 4 Kr. (56 cents) to 7 Kr. (98 cents); always half price for children. For information phone PA 3105.

THE SEARCH FOR THE PRINCESS BEGINS

Hans Christian took pride in his punctuality. He arrived at Amalienborg Palace just as the guests were beginning to make their entrance. When he saw all the lovely people all handsomely attired he rushed out of the ballroom and later wrote: "I flew out and up to my room, went to bed, cursed my fate for not having fine clothes . . . the carriages rolled past and inside my head ideas rolled around." Before leaving the main entrance he stopped before the painting of a fair lady long dead. "Oh that she were alive!" he thought. And then in his diary he wrote, "Give me a bride. My blood needs love as my heart needs it!"

And then, at twenty-five, he thought he found his princess. In the summer of 1830 he met the sister of a student friend of his while he was on a holiday. Twenty years old, Riborg Voigt had a sweet, serious face and she greatly admired Hans Christian's published works. He arrived so early in the morning to see his friend that no one was ready to receive him except Riborg. She laughed and joked about her lazy brother and Hans Christian thought her witty as well as exquisite; he exerted himself to please and soon felt surprised at the ease and joy between them. Days passed filled with picnics, singing, laughter, and coy feminine tributes to the young poet. He was captivated, yet with a terrible desire to run away. As he departed he gave her a poem, and she gave him a nosegay and waved from her window, as the carriage rolled away.

Later she came to Copenhagen and Hans Christian rushed to see her at the Hotel Royal, the fine building at Ved Stranden 18. Although she was already engaged to be married, he proposed to Riborg, and was refused. Her farewell letter was found in a leather purse around his neck when he died. By his order it was burned unread. This first of many loves may in later years have inspired him to write "The Princess and the Pea." The enchanting story tells of a Prince who searched for a "real" Princess. To make sure of each contestant's sensitivity a pea was placed under a pile of twenty mattresses. When a bedraggled girl soaked from a rainstorm appeared at the door claiming to be a "real" Princess she was put to the test. In the morning she was asked, "Did you sleep well?"

"Oh, terribly badly!" said the Princess. "I seemed to be lying on something very hard, and my whole body is black and blue this morning."

So the Prince took this Princess to be his wife, for now he was sure that he found a "real" and natural princess. And as the story goes—"the pea was put into a museum, where it may still be seen, if no one has stolen it."

Hans Christian's initial quest for a princess was overly dramatic. Riborg was neither his greatest nor his deepest love but merely his first. Scarcely had she turned him down when the reviewers of his books also snubbed him. To recover his spirits he decided to travel and in the spring of 1831 he set out with his savings to visit Germany. It was the turning point of his career. For when he returned to Copenhagen he wrote his impressions into books which were successful. Again his troubled heart met with a fresh defeat when Louise, the daughter of his sponsor and dearest friend Jonas Collins, became engaged to someone else. He had secretly loved her. Travel again was the only way to escape. He journeyed to France and Italy, where he visited the most famous people of the day. This voyage inspired him to write his novel *The Improvisatore*. The story of Antonio, a poor child from the country who is given an education by a nobleman and becomes a poet, was his own life changed to an Italian setting with ruins, blue skies, orange trees, serenades, and bandits. It was a popular success, followed in the same year by the first little book of fairy tales. The small gemlike stories were also part of his life's tale.

All was going well except his search for his "real" princess. Then he met Jenny Lind, a remarkable singer making her European debut in Copenhagen. He was entranced by her singing and moved by the similarity of their humble backgrounds. During the three weeks of her stay he sent her poems, bouquets, presents. Indeed, what more happy combination than a poet and a singer? For a while Jenny lived in Nikolaj Plads. Then on October 21, 1845, she gave a farewell dinner for her friends at the Hotel Royal, the same spot where Riborg had informed Hans Christian of her intention to marry someone else. Binding Jenny and himself together, he wrote, almost in one sitting, "The Nightingale." This is the tale of the little bird from the woods who by far outdistanced in popularity the ruby- and diamond-trimmed music box mechanical bird.

"And the Nightingale sang so sweetly that tears came into the Emperor's eyes and rolled down his cheeks. Then the Nightingale sang still more sweetly, and it was the Emperor's heart that melted. . . . The whole town talked about the marvelous bird, and if two people met, one could scarcely say 'night' before the other said 'gale,' and then they would sigh in unison without words. Eleven pork-butchers' children were named Nightingale, but not one could sing. . . . 'Only one thing I ask you,' said the Nightingale. 'Tell no one that you have a little bird who tells you everything.' Then the Nightingale flew away. The attendants came in to look after what they thought was their dead Emperor, and there he stood, bidding them 'Good Morning!'"

HIS SUCCESSFUL YEARS

Hans Christian changed addresses many times but he was particularly fond of Nyhavn. The throbbing life of the harbor and the many ships stimulated his unfailing desire to travel. He moved into an apartment on the second floor of Nyhavn number 20 in 1834 and here wrote his first fairy tales. Among the four in the volume was "Great Claus and Little Claus." Money being very scarce, it played an important part in his thinking. This folk tale was told from his own pressing needs. Two men with the same name were distinguished by their neighbors by the number of horses each owned. "Great Claus" owned four; "Little Claus" owned one. All week long Little Claus was obliged to plow for Great Claus and to lend him his one horse. But on Sunday Little Claus had all five and was so proud that he cracked his whip and cried out "Gie-up, my five pets."

"I must really beg you not to say that again," said Great Claus. "If you do, I shall hit your horse on the head so that he will drop down dead on the spot." And this was what he did when Little Claus had a slip of the tongue. The rest of the tale explains how Little Claus outwitted Great Claus by enticing him to seek sea cattle at the bottom of the river. As he walked away from the riverbank, having just put a big stone into the sack containing Great Claus, he said, "I'm afraid he won't find any cattle where he's going," as he drove his own real herd back home.

In 1848 Hans Christian moved to Nyhavn number 67 and then to his last apartment at Nyhavn 18. Often he would walk about to enjoy the sights of his favorite part of the city. Here the sailing ships tie up to the pier. The canal streets are popular with sailors and filled with dark dives and tattoo parlors. The enormous anchor at the end of the canal has sailed the seven seas on a Danish frigate and is now a monument to the sailors who lost their lives during the Second World War. Almost daily flowers are placed here by unknown donors. Walk along until you come to Lille Strandstraede, an interesting street, where you turn left. Wander under the archway of number 6 to a small courtyard, where you will find a timbered house looking like "old Copenhagen."

Toward the end of his life the aging writer was often ailing and stayed at home. On his seventieth birthday Crown Prince Frederik came to see him, and the previous day the King had sent a carriage to fetch him and bring him to the palace. In his diary Hans Christian wrote: "When I told the King how during my early afflictions I had eaten a piece of bread for dinner every day on a bench in Kongens Have, and now I was to see a statue of myself put there, his eyes became wet with tears. . . ."

Rosenborg Palace, Øster Voldgade, May 1 to October 20, 11 A.M. to 3 P.M. every day; October 21 to April 30, Sunday, Tuesday, and Friday 11 A.M. to 2 P.M. Fee: 2 Kr. (28 cents), children .50 øre (7 cents).

The red brick castle was another of King Christian IV's favorite buildings. It is the home of the mementos of the Danish royal family (odd pieces such as ivory coronation chairs and Frederick VII's baby shoes). The crown jewels in Christian V's room, number 6, are spectacular. The crown of Christian IV is a superb piece in gold and multicolored enamel, set with diamonds and pearls. It has been kept here for three centuries. The Collar of the Order of the Garter is from England and dates back over three hundred years. It was given by Elizabeth I to Frederik II, and consists of twenty-six blue-enameled garters with red roses, and shows St. George slaying a dragon. The Oldenburg, Germany, Gilded Drinking Horn is Rosenborg's oldest (1448) and most celebrated treasure. The detailed figures represent Gothic castles and battlements, musicians and shield-bearers. According to legend, it was given to an early Danish king by elves.

Don't miss the KNIGHTS' HALL, room number 21, with its elegant coronation chair, used since 1671 and guarded by three silver life-sized lions. ROOM NUMBER 6 was Christian IV's and contains his lavish coronation saddle and black-velvet riding habit trimmed in gold, pearls, and diamonds.

The KINGS' GARDEN (have) surrounds the castle. Down the old avenue of lime trees stands Hans Christian's statue. It is a fitting place for his memorial, for he loved visiting the peaceful country. "In this world of quiet lakes in the woods, and the green grass fields where the game leap and the stork saunters on his red legs, only nature around me and within me preaches. . . ." He often wrote about these moments, as in "The Little Fir Tree." "Far down in the forest grew a little fir tree that yearned to become big and be a part of the outside world."

"Rejoice in thy youth," said the sunbeam. And the wind kissed the tree and dew watered it with tears. Finally the little fir tree grew large enough to become a handsome Christmas tree in someone's home and it listened carefully to wonderful stories and rhymes such as "Humpty Dumpty." After all the happy festivities were done it was thrown aside and chopped into small pieces which were placed in a fire under the kettle. The tree sighed so deeply that each sigh was like a pistol shot. "Pop, pop," it cried. With each "pop" the tree was thinking of a summer day in the forest, or of some winter night when the stars shone brightly, and of Christmas evening and of "Humpty Dumpty," the only story it knew how to relate.

The Botanical Gardens, across the street, open every day 1 P.M. to 4 P.M. (to 3 P.M. October to March), free, is filled with wonderful rare plants and trees.

THE NIGHTFALL OF HIS LIFE

The evening of Hans Christian's last birthday was spent at a gala performance in his beloved Royal Theater. Afterward he wrote: "What a lovely, magnificent day, how frail my body is to bear such blessings. . . ." The frail body grew weaker and weaker, and then a few months later on August 4, 1875, he died. Although he never found a princess, he did win over most of the world with his 168 fairy tales, of which 156 were printed during his lifetime.

Vor Frelsers Kirke (Our Savior's Church) at Prinsessegade on Christianhaven was where Hans Christian's funeral services were held. If you are nimble and have a good head for heights, climb the circular outside stairs on the twisting steeple. You may recall that the heroes of Jules Verne's book *The Voyage to the Center of the Earth* did this in preparation for their exploration of the middle of the world. The tower is open May to September 10 A.M. to 4 P.M. daily, Sunday noon to 4 P.M.; October to April 10 A.M. to 2 P.M. daily, Sunday noon to 4 P.M. Fee: 1 Kr. (14 cents), children half price.

The Assistens Cemetery, Jagtvej, is Hans Christian's final resting place, where he is surrounded by the graves of many of the people who were to figure in the fairy tale of his life. Today, nearly one hundred years later, his marker is never without flowers, his stories never out of print, his home in Odense is never without visitors. Somewhere in the world a young person is joyfully discovering his books for the first time as Hans Christian Andersen continues to weave his magical spell.

ABOVE ALL, COPENHAGEN MEANS TIVOLI

Tivoli is music, lights, flowers, and murmuring fountains all made to resemble a fairy garden filled with innocent merrymaking. The proper way to enter is by the festive main gate passing by the Chinese Theater into the heart of Tivoli. Tivoli opens at 9 A.M. but at 4 P.M. people begin to arrive in numbers. Admission is 2.50 Kr. (about 35 cents) on weekdays and 3.50 Kr. (49 cents) on weekends. The season starts May 1 and lasts until the second Sunday in September. The special attractions of the day are posted outside and inside the main entrance.

The Tivoli Guards come marching through the garden on Saturday and Sunday at 6:30 and 8:30 P.M. and give concerts at 3 P.M. on Sunday on the open-air stage. These ninety boys between the ages of nine and sixteen parade about in their scarlet tunics and bearskins playing their drums and fifes. It is a great honor to be selected for this corps. Fireworks are displayed at 11:15 P.M. on Wednesday and 11:45 P.M. on Saturday, Sunday and holidays.

The Pantomimeteatret (Pantomime Theater) is one of Tivoli's true glories. Performances of ballets and mimes are given in the afternoon and at 7:45 every evening. The Chinese-style theater has wooden dragons twining over the roof ridge. As the show begins the splendid peacock-tail curtain spreads apart and disappears into the floor. This is one of the last places in the world where you can still see the old classic Italian pantomimes with Pierrot, Harlequin, and Columbine played exactly as they were hundreds of years ago. It has become the custom that seemingly slow-witted Pierrot is called before the curtain after the show to the shouts of "Say something, Pierrot" from the audience and that the dumb white clown must admit that he can speak. The true spirit of the theater is written in Chinese characers about the stage: "It pleases me to please others." The same sign appeared above Hans Christian Andersen's own miniature theater models. Seats can be reserved in advance at the ticket office on the left by the main entrance. Price only 1.50 Kr. (21 cents), but you can stand and watch the show free.

Punch and Judy shows, modern-style, are given daily in the afternoon next to the Pantomime Theater. The **Kunstnerplaenen** is the open-air stage in the center featuring all kinds of acts (tumbling, clowns, acrobats, aerialists). Ticket prices range from 1.50 Kr. (21 cents). Show time is 7 and 10:30 P.M. The music halls in the eight-sided building feature international singing and dancing stars. Shows are at 7:30 and 9:30 P.M. and cost from 6 Kr. (84 cents). The concert hall near the cluster of splashing fountains has famous artists. Show time is 7:30 and 9 P.M. Good seats start at 4 to 7 Kr. (56 to 98 cents).

The Children's Playground is one of the most unique in the world! Climb upon a "fireworks tree," hundreds of electric lamps flash; go through "The House of Forbidden Games," where you're allowed to do all the things you're not supposed to do at home; and explore the carved wooden figures of a rocking fish, a porcupine, and birds that act as seesaws. There are about eighty regular rides and attractions, ranging from roller coasters to Ferris wheels to a crazy kitchen where you smash pieces of china.

You can choose from twenty-three restaurants. **Groften** is in the hollow on the right side of the Pantomime Theater. Most people eat outdoors under the leafy linden trees to the sound of chirping sparrows. This restaurant has one of the best dinner buys in Tivoli, average cost 10.50 Kr. ($1.47). Lunch prices for triple-decker sandwiches, 5 Kr. (70 cents). **Faergekroen** is by the lake, the remains of the old moat that once circled Copenhagen. The building is like an old half-timbered inn. Triple-decker sandwiches are their specialty, 5 Kr. (70 cents), and so is "Lobscouse," a meat and potato dish spiced with butter and bay leaf, 6 Kr. (84 cents). Rousing singsongs are heard in the evening. **Pjerrot Maelkebar** (milk bar) is like an outdoor bazaar with hanging baskets and canvas canopies. Light snacks are best, hamburgers 2.50 Kr. (35 cents) and special delicious ice cream 1.75 Kr. (25 cents).

MORE, JUST FOR FUN

Circus Schumann, Jernbanegade 8, a few steps from Rådhuspladsen, is filled with clowns, animals, and tumblers and is done in the grand old style. The top spot is reserved for the performing horses. Seat prices range from 8.50 Kr. ($1.19) to 12 Kr. ($1.68).

Dyrehaven (Royal Deer Park) and **Bakken (Amusement Park)** are a short twenty-minute ride by electric train from the center of the city. The two thousand deer that live in Dyrehaven wander about freely and can be seen alone or in groups. You cannot feed them but they are well supplied with food and are quite harmless if you follow the rules. Many of the deer will approach within a few feet.

All kinds of surprises are in the park—like a little hunting lodge, EREMITAGEN built by a king over two hundred years ago. It is a miniature castle and has many unusual features, such as a hole in the kitchen ceiling through which a lift carries the food up to the dining room. Take a drive through the woods and parklands in an old-fashioned horse-drawn carriage, or in the winter in a sleigh, which you can rent just outside Klampenborg station, where the train arrives.

Bakken has every kind of entertainment that you can wish for —a ghost train, unusual rides, and all sorts of games. Most of all, it has the BIG TOP. Denmark's best performers, like Professor Tribini, a remarkable juggler, appear here. There are other light-hearted shows to enjoy, like *Summer Delight* and *The Merry Juggler*. There is no need to go hungry or thirsty, with restaurants like LITTLE PETER and THE BALCONY. Bakken is open April 20 to August 28 every day; Dyrehavn is open all year.

The **Royal Theater** at Kongens Nytorv is charming. The chubby cupids on the classic curtain put you in a happy mood before the show begins. The Royal Danish Ballet Company is world-famous, particularly for their over-one-hundred-year-old story ballets by Bournonville. Performances are given all year except during July and August. Tickets range from 7 to 25 Kr. (98 cents to $3.50). Curtain time is 8 P.M.

Castle hopping can be done in one afternoon on a special tour. Ask at your hotel about the tickets (price about 35 Kr., $5). The three regal residences in some of the tours include Rosenborg, Frederiksborg (the coronation setting), and Kronborg (Hamlet's home).

Frederiksborg Castle (Museum of National History) at Hillerød. Open every day May 1 to September 30, 10 A.M. to 5 P.M.; October to April, 11 A.M. to 4 P.M.; closes one hour earlier in winter. Fee: 1 Kr. (14 cents).

Climb the spiral staircase of the KING'S TOWER. The walls are covered with the coats of arms of the Knights of the Grand Cross. Enter the splendor of the gilded CHAPEL where Danish kings were once crowned, a formality no longer observed. Notice the King's pew and the famous mammoth wooden organ made in 1610. It has 1001 rectangular pipes; the keys are of solid ivory covered with engraved silver. Two men have to work together to play it; one controls the bellows, the other the keys. Ordinarily the chapel organist gives a recital every Thursday from 1:30 to 2:00 P.M. The gallery is hung with the coats of arms of the Knights of the Order of the Elephant. Being made a member of this order is the highest honor a person can receive from the Danish Government. Most of the people who have been chosen are royalty, with the exception of President Eisenhower, Sir Winston Churchill, and a few others.

As you pass through the rooms in the KING'S WING you'll see large chests decorated with coats of arms. They were generally made for girls of noble rank shortly before their marriage, and held a precious dowry. The WINTER PARLOR ceiling has another portrayal of the giantess Gefion and her four sons plowing their portion of the Danish Islands out of the soil of Sweden. The most curious item in all the rich treasure is in ROOM 42. To the right of the enormous canopied bed is a small statue of a dwarf. This is not unusual, for dwarfs were favorites at court, considered good luck. Inquire from the guard if you can look closely at the statue's pocket flap. There you'll find a little slit. Besides being an ornamental piece, it was also a bedside bank. The thought of a king keeping his money close to him while he slept is indeed odd.

Before completing your tour, stop in at ROOM 56 to see the portrait of Hans Christian Andersen. It is appropriate that his picture be hung here. The faraway look in his eyes suggests that he may have been thinking about "The Emperor's New Clothes," the story of the vain emperor who was so fond of new clothes that he spent all his money on them. "He cared nothing about his soldiers, or the theater, or for driving in the woods, except for the sake of showing off." Two swindlers pretended to be weavers of cloth that would enable him to discover which men in his kingdom were unfit for their jobs. When the Emperor took off all his clothes the impostors pretended to fasten on different articles of clothes. Finally they proclaimed, "How gorgeous your new robes look." The Emperor paraded through the streets as the astonished crowds looked on, daring not to say anything but "What splendid clothes." From way inside the mob a tiny voice piped up, "But he hasn't got anything on." The Emperor stopped, for he knew what the child mumbled was true. But he thought, "The procession must go on now." So he held himself high, and his chamberlains twisted and turned the invisible train.

"And the procession goes on still!"

Hans Christian had actually written the story as a deadly barb about one of his rivals for a sweetheart. The man always wore fine outer garments but Hans Christian added, "heaven help him if anyone ever saw him in his undershirt."

Kronborg Castle at Elsinore, called "Hamlet's home," is open

May 1 to September 30, 10 A.M. to 5 P.M.; October to April, 11 to 4 P.M. Fee: 2.50 Kr. (35 cents).

The castle was built by King Frederik in 1412 as a stronghold to protect the sound, Øresund, and to collect tolls from every foreign ship that passed through it. The King was in need of funds since the royal treasury was beginning to dwindle. The castle is built on a rocky elevation only three miles from Sweden, twenty minutes by motor ferry. Before the castle and extending along the sound is the FLAG BATTERY, with its ancient guns and pyramids of cannon balls. This is the "platform" on which Prince Hamlet was supposed to have seen his father's ghost. There is no record that Shakespeare himself ever visited the castle, but it is known that one of his best comic actors, William Kempe, often did. If the playwright never saw the towers of Kronborg he heard enough stories to fire his imagination.

Wandering through the drafty, bleak rooms, you can almost see Hamlet's drama come alive. Perhaps the great KNIGHTS' HALL was Shakespeare's backdrop for the strolling players who were invited by the Prince to re-enact his father's murder as he accuses his uncle, now his stepfather, of the dreadful deed. In the play, what begins as a joyful party ends up a graveyard, as even Hamlet's mother is accidently poisoned. This huge hall is over two hundred feet long. The windows opening to the court and those looking out to the sea are so deep-set in alcoves that the light coming from them in snowy winter or full summer casts a kind of spell upon the room.

The other highlights of the castle are: the chapel with original oak furnishings; the private chambers of kings and queens (the TURRET ROOM off the Queen's Chamber on the second floor served as a prison in 1772 for Queen Caroline Mathilde, because she fell in love with a court diplomat); the wool and silk tapestries depicting Danish kings in various settings; and the TRUMPETER'S TOWER, in the southwest corner, with its commanding view of the sound, busy with ships coming to and from

Sweden. Two paintings of special note are: "Children Departing for School" by Frantz Clein and "A Lecture in a Noble Academy" by Reinholt Timm. A spooky treat awaits you in the basement, the garrison-prisons. Here sits a statue of Holger Danske, a legendary hero, who with sword and shield is supposed to awake at a moment's call to defend his country against all dangers.

The Danish Maritime Museum, housed in a wing of the castle, vividly illustrates the history of Danish shipping from prehistoric days through the Viking period and on to the present time. Two unusual exhibits are: a brick with a picture of a ship scratched out in 1450 by the workmen who built the Carmelite monastery nearby, and the rather humorous painted clay figures with their false hair. The latter are rare portraits of European merchants and of seamen with very grim expressions.

FARMING SIDE TRIP

Frilandsmuseet (Farmland Open-Air Museum), situated nine miles from the central Station to Sorgenfri is ninety acres of oldtime country life reassembled exactly as it had been from various parts of Denmark. There is a whole range of buildings, including primitive "long houses," tower windmills, and nineteenth-century pottery workshops. There are two unusual things to look for. One is the thatch-roofed farmhouses from Laesø, which are made of seaweed a yard thick. Straw was scarce and had to be saved for fertilizing the soil, while seaweed was commonly washed ashore. The other oddity is the houses from Fanø. The people who lived here were farmers, fishermen, and sailors and often traded with Holland. Therefore the walls of the houses are covered with Dutch tiles and the pottery and china imported from there. Inquire at the Danish Tourist Office in Copenhagen about the time and dates of the folk singing and dancing performances and the demonstrations of handicraftsmen. The RES-TAURANT has a lovely pastoral view of farm animals grazing in the field. Meals are inexpensive, about 10 Kr. ($1.40). The park is open daily May to September 10 A.M. to 6 P.M.; winter mostly Sundays 10 A.M. to 3 P.M. Fee: 1 Kr. (14 cents).

TO ODENSE: HANS CHRISTIAN ANDERSEN'S BIRTHPLACE

A train, a ferry ride, and another train and then two and a half hours later you're in the home town of Denmark's favorite son. Though a long journey, it is well worth it. If you start early in the morning you can complete the visit in one day, but it is exhausting. Consider staying overnight in the Grand Hotel for some extra glimpses of this charming city.

A LEGENDARY GOD

Besides Hans Christian there are two other famous people from this area, the first legendary and the other a historical person. The very name of the city comes from the ancient one-eyed chief god of Scandinavia, Odin. He and his two brothers Vili and Ve slew the giant Ymir and out of his body formed the universe. Then Odin created day and night and set the sun and moon in the heavens. Afterward, the story goes, he and his brothers made man out of a branch of an ash tree and woman out of an elm. Sitting on his throne surrounded by fallen heroes, Odin listened to his ravens, who flew over the world to give him the news. When he went to war he rode his eight-legged horse, wore his eagle helmet, and carried his magic ring and all-powerful sword.

The Fyens Stiftsmuseum (Country Museum), Jernbanegade 13, near the Grand Hotel, has a good collection of relics from this bygone period. It's open daily April 1 to September 30, 10 A.M. to 5 P.M.; October 1 to March 31 weekdays 10 A.M. to 3 P.M., Sunday till 1 P.M. Fee: 1 Kr. (14 cents).

A HOLY KING

Years later King Canute the Holy ruled Denmark. His powerful body, his piercing eyes, and his long, fair hair made him look every inch a warrior. He was the nephew of Canute the Great, whose military success was so great that his followers thought he had divine powers. To prove them wrong, he ordered his chair placed by the seashore as the tide rose. When the water did not recede at his command he told his courtiers, "One being alone cannot say to the ocean, 'Thus far thou shalt go and no farther.'"

Canute the Holy was killed in front of the high altar of St. Alban's Church while defending the country and became a saint in the eleventh century. We'll visit the church named after him later on in our tour of the city.

A short walk from the station leads to Odense Castle in Kongens Have, the King's garden where Hans Christian, the son of a poor shoemaker, was received by the Crown Prince. Follow Jernbanegade Street to the Odense Theater and left on Vestergade to the Rådhus (Town Hall). The mighty statue of Canute, the patron saint of Denmark, stands tall and ready to defend his country against all foes. Continuing along, you will see that Vestergade changes its name to Overgade. Turn on the Bangs Boder corner to the end of the street, Hans Jensensstraede 39–43, and find a little yellow house with a nice red roof. This is the birthplace of our famous storyteller.

Hans Christian Andersen's House (Museum). Open June to August daily 9 A.M. to 9 P.M.; rest of the year times vary, generally 10 A.M. to 5 P.M. Fee: 1.50 Kr. (21 cents).

The original entrance to Hans Christian's home is to the right in the Remembrance Hall. THE GROUND FLOOR has the school notebooks from Hans Christian's grammar schools at Slagelse and Elsinore where he was cruelly dominated by his headmaster. There are pictures and letters from Mr. Guiseppe Siboni and Jonas Collins, the Copenhagen people who supported him, and the leather bag which carried his first love's (Riborg Voigt) farewell letter. From his more successful period there are: furniture from his apartment in Copenhagen; his top hat; screens made of pictures, cut out and pasted together by himself; his old extra-large boots; a fan with scribbled sentences written for a lady he admired; and statues of his likeness. Tributes to his renown include medals and gifts from many foreign countries. The most interesting are a big dock leaf with a snail made in silver, a gift from the pupils of Nathalie Zahle School, and a letter enclosing a dollar note from Abigail Tompkins "to pay off the debt American children owe you as their favorite author, and to obtain for you, 'old man,' a comfortable old age."

UPSTAIRS are his fairy tales, told in many different ways. Especially interesting are Hans Christian's pencil drawings from his travels in southern Europe. Although they look as though a young child drew them, he gets across a different feeling for each country. The showcases also have some funny things: his traveling stuff (two big trunks, a small bag, a stick, an umbrella, his hatbox) and an original fire escape (a long rope). He took the latter with him wherever he went because he was terrified of flames. Fortunately he never had to use it. THE DOME HALL depicts in wall paintings, frescoes, the story of his entire life: (1) childhood in Odense; (2) parting from his grandmother for Copenhagen; (3) questioning during student examination; (4) visit to Italy; (5) reciting his poems to his benefactors, the Collins family; (6) visiting fancy manor houses and friendship with the noted sculptor Bertel Thorvaldsen; (7)

listening to Jenny Lind; and (8) the torchlight parade in Odense honoring their favorite son on December 6, 1867.

After leaving the museum double back on Bangs Boder Street till you come to the corner of Overgade and Paaskestraede.

The Odense Charity School was at Number 19. Hans Christian was scarcely ten years old when he attended it. He was not the best of students. "I hardly knew how to spell a single word properly. At home I never learned my lessons, just a little bit on the way from school. My mother praised me, at the expense of the boy next door, because I was quick at learning."

The end of Paaskestraede has a bit of the riverbank where Hans Christian's mother, Anne Marie, went through her daily drudgery of washing other people's laundry. In icy water up to her knees she stood with the linens on a washing bench or a stone, beating them with a bat and then putting them in a tub of soapy water. The process was completed after they were rinsed in the water. It was just the same summer and winter, often bitterly cold. In Hans Christian's fairy tale "She Was Good for Nothing" he recalls this tragic part of his early childhood. "I was nearly done for," said the washerwoman. "Got something for me?" The boy produced the bottle, and the mother put it to her lips. "Ah, that's what I wanted—how it warms me up. Take a drink, my son—you look so pale, you must be shivering in those thin things. But you mustn't get into the way of this, my poor penniless child! . . ."

The Albanigade Bridge is next. On the east side of the bridge is the part of the river known as "The Bell-Deep," the river's deepest spot. In Hans Christian's story he writes, "When you hear a bell sounding in the deep, then it is the sunken bell telling tales to while away the time for the lonely River-Man who lives down below." Where did the actual mysterious church bell come from? Old St. Albani Church, which no longer exists. Albani Torv (Albani Market) on the top of the hill is where it stood.

St. Canute's Church is facing you on the left as you cross the bridge from Paaskestraede. Down in the crypt are two showcases displaying the remains of Canute the Holy and Prince Benedict, almost five hundred years old. Two other Danish kings are also buried here. The altarpiece above the crypt is another remarkable feature of the church, with its hundreds of figures from the Bible and Danish history. The church was significant to Hans Christian. Here his beloved father was buried and he received his confirmation. He wrote about this event in his book *The Story of My Life*. One of his father's suits was altered for him and for the first time he got his own pair of boots. "I only feared that not all should see that they really were boots, and so I held up my trousers and thus went up the church aisle. The boots creaked, and I was very much delighted that the congregation could hear that they were new." Before leaving the church climb the steeple for a splendid view.

Take a restful moment and saunter through THE FAIRY TALE GARDEN behind the church. In Odense offices close between 12:30 and 2 P.M. for lunch, and the park is full of people basking in the sun, eating a picnic lunch, or just dozing off to sleep. With its back to the church and looking over the river stands the statue of Odense's famous son: Hans Christian Andersen. Every year on the second of April, Hans Christian's birthday, little children dance around the statue and leave him bunches of flowers. On his birthday too, and throughout the world, International Children's Book Day is celebrated. When you leave the park don't forget to notice the sculpture of "The Wild Swan," fashioned after the fairy tale of the same name.

Hans Christian Andersen's Childhood Home, Munkemollestraede Monk Mill Street 3-5, is open daily April to September 10 A.M. to 5 P.M.; October to March noon to 3 P.M. Fee: 25 øre (4 cents). Ring the bell and the old keeper will welcome you. Hans Christian lived here from the age of two until he ventured to Copenhagen at fourteen. Four families resided in the building, each one having one room and a kitchen. Today the room is empty, but on the walls different pictures tell about the old Odense, Andersen's Odense. Use your imagination to furnish the room in your mind's eye. Under the window the father had his shoemaker's workshop. On the gable wall were bookshelves holding Shakespeare's plays and wonderful stories like *The Arabian Nights*. The evenings when his father read the books aloud to him and his mother were the high points of Hans Christian's life. In the alcove to the left the parents' double bed was placed, and Hans Christian slept in a make-do thing on the opposite side. The next room was the kitchen, and a ladder led to the loft. Then straight ahead is the back garden. The first thing you'll see is a gooseberry bush. If you ask the keeper whether it is the same bush under which Hans Christian sat dreaming he will answer you, "Oh no, to be honest it is not the same bush, but it is a cutting of it." The garden could very well be the one Hans Christian envisioned in "The Snow Queen" for often his father would heat a copper coin and place it against the frosted window. For a moment the cleared peephole looked into a different world, especially when the sparkling snowflakes danced about.

IF TIME PERMITS

Cruise on the Odense River from May 1 to September 1 daily, from Munke Mose to the Zoo and Funen Village. Detailed information about the timetable is available at the Tourist Office, phone 13-03-83 or 12-83-83. The trip takes about twenty to thirty minutes and costs 2 Kr. (28 cents).

The Funen Village (Farm and Country Building Museum), Sejerskouvej, via bus line 2, open at 10 A.M. with varying closing times through the year (4:30 P.M. is the earliest). Fee: 1 Kr. (14 cents). The reconstructed old village has buildings from different parts of the island: a wayside inn; a weaver's house; a mid-eighteenth-century hospital; an old mill farm; and lots more, all complete with furnishings and furniture. THE OPEN-AIR THEATER has a month-long (July–August) Hans Christian Andersen festival of plays performed by local children. Past successes were *The Tinder Box, The Swineherd*, and *Simple Hans*. Performances are daily at 2 P.M. in English and at 7:30 P.M. in Danish. Length of the show is approximately seventy minutes and the cost is 3 Kr. (42 cents) for young people up to twelve. Adults pay double.

BO: TO STAY

Copenhagen room rates are for doubles with bath and include breakfast.

Hotel Hafnia, Vester Voldgade 23, is a small hotel just a short one street away from the Rådhuspladsen (Town Hall Square). An old-fashioned open elevator takes you to a comfortable, up-to-date room with good Danish modern furniture. The courtyard restaurant has a large tank of fish where you can select your evening's meal. Rates start at 129 Kr. ($18.06).

The Astoria, Vesterbrogade 7B, is an excellent choice if you want to be close to Tivoli and the Central Station. Rooms begin at 100 Kr. ($14.00).

The Alexandra Hotel, H. C. Andersen's Boulevard 8, is quiet and modest yet still in the center of activity. The people who work here all try to be helpful, giving the hotel a homey atmosphere—including a joyful fire in winter. The three-window corner rooms are especially large. Rates start at 114 Kr. ($16).

Breakfast has one available dish that can be claimed nowhere else in the world—real Danish pastry served with real Danish butter. What a delicious morsel! The meal is light, with perhaps a soft-boiled egg, a glass of cold milk, and a few slices of some mild cheese. (Breakfast-in-bedders beware, the Danish rolls are very crumbly.) If you're not eating in your hotel try the nice outdoor cafés at Kongens Nytorv (the square at the other end of Strøget) or Rådhuspladsen (Town Hall Square).

Lunch is usually simple, a few smørrebrød, the famous open-faced sandwiches. Many Danes prepare their own at home and carry them to school or work. Others buy a package at the smørrebrød shops or from the street vendors, spread a paper napkin on their desk or lap, and eat almost on the run. Lunch lasts no longer than thirty minutes. All restaurants, however, serve delicious smørrebrød. If you want the waiter's attention wave or call "Tjener" and he'll reply, "I'll be right with you," which means "Don't be in a hurry. I'll be there in a suitable amount of time."

Oscar Davidsen, Søpavillonen, Gylden Løvsgade, is the paradise of smørrebrød lovers. The yard-long smørrebrød menu is yours to take with you when you go. The sweet tiny shrimps, smoked salmon, or, if you're adventurous, eel are all tasty. Remember smørrebrød is very filling and two are usually enough for most hungry people. Each open-faced sandwich costs about 3 Kr. (42 cents).

Restaurant Kongens Have, Kronprinsessegade 13, has an entrance from the nearby park or from the street. The management is particularly cordial to young people. Cost about 10 Kr. ($1.40).

Fiskehuset, Gammel Strand 34, is the ultimate in seafood. Try the "skipperlobeskoves," a delicious Danish stew. The view across the canal is splendid. The old fish market used to be in the street outside. There are only a few old fisherwomen left now. One has turned to stone, a statue, of course. Cost about 35 Kr. ($5).

Dinner is at about six. On the menu are a number of dishes marked with frames. These dishes can be served quickly and are less expensive than others on the menu.

7 Smaa Hjem, Jernbanegade 4, just off Rådhuspladsen, has a pint-sized room and an atmosphere with lots of charm.

Scott, Grabrødretorv 15, is a short stroll up Klosterstraede from Strøget and then right into a pretty little square. Danes in the area, including professors and students from the university, dine here. Cost of a dinner about 20 Kr. ($2.65).

PENGE AT GIVE UD: MONEY TO SPEND

Here the basic unit is the krone (Kr.). One Krone is about 14 cents and will buy a delicious hot sausage from the street vendor. Roughly, 7 kroners equal a dollar and can purchase a lovely souvenir ash tray or a wooden Tivoli guard doll. Each krone is made up of 100 øre. A 10 or 25 øre coin is needed to use the telephone and 50 øre fetches a package of world-famous Dandy chewing gum.

GAA PAA INDKOB: TO SHOP

Stroget (pronounced "Stroyet"): loosely meaning "the stretch," is Copenhagen's most famous shopping street, connecting the capital's two main squares, Kongens Nytorv (King's New Market) and Rådhuspladsen (Town Hall Square). You won't find the name on any street sign since it is a nickname for the mile and a half stretch. It is made up of five old streets—Frederiksberggade (which runs into the large square Gammel Torv on the left and Nytorv on the right), Nygade, Vimmelskaftet, Amagertorv, and Østergade. No one knows exactly how old Strøget is. A three-thousand-year-old flint tool has been found under Frederiksberggade, so the street may very well have been the place to shop for exclusive flint axes long ago. It is known that the present narrowish streets wound their way among houses and inns since the Middle Ages, over a thousand years ago. Now Strøget is free of all traffic on wheels except baby carriages and bicycles, and is a favorite for shopping and strolling.

Shopping hours generally are Monday to Thursday 9 A.M. to 5:30 PM., Friday till 7 P.M. Closing time on Saturday is between 1 and 2 P.M. On Sunday, bakers, confectioners, florists, and newspaper stands are open.

Let's stroll! The shops are listed in the order in which you might come upon them rather than by subject. At the Frederiksberggade entrance, where the street is almost straight, the merchandise tends to be less expensive. The closer to Kongens Nytorv at the other end, the higher the prices.

FREDERIKSBERGGADE

Engelsen and Schroder, No. 15, has books, maps, souvenirs, and, best of all, delightful Danish Christmas cards costing about 6 Kr. (84 cents).

The Bristol Music Center, No. 25, in two floors, is Copenhagen's largest specialty store for classical and pop records. Each customer has his own turntable.

Rytterstuen, around the corner at Gammel Torv 22, is especially for horse lovers. You might like to get a beautiful crop or a pair of spurs, approximately 20 Kr. ($2.80).

The square you are now in is really two squares, Gammel

Torv (left) and Nytorv (right). On the Gammel Torv side notice the fountain with a bronze lady and children who spurt water. On the King's birthday, March 11, golden apples leap on the top of the cascades of water. On the Nytorv side notice the fronts of the buildings. These are ornately decorated law courts. The open square was once the setting for the Town Hall of old Copenhagen. Where the present Town Hall Square stands was considered the outskirts of the town.

NYGADE

No. 6 has one of the yummy chocolate shops that abound in Copenhagen.

VIMMELSKAFTET

Thorngreen, No. 34, has three full stories of toys. Study the windows carefully before entering—girls and mothers on the left and boys and fathers on the right. Prices: Viking dolls 4.85 Kr. (68 cents); soldiers 6.85 Kr. (96 cents); and folk-costumed dolls and miniature Danish furniture 40 Kr. ($5.60).

Fona, No. 46, calls itself Scandinavia's largest record shop. Whether or not this is true is unimportant, for the shop has thousands of records from which to choose.

Trianon Bageri, No. 37, has a wonderful display of Danish pastry. Drop in a moment to inhale the heavenly aroma.

AMAGERTORV

Jordbaerkaelder (Strawberry Cellar), No. 27, is just that. You can rest your tired feet here and enjoy strawberries and cream, or any other fruit you fancy. The custom has been going on for generations.

Toward the end, the street widens and begins to look like a market. In the middle of the street, vendors sell hot sausages and fruit near a funny old Victorian fountain made up of storks and frogs. Here nurses in the annual graduating class traditionally dance after passing their final exams.

ØSTERGADE

Illum, No. 52, is a famous department store with practically everything stocked.

Pariser-Magasinet, No. 22, has more toys and souvenirs, but the specialty is dolls of all kinds, prices from 7 Kr. ($1).

Crome & Goldschmidt, No. 32, is another department store, less spacious and less fancy.

The rest of Østergade is full of specialty shops of various kinds. One not to pass up is **Marburger,** No. 17–19, a top-notch delicatessen shop. A whole wall is graced with hundreds of sausages. Try a little bit of each kind. At the end of the street is the big square called Kongens Nytorv, the outskirts of Copenhagen in the Middle Ages. King Christian V still stands in the middle of the square inside the ring of trees. His statue is popularly known as "The Horse." The unpleasant gentleman the King's horse is treading on is supposed to be Envy. Students from the university celebrate the end of their exams here by holding hands and running three times around "The Horse." You can see this if you're here the last week in June. Continuing across the square, you'll find hundreds of pigeons. They are so tame you'll have to be careful not to trample them. Buy a packet of smørrebrød from the street vendor and share a snack with your quickly made feathered friends.

MODE: TO MEET THE YOUNG DANES

Young people go to school from eight in the morning until two in the afternoon. Lessons last forty-five minutes each, just long enough for young brains to concentrate on one subject.

Each lesson is followed by a fifteen-minute break except at eleven o'clock, when thirty to forty minutes are allotted for eating smørrebrød and for playing outdoor games. When the youngsters go home a second meal of smørrebrød is waiting. Homework is done and there's plenty of playtime. Recreation holds as important a place in their life as work. There seems to be an easy give-and-take between young people and their parents, free from fighting and bickering.

After the primary grades, "Basic School," students go to the "Middle School" from about eleven until fifteen or sixteen years of age. To qualify to go on they take an examination for the "Gymnasium," which prepares them for a university career. Third-year Gymnasium students who have successfully completed their exams wear red and white "students' caps" stating boldly to everyone "I am going on!" On the whole, young Danes receive a solid education which is lively and attractive yet not too bookish and which includes cooking and house management and visits to farms, churches, and other community projects. This is not too unlike the education of the early Vikings. Teachers and professors have a great deal of liberty in their methods. They are on friendly and familiar terms with their pupils, usually calling them by their first names. There are seldom more than twenty-four children in a class—a rule that is closely adhered to. All in all, both boys and girls seem to have tremendous outgoing energy and vitality and when asked a question give direct and straightforward answers. It's all part of a special easygoing quality that all Copenhageners have.

The Danes, who pioneered the meet-the-people programs after World War II, making it easy to visit a Danish family at home, extended the hospitality to workshops, factories, schools, and industries. These tours are called "Lifeseeing." But if you want to meet a young person your age personally, contact as soon as you arrive the Danish Tourist Board, 7 Banegaardspladsen, at the Central Station, or telephone 11-14-15. They are open Monday to Friday 9 A.M. to 5 P.M., Saturday until noon. All services are free.

FARVEL: FAREWELL HAPPILY . . .
(but not ever after)

Don't be surprised to find that Copenhagen has real elves, sprites, hobgoblins, trolls, and mermaids. There is something childlike about the Danish personality that may explain their fondness for fairy tales. Their naturalness and spontaneity are lovely qualities that all adults would do well to retain. Even as young children the Danes glory in each festival and birthday, in giving and receiving presents. Schoolfellows are urged to join in as the teacher substitutes songs and games for work. And after the Danes reach adulthood birthdays continue to be a source of joyous pleasure—they are announced in the daily papers and in broadcasts, and flags are gaily hoisted in salute of the big event. Grownups and young people alike love being amused, and if it sounds as though they are laughing loudly at the smallest joke it is only that they are enjoying it to its fullest.

And what of the Viking side of the Dane? There is still the heartiness (contentment in devouring a king-sized meal), simplicity (love of wandering the countryside), and style (an elegant lady whipping out a large black cigar and relishing each puff). The modern Viking still yearns to travel. Although he loves his country, he is happiest exploring new places. The next best thing to going away is having visitors from other lands. The openhanded Danes welcome everyone into their homes with enthusiasm and soon dispel any feelings the visitor has of being a stranger. Shopkeepers, hoteliers, and restaurateurs may at first regard you indifferently, but as soon as they know you're from another country their faces light up and you become a treasure from the outside world. It is the fun, food, and fairy tales that make Copenhagen different, but the people make it "hyggelig" (comfortable, pleasant) and a "once upon a time there *is*" experience.

AT TALE: TO SPEAK

ENGLISH	DANISH	PRONUNCIATION
Good morning	God morgen	Go morn
Good afternoon	God aften	Go aft-n
Good night	God nat	Go nat
Goodbye	Farvel	Far-vel
So long	Farvel så laenge	Far-vel saw ling-eh
Yes	Ja	Yă
No	Nej	Nĭ
My name is	Mit Navn er	Mit nawn air
May I ask your name?	Ma jeg spørge om deres navn?	Maw yi sperr-reh om deh-res nawn
How are you?	Hvordan har De det?	Voh-den hahi dee de
Fine, thank you, and you?	Tak, godt; og De?	Tak, got; aw dee
Please speak slowly	Vaer så venlig at tale langsommere	Vehr saw ven-lee aw ta-leh lahng-som-reh
I speak only English	Jeg taler kun engelsk	Yi taler kohn ehng-elsk
How much is it?	Hvad koster det?	Vă kos-ter de
Please show me the way to	Vaer så venlig at vise mig vejen til	Vehr saw ven-lee aw vee-seh mi vi-en til
Right	Høre	Hoy-reh
Left	Venstre	Ven-streh
Straight ahead	Lige ud	Lee-eh-ooth
Open	Åben	Aur-ben

ENGLISH	DANISH	PRONUNCIATION
Closed	Lukket	Logh-geth
Entrance	Indgang	In-gahng
Exit	Udgang	Ooth-gahng
Drugstore	Apotek	A-pooh-ték
Barbershop	Barber	Bahr-ber
Bathroom	Badevaerelse	Ba-the-vehr-el-seh
1	een	een
2	to	toh
3	tre	tré
4	fire	fee-reh
5	fem	fem
6	seaks	sex
7	syv	sewv
8	otte	aw-teh
9	ni	nee
10	ti	tee
11	elleve	el-veh
12	tolv	tol
13	tretten	tret-ten
14	fjorten	fyohr-ten
15	femten	fem-ten
20	tyve	tew-veh
50	halvtreds	hăl-tres
100	hundrede	hoon-reh-the

HELLIGDAGE AT HUSKE: HOLIDAYS TO REMEMBER

January 1	**Nytårsdag** (New Year's Day). Attending church and visiting friends.
January 6	**Hellig-Tre-Kongers-Dag** (Day of the Three Holy Kings). Christmas tree and ornaments dismantled. Young girls play fortunetelling game: walk backward, throw shoe over left shoulder. Man who appears in dream will be future husband.
February 14	**Fjortende Februar** (Fourteenth of February). School friends exchange verse cards called "gaekkebrev,"

joking letter, signed by series of dots—one for each
letter in sender's name. Boy guessing name sends
chocolate or sugar egg at Easter. Failing to decipher
name means serious forfeit.

February-
March
(Monday
before Ash
Wednesday)

Fastelavn (Shrovetide). School holiday celebrated
by eating of "Fastelavnsboller," Shrovetide buns.
Young people rise early (5 A.M.) and wake parents
for buns and candies. Then they dress in fancy costumes and masks, carry collection box, and chant:

> Buns up, buns down,
> Buns for me to chew!
> If no buns you give
> I'll rattle till you do!

Adults play games too—"Slå Katten of Tonden"
(knocking the cat out of the barrel). Player armed
with stick tries to smash artificial cat (in ancient
times live). Winner is "Cat King" and gets prize.

March-April

Påske (Easter). Eggs to eat and for games. **Anden**
Påskedag (Second day after Easter). Stores closed
but amusements wide-open and filled to capacity.
Store Bededag (Great Prayer Day—fourth Friday
after Easter). People promenade in best finery and
eat traditional "varme hveder," a small, square, hot
wheat roll. **Pinse** (Whitsun—the fiftieth day after
Easter). New summer clothes are worn. Excursions
to the country and woods to bring young birch
branches home for decoration, symbolizing welcome
to early spring. Customary to go to Frederiksberg
hill and watch the sun rise by 6 A.M. Singing societies
are particularly in tune.

April (late)–
August (late)

Dyrehaven (Royal Deer Park) and **Bakken** (Amusement Park) are open.

May 1–
September 16

Tivoli open.

June 23

Sankt Hans Aften (St. John's Eve). Shortest night
in year celebrated with bonfires, singing, fireworks,
dancing, and burning of witches' effigies.

November 10

Mortensaften (St. Martin's Eve). Harvesttime. Family

goose dinners. Legend says goose's quack squealed on St. Martin hiding in a barn.

December 24   **Juleaften** (Christmas Eve). Bunches of grain tied outdoors to honor birds and animals that stood at midnight to celebrate baby Jesus' birth. Lavish supper includes "risengrød," a big rice pudding with one almond, considered a special prize for the person who finds it, and who is then given a gift of marzipan or other trifles. After dinner games, carols, and presents. Jule-Nisse, the mischievous gnome said to live in attics and barns is no longer part of the celebration—only on Christmas cards and holiday decorations. **Juleday** (Christmas Day). Quiet visits with friends and relatives.

December 31   **Nytårsaften** (New Year's Eve). Worthless earthenware collected all year is smashed at appointed time. Fireworks explode amid laughter, fun, and relaxation.

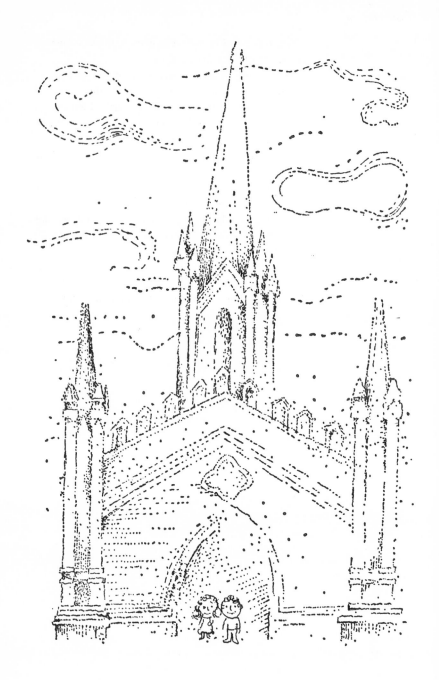

4. DUBLIN

The Rebellious Ones

"Céad Mile Fáilte!" A hundred thousand welcomes! That's the largest number of greetings you'll get anywhere in Europe. The Irish are never halfhearted about anything. A sad Dubliner is the most sorrowful person in the world, while a happy one is the most elated. And while there is no such thing as a typical Irishman, they are usually lively, friendly, and always ready to talk to strangers. This facility with words has given Dubliners, and for that matter all the Irish, a considerable reputation for effective speaking and writing. Queen Elizabeth I is said to have started the phrase "Blarney talk," referring to the eloquent pleas of the Lord of Blarney, Cormac MacDermod McCarthy. The legend grew that whoever kissed the Blarney stone in the castle at Blarney, County Cork, would receive the gift of magnificent speech.

It is amazing that there are so many significant Irish writers, considering the small size and population of the country— Oscar Wilde, George Bernard Shaw, W. B. Yeats, Oliver Goldsmith, Sean O'Casey, James Joyce, and Jonathan Swift, who wrote *Gulliver's Travels*. (You'll find out a great deal about Swift in your tour of the city.)

The love of drama in the form of storytelling lives on today. Traveling storytellers ("seanachai" in Irish) evoke ancient heroes before spellbound audiences. The Irish enjoy conjuring up the past, for their history is rich with heroes, saints, scholars, kings, warriors, bards, and poets. But fairies, or "sidhe" (pronounced shee) in Irish, are what most of the storytellers tell about. According to the Celts (the earliest Irish), fairies hid in small hills surrounded by forests of tall trees. The best-known fairy is the leprechaun, the shoemaker who owns the original crock of gold. Only a fixed stare can part him from the treasure, but somehow he always manages to escape and still hold onto his gold. Another mysterious creature is the banshee, or female spirit. She foretells death by her low wail. The stories of these fanciful folk, along with those of more historical heroes, add color and spice to what might be ordinary conversation. Though the modern Dubliner tells you he doesn't believe in hearsay or fairies, he may add ". . . and I hope *never* to run into one."

THE CITY PLAN TODAY

Getting around Dublin is easy. The river Liffey with its nine bridges is a central point to refer to when identifying the location of streets, places, etc. Its important bridge is the one on O'Connell Street. Beyond the bridge is Westmoreland Street, leading to bustling Grafton Street, the main shopping area. The best way to see the city is on foot or by taking short hops on the big, lumbering, two-decker buses. Their routes cover the entire city and suburbs. The cost ranges from only a few copper pennies to a shilling (1 to 12 cents). The conductors will cheerfully point out your closest stop and often remind you when you have to get off.

THE EARLIEST PEOPLE

The first settlers are believed to have been the Larnian race, who lived about six thousand years before Christ. Although small in size, they were sturdy, excellent sailors. They came from southern France, traveling up to the coast to Brittany in their frail dugout canoes and across the stormy Irish Sea. They lived quite simply on berries and varied their diet by catching wild birds and fish. It is said that some of their settlements were washed away when the level of the Irish Sea rose.

By 4000 B.C. farmers had come to Britain and Ireland from the Mediterranean area. The people were small, slight, olive-skinned, with long heads, lean faces, and narrow noses. Another migration wave brought other Mediterranean people. This time they were tall, fair, and blue-eyed and builders of the great tombs of the Stone Age. On the river Boyne, just thirty miles north of Dublin, is Newgrange—one of the most remarkable burial mounds in the world. The circular shrines were made by putting giant capstones weighing many tons across the tops of three or four large upright stones. No one knows how the stones were moved, for even today if the strongest men in the world tried to lift the capstones they would not be able to budge them an inch. Engineers feel that very clever mechanical means must have been applied. Scholars have discovered that the tombs served as instruments of astronomy detailing the days of the year.

After the Stone Age, workers skilled particularly in metal-work flourished, and left evidence of their activity. Disc-shaped pieces of gold have been found in tombs, suggesting that sun worship was practiced. Other gold artifacts have been un-covered, including paper-thin necklaces, brooches, belts, and earrings. Each piece was delicately worked into patterns of triangles and diamonds.

The next people to arrive were the Celts, whose use of iron gave the Iron Age its name. They came from the Rhineland, Germany, with improved sturdy metal farm tools such as the plowshare and the two-ox plow. A second group left northern France and Brittany and became miners, traders, horse breeders, and cattle farmers. Their smiths forged iron and bronze into swords, shields, and horse armor. They probably introduced chariot warfare to Britain and Ireland.

You can see the amazing display of Irish achievement in art and craftsmanship from pre-Christian times through the ages by visiting one of Europe's most impressive museums.

The National Museum, Kildare Street, open Tuesday to Saturday 10 A.M. to 5 P.M., Sunday 2 P.M. to 5 P.M.; closed Monday. Free.

Begin your tour in the main room on the first floor and trace the story of man in Ireland. In the STONE AGE (6000–3500 B.C.) all hunting and fishing was done with primitive tools and weapons made of flint and stone. The exhibits shown include stone axes, clubs, scrapers, knives, arrowheads, and a particularly interesting flint knife with its original handle of dried moss. Also shown are some stones with strange, magic-like designs from the mound of Newgrange. THE BRONZE AGE (3500–1000 B.C.) introduced metal used for tools, weapons, and jewelry. A number of the original stone molds are shown alongside the objects they formed. The splendid collection of gold ornaments shows great artistic skill as well as enormous wealth. Note the "lunula" or crescent-shaped gold disc which was worn as a necklace; the round, curved bars with funnel-shaped ends, used as dress fasteners; and the fancy jewelry worn at the end of locks of hair. Along one wall find the prehistoric graves transferred in their entirety to the museum and encased in glass. By the IRON AGE (1000 B.C.–A.D. 500) gold seemed to cease being available. Simple patterns on weapons and artifacts gave way to curves and spirals. Color played a new part in the design. Red was used to dramatize certain features of a design. The collection includes swords, spears, two great bronze trumpets, and an especially unusual gold collar with an ingenious locking device, found in Broighter, County Derry. THE EARLY CHRISTIAN PERIOD (A.D. 500 to 1200) is marked by fine flowery Irish art. The Tara Brooch and the Ardagh Chalice are two of the finest pieces on display. With the help of magnifying glasses placed in the case close to each piece, you can see all the lovely details.

Other sections of the museum feature: the Viking period (tools, weapons, and the processional Cross of Cong, dating back to A.D. 1123); the folk collection of costumes in settings of old houses; and the rooms devoted to the English-Irish War of 1916, with uniforms, pictures, and some sad farewell letters from those executed after the Rising.

If you have any questions or would like to learn more about a specific portion of the museum, ask for the museum's staff officer, Joseph Murphy, or telephone ahead for an appointment, 655-21.

The Natural History Building next door has an entrance on Merrion Street. It's open 11 A.M. to 5 P.M. daily including holidays and 2 to 5 P.M. on Sunday. Free.

There is a fine collection of Irish birds with their nests and eggs, many of them in their natural settings. A rare Irish giant deer, which roamed the country about four thousand years ago, has been preserved stuffed and is a principal attraction of the Natural History Building.

THE FOUNDING OF THE CITY

The first account of Dublin, about two thousand years ago, described it as being beyond the river Liffey out to the edge of marshland. The original name for the city, "Baile Atha Cliath," means "the town of the hurdle ford," for at a shallow place in the river chariots could be driven across if sticks were spread on the muddy bottom. By the eighth century the Vikings, who were concerned with the harbor rather than the ford, had taken over the city, and it became known as Dubhlinn, or "dark pool," for the color of the peat-filled waters. The port became a naval base for the Viking raids. A settlement of wooden houses sprang up as trade started with the rest of the growing Viking empire.

Earlier, in the fifth century, the Romans, who had conquered most of Europe, tried to invade Ireland but were unsuccessful. The Irish were known as fierce warriors and plundered the western part of the Roman Empire (Britain and Gaul, or France), carrying off captives to use as slaves. Among the prisoners the Irish captured was a sixteen-year-old boy who was sold and put to work tending sheep. At the end of seven years he became as much of an Irishman as if he were native-born. Although he was not ever considered a meek youth, he had gained, during these slave years, a bit of the hot-blooded Irish temper. One day he had a vision telling him to escape to Gaul. He set out at once, even though the port where he was told his ship would be waiting was hundreds of miles away. On the way, he thought to himself how he loved the island, the people, and the three-leaved shamrock which made the land so green. But some things he hated, such as the poison snakes, whose venom was a danger to life, and the Druid priests, whose magic held people in a constant state of fear.

Back in his homeland, he had a dream one night. He heard the Irish crying out, "We pray thee, holy youth, to come and walk amongst us as before." This, the young man decided, was a missionary call. Fourteen years later he returned to Ireland with the title of Bishop and the Pope's blessing. He began the work which was to make him known as St. Patrick, the patron saint of Ireland. He built churches and monasteries and converted people to Christianity. Many legends sprang up as he traveled throughout the country. Among them is the story of how he forced the snakes and toads of Ireland to fling themselves into the sea. It was also claimed there was no night for twelve days after his death and that he lived to be 120 years old. In Dublin St. Patrick is said to have produced miraculous springs which had special healing powers. The two wondrous wells were located at St. Patrick's Cathedral and the end of Nassau Street (which, in Irish, is called St. Patrick Well Street). Today the water from these springs is used as the main ingredient for a world-famous soda water. The day of St. Patrick's death, March 17, is honored by Irishmen throughout the world. Practically every Irishman wears a shamrock on that day because it is said that St. Patrick used his beloved three-leaf plant to illustrate the meaning of the Holy Trinity (the Father, the Son, and the Holy Spirit).

For three centuries after St. Patrick, art and religious learning flourished. More monasteries and churches were built and Ireland earned for itself the name "Island of Saints and Scholars." Wonderful examples of the art of this period can be seen today.

Trinity College Library, College Green, is open year round 10 A.M. to 4 P.M. weekdays; and, in addition, until 1 P.M. on Saturday and Sunday from mid-July to September. Free.

The prize possessions are the collection of ancient books of Ireland made by hand twelve hundred years ago. Not until the coming of Christianity was any widely known writing used. Law, legend, and history were preserved by word of mouth from one generation to the next. The new religion preaching equality proved immensely popular with the poor but unpopular with the ruling families, who felt strict regulations and lack of knowledge were the best way to keep the working people in their place. Many monks dedicated their lives to the transcription of the teachings of Christ, making copy after copy of the Latin texts. The devoted scribes took pride in making their work as beautiful as possible. The results were extraordinary illuminated manuscripts made on fine animal skin (vellum) and painted with the brightest colored inks. THE BOOK OF KELLS is considered the most remarkable masterpiece to survive from this period. In poorly lit cells in the Monastery of Kells, back in the eighth century, the monks painstakingly executed all 680 pages. A different page with a portion of the Scriptures is turned each day but copies of the other pages are on display. The page with the eight-circle cross, which faces a portrait of Christ, is unique. There are elaborate spirals, whirls, and trumpet patterns that are never repeated. The best-known page, Chi Rho, has a wealth of detail calling for a close look. Try to locate several human heads, an otter with a fish in its mouth, a moth or butterfly, and a cat and mouse scene.

Another treasure, THE BOOK OF DURROW, a copy of the Gospels, has been described as the "elder sister" of the Book of Kells, although the actual date of its creation is unknown. Each of the four parts begins with an unusual drawing of Matthew, Mark, Luke, and John, the Evangelists who preached the teachings of Christ. Each drawing is followed by designs of interwoven curves, spirals, and small, fantastic animals with extra long bodies. Only four colors are used throughout the decoration. The three main ones are orange-red, a vivid green, and golden yellow.

One last rare exhibit is the O'NEIL HARP. This instrument is the national emblem of the country. Although the harp is the oldest known musical instrument, the Irish did not introduce it to Europe until around A.D. 700. Bards (or wandering minstrels) traveled throughout the country singing the news of the day in the form of ballads accompanied by their harp. As you can see, the O'Neil Harp is much smaller and more compact than the large ones played on the concert stage today. The bards carried them like hand luggage as they moved from castle to castle performing before kings and chieftains, depending on their host's generosity for their living. If the hospitality was good the bard composed verses praising the host and sang them everywhere he went. If the reward was not up to the bard's expectation the verses were not complimentary and nasty rumors were spread far and wide. The pleasant vagabond life and the power over rulers attracted many young people to join the ranks of the bards. Eventually there were so many that they could not earn a living, and the number of bards was greatly reduced. Before leaving the library, locate the bust of Jonathan Swift. Before you leave Dublin you will learn about this man and his part in the struggle for Irish freedom.

SEEDS OF THE UPRISING

By the eleventh century, Brian Boru, then High-King of Ireland, and earliest relative of the late President Kennedy, rallied his troops and defeated the ruling Vikings. Unfortunately Boru died in battle and the leaders started fighting among themselves. This left the country in a weakened condition. The Normans, from France, had already taken over England and had their eyes on Ireland. To the surprise of the potential invaders, the Irish King of Leinster (the area around Dublin) invited the Norman King Henry II to help him regain some lands which had been taken away from him. In 1169 Henry sent English Richard de Clare, Earl of Pembroke (known as Strongbow), to Ireland, supposedly to assist the King of Leinster. But Strongbow had far more ambitious plans. He swept across the country and claimed everything in his path, including the King of Leinster's daughter, whom he married. The castles, forts, and keeps seen throughout the country are lasting reminders of the Normans' stay.

King Henry, nervous about Strongbow's conquests because

they had gone so far beyond the purpose of his original mission, went to Ireland determined to secure the country as his own, not Strongbow's. Henry brought with him the promise from Pope Hadrian IV, the only English Pope, that he could rule the country if he captured it. Thus began a struggle between the Irish and the English which lasted for seven hundred years. The Normans and the Irish were brought under control and the English firmly established their power. The Irish chiefs fled the country—their property taken over by the English and changed into "plantations." These lands were given to English settlers or to someone back in England as a reward for services to the crown. The land was rich and tempting and at first that was all the English wanted. But when Henry VIII introduced the reformed (Protestant) religion and the Irish remained as staunchly Catholic as ever, the conquest took on a different tone. By this time the songs of the bards and the sound of the harp were almost forgotten. In their place the Irish rallied their spirits and muskets to defend themselves.

When in 1690 a decisive battle against William of Orange was lost by the Irish, a severe penalty was "bestowed" upon them—the Penal Laws. These laws took away civil and religious rights from Catholics, barring them from voting, holding office, or being eligible for election to Parliament. They were forbidden to hold positions in the legal and teaching professions, to bear arms, or to own a horse worth more than fifteen dollars. Catholic schools and teachers were banned and children had to be educated in so-called "hedge schools," held in open fields. The teachers traveled from place to place, teaching as they went. Landowners were forced to subdivide their property equally among their sons, decreasing their small holdings to minute plots. With no way out, the Irish, some descendants of kings, were forced to live as unprotected tenants on lands of absentee landlords. They were charged huge rents for the privilege of dwelling side by side with their animals in windowless huts (taxes were levied according to size of windows), unable to educate their children and with little but potatoes and buttermilk for food.

There are two awesome places in Dublin which contain many reminders of this period.

Christ Church Cathedral, off Lord Edward Street is open, May to September 9:30 A.M. to 5 P.M.; October to April till 4 P.M.; Sunday for services only.

The oldest part of Dublin is on the rise overlooking the Liffey River between this cathedral and St. Patrick's, only a quarter of a mile away. Christ Church was first completed about 1038 by the Viking settlers. Then when the Normans arrived they quickly established St. Patrick's in order to counter the influence of the older church.

The fine stone interior is awe-inspiring, and the nave with its crisscross high arched ceiling is the best example of Gothic architecture in Ireland. But the showplace of the old church is Strongbow's tomb. Strongbow had the church rebuilt in 1172. The stone figure of Strongbow above his crypt is quite strange. The legs are suspiciously crossed, with one leg oddly turned out in the wrong direction. It is thought that perhaps he had a clubfoot. Another peculiarity is his full armor without an evident sword. Looking closely, you can detect the end of the sword placed beneath him. The half figure alongside Strongbow is explained by two different stories. One says that it is Strongbow's son, whom he killed in anger for showing fear and cowardly feelings on the field of battle. The other story claims it is Strongbow's wife Eva. The statue's legs were broken and lost after a church wall collapsed. It is also said that the hollow in the head of the small figure was used as a place to put coins.

Other things of particular note in the church are the passages between the walls used as walkways by the monks, the chapel pews with the names and dates of the owners going back to

1400, and the beautiful tile floors, many with intriguing patterns. Find the one showing the figures of begging friars represented as foxes. No doubt they are represented by the cunning animal to honor their skill in getting alms throughout the country. The crypt below, the oldest surviving portion of the building, has the most lively exhibits: a fossilized cat chasing a tiny mouse, preserved exactly as they were found in 1846, wedged in between the organ case and the pipes; and an ancient stock which stood in 1670 right above its present position. The stocks were used by the dean of the cathedral as punishment for offenders committing petty crimes. The giant-sized collection box at the front door is an old treasure chest from one of the wrecked ships of the Spanish Armada.

Dublin Castle, entrance off Castle Street, was built in 1208 on the site of a Viking fortress erected some four centuries earlier. The castle was the center around which the city grew. Originally four towers rose above each corner. (The Record Tower is the only one that visibly remains.) In Elizabethan times (about 1560–1600) the castle fortress was as grim as the Bastille and the Tower of London. Its spiked gate, now destroyed, was seldom unadorned by the heads of enemies.

The State Apartments are open Monday to Friday 10 A.M. to noon and 3 to 4:30 P.M. Fee: one shilling, written 1/- (12 cents). Regularly conducted tours last about thirty minutes. Don't be discouraged by the dull exterior. Inside are some of the finest rooms in Ireland. ST. PATRICK'S HALL—called this because the knighthood ceremonies took place here—has banners of the Knights of St. Patrick, along with crests, helmets, swords, and stall plates bearing the arms of each man. This gracious room is where the first President of Ireland, Dr. Douglas Hyde, and his successors were sworn into office. One last note about the castle: Husbands were hard to come by in Ireland and mothers felt it was an excellent investment to dress their daughters in the most expensive gowns and send them to the elaborate balls given here. The returns were hoped to be a captain for a son-in-law or at least someone with high prospects for the future.

The Genealogical Office and Heraldic Museum, in another part of the castle grounds, is open Monday to Friday 9:45 A.M. to 1 P.M. and 2:15 to 5 P.M. Free. If you have Irish ancestors and would like to trace your family tree, the staff will help you find out all about your relatives. And don't leave without visiting the **Castle Church,** a miniature gem of oak carvings and stained glass. It is open on weekdays from 9 A.M. to 6 P.M. Free.

And so to lunch? **The Old Stand** at the corner of St. Andrew's and Exchequer streets is very English but it serves good hot meals. Seafood is the specialty ("Lobster bonne femme" particularly good), and delicious soups. The cost should be under 12/- ($1.44). Another suggestion is **Bewleys** at 138 Great George Street South. A wide variety of snacks and light meals should not come to more than 5/- to 10/- (60 cents to $1.20), and your meal can be topped off with their yummy chocolates, which have been popular with young and old Dubliners for generations.

MORE ABOUT THE PEOPLE AND THE RISING

JONATHAN SWIFT (1667–1745) is the creator of Lemuel Gulliver, perhaps the most famous traveler in fiction, "first a surgeon and then a captain of several ships." This celebrated voyager never existed except in the mind of the author of *Gulliver's Travels.* Although the places depicted in the book were fantasy, many readers believed them to be fact. One sea captain claimed that he knew Captain Gulliver well. The book describes Gulliver's four voyages to lands inhabited by strange beings. On his first trip he is shipwrecked in the country of Lilliput, where the people are six inches tall. Gulliver succeeds in helping the Lilliputians rid their land of an enemy. On the second voyage, to Brobdingnag, he encounters humans sixty feet tall who are gentle and kind. Gulliver's terrifying adventure here has him meeting a giant pet spaniel who carries him off in his mouth. The third sea journey takes Gulliver to several remote places, including the flying island of Laputa. The philosophers and scientists of this land are so absent-minded that they hire boys to wake them by special devices when their minds wander. On the last trip, Gulliver is in the country of the Houyhnhnms (hōō-ĭn′ ŭms), intelligent horses with the best human qualities. Their servants, called Yahoos, are horrid human beings with the worst animal traits. Although the book is enjoyed for its amusing and fanciful story, underneath its playfulness is one of the harshest criticisms of human beings ever written. All the follies of mankind are attacked by Swift in this book.

Jonathan Swift, from his early youth, was bitter and resentful. He was born in Dublin of English parents. Eight months before his birth his father died. When he was one year old his nurse took him away from his mother and went to England. Surprisingly, Mrs. Swift raised no objections, and the baby remained in England for three years. Shortly after he returned to Dublin his mother went to England, and he was left completely dependent upon his uncle, who was, the boy thought, "stingy." He was sent to Kilkenny School, "the Eton of Ireland," where he spent eight friendless years, and then to Trinity College, where he experienced even less happy times. After the Irish rebellion against the English in 1688, anyone of English background was not made to feel very welcome in Ireland. Jonathan went to England to seek employment. His uncle helped him obtain a position as a secretary to William Temple, a retired Anglo-Irish statesman. Although Temple was kind, Jonathan resented being dependent on someone else once again. His chief comfort in this galling situation was his friendship with a child,

Esther Johnson. Her mother had been the companion of Temple's sister. Esther was only eight when they met, and Jonathan was fourteen years her senior. He taught her to read and write, and as long as she lived was her closest friend. He nicknamed her Stella. Some accounts say they were secretly married in 1723 but never lived together as husband and wife.

In 1699 Temple died and Jonathan returned to Ireland with Stella. Six years earlier, he had taken holy orders in the Church of England and was now given a small parish in his native country. It was so insignificant that the story is told that the sole member of his congregation was his sexton and his sermons began: "Dearly beloved Roger ————." During the years that followed, he became an outspoken critic of England's policy toward Ireland, writing protest articles, pamphlets, and books. In 1710 Jonathan became the editor of the Tory Party's newspaper, the *Examiner*. In it he carried on a blasting campaign against one of the British generals, Marlborough, causing the general's downfall. This is probably the first example of the influence of the press on English politics. When the Tory ministry fell in 1713 Swift retired from politics and became dean of St. Patrick's Cathedral in Dublin. But again in 1729 his anger lashed out, this time in the most terrible of his satiric pamphlets, "A Modest Proposal"—that the people of Ireland eat their children as the only way to keep England from starving them to death. After that he suffered from a sickness that caused attacks of deafness and giddiness. For the last three years of his life some claim he was insane. His concern for his sanity may have been the reason that he left the bulk of his money to the building of St. Patrick's Hospital for mental patients. There, he swore, the atmosphere would not be like that in the existing asylums, where patients were beaten, chained, and exhibited to the public as freaks. Although Jonathan Swift raged against people's weaknesses, he passionately defended their human rights.

St. Patrick's Cathedral, Patrick Street, is open daily 8:30 A.M. to 6 P.M. Free.

Once you see the towers you are walking in the footsteps of Dean Swift. He was born in a house now torn down, off nearby Werburgh Street. The cathedral is said to be built on the site where stones from one of St. Patrick's miraculous wells were found. The church has had its share of tumultuous historic events. When Oliver Cromwell arrived from England in 1649 to take over Dublin, his troops stabled their horses right in the cathedral.

A river flowing underneath often completely flooded the church, but the building was permanently restored and the foundation secured about one hundred years ago. The best-known crypt is Jonathan Swift's, marked by a brass plate in the floor. His dear friend Stella is next to him. Another touching proof of Swift's warm humanity is the inscription to his servant nearby—"Here lies the body of Alex McGee, servant to Dr. Swift, Dean of St. Patrick's. His grateful Master caused this monument to be erected in memory of his discretion, fidelity, and diligence in that humble station." It is said that Swift was, with difficulty, persuaded to omit the words "and friend" after "Master" and that he wept during the funeral for his faithful servant, "Saunders." Yet Swift's own epitaph is less gentle. It is over the robing room door and reads:

> Swift has sailed into his rest;
> Savage indignation there cannot
>   lacerate his breast.
> Imitate him if you dare,
> World-besotted traveller; he
> Served human liberty.

Another corner of the church is devoted to Swift's memory; it has his pulpit, horsehair chair, death mask, and chalice. Nearby is an interesting memorial to the Irish soldiers who, in

1814, fought in South Africa, China, and Burma. The carved scenes show hundreds of men "Storming the Pagoda at Rangoon." The monument is protected by life-size porcelain statues of wolfhounds, the mascot of the troops. Another curious exhibit is the "Door of Reconciliation" in the south transept. The door is from an old chapter house (the section of the church where business was conducted). In 1492 two feuding chieftains would not concede that either had committed any wrongdoings. To make it easier for them to resolve their differences, a hole was cut in the door so that, standing on opposite sides of it, the chieftains could shake hands without losing face. Another highlight, and a constant source of wonder, is the organ. Built in 1902, it is one of the world's most perfect instruments. The St. Patrick's choir is considered as worthy as the organ and can be heard weekdays at 10 A.M. and 5:30 P.M.; Saturday at 10 A.M. Beyond the church is a delightful little park usually filled with children playing, mothers gossiping, and old pensioners remembering old wars.

Marsh's Library, adjoining St. Patrick's, is open Monday, 2–4 P.M. Wednesday, Thursday, and Friday from 10:30 A.M. to 12:30 P.M. and 2–4 P.M. Saturday 10:30 A.M.–12:30 P.M. Tuesday closed. Closed during July. Free.

This is the oldest public library in Ireland. It has changed little over the past 250 years and is well worth a visit. You will see the old shelves with the remains of sockets that held chains leading to the volumes—in those days, books were scarce and had to be chained down against light-fingered scholars. Notice the three wired booths, where eighteenth-century readers were locked in while they studied particularly valuable books. There are thousands of volumes in every known language, and some twelfth-century hand-lettered manuscripts. The guest book contains many famous signatures, including that of the noted author James Joyce. The glass cases hold rare letters and diaries, including Dean Swift's comments on some of the members of his

choir. "Mr. Fox, whose cold disturbed the performance . . ."
"Very indecent in behavior. Openly laughing, grinning, whispering in time of devine services." Hearsay is that Dean Swift's
ghost roams the library at night searching for a letter he wrote
to Stella and left in a book by mistake. His house was just
across the street and he was in the library often. For more
details about the library ask for the Deputy Keeper, C. R. J.
Bradley, who will show you where bullets struck the walls and
shelves during the 1916 Uprising; a few are still lodged in some
of the books.

THE TENSION MOUNTS

The eighteenth century saw the peasants sinking into poverty,
misery, and despair. Then in 1775 the American War for Independence against the British gave the Irish new hope. They
were not only stirred but felt great sympathy for their many
countrymen who had fled to America seeking freedom from
English suppression. Indeed, these exiles played a prominent
part in the struggle for American independence—the signers of
the Declaration of Independence included four native-born Irishmen and four of Irish extraction. Now it was Ireland's turn to
rebel. The first step seemed innocent enough. The English were
so terrified of the French-American alliance and an invasion of
Ireland, which the French might engineer in an attempt to
surround England with its enemies, that they quickly granted
the Irish request to raise a voluntary army. Swiftly the ranks
swelled to over eighty thousand. As soon as invasion threats
disappeared, the cry for "free trade" and an end to tariffs crush-
ing Irish industry was sounded. Popular feeling against the
British ran high. The volunteers continued to meet and drill,
and formed resolutions demanding the right to manage their
own country.

THEOBALD WOLFE TONE (1763–98) led the new political party called the Society of United Irishmen. It took up the more extreme demands of the volunteers for religious freedom and political equality. As the membership grew so did the number of arrests and prosecutions, making secrecy a necessity. Tone himself had to flee to America for safety in 1795, but within a few months he returned to France to agitate for the cause. The French dispatched a small force to the west coast of Ireland. Bad weather scattered the ships and prevented a landing. The Irish revolutionaries looked for a sign, any sign of encouragement. When reports were heard that the French were going to invade England, they anxiously awaited the outcome. The citizens' army trained night and day as the country blacksmiths forged crude weapons. Napoleon did lead his great forces, but to Egypt, not Britain. Now the United Irishmen numbered half a million. The tension was rising, informers were at work, leaders were threatened, but the rebellion had to break through. In May 1798 Tone arranged in Paris for a small force to raid different parts of the Irish coast. The naval battle raged but was quickly quelled by a superior English fleet. The French were defeated and Tone was taken prisoner. As a military officer, he demanded execution by firing squad, but was sentenced to be hanged. Early that last morning he took his own life, confident that his followers would fulfill the demands he shouted at his trial, for a "fair and open war to procure the separation of the two countries." The English retaliated in 1800 with the Act of Union, abolishing the Irish Parliament and formally bringing Ireland into the United Kingdom.

ROBERT EMMET (1778–1803) was too young to take part with his brothers in the '98 rising. After proving himself a brilliant student at Trinity College, he too took up the fight. In 1802 he visited Paris and interviewed Napoleon, once again enlisting his support. Relations between France and England had reached such a boiling point that Napoleon was ready to encourage any kind of disorder in Ireland. Napoleon even suggested a suitable flag for the movement—tricolored, with "République Irlandaise" blazoned across it. Emmet returned to Ireland and organized another rising for a summer evening in 1803. His elaborate plans called for extensive street fighting and the use of a newly developed weapon, the rocket. But everything seemed to go wrong. An accidental explosion of an army depot triggered the attack too early and the one hundred followers (this small number was necessary to ensure secrecy) were not sufficiently prepared to make the necessary adjustment. The battle turned out to be merely a street brawl. Emmet, twenty-four years old, betrayed by an unknown spy, was captured and taken to Kilmainhaim jail. Later he was "hung, drawn and quartered" in the streets of Dublin. Almost every Irish home had a picture of the trial showing Emmet giving his famous speech ". . . when my country takes her place among the nations of the earth, then, and not till then, let my epitaph be written."

DANIEL O'CONNELL (1775–1847), a big, athletic man, sparkling with life, set out to force the British to change the Test Act, which prevented Roman Catholics from holding office. To raise funds, a subscription of a penny a month was asked and collected at church doors. The response was so great that soon a thousand pounds was raised (worth at that time about $5000), and O'Connell was elected in 1828 to the Parliament at Westminster, England. The Test Act prevented him from taking his seat, but the uproar which followed helped to bring about the repeal of the act. O'Connell's next target was the elimination of the Act of Union so that Ireland could decide her own domestic affairs. Here he found less sympathy among the wealthier, influential circles and decided independence was closer to the heart of the humblest Irish citizens. He took his cause directly to them. By 1843 he was holding a series of huge meetings all over the country, attended by thousands. With the tremendous weight of public opinion on his side he was sure he could win, but the

British watched calmly. Toward the end of the year the British banned what was to be O'Connell's greatest gathering, arresting him for a term of imprisonment. The people of Ireland affectionately refer to O'Connell as "The Liberator."

CHARLES STEWART PARNELL (1846–91) was born in the year of Ireland's worst catastrophe—the Great Famine. The country's population had soared to an all-time high of 8.5 million people. Every possible inch of soil was used to plant potatoes— the main source of food. Each year the crop grew without the help of fertilizers or chemicals. Suddenly that summer in district after district, the stems of the plants collapsed; the leaves sank into the earth and the air quickly filled with the stench of decay. For three whole years the potato crop continued to fail, causing the death from starvation of over a million people. Another million left their country in despair—mostly to go to the United States. Any revolutionary efforts at this time were easily arrested by the British Government, except for one by the exiles in the United States through an organization known as the Fenian Brotherhood. They recruited an oath-bound Irish republican army, drilled and disciplined, ready to liberate their country. An attempted rising in 1867 was unsuccessful, but it kept alive the spirit of revolt.

By 1874 the political leadership was taken up by Charles Parnell, then a member of the Irish representation in the British House of Commons. He headed a bloc of sixty countrymen known as the Irish Party who were trying to establish an Irish national assembly that would have authority to deal with local matters, "Home Rule." Parnell cleverly devised a tactic to delay all House business, hoping to force the English members into favoring his cause. The strategy almost worked.

During the Irish famine, landlords tried to drive the tenants from their farms. Parnell encouraged people to have nothing to do with the landowners who were doing the evicting. One such landlord had an agent named Captain Boycott. He got an isolation treatment which gave rise to a new word—"boycott." Parliament tried to force the Irish into complying by passing a bill. Parnell fought back by delaying all House business. He was jailed. Irish disorders flared up and Parliament insisted that the two factions compromise. Parnell was freed. Home Rule was almost in sight when the Chief Secretary of Ireland and the Undersecretary, both British, were assassinated in Phoenix Park, Dublin. The shocking incident started the old quarrels all over again. The London *Times* printed a letter supposedly written by Parnell, which proved he encouraged violence and the murders. When the letter's forger confessed, Parnell's popularity increased. Again, Home Rule seemed near.

Then in 1890 Parnell was accused of interfering with the marriage of one of his party aides, William O'Shea. A divorce followed and Parnell married Katherine O'Shea. The scandal charges created a storm of protest in England and Ireland. The Irish Party was forced to dismiss Parnell, but to this day the people often refer to him as the "uncrowned King of Ireland."

If you want to get a feeling of the full impact that these four leaders had on Dublin, take a look at your map and locate the numerous places named in their honor—Wolfe Tone Quay, Emmet Road, and Parnell Street, Road, and Square. The city's main thoroughfare is named for Daniel O'Connell, whose statue stands at one end of the street while Charles Parnell's monument guards the other. Let's go to some of the places identified with this period.

The Old Parliament House (now the Bank of Ireland) in College Green is rich in history. The walls echo with the speeches of men who were known for the art of oratory. As the fight for independence went on, the leaders became popular idols. Their speeches were printed for large crowds who read each word eagerly. The most dramatic scene ever enacted here was the passage of the 1800 Act of Union, giving complete control of Ireland to the British. Many opposed the decision but none more passionately than one representative, Henry Grattan. (His statue is immediately outside the Bank.) On the final day of the debate he appeared in the House aged and frail, dressed in his old Volunteers uniform. Leaning on the shoulders of two friends, he took leave of the Parliament he had helped to create with these parting words: "Yet I do not give up my country— I see her in a swoon, but she is not dead—though in her tomb she lies helpless and motionless, there is on her lips a spirit of life and on her cheek a glow of beauty."

The interiors were altered when the House was converted to the Bank. The cash office is where the Commons Chamber was. The House of Lords, which remains practically unchanged, is now used as the Board Room. It contains several unique features, including a splendid chandelier. The last Speaker of the House also thought this chandelier was special. He removed it to his own home for safekeeping. After many years it turned up in London and was brought back by the Bank. The intricate stone-work ceiling is quite unusual, and so are the two great tapestries woven about 1734. The chairs and table were also here when the Irish peers assembled.

You can tour the building during banking hours. An elegantly dressed attendant will show you around. Perhaps he will even explain the reason for the absence of windows.

GEORGIAN STYLE

The old Parliament and the customhouse nearby are examples of the elegant eighteenth-century architecture for which Dublin is famous. During this period, although the farmers lived poorly, the city was flourishing. The English were in political power and they decided to build noble buildings and graceful squares similar to those popular in London. The style is known as Georgian, after the reigning four Georges, kings of England.

The long rows of look-alike houses are the most typical. The origin of this pattern is rather interesting.

After London's 1666 Great Fire the government set certain regulations on the rebuilding of homes. Construction was to be of stone or brick (previously, buildings were of wood), four stories high with a gabled front. The problem was that overcrowded London had to find space for the large number of merchants and professional men, all with large families, near their places of business. The happy result was the discovery of two elements in modern town planning—the square and the terrace. Although the houses were sandwiched together, the center square gave a country feeling with its gardens of plants and greenery. The narrow frontage of the house was fine with the owners, since they were taxed according to the footage overlooking the street. The narrowness was compensated for by building the houses two or three times longer than their width. The back terrace—another touch of the country—was small-carpet-sized or large enough for a stable and coach house. The vivid colors of the doors and the unique doorknobs were the owner's personal touches. But his real individuality was saved for the interiors. Elaborate stairways dominated the center hallway and delicate plasterwork in lovely pastel shades decorated the walls and ceilings with harps, cupids, and flowers. Merrion Square and St. Stephen's Green have outstanding examples of these Georgian town houses. For a close-up tour of an interior, go two streets away from St. Stephen's Green to a charming building that houses exhibits of Dublin's yesterdays.

The Civic Museum, City Assembly House, South William Street, is open Tuesday to Saturday, 10:30 A.M. to 6 P.M.; Tuesday till 8 P.M.; Sunday 11 A.M. to 2 P.M.; Monday closed. Free.

THE OCTAGONAL ROOM, where most of the displays are shown, has a beautifully decorated ceiling and cupola. On the walls are hung delightful prints of eighteenth-century Dublin. The

wax models for the ornaments on the arches in the customhouse
are emblems of Irish rivers. Don't miss the armor crest and silver
mounts for the Lord Mayor's state coach, or the assortment
of old brass door knockers.

The Brazen Head Hotel and Pub is the pleasantly sinister setting where Robert Emmet and his conspirators plotted many of
their moves. Even the entrance is hidden away, just off the quays
on lower Bridge Street and tucked in between a vegetable store
and a sundries shop. The hotel and pub are considered the
oldest in Dublin, dating back to 1786. The courtyard was once
a busy stable yard for horses and carriages as well as the way
station for dashing highwaymen en route to robbing their next
traveler. Inside, just above the first flight of stairs, is a window
with the signature of one of Ireland's most famous road bandits,
John Lonegoon Waterford. He scratched his name on the glass
with his diamond ring. Above the landing are the doors leading
to Emmet's room. During one encounter with the authorities,
Emmet is said to have hidden in the linen closet for ten hours,
almost smothering to death. Then when all was clear he made
a successful escape, it is believed through a tunnel under the
hotel that led to Christ Church. The pub has the look, smell,
and feel of ancient good cheer. One of the customers or the
barmaid will be pleased to describe the background of the old
pictures (Emmet's trial) and furniture (Emmet's writing table).
It is usually quite empty during the day and young people are
welcome to look around.

Young Emmet was hanged right in front of the **Church of St.
Catherine** in Thomas Street. It was a spine-chilling scene. The
betrayed young man stood on the gallows plank with a sack
over his head. The silent, terrorized mob stared in disbelief
and Emmet's young girl friend fainted. She became insane from
recalling that terrible day. The plank was kicked away by the
hangman, who eventually cut Emmet's head from his body.

St. Michan's in Church Street (near the Four Courts), is said to contain the unmarked grave of Emmet and is the place where Charles Parnell's body was brought for final services. But what is most interesting are the underground vaults. Here you see the mummified bodies of members of many noble families. The skin is like leather and the knees and other joints are still movable. No one can explain the exact reason for their state of preservation. The chambers are absolutely dry and remain at exactly the same temperature. Although it is not certain how long the bodies have been here, one vault has a little child known to have been buried 150 years ago. Another one has a huge man, over eight feet tall, who may have been a knight Crusader. His leatherlike hands have become shiny from the custom of visitors shaking hands with him. A last oddity is that no animals live below except spiders, who have woven a most wonderful veil in one of the vaults. Tours are conducted Monday to Friday 10 A.M. to 1 P.M. and 2 to 5 P.M.; Saturday 10 A.M. to 1 P.M. only. Fee: 1/- (12 cents), half price for children.

NOW! 1916

Small uprisings. A few rebellions. These were not enough. The Irish yearned for what they had fought for since Brian Boru —independence. By the mid-1800s secret societies had sprung up everywhere. Each one had a different plan but all with the same idea, return Ireland to the Irish. The Gaelic League set out to restore pride in the Irish language, which had been forgotten. Under British rule, all education and business was conducted in English. The League, still functioning today, sponsors festivals of poetry, music, dance, drama, Gaelic sports events, and is responsible for road signs being written in both the English and Gaelic languages.

Another organization was convinced that there was a more direct way to get Ireland's freedom. The Irish Republic Brotherhood (IRB) and its political arm, the Sinn Fein Party ("we ourselves"), believed in taking it by force. Dublin on Easter morning 1916 was the appointed time.

The General Post Office on O'Connell Street was the first target. It was to become the headquarters. Today, the battle maneuvers may seem a bit homemade, but to the Irish Volunteers it was a defiant stand. Picture the small band of 150 men dressed in bits and pieces of makeshift uniforms, proudly marching in what would seem, to a casual stroller, a holiday parade. One man in the ranks waves a drawn sword. Others carry rifles and some go empty-handed. Following close behind is an overloaded taxicab jammed with pikes, pickaxes, sledge hammers, and hampers of food and provisions. The order is given. The men halt, break ranks, and storm the post office. The employees and stunned people mailing letters or buying stamps are chased onto the street. Windows are smashed and guns propped out on the ledges. (More men are wounded from the shattered glass than from enemy bullets.) Immediately two flags are hoisted and Patrick Pearse, the commander in chief, stands between the front columns reading a proclamation that ends, "Irishmen and Irishwomen: In the name of God and of the dead generations from which she receives her old tradition of nationhood, Ireland, through us, summons her children to her flag and strikes for her freedom." Seven men sign the document, knowing they are probably putting their names to a death notice. Copies are posted on the outer walls of the post office for the curious onlookers. Barricades of automobiles, streetcars, flour and sugar sacks, and rolled newspapers are placed at strategic places. Although rifle shots are heard throughout the city, the majority of Dubliners go about their daily routines as if nothing is happening. They are careful to avoid the streets known as trouble spots. The valiant men hold onto the post office for six days. Finally a British gunboat, anchored in the river Liffey, opens fire. The building is aflame and the men are forced to evacuate.

The scars of the battle are still evident. On the outside walls of the post office you can see where the bullet holes have been carefully patched.

In the center of the main hall is the bronze statue of the dying Cuchulainn—Ireland's most colorful mythical hero, whose tales of fantastic strength date back to prehistoric times. The monument honors the men who died in this building in the 1916 Rising. Legend says Cuchulainn courageously defended Dublin and all of the Province of Ulster from many dangers. Once evil Queen Maeve was determined to capture the most precious religious object—the sacred animal, the Brown Bull. Cuchulainn mounted his chariot and set forth for battle. He journeyed "over the Plain of Speech, beyond the Tree of Triumphs" until he came to a clearing crowded with black tents. Cuchulainn drove his chariot in ever widening circles as black-clad enemies sprang up in front of him in endless numbers. Behind each group there seemed to be more: ". . . almost as innumerable as the blades of corn in a field or the stars in an autumn night; grim and gaunt their blood-red horses, with fiery manes, charged on." It seemed to Cuchulainn that the smell of blood was in the air, but instead of daunting him, it gave him more courage and anger. Then, as he felt his battle rage come upon him, his entire body changed. It is said that one of his eyes retreated into his head while the other stuck out as big as a fist; a column of red smoke sprang from his head and his body became so hot that it burned those near him. Without a pause and in his wild, ferocious rage, Cuchulainn leaped upon his shapeless foes and slew them by the thousands.

His considerable reputation for physical prowess started when he was a child of seven. He accidentally killed a fierce watchdog belonging to the House of Culan. To compensate the owner, Cuchulainn volunteered to guard the house himself until one of the watchdog's puppies was old enough to replace him. The incident earned him his name, which means "hound of Culan." The statue in the post office shows Cuchulainn after he was fatally wounded in battle by the sons of a king of Ulster and by the daughters of Calatin the wizard, both of whom had been killed by Cuchulainn. He had tied himself to the pillar so that he might die on his feet. The bird getting ready to fly may be his faithful wife or Queen Maeve; mythical characters were well known for their ability to change shapes by just a wink of the eye.

St. Stephen's Green, at the top of Grafton Street, was another major battle area. At midday that Easter Monday, a group of about one hundred Sinn Fein Volunteers stood outside the entrance gate. At the appointed signal, the men and a remarkable woman, Countess Markiewicz, quietly moved in and cleared all the civilians out of the park. In half an hour trenches were dug and the buildings commanding the approaches to the park were taken over. As night fell, the sniping began. News of the Rising was sent to well-wishers in the United States in a coded message —"John [Bull] Has Been Successfully Operated On Today." But by the next day the British organized and took over the Shelbourne Hotel facing the park. Their machine-gun fire raked the Green as the fighting raged on. By Thursday the communications between the various rebel units broke down. The British, who had first moved slowly, were now surging ahead, breaking through walls and taking over one building after another. The rebel forces, shelled and bombed, were weary from hunger and lack of sleep and were running short of ammunition. The end was near. Saturday morning Patrick Pearse sent a white flag of surrender to the British commander and a note to his various garrisons. The rebels were stunned with disbelief when they were told the Rising was over in a message from their leader that read: "It is not my wish to surrender. If we do not, they will show no mercy to those who are prisoners."

Today the Green is anything but a battlefield. Originally
it was the recreation ground of those who lived in the splendid
houses surrounding the park. Now it is open for everyone to
enjoy the delightful trees, the flower beds, the waterfall, and the
lake with its miniature islands. A favorite pastime is feeding the
ducks. There are a number of statues throughout the park,
ranging in style from very modern (Theobald Wolfe Tone at
the corner by the Shelbourne Hotel) to old-fashioned (Countess
Markiewicz). In the middle of St. Stephen's, in a fussy enclosure of stone, stands an unusual memorial to William Butler
Yeats, the poet. It was created by the famous English sculptor
Henry Moore. He named it "Knife Edge" and if you walk
around the piece several times, you can see the flashing blade.

St. Stephen's is open during daylight hours from 8 A.M. on
weekdays and from 10 A.M. on Sunday. Be sure to stroll around
the outside of the park for a look at the attractive Georgian-
style houses. At numbers 84 and 86, now the property of
University College, you will be allowed to look inside at the
splendid plasterwork.

The Mansion House, on nearby Dawson Street, has been the
residence of Dublin's Lord Mayor since 1715. It has been the
scene of many important events. In the ROUND ROOM at the
first session of the Dáil, the Irish Parliament, the Declaration of
Independence was adopted in January 1919. Also, the signing
of the truce between the English and the Irish became official
in this very place in 1921. To tour the building you must
write ahead to the Secretary to receive permission.

Time for a light refreshment? **Bewleys,** 78 Grafton Street, is
great at 4 P.M. for high tea and delicious cakes. **The Country
Shop,** on the northern side of St. Stephen's Green at number
23, has two floors of homey atmosphere (large fireplace, country-style furniture) and the best homemade food. Lots of splendid
small baked pies (steak and kidney, chicken and ham, cheese
and tomato) and wonderful freshly baked brown bread. The

food is not fancy but just plain good. Prices about 6/2 (74 cents); open only for lunch and afternoon tea until 6 P.M. The restaurant is run by the Irish Countrywomen's Association, which encourages farm ladies to produce and sell their own wares. The small shop in front sells beautiful, inexpensive hand-made items.

Kilmainham Jail, Kilmainham, is a ten-minute bus ride from the center of the city. Conducted tours of the newly converted museum are given each Sunday from 3 to 6 P.M. To visit at other times or days, contact the Secretary of the Restoration Society, Seamus Brennan, by telephoning 375-080.

A chilling experience will be a fitting end to your tour trailing the rebellious ones. You'll enter the horrible, tiny cells in which the revolutionaries spent their last hours. If ghosts did exist, they would re-echo the countless miserable footsteps of those who fought for Ireland's freedom from the first prisoner in 1787 to the last in 1924. Some of the tour guides have been prisoners here themselves and will give you their own personal account of their terrible period of captivity. The stone carving over the entrance sets the tone—five ugly serpents, each repre-senting the demons of crime, are chained by Law and Justice. Once beyond the front door, glance at the giant-sized locks, which were immediately bolted as prisoners were brought in or out. The four-foot-thick walls and the cramped, cagelike cells shut the inmates completely away from the outside world. Their only contact was the one letter a month they were allowed to send and receive. And all mail was strictly censored.

The large cell with two windows looking out to the stone wall is where Charles Stewart Parnell was imprisoned. His like-ness in the form of a bust is there and an interesting inscription is cut into the window sill. You proceed through the exercise yard and into the bleak section where some of the men of the Rising faced the firing squad. One victim, James Connolly, was badly wounded and carefully nursed in a hospital until he was well enough to sit up in a chair for execution. Row upon row of small cells were totally bare except for three planks of wood placed on the icy stone floor as a bed. Shoes and bits of clothing served as pillows or bedding.

Twenty-one-year-old Anne Devlin, a faithful friend and assistant to Robert Emmet, spent four torturous years confined in a below-ground cell, in total darkness. Shortly after the Rising, Anne was dragged from her house, pricked by bayonets until she was covered with blood, and half hanged in an attempt by the English to obtain information about Emmet. Released from prison at the age of twenty-five, she looked like a gray, withered old lady. Another cell held Countess Markiewicz, the founder of Fianna Eireann, the National Boy Scouts, and an early supporter of the 1916 Rising. Although the Countess was sentenced to death, the English did not kill her for fear the world would react harshly to the execution of a woman. While still a prisoner, she became the first woman to be elected to the Irish Parliament.

The MAIN COMPOUND, completely redone, is a museum that serves as a grim reminder of the fight for liberty. It contains Wolfe Tone's death mask, Emmet's execution block, tearful letters from prisoners, a cell covered with murals belonging to a Mrs. Plunket, and hundreds of other sorrowful exhibits. Fresh air will take on new importance by the completion of this tour.

THE OUTCOME OF THE RISING

For sixteen men the 1916 Rising meant the firing squad at Kilmainham Jail. Patrick Pearse, their leader, was among the unlucky ones. But the severity of the sentences received international attention and inspired sympathy for the Irish cause. The Sinn Fein Party was able to win a majority of seats in Parliament. But they never accepted them. Instead, in 1919, they declared they were establishing their own National Parliament

("Dáil") in Dublin. Eamon de Valera, American-born, was elected president.

Now open war between the Irish and the English was official. The British sent in troops of ex-servicemen. They were called Black and Tans because, lacking complete uniforms, they dressed partly in khaki and partly in dark clothes of the Royal Irish Constabulary (police force). The Irish secretly built up the Irish Republican Army (IRA) and resisted with savage guerrilla fighting. The war raged on for two years, and hundreds of people were killed. Finally a treaty was signed giving Ireland the right to rule itself, with the stipulation that it remain in the British Empire. Six counties in Northern Ireland decided to remain part of the United Kingdom. Then, on Easter morning, April 18, 1948, thirty-two years after the motley crew of Dubliners openly rebelled and hundreds of men on both sides lost their lives, southern Ireland got its complete freedom from Great Britain. The name of the country was also changed from Eire to the Republic of Ireland.

FOR YOUR AMUSEMENT

Dublin Zoo, in Phoenix Park, Parkgate Street, a short distance from town, is open from 9:30 A.M. to 6 P.M. in summer; to sunset in winter; Sunday noon to 6 P.M. Fee: 4/- (48 cents) children 1/- (12 cents).

One of Europe's finest, it is delightfully laid out, full of all manner of beasts, from elephants to white mice. The zoo is famous for its breeding of lions, which are kept in simulated natural surroundings. The original mascot lion for the Metro-Goldwyn-Mayer motion picture studio came from Dublin. During World War II many European countries sent their lions here to board. The deer, llamas, and wallabies (small Australian kangaroos) roam freely in enclosed fields. Two islands are filled with families of gibbon monkeys, swinging and chattering from tree to tree and occasionally coming to the edge of the water to beg for apples and nuts. Feeding is allowed. Albert the hippopotamus wallows in his bath next to the elephants, who work untiringly each day standing up on their hind legs for pictures or carrying young people on their backs. THE PET CORNER has lots of gentle animals, guaranteed not to bite. Here you'll find lambs, kids, rabbits, birds, monkeys, and even a lion cub or two.

There are many other attractions in Phoenix Park itself. A restaurant in pleasant surroundings serves inexpensive meals. Polo, a form of hockey on horseback, is played from the end of April to the beginning of September every Tuesday, Thursday, and Sunday at about three o'clock in the afternoon. It is one of the most difficult, fastest, and most fascinating sports to watch. Two teams of four players each, on horseback, try to hit a small wooden ball through the opponent's goal with long-handled mallets. Everything is fair except fouls or dangerous riding. Cricket matches are common within the park, as well as hurling, a most popular game similar to field hockey. "Hurley" refers to the stick used to strike the small leather ball, which travels at such fantastic speeds that it is sometimes difficult to follow its flight.

Riding enthusiasts can rent a horse for about 10/- ($1.20) per hour at the Phoenix Park Race Course Stables. Call 300-837 for detailed information. You will find free entertainment and music every Sunday around the bandstand. And most interesting, in more desolate sections, you can watch farmers bring their cattle here for grazing.

A FEW DAYTIME SUGGESTIONS

Sea fever can easily be catered to with a tour of the docks conducted by a harbor master. Write to: Harbor Constable,

Alexandra Basin, Dublin 1, or telephone 48772. What a sight, as the mammoth ships are loaded and unloaded.

The Bottle Museum, in cellars beneath Kingsbridge Station, is really unique. It contains bottles of every size, shape, and form, old and new, from all over the world. Hours are 10 A.M. to 12:30 P.M. and 3:30 P.M. to 6 P.M. Monday to Friday. Admission is free and a knowledgeable guide provides interesting background information.

The Moore Street open-air market, below the General Post Office, is held early every morning except Sunday. Listening to the broad and unusual accents is a treat; don't be confused— it is English. Careful shoppers can find a bargain or two.

AND THE EVENING . . .

The Abbey Theatre, in its new home on Lower Abbey Street, is justifiably world-famous. Seeing a performance of J. M. Synge's *Playboy of the Western World,* Sean O'Casey's *Red Roses for Me, Shadow of a Gunman, The Plough and the Stars,* or Brendan Behan's *Borstal Boy* (life in a boy's reform school) is a rare and splendid experience. The Theatre often reflected playwrights' vivid accounts of the ardent spirit displayed during the risings. At some premieres the audience would get carried away, shouting, booing, hissing, stamping, and in some cases actually rioting. Today the actors perform with the same zeal but the audiences relive the past in a calmer fashion. Seats should be booked in advance by writing—or you can try your luck at the box office. The best seats seldom cost more than 12/- ($1.44) and often less. The curtain rises at 8 P.M.

Singing pubs preserve the tuneful and entertaining old Irish ballads. Some have regular performances; others rely on audience participation. Young people accompanied by adults are welcome to join in the fun, which starts at about 8 P.M. **O'Donoghue's,** 15 Merrion Row, is the most central. You may be intrigued by the age of the waiters (and some bartenders), who are about fourteen years old. **The Bark Kitchen,** 1 Sarsfield Quay, has nightly singing competitions in the upstairs lounge. A surprising number of good singers show up. Three other exceptionally good places in different areas of the city: **Abbey Tavern** in Howth; **Old Shieling** in Raheny, and the **Embankment** at Tallaght. If you really enjoy this type of folk music, there are a few other places (a little more rustic) that perform it to perfection: **The Ould Triangle,** 81 Lower Mount Street (Wednesday, Friday, and Sunday at 9:30 P.M.); **Fiddler's Club,** 153 Church Street (Friday and Saturday at 9 P.M.); and **Piper's Club,** 14 Thomas Street (Sunday at 9 P.M.). Admission about 1/- to 2/6 (12 to 30 cents.)

SOME SPECIAL INTERESTS

BOWLING (Tenpin)

Stillorgan Bowl, Stillorgan. Open daily 10 A.M. to 2 A.M.

CHESS

Dublin Chess Club, 20 Lincoln Place, Dublin 2. **U.C.D. Newman House,** 86 St. Stephen's Green, Dublin 2.

FENCING

Irish Amateur Fencing Federation: c/o Royal Bank of Ireland, 54 Lower Baggot Street, Dublin 2. Telephone 62721

STAMP COLLECTING

Dublin Philatelic Club: Contact Secretary A. L. Stokes, 25 Pembroke Park, Ballsbridge, Dublin 4.

Rates are for a double room with bath and include breakfast.

Russell Hotel, right on St. Stephen's Green at number 102–4, is in the center of most of your activity. This smallish hotel has been adding new rooms, making it a kind of fun maze when you try to find your room. It has one of Dublin's best restaurants but it is fairly expensive. The price of a double room is 160/- ($19.20).

Jury's, on College Green, is close to Trinity College and an interesting place to see the students in action. Some of the old-fashioned decorations are still intact. The roof garden is very pleasant. Rates for a double room are about 120/- ($14.40).

Wynn's, 35/39 Lower Abbey Street, overlooks the river Liffey, where you can spend many adventure-filled hours investigating the quays. It is centrally located—right next to O'Connell Street—and is a convenient family-size hotel (only sixty-two rooms). Rates are about 90/- ($10.80).

CHUN GREIM LE NITHE: A BITE TO EAT

Breakfast is usually enormous (hot cereal, farm-fresh eggs, marvelous crunchy bacon, thick slices of homemade bread, and good tea or milk), followed by an eleven o'clock break for tea and pastry. Lunch is the big meal of the day (four to six courses). High tea at about 4 P.M. includes little snacks consisting of cakes, scones, or sandwiches. Dinner, around seven, is light.

The Soup Bowl, 2 Molesworth Place, is a happy discovery. The whole place looks like one *large* living room complete with a cozy fireplace. The Irish potato soup is a delight. Price for an average meal is 18/- ($2.16).

India Tea Center, 21 Suffolk Street, serves interesting Indian food and is a popular meeting place for students and young people for lunch and snacks. Closed after 5:30 and all day Sunday. Price for a meal about 7/9 (93 cents).

The Unicorn, 11 Merrion Row, serves an interesting variety of German, Italian, and Irish dishes. Here's a chance to try Irish stew (made without carrots) and particularly good soda bread. The upstairs room is especially homey. Lunch is served from 12:30 to 3 P.M. and dinner from 6 to 10:30 P.M.; closed on Sunday. Price for a meal about 18/- ($2.16).

RUD ÈIGIN A CEANNACH: TO BUY SOMETHING

The pound (written "£") is the basic unit and worth $2.40, enough to buy an Irish peasant doll. It is made up of 20 shillings (written "s" or "/"). Each shilling is worth 12 cents and will pay for a ticket on the double-decker bus all the way to Dún Laoghaire (six miles). There are 12 pence ("d") in each shilling. Pence is plural for penny and each is worth 1 cent. It takes 4 pence for the telephone and 6 for a chocolate-covered wafer or an ice cream.

AG SIOPADÓIREACHT: SHOPPING

Business hours during the week are 9:30 A.M. to 5:30 P.M., half day on Saturday.

CLOTHES AND TOYS

Brown Thomas & Co., Ltd., Grafton Street. Just about anything you want at a reasonable price.

Clery's, O'Connell Street. An entire basement full of toys. Especially lovely are the dolls dressed in traditional costumes. Price about 29/- ($3.50).

His 'n Hers, South Anne Street, off Grafton, is strictly for mod clothes.

W. J. Kelly, Grafton Street, specializes in boys' and men's sweaters from about £2–10 ($4.80 to $24) and Irish Aran "fishermen" ones for £5 ($12). Irish tweed ties are 7/6 (90 cents).

Irish Jewelry, 11 South Anne Street, makes keen copperwork. Necklaces are priced from 15/- ($1.80).

PET SHOPS

Uncle George's, Marlborough Street, has something special for your favorite animal.

RECORDS

Pigott's, on Grafton Street, has a vast collection of Irish ballads. Albums of the "Dubliners" and "The Rafters Abbey Tavern Singers" are outstanding. Cost for an album about 33/- ($3.96).

SOUVENIRS

The Cluna Studio, St. Stephen's Green. Famed Connemara marble, handmade jewelry inspired by designs in the Book of Kells, bracelets, and rings range from £1–5 ($2.40 to $12).

MEET THE YOUNG IRISH

You can arrange with any of the Irish Tourist Board offices in the United States to get acquainted with someone of your own age and similar interests. The completed application should be returned to the Board at least one month before your departure. If you arrive in Dublin without previous arrangements, contact Bord Fáilte Eireann (the Irish name for the tourist office), Baggot Street Bridge, Dublin 2, or telephone 65871.

SLÁN: FAREWELL

The Irish have an old saying, "When God made time, He made plenty of it," and in Dublin this is particularly true. Life is not a gallop but something to be enjoyed, like a long, leisurely stroll. And the Dubliners wish to keep it just that way. Once you've accepted the old gracious look of the city and the unhurried attitude of the people, it is easier to enjoy.

But Dublin is not typical of Ireland. Once outside the capital the gently sloping hills and stone walls spring up everywhere. Thatch-roofed cottages line the roads. Motorists, walkers, and climbers find the roads completely uncrowded except for an occasional herd of sheep or cows. Ireland is a land of contrasts. Even the countryside is made up of opposites. It is called the "Emerald Isle." The sections that are green are as green as you'll see anywhere. Much of the rest of the land is hills of purple and black bogs. The square pieces cut out of the bog land are known as peat or turf and are ingeniously used for heating and cooking. Peat gives off a pleasant aroma and makes Irish homes cozy and warm in the winter.

Connemara is on the wild west coast. Here, amid some of the most splendid mountain scenery in the world, are brilliant blue and clear green lakes surrounded by meadow flowers and golden, swaying daisies. This is the region where Irish is spoken as an everyday language and many old crafts and traditions are kept alive. It is also the original home of the famous ponies of the same name. The tiny village of Renvyle has one splendid hotel from which you can go swimming, boating, hunting, fishing, bird watching, exploring—or you can just listen to the quiet all around.

Want a unique way of getting to Connemara? How about traveling like a gypsy in a horse-drawn caravan? A caravan looks like a covered wagon with rubber tires instead of spoked wheels. Companies such as the *Carefree Caravans* (354 Clontarf Road, Dublin 3) can take care of everything. The equipment comes complete with free lessons in harnessing and unharnessing the horse and driving instructions. Best of all, you and your family can take turns driving across country at your own pace. And everywhere you go you're sure to hear well-wishers call out, "Go n éiri an bóthar leat"—May the road rise with you.

RUD ÈIGIN A RÀ: SOMETHING TO SAY

English is spoken everywhere in Dublin but here are a few Irish words you might like to try.

ENGLISH	IRISH	PRONUNCIATION
Hello	Dia dhuit (God be with you)	Dee-ah gwuit
Reply to hello	Dia's Muire dhuit (God and Mary be with you)	Dee-ah śmuire gwuit
Goodbye	Slan leat	Slawn loath
Thank you	Go raibh maith agat	Gah rev ma agut
Tea	Té	Tay
Milk	Bainne	Bonnyeh
Butter	Im	Imm
Bread	Arán	Arawn

CÚRSAÍ: EVENTS

March 17	**St. Patrick's Day.** Cavalcade parade of floral floats, drum majorettes, brass and pipe bands, traditional

Irish dancers in costume, and children's choirs. Great annual dog show on the Royal Dublin Society grounds. In Croke Park, a festival of the national games—hurling and gaelic football. Children hunt shamrocks. Friends and family gatherings, with toasts to those absent.

March-April   **Easter.** Colorful egg gift giving. Easter, 1916 Rising celebrations.

May (first week)   **Spring Show.** A mammoth country fair. Horse shows, folk singing and dancing, and exhibits galore.

June   **Irish Fencing Championship.**

August (first Tuesday through Saturday)   **Dublin Horse Show.** Main social and sporting event of the year. Concerts and splendid floral displays. Jumping events and children's competitions.

October (early, for two weeks)   **Theater Festival.** All theaters are filled with exciting productions—both Irish and foreign playwrights.

October (last weeks)   **Oireachtas** (Celtic Festival). Every aspect of Gaelic life shown. Competitions of Gaelic football, hurling, ballad singing, country dancing, harpists, pipers, fiddlers, and lots more.

October 31   **All Saints' Day** (Halloween). "Bairin breach" (fruit bread or cake) baked with novelties inside. Finder of ring is first to be married.

December 25   **Christmas.** Large candle set in front windows. Merchants give their shoppers gifts of tea, sugar, raisins, jam, currant bread, etc. Special pantomime shows in the theaters.

December 26   **St. Stephen's Day.** At dawn children dress in improvised costumes and go from house to house singing rousing ballads. Spirited chorus known as "wren boys" collects money, cakes, and other traditional Christmas fare.

5. LONDON

A Royal Past with a Swinging Present

Ha'cher! Here's cheer! To London town. Ride a red *jam-jar* to Temple Bar. Set your *bird-lime* at ten to the sound of Big Ben. Have *Jack-the-Rippers* at seven, *Jenny-Lee* at eleven. With *Oxford scholars lollypop* for mod shirts with wild collars. Meet an Eton *china-plate* at the Gallery Tate. As the *sunshine and rain* lands, you'll know we all mean—"Welcome, welcome to the slightly mad but old, old London scene."

That's your cockney invitation to discover London. The cockneys are natives of the city and have a distinct way of speaking. Your greeting contains rhyming slang from their special language. Decipher the message by using these words for the italicized ones: tramcar, time, kippers (a breakfast fish), tea, dollars, shop, mate, and plane.

The English enjoy things in a set order and probably have the best manners in the world. You'll find 50 million gentlemen (and ladies)—banker gentlemen, road-cleaner gentlemen, shop-keeper gentlemen, and even fishmonger gentlemen. They are all polite in their own quiet manner. At theaters and bus stops long lines of people automatically "queue up" to wait their turn.

The sense of order is part of tradition, something that has been handed from one generation to the next. Do all Englishmen smoke pipes and love dogs? No, but millions do just as their fathers did before them. Keeping tradition alive makes the Londoner feel he has a link to the past and a better way to understand the future. Ancient ceremonies are re-enacted as they were hundreds of years ago. The manner of carrying out official acts rarely differs. When it does, a new tradition is instantly born. One year a small, misplaced item altered a historical event. Queen Elizabeth I was fond of knitting. When the list of nominees for sheriff was shown to her it was customary to pick up a quill and check off her choice on the scroll. A pen was not handy. Instead she picked up her knitting needle and pricked a hole next to the favored names. Today Elizabeth II still appoints her sheriffs by piercing a hole next to the names of her appointees.

Feel like an Englishman, thrill and cheer to the ceremonies, brilliant parades, and spectacles passing by just as people have for centuries. Follow the guide to royal London, as you delight in the turned-on atmosphere of swinging London.

HOW IT ALL BEGAN

Over two thousand years ago, ancient Britons discovered two small hills beside the sluggish river Thames, which flowed through a marshland. Much of the marsh is still there. Today the buildings near the river stand on great piles driven into soft, wet clay.

Homes were built on top of the hills, which are now called Cornhill and Ludgate Hill, and also on the nearby high ground. When the Romans conquered Britain, they decided this site was perfect for their own city, Londinium. The river Thames served as a great highway to the sea, connecting Britain to other countries. A thick wall was built to surround the city, with forts and gates and great roads leading to the other towns. During the three and a half centuries of their rule, the Romans conquered more and more of the surrounding lands and built lavish houses, forums, and temples. Many of these buildings had what would be considered today modern conveniences—central heating and hot water baths.

When the Romans left in the fifth century, many other people ruled Britain. Finally the Saxons, an ancient German people, occupied the area and changed the name of Londinium to London.

By the ninth century a very unusual king had become a dominant force in London's history—Edward the Confessor. His strong belief in religion accounts for his nickname "Confessor." He is said to have had snowy white hair and a beard, and long, almost transparent fingers, which were able to heal people. As one of the few early kings to rule over a united England, he lived through twenty-five years of peace and saw the wealth and strength of the kingdom spread abroad. He was interested in building and during his reign Westminster Abbey was begun.

Later the Normans came from what is today France and invaded the country. Their leader, William the Conqueror, was crowned in the abbey at Westminster. He found the city so powerful that he decided to control it by building a great castle to serve as a fortification close to the banks of the river. This was the White Tower, which became part of the Tower of London.

William changed the whole shape and color of English life with a new language, new laws, and a new prosperity. One of his first deeds was to promise the citizens that they would remain under the same law as in King Edward's day and that every child would be heir to his father's property.

Then like two pebbles dropped in a pond, separate sets of ripples began to spread until they met—two different sections established themselves at the same time—the city of London and the city of Westminster. They both continued to grow close to the banks of the river Thames. Eventually they overlapped and formed central London, known as the "City."

In the City merchants became strong and trade guilds flourished. The kings remained in Westminster, where they felt they could reach the City easily on the river. In 1264 the national Parliament was established in Westminster and became the forerunner of English government.

During the reign of Elizabeth I the people involved in both politics and business decided to be closer to both London and Westminster. They moved into the area now known as the fashionable West End. Lawyers settled in the section called the Temple and newspapers were printed on Fleet Street.

Theaters were forbidden by religious leaders who thought plays were the work of the devil. Elizabeth I didn't agree. She loved splendor (even her nightcaps were sewn with spangles) and she willingly encouraged the Londoners' love of pomp and pageantry. In spite of the frowns of the Lord Mayor and the aldermen, Elizabeth allowed the building of the famous Globe Theatre at Southwark at the end of London Bridge. Crowds poured into the circular wooden building to watch long historical dramas full of shouting and swordplay. When the dreaded plague struck the city, authorities were pleased to close the playhouse. The plague, they said, was sent by God to punish theatergoers for the sin of attending performances.

On September 2, 1666, a fire broke out in a bakery near London Bridge. A strong east wind spread its flames rapidly. Before anyone realized what had happened, the ancient city was a ruin. But the fire helped to destroy the plague. To rebuild the city the King summoned the architect Christopher Wren.

A proclamation was issued. No more wooden houses; no more narrow, twisting lanes; and no more trades using fire crowded into a small section. Christopher Wren designed St. Paul's Cathedral and fifty-two other churches.

The eighteenth century saw the West End continue to enlarge and become known for squares such as Berkeley, St. James's, and Hanover. The Regency period brought a new style in furniture and buildings. Houses were constructed with stucco exteriors. The designs included bay windows and balconies. Other small villages sprang up in nearby Chelsea, Kensington, and Hampstead, and London prospered.

Today there are two Londons. The first is the City, which has its own Lord Mayor, its own police, its own courts. It consists of one square mile on the north bank of the Thames. It teems with workers going to and from the business center. The bowlers and top hats, black suits and umbrellas have been livened up with short skirts, wild trousers, and bright shirts. The second London is governed by the Greater London Council and has about 10 million people living in it; it encompasses an area of 735 square miles.

The majority of interesting places described in this chapter are located in a two-mile area. Charing Cross is the official center. As you travel about the city try to imagine what old London looked like. Many signs that read "High Street" mark thoroughfares of what used to be separate villages. Most street names have special meanings. Small notices on the walls will give you a clue. On some roads kings and queens and whole armies moved, and highwaymen rode too. In another spot Londoners played games and had holiday fun or a rich nobleman built an estate. A quiet area may have been the site of an ancient church or monastery. Begin by exploring what remains of Roman London and then visit one of the city's earliest landmarks, West-minster Abbey.

London Wall is the section of the city where the ancient enclosure was built. You can see where the gates and the wall once stood near St. Paul's Cathedral and the ruins of a Roman temple by the Bank of England. Although London Wall has been repaired and strengthened, its course has never been altered. Until the time of Queen Elizabeth I, every traveler approaching London had to enter through one of the six gates in the wall—Aldgate, Bishopsgate, Moorgate, Cripplegate, Aldersgate, and Ludgate. All were closed at midnight. Finally in the 1760s during the reign of George III the gates were pulled down and sold. Their names, however, exist today on signs over the double-decker buses, and the boundary of the City of London is still the same square mile of territory enclosed by the Romans nearly two thousand years ago.

The statue of Queen Boadicea—or Boudicca, as the Romans called her, stands in her warlike chariot at the northern end of Westminster Bridge, facing the Houses of Parliament. In A.D. 61 she led a tribe of Britons in an attack on Roman-occupied London and set it on fire. The Romans crushed the rebellion, and Boadicea to show her defiance took poison.

Westminster Abbey. Amid the splendor of this building, all the kings and queens of England have been crowned since Edward the Confessor founded the ancient abbey in 1065. Near his shrine in the Royal Chapel is the Coronation Chair made at the command of Edward I to enclose the sacred Stone of Scone, which the old kings of Scotland sat on when crowned.

Elizabeth II and all other monarchs except two Edwards, V and VIII, have been crowned ruler of the kingdom seated in this chair. It is moved into the sanctuary for the colorful ceremony exactly as is, with only a small pillow added to the seat for comfort.

Close by are Edward's sword and shield, which he used in

battle against the French. The sword must have been difficult to maneuver since it is seven feet long and weighs eighteen pounds.

THE HENRY VII CHAPEL holds the stalls and brightly colored banners of the Knights of the Bath, one for each knight. In back of each stall notice the small plate of copper with the knight's coat of arms. Below the stalls are seats for the knights' coat of arms. Below the stalls are seats for the knights' squires (three to every knight), with their own arms engraved.

THE NORTH AISLE has the white marble tomb of Elizabeth I and a section called The Innocents' Corner. The marble urn is for the two little princes some people believe were murdered in the Tower of London by their scheming uncle, Richard III. The cradle is for Princess Sophia who died after living only three days. Her sister Princess Mary, age two, is shown resting on her elbow near her.

The tombs of famous people and some unknown ones will be found throughout the abbey, but the most unusual is in the south walk of the cloister. A large blue stone is supposed to cover the lady giant "Long Meg," who lived in Henry VIII's reign, and twenty-six monks who died of the plague.

Don't miss a chance to see the waxworks in the NORMAN UNDERCROFT abbey museum. It was a custom at funerals of noted people to have a wax likeness of the person who died at the head of the funeral procession. The figure would be dressed in clothes worn when the person was alive. In the museum you'll see William Pitt, the great statesman, wearing his parliamentary robes, Queen Elizabeth I, and Lord Nelson with his naval medals and nearby his cocked hat with its green shade, which he wore after the loss of his eye. The figure of King Charles II is in its original showcase (1685), dressed in Garter robes and feathered hat. Many other interesting figures and exhibits are also on view, including the coronation chair of Queen Mary II, used only once when she and King William III jointly ruled.

CITY WITH A ROYAL PAST

Today, as in the past, the reigning monarch is the symbol of the country. All state discussions are carried on in the name of the monarch. But elected officials make the important decisions. In this way the monarch remains above politics and offers historical continuity. Londoners thoroughly enjoy seeing the colorful pomp and ceremony surrounding royalty.

State ceremonies are still held at the Court of St. James, where ambassadors from foreign countries present their credentials. Ministers "kiss hands" on their appointment and receive their seal of office, which they must return when they leave.

The reigning monarch presents official titles to peers, and as head of the armed services, must be familiar with all phases of military service. He is also head of the Church of England and appoints bishops. This custom began when the Roman Catholic Church would not allow Henry VIII to divorce his first wife. He insisted that Parliament grant him this power. He was anxious to remarry and have a male heir to his throne. It took five years, several deaths, and many changes of government before Parliament would agree.

Here are highlights of the lives of a king and two queens whose customs and traditions still exist, and some of the places most clearly identified with them.

HENRY VIII (1491–1547) At the age of seven the future king paid a formal visit to the city. After receiving a pair of silver goblets he gave a delightful little speech of thanks. The Lord Mayor and the aldermen never dreamed that when this sturdy, attractive red-haired child would grow to manhood he would alter the entire social and religious life of the country.

When the new king came to the throne as Henry VIII, his first act was to hang two hated tax collectors, Empson and

Dudley, who had done his father's bidding in squeezing money out of the city. The people were also pleased when he married his brother's widow, the Spanish Catherine of Aragon, whom everyone liked. Now England would enjoy Spain's support against France as well as trade with the New World. The cheerful, popular King was often hailed as "Hal" or "Harry" as he passed in review.

The middle and later years of Henry VIII's reign were difficult and dangerous. The citizens had no sympathy with his efforts to divorce Queen Catherine and marry one of her ladies in waiting, Anne Boleyn. With angry eyes they watched Thomas Cardinal Wolsey, Henry's able and ambitious chief minister, ask Pope Clement VII to annul the King's marriage. Wolsey argued that it was wrong for Henry to have married his brother's widow. The people had no pity for Wolsey when his failure to secure the divorce brought him dismissal from Henry's court.

The King was determined to have his divorce. He denied that the Pope had authority over England and secretly married Anne Boleyn in 1533. Everyone knew Henry would let nothing stand in his way. At Henry's insistence, Parliament passed two acts— the Pope had no authority over England and the Church of England was a separate institution with Henry as its head.

Henry had no wish to see reform ideas in religion spread, but the break with Rome forced him to destroy shrines and churches. No man uttered a word of protest. Life became more and more difficult and dangerous. No one knew which way the royal mind would turn next, but it was necessary to be prepared for any change to keep your head on your shoulders.

On the outside, the city prospered. Merchants sold the latest court fashions, elaborate and heavy, unlike the slender styles of before. Yet life had changed considerably for young people. All of the schools in London had been supported by a church. When Henry changed the course of events, few schools were able to find new sponsors. It was a long time before children's education recovered from the blow dealt by the upheaval. Among those schools which did survive were St. Paul's, founded in 1509. The boys of the cathedral school were nicknamed "Paul's Pigeons." They often fought with "Anthony's Pigs," the pupils of a rival school on Threadneedle Street. Briefcases were the common weapon of war.

It was even more difficult for the girls, who received their education in nunneries, which were quickly abolished. At least at the school of St. Helen's, Bishopsgate, girls were taught good manners, fine embroidery, some French and Latin, and church singing. For a long time after, a girl's education was left to her parents or to chance.

Henry's marriage to Anne Boleyn did not produce the happiness he sought. Instead of the son he so desperately wanted, Anne bore a daughter, Elizabeth. Then in 1536 the impulsive Henry had Anne beheaded to make way for a third wife, Jane Seymour. At last a son, Edward VI. But Jane died shortly after giving birth.

Henry had six wives. The last one, Catherine Parr, outlived him, and, it is said, henpecked him to death.

ELIZABETH I (1533–1603) Ships on the Thames fired ear-shattering salutes, flags flew from the steeples, fountains flowed with wine, and merchants in long, colorful parades joyfully greeted their soon-to-be-crowned Queen. Elizabeth I was enjoying every minute but she was too preoccupied with selecting her coronation robe and talking with her astrologer, Dr. John Dee, to decide the luckiest day for the celebration.

Why were the Londoners so willing to welcome the young Elizabeth? Mary Tudor, Elizabeth's half sister, had succeeded their sickly half brother, Edward VI. Mary believed she was chosen to restore England as a Catholic country. Within one year, and against the advice of the Pope, she had 288 victims burned alive for refusing to accept the supreme authority of the Church of Rome. She died in 1558, a most unhappy queen.

The people felt Mary Tudor's devotion was divided among Rome and Spain, her husband's country, and England. Elizabeth was all English and her subjects would soon learn that the fiery, red-haired sovereign had a keen mind. She was cautious, astute, and economical like her grandfather but still had some of the bravado of her father, Henry VIII.

Elizabeth's first Parliament questioned her about marriage. They were afraid that if she died, her nearest relative, Mary Stuart of Scotland, would become queen. Elizabeth was clever. She kept her foreign suitors, Philip II of Spain and the French Duke of Anjou, waiting for a long time to receive her answer, dangling the reply like bait on a hook and using it to her political advantage. In the end she remained unmarried.

The London of Elizabeth I was still a medieval city. The narrow streets and small, low-pitched dwellings were ill fitted to the growing population. To relieve the overcrowding, the Queen forbade the building of new homes within three miles of the gates.

Sir Thomas Gresham, a prominent financier, convinced the Queen that London needed a bourse, a place where merchants might meet to do business and merchandise could be stored. It was built and named the Royal Exchange. Shops were included in the quadrangle—apothecaries selling mysterious drugs from distant lands, goldsmiths, armorers. Other shops sold tiny items like mousetraps, birdcages, shoehorns, and anything else one could possibly want to buy. Soon the merchants' wives found this an excellent place to gossip. They would spend two or three hours preparing for their walks, cheeks painted, false hair in place, and their ruff (a huge three-tiered stiff collar) all set. They would carry a fan, a shopping bag, and a spice container as they set about to hear the latest news. The original Royal Exchange was destroyed in the Great Fire of 1666. The present exchange, at Cornhill, E.C. 3, still bears Thomas Gresham's crest, a golden grasshopper.

"Good Queen Bess," as she was affectionately referred to, became a legend. She brought a feeling of confidence and pride to England. During these years Shakespeare wrote his plays, Spenser wrote his famous poem *The Faerie Queen* and Francis Bacon wrote his essays. But the Elizabethan Englishman was someone who wanted action. Sir Francis Drake brought pirated treasures from the New World on his ship the *Golden Hind*. Sir Walter Raleigh roamed the seas in search of new lands and wealth. England's empire began to grow.

With the exception of her relationships with close companions, all was going very well for the Queen. Elizabeth's favorite was the Earl of Essex, who was many years younger than she. She had sent him on several successful expeditions, but one mission was a disaster. He was put on trial for the blunders he had committed when he went to Ireland to suppress a rebellion. Sentenced to prison, he was stripped of all his wealth. Elizabeth soon relented and had him set free. He took up quarters in a house in the Strand, where the name "Essex Street" still marks the site. But he would not keep quiet and his friends kept prodding him to rebel. He was once again placed on trial. Word spread rapidly that Essex had been holding secret communications with the King of Scotland and had been making unkind remarks about Elizabeth's fading beauty. He was executed.

In her last years Elizabeth made fewer appearances before her devoted people. Rumors circulated that she would go through periods of forced gaiety and then complain that she could not sleep at night. Some courtiers sorrowfully related that they saw her sitting in her dark room way into the morning weeping for Essex.

Elizabeth was seventy when she died. She had lived longer than most of her contemporaries. She still fascinates historians. Vain and deceitful, she managed to gain and hold the love of her subjects to the end of her life. The Elizabethans must have been convinced that their Queen was responsible for England's great expansion during the sixteenth century.

The Tower of London, Tower Hill. Open Monday to Saturday 10 A.M. to 5 P.M. in summer (until 4 P.M. the rest of the year); Sunday 2 P.M. to 5 P.M. during the summer only. Fee: 2/- (24 cents), children five to fifteen, half price. Wakefield Tower (crown jewels) 2/- (24 cents), children half price.

You can go to the Tower by river steamer, which leaves frequently from Charing Cross Pier and Westminster Pier. Telephone MAYfair 9191 for information. As you sail along, there is a splendid view of Big Ben, the Houses of Parliament, and St. Paul's Cathedral. Then slowly the medieval gray Tower comes into sight with battlements, flags, and iron gates. The nearby Tower Bridge should be seen in action. The drawbridge lifts when a bell rings.

Nearby, during Henry VIII's reign, the Lord Mayor and, the aldermen duly attended a water pageant in honor of the King's second marriage. Fifty barges with saluting trumpets and hung with cloths of gold took part in the show. One Londoner firmly refused to join any of the celebrations—Thomas More, onetime member of Parliament, later Speaker of the House of Commons and finally Lord Chancellor. Many tearful faces glanced toward the Tower of London when it was known that Sir Thomas was arrested for refusing to acknowledge the King as supreme head of the church. A year later Sir Thomas' head was hoisted above London Bridge.

THE YEOMEN WARDERS, familiarly called "beefeaters," are honorary yeomen of the guard, or members of the Queen's bodyguard. Actually, they are retired army sergeants full of honors and, as yeomen, part of the oldest military body in Europe. There are thirty-five to forty of these men who attend the Tower wearing approximately the same uniform designed for them by Henry VIII close to five hundred years ago. It consists of a red knee-length tunic, trimmed in black and gold, and a Tudor hat and ruff. The royal badge is embroidered across the center of the tunic. A beefeater carries a gilt, long-handle ax with a tassel. The chief warder carries his badge of office, a staff topped by a silver model of the White Tower.

The nickname "beefeater" is from a casual remark from Count Cosimo, Grand Duke of Tuscany, who when visiting the court in 1669 wrote that the yeomen "are great eaters of beef, of which a large ration is daily given them. They might be called beefeaters."

One yeoman takes care of the six ravens always at the Tower. He feeds them with horsemeat on a 2/4 (28 cents) weekly ration. Tradition says that the day there are no ravens at the Tower, it and Great Britain will collapse.

Although the original purpose of the Tower was protection, it is as retired from military duty as its yeomen. Actually it is a museum and the yeomen act as guides and guardians of the crown jewels.

To know of the events that took place in the Tower of London is to know what a poet described as "London's lasting shame." Its prisoners have been a King of Scotland (seventeen years), a King of France (two years), a King of England (Henry VI), and queens, princes, pretenders, and a long list of nobles who argued with their kings. Most of them left the Tower only to walk to the headsman's block on Tower Hill.

The Tower has been used in many ways—as a fortress, a palace, a royal mint, an observatory, and, of all things, an animal menagerie. Monarchs stayed in the Tower before their coronation and then rode from there in a parade to Westminster Abbey. Each Tower and building has a story of its own.

TOWER HILL. This is the site of the first permanent scaffold where many famous people were beheaded, including Queen Elizabeth's favorite, the Earl of Essex. In this area are the homes of the governor and the yeoman gaoler (jailer). These are the old gabled and red-tiled houses which have played a part in history. From one of these windows sad Lady Jane Grey saw her husband's body carried away from Tower Hill. Queen Elizabeth I, before she was crowned, was held captive here by her sister. The area she used for exercising is now called "Elizabeth's Walk."

LION TOWER formerly housed leopards, bears, lions, and even elephants, which were domesticated pets.

BELL TOWER was the prison for Princess Elizabeth, Sir Thomas More, and others. Guy Fawkes, who with two fellow plotters tried to blow up the Parliament Building, was examined here by the Council in 1605 before trial at Westminster.

BLOODY TOWER was originally known as the Garden Tower but is famous for a horrifying reason. It is believed that here little Prince Edward and his brother, the Duke of York, were smothered to death with a pillow by order of their crafty uncle, Richard III.

Sir Walter Raleigh, whose portrait hangs over the fireplace, was a comfortable captive for twelve years while he wrote the *History of the World.*

JEWEL TOWER is the strongest fortress in the land. It holds the brilliant crown jewels used during coronation ceremonies. Many of the pieces date back to 1660 and were first made for Charles II. The original pieces were melted by Oliver Cromwell, who tried to do away with kings and queens.

On exhibit is Edward the Confessor's crown, the oldest in Britain and last worn by Elizabeth II at her coronation. Look for the magnificent ruby in Queen Victoria's crown, said to have been given to Edward the Black Prince (known for his black armor) by Pedro the Cruel of Castile, Spain. The entire crown contains over three thousand precious stones, mainly diamonds and pearls. The biggest diamond in the world, weighing 530 carats, is called "The Star of Africa" and is set in the royal scepter. Remember that on summer weekends the lines to see these jewels are very long. Try to arrive promptly at 10 A.M. or to go during the week at working hours.

THE ARMORY has a collection of beautifully made old guns, knives, and swords as well as the original wooden execution block.

There are several suits of armor worn by Henry VIII. Each uniform in the armor exhibit looks small but is tremendously heavy. Often the warriors had to be lifted onto their horses. The smallest sizes fitted young boys of thirteen who went off to war.

THE RECORD ROOM has two daggers belonging to Colonel Blood, who tried to steal the crown jewels. He was so full of tricks that a poem was composed for him after his death.

> Thanks, ye kind fates, for your last favor shown.
> For stealing Blood who lately stole the crown!

BEAUCHAMP AND SALT TOWERS have pathetic inscriptions drawn on the walls by their prisoners. Cell number 66 housed Thomas Abell, the faithful servant of Henry VIII's first wife, Catherine of Aragon. He acted as her chaplain for the divorce. This offended Henry, who sent the poor man to his death.

In the Salt Tower, Hew Draper of Bristol (1561), who was accused of witchcraft, drew his horoscope on the wall.

CEREMONY OF THE KEYS. Each night from approximately 9:40 P.M. until 10 P.M. an age-old ceremony is re-enacted as it was over one hundred years ago. The Chief Yeoman Warder joins three men who assist him in closing the three gates. When the keys are returned the sentry calls:

"Halt! Who comes there?"

"The keys," answers the Chief Warder.

"Whose keys?"

"Queen Elizabeth's keys."

"Advance, Queen Elizabeth's keys. All's well!"

The party then advances through the archway. The officer in charge of the guard orders the guard and escort to "Present arms!" and the Chief Warder, taking two paces forward and removing his Tudor bonnet with a fine flourish, cries: "God preserve Queen Elizabeth!"—to which the guard and escort answer "Amen." Finally, as the barracks clock strikes ten, the bugler solemnly sounds the last post and the Chief Warder collects his lantern and proceeds to the Queen's House. There he hands the keys into the safe custody of the Resident Governor.

To see this ceremony write well ahead to the Resident Governor and Major of the Tower, Constable's Office, H.M. Tower of London, London E.C. 3.

Hampton Court Palace, Teddington, Middlesex. Ten miles from London, by train from Waterloo Station, by boat (April to September) from Westminster. Cost about 15/1 round trip ($1.81), children under fifteen half price. The palace is open May to September weekdays 9:30 A.M. to 6 P.M., Sunday 11 A.M. to 6 P.M.; shorter hours the rest of the year. Fee: 2/6 (30 cents), half price for children.

Here is England's most beautiful and Henry VIII's favorite royal palace. It was built in 1515 as a residence for Cardinal Wolsey, but was taken over by Henry when the Cardinal fell into disgrace. Cardinal Wolsey chose Hampton because his doctor told him it was the healthiest place within twenty miles of London. He was terrified of illness. It was a safe retreat from the crowded streets of London during the plague.

Wolsey had good taste and enjoyed having countless servants. The master cook dressed in velvet and wore medals showing his office. You can see the little room where he drew up his menus. Under him were eighty assistants, which means that mealtime was quite busy.

Henry VIII enlarged and enriched the palace and brought all six of his wives to live here.

At the SECOND COURTYARD there is a rare astronomical clock

on the inner side of Anne Boleyn's Gateway. The clock was made for Henry in 1540. In addition to telling time it indicates the phases of the moon and the tide recorded from London Bridge.

Enter the palace by way of the GREAT HALL and go through the few remaining Tudor rooms with their original tapestries, oak chairs, tables, sideboards, and clocks. Lavish banquets were held here and perhaps Shakespeare's troupe performed new plays. Today state dinners for prominent leaders are still given.

Ghosts are said to live in the HAUNTED GALLERY, after the Cumberland Suite. Two are Henry's wives. Catherine Howard, her loose hair flowing, has reportedly been seen wandering about in a long white dress. Her terrified screams recall when she was led to death at the Tower of London. Jane Seymour, another wife, has perhaps been seen entering from the Queen's Room carrying a lighted taper. Mistress Sibell Penn, nurse of Henry's son Edward VI, may have appeared accompanied by the sound of a spinning wheel. The whirring was heard by many people. Recently the palace was being fixed and a workman found an unknown locked room. When the door was opened, he discovered a spinning wheel whose foot pedal had worn a groove in the floor.

Don't miss the lovely gardens laid out in formal Dutch style going back to the seventeenth century. THE ROYAL TENNIS COURT, built by Henry VIII in 1529, adds another interesting historical note. The King was the first person in England to wear tennis shorts. Even today his red silk or velvet drawers slashed at the sides and edged with gold would seem a bit "way out" for the tennis courts. The King started his tennis career using a padded glove for a racket and a hard ball stuffed with compressed wool. The tennis net was a fringed cord drawn across the court. The match in the indoor court is played today just as in Henry's time, bouncing the balls off the wall.

Clever at solving puzzles? Try the cunning maze made from formal shrubs.

Windsor Castle. About twenty-five miles from London, fifty minutes by train from Paddington or Waterloo, and you are at the most romantic castle in the world. If you have time, you can visit nearby the most widely known of all English schools, Eton.

Windsor Castle is the part-time home of British kings and queens. Legends declare that King Arthur and the Knights of the Round Table met at the very place where the castle stands. Merlin the magician studied the stars from this vantage point. Certainly William the Conqueror built his fortress in wood, changed to stone by his sons. Three hundred years later Edward III built the solid Round Tower. The monarchs who followed made changes and improvements.

Much of Britain's history has been made within the solid gray walls of this castle. Here Henry VIII's roving eye alighted on poor Anne Boleyn. Through the cloisters Shakespeare may have hurried when he went to produce the play *The Merry Wives of Windsor* for the entertainment of Elizabeth I. Queen Anne was sitting by a window, one day in 1704, when they brought her the news of the Battle of Blenheim. The cards she was playing are still on the window sill. On an autumn day in 1839 the young Queen Victoria, strong-willed yet romantic, stood at the top of the staircase. She was to catch her first glimpse of Prince Albert as he arrived in his stately carriage. That night she wrote in her diary, "It was with some emotion that I beheld Albert, who is beautiful." She later proposed marriage to him.

To the present Queen Elizabeth, Windsor Castle has always been a second home. She played happily there as a child with her sister Margaret, sometimes boating among the water lilies or playing in the model thatched Welsh cottage. And it was at

Windsor that the Queen met the man she would marry, Prince Philip.

One of the first buildings you may visit is ST. GEORGE'S CHAPEL, the imposing setting for the ceremony conferring the Most Noble Order of the Garter, which was founded six hundred years ago. The popular story has it that at a ball in the Round Tower the Countess of Salisbury lost her garter while dancing. To silence the snickering courtiers, Edward III picked it up and placed it on his own knee. Then he spoke the French words that have been the motto of the Order, *"Honi soit qui mal y pense*—Evil to him who thinks evil." The Garter is the most important honor bestowed by the crown. The letters "K.G." after an Englishman's name mean that he has received this award. In the richly decorated choir loft are the statues of the Knights of the Garter. Read the plates bearing the names of the past and present members. An underground passage leads you to the Tomb House. The reclining monument to Prince Albert in white marble has his favorite dog Eos (goddess of dawn) close by his side.

Now let's go to the castle. In the STATE APARTMENTS are the guest rooms for foreign kings and queens. On the landing of the Grand Staircase is a statue of King George IV in the robes of the Order of the Bath (a military honor). Beneath this statue is an enormous suit of armor made for Henry VIII. Above the stairs are additional exhibits of medieval armor and weapons.

KING CHARLES II'S DINING ROOM is impressive. Look inside the Italian cabinet for the nightgown and cap worn by Charles I and beneath it for the stool on which he knelt for his execution.

THE GUARD ROOM has many souvenirs of British battles. Over a marble figure of the first Duke of Marlborough hangs the fleur-de-lis banner, the "rent" paid the crown for Blenheim Palace.

THE GRAND RECEPTION ROOM is the most handsome in the castle. The tapestries on the wall tell the Greek myth of Jason and the Golden Fleece. In the GRAND VESTIBULE leaving the State Apartments are a clock and table service taken from Napoloeon's coach at Waterloo. Next to the State Apartments is the room which has the Queen's Doll's House, a model of a tenth-century house. The items inside are one twelfth actual size.

THE GREAT PARK has many bronze memorials to Queen Victoria's dogs. One thing you may not see is the ghost of Herne the Hunter, a forest warden under Henry VIII. He was suspected of witchcraft and hung himself. Some people claim he prowls at night near the site of the ancient oak which bears his name.

Eton, just across the river, is one of England's most highly regarded schools. More than five hundred years old, it has traditions of a special world and way of life. Through the courtyards and across the streets surge boys of all sizes, small ones in big white collars and short black jackets like picture-book scholars. The big ones are in black tail coats with white ties tucked under their collars. This is the style of the uniform worn since the nineteenth century. Shiny black top hats are worn on special occasions.

Rowing boys are known as "wet-bobs," while cricketers are "dry-bobs." A few boys stride like peacocks through the streets, wearing bright waistcoats and looking very important. They are the twenty members of the "pop" club and act as monitors with powers of beating and levying fines.

One of the traditions of the school is that each year on the birthday of its founder, Henry VI, a group of students makes a trip to the Tower of London to place a rose on the spot where the King died.

Eton is a "public school," the type Americans speak of as a private school. A high tuition is charged. Eton places heavy emphasis on sports as well as studies. The Duke of Wellington was not exaggerating when he made his famous statement, "The Battle of Waterloo was won on the playing fields of Eton."

Daily you can enter the school yard and cloisters from 2 to 5 P.M. The chapel may be visited from 2:30 to 4:30 P.M. During schooltime choral evensong, which guests may attend, is sung at 5:15 P.M. on Tuesday and Thursday and lasts about forty minutes. Go to the school office, just inside the main entrance, for admittance.

The school yard has a statue of Henry VI. The top level of the building is the Upper School with statues of famous graduates. Notice the names of the boys who carved their initials in the wood. On the playing fields you can watch a special sport called the "wall game," a style of football played only at Eton.

The Cock Pit Restaurant, 47 High Street, is a meeting place for Eton students who enjoy eating inexpensively. Take an old-fashioned English cream tea here with buttered scones, home-made jam, and cakes baked right in the kitchen. It costs about 4/6 (54 cents). Be sure to ask for a look at the knucklebone yard out back.

QUEEN VICTORIA (1819–1901) Victoria proved to be one of the greatest rulers in English history. She was Queen of the United Kingdom of Great Britain and Ireland and Empress of India. The Victorian era named for her included most of the 1800s and saw Great Britain reach the height of its power.

In 1840 Victoria married her handsome twenty-year-old cousin, Prince Albert. The pleasure the match gave the people was shared by Victoria and Albert, who developed a deep and lasting affection for each other. From the beginning Albert played an active part in taking care of all phases of Victoria's life, public and private. He had an overdeveloped sense of right and wrong and brought a very rigid tone to the Victorian age.

London was changing. Ladies in wide crinolines and gentlemen in tall stovepipe hats strained to see the arrival of a giant clock, Big Ben. By 1834 a novel "gadget" had appeared on the scene, a comfortable, neat, two-wheeled carriage drawn by a sure-footed horse. It was called the hansom cab, named after its inventor. The merry clip-clop and jangle of bells remained a part of the sounds of London a little beyond Queen Victoria's reign. The underground railway made its trial run in 1863, whisking gentlemen waving their hats in unroofed cars. Many were terrified that the tunnel would collapse.

In the summer of 1851 Londoners had a new and wonderful experience which they owed to the imagination of Prince Albert. It was the Great Exhibition, in which the nations of the world would meet for the first time to display their arts, crafts, and industry. The Prince had to fight hard to get his project started, as people who viewed the outside world suspiciously felt that the exhibition would attract the ruffians and revolutionaries of Europe. Religious people thought exposure to worldliness would encourage sin. Some predicted financial disaster. The Prince was determined to carry on.

The opening day was brilliant. Queen Victoria glowed with pleasure and excitement in her rose-colored silk gown. Prince Albert donned the uniform of a field marshal. Their family proudly assembled to enjoy the festivities. Vast choirs sang the "Hallelujah Chorus." The splendid procession examined with great interest the overwhelming number of exhibits, from the Koh-i-noor Indian diamond to a Canadian birchbark canoe, from a cream ladle shaped like a buttercup to a machine for threshing corn, from a fountain of scented soap to a life-size statue of a slave girl.

The skeptics were defeated. The Great Exhibition was a huge success artistically and financially. Profits were used to build the Victoria and Albert Museum and Albert Hall. The Prince's role in the project is dramatized by the Albert Memorial near the museum. It is made of marble, bronze, and a mosaic of colored stones which took twenty years to create. It pictures Prince Albert triumphantly viewing a larger-than-life catalogue of the Exhibition.

The year 1861 was a tragic one for Victoria, when after a

short illness the Prince died from typhoid fever. She was bowed with grief and went into deepest mourning for the remainder of her life. When she was urged to open Parliament, she said it was unkind for her "dear people" to see their Queen "a poor brokenhearted widow." She would much rather they remember Prince Albert and herself in happier times.

The only person who succeeded in bringing her out of her retirement was Benjamin Disraeli, whom she called "Dizzy." He became one of England's most colorful prime ministers and won the Queen's affection and regard with his keen political sense, warm wit, and gentle chiding. Near the end of her reign the affection of her people was shown by the Golden and Diamond Jubilee celebrations in 1887 and 1897.

Kensington Palace Museum, Kensington Palace (part of London Museum). Open March to September 10 A.M. to 6 P.M.; October to February 10 A.M. to 5 P.M. Sunday 2 to 5 P.M. Free.

Victoria was born in this palace, which has a fine Victorian collection. It is also the setting for the most famous event of Victoria's life.

"Open these gates at once!" two men shouted outside the palace one pleasantly warm morning in 1837. The men had driven all night from Windsor to tell a teen-age girl her uncle William IV was dead. The suspicious porter allowed them to enter. They asked for an audience with Princess Victoria. The Archbishop and Lord Chamberlain waited and waited and waited. The servant returned saying that the Princess was sleeping so sweetly that she could not be aroused. The two men exploded, "We have come to the new Queen on business and even her sleep must give way."

Soon the two men were kneeling before an eighteen-year-old girl wearing a white dressing gown and shawl, her hair loose around her shoulders. She was half awake. That was the world's first look at Queen Victoria and the beginning of a new era.

Two hours later the Lord Mayor, as part of the Privy Council, had an opportunity to admire the grace and composure of a dignified queen. The dress she wore on this occasion can be seen next door in the London Museum. The black silk is a bit rusty brown, but the huge balloon-shaped sleeves, the tiny waist, and the long, narrow skirt give you an idea of her appearance when the Lord Major knelt to kiss her hand.

Enter the palace and climb the Queen's Staircase, find the KING'S PRIVY CHAMBER. Here are two special showcases, one containing rare china and porcelain, and the other ornaments, fans, and figurines associated with the Queen.

In another part of the room locate a miniature porcelain tea service used by Victoria as a child. A china tea service pictures her playing with the Prince of Wales at Windsor Castle. A painting on the wall depicts "The First Council of Queen Victoria," which took place in what is now the entrance of the London Museum.

The next room is the QUEEN'S BEDROOM. Furniture, prints, and drawings connected with Queen Victoria are on display and the wallpaper has been printed from the original blocks. The most extraordinary thing in the room is a pair of Indian clubs on a ledge by the fireplace. The sight of Victoria as a young girl or an older woman twirling them would surprise a lot of us.

THE ANTEROOM was originally part of the King's Gallery. The doll's house and toys are Victoria's playthings. A needlework picture of Queen Victoria and two children hangs above the doll's house.

THE NURSERY is a perfect reproduction of a Victorian room. It is not exactly a place where you could sink into a chair and relax, but comfort was not characteristic of the period. It was a time when to show an exposed ankle would cause a scandal.

London Museum, Kensington Palace. The same days and hours as the palace next door.

This museum gives a fine, sweeping impression of London's

colorful past. The exhibits are arranged to show the development of the city from Roman times to the nineteenth century, dramatized by vivid dioramas showing the important events. Also there are models, clothes, toys, and dolls, including ones dressed by Queen Victoria, and an elegant collection of coronation regalia and theatrical costumes and properties.

The TUDOR COLLECTION beginning in Room 13 is outstanding. Elizabethan clothing, both the fashionable attire of the courtier and the flat woolen caps and leather boots of the merchants and apprentices, is displayed. A model of Sir Thomas Gresham's original Royal Exchange is exhibited. Other models will give you a feeling for the crowded conditions of the city, which made the Great Fire of 1666 the terrible disaster it was.

View the Elizabethan jewelry and uncut stones found buried in a wooden box in 1912. The collection includes a cameo with the Queen's likeness, an emerald with a watch set into the heart of it, and some fine chains of gold.

Since the museum is divided into different sections—Roman, Medieval, Tudor, Stuart, Georgian, and Victorian—special talks are given for each of the periods. The front desk will provide you with interesting work sheets to help you remember the highlights of each section. In addition you can arrange to examine some of the objects close up. Talks are also given to older girls about the costumes.

To participate in any of the activities, write in advance or phone the Schools' Officer, Mrs. Mary Speaght, London Museum, Kensington Palace, W. 8. Telephone: WES 9816.

Kensington Gardens. When you leave the London Museum take time for this special park. On the west bank of the Long Water is the statue of Peter Pan with his pipe and friends. The Round Pond is perfect for meeting new friends while they sail their model yachts.

Londoners love a parade. England's army was a part-time job for the wealthier people. Being in the military was, and still is in some ways, important to the London social scene.

Changing of the guard. Foot guards at Buckingham Palace parade every day including Sunday at 11:30 A.M. There are five different regiments which may participate. How do you tell them apart? Look closely at the uniforms when the guards go marching by. The men wearing these uniforms are among the toughest fighting soldiers in the world. Watch the colors of the plumes in their bearskin caps: Grenadier Guards (white), Coldstream (red), Scots (no plumes), Irish (blue), and Welsh (white, green, white). Examine the spacing of their jacket buttons. The Grenadiers have single buttons regularly spaced; the Coldstream buttons are in pairs; Scots in threes; Irish in fours; Welsh in fives.

If the Queen is in London her color, "Queen's Color" (crimson), will be carried. If not, the guards will be carrying their own company colors, the "Regimental Color."

As the new guards are in the palace forecourt the old guards are formed facing in front of them. The new guards march in slow time, pointing their foot, pausing, and then moving forward. After presentation of military compliments, the keys of the palace are presented by the captain of the old guard to his replacement. The band plays popular tunes while the sentries step into place. The old guards march away.

You can't visit the palace, but you may go to ROYAL MEWS, Buckingham Palace Road, which houses the royal coaches and horses. You can see the State Coach, used for coronations; the Glass Coach, used at weddings; and the Irish Coach, which appears for the state opening of Parliament. It is open every

Wednesday and Thursday 2 to 4 P.M. Fee: 2/6 (30 cents), children 1/- (12 cents).

The Horse Guards at Whitehall parade every day at 11 A.M. (10 A.M. on Sunday), the Royal Horse Guards known as the "Blues" from their blue uniforms, and the Life Guards, or "Tins," in their scarlet uniforms. Both wear armor reaching down to their waists (cuirasses). The uniforms are complete with buckskin breeches, black jack boots, and spurs.

If the Queen is in London there is more to see since the "long guard" is performed with its complete number of men. The guard is commanded by an officer in charge of sixteen troopers, a corporal horse, a corporal major, and a trumpeter who rides a gray horse. The others ride black chargers. First the old guard is dismissed. It is drawn up in the forecourt, facing south. With the arrival of the new guard, the trumpets sound a call. The two officers salute and then stand their horses side by side while the guard is changed. The ceremony lasts fifteen minutes.

It's easier to see both changing ceremonies on Sunday but possible to do so on weekdays if you really hurry.

Trooping the color is a royal event. The Queen celebrates her official birthday usually on the second Saturday in June. It takes place on Horse Guards Parade in Whitehall at 11 A.M. The pageantry is of rare splendor with the Queen riding side-saddle on a highly trained horse.

The colors of all five regiments in their special ceremonial uniforms are on show. The troops stand especially rigid as they await the Queen's inspection. Then the precision marching takes place. It is an unforgettable experience.

A limited number of people are able to watch from special seats on either side of Horse Guards Parade. Admission for a seat is by invitation only, chosen by a drawing. Entries for the drawing should be sent to Household Brigade, Horse Guards,

London S.W. 1, and must be mailed before February. If you don't get a ticket, watch the magnificent parade along the Mall. But get there very early.

The opening of parliament is another royal event. Every year, usually in early November, the Queen in her golden Irish State Coach rides in a stately procession from Buckingham Palace to the Houses of Parliament to open the first session. She is escorted by the brilliantly uniformed Household Cavalry Guards. Upon her arrival at the Palace of Westminster she is received by the Great Officers of State and then proceeds to the robing room. When she emerges in her elegant robes and jeweled crown a hush is broken by the sound of trumpets. The House, rich in color with splendid costumes worn by peers, judges, bishops, ambassadors, awaits her entrance.

The Queen moves slowly, ascending the throne in the House of Lords. She delivers her speech, presented to her by the Lord Chancellor. It contains the government's program for the new session. At the end, the procession moves quietly out of the chamber, recalling perhaps that Parliament has opened in just this same way since at least 1523.

Searching the vaults is another custom of the state opening of Parliament. It is done by the yeomen warders early in the morning. This is a reminder of the seventeenth-century Gunpowder Plot, when Guy Fawkes and his fellow conspirators made plans to blow up the Houses of Parliament. It is said at the last moment the King cried out, "I smell smoke!" He must have had a very keen sense of smell. The guards found the gunpowder and fuses in time to stop the plot.

Guy Fawkes Day Celebration. English children look forward to celebrating this event on November 5 every year with fireworks and bonfires. Days in advance young boys ask "Penny

for the guy, sir?" They stand hopefully and proudly next to a
tattered bundle of old clothes stuffed with straw and rags with
a mask serving as a head for the "guy" (Guy Fawkes). The
pennies buy fireworks and on the evening of November 5, all
over the country these and hundreds of bonfires go off. As the
flames blaze an old chant is heard:

> Remember, remember the fifth of November,
> The gunpowder treason and plot.
> We see no reason why gunpowder treason
> Should ever be forgot.

Touring Parliament: Her Majesty's government. Conducted
tours with an official guide are available on Saturday, Monday,
Tuesday, and Thursday in August between 10 A.M. and
4:30 P.M. During the rest of the year you can visit the building but conducted tours are not available.

The tallest tower, Victoria, is 336 feet high. The clock tower
contains "Big Ben," named after Benjamin Hall, the man who
commissioned the works to be made. You can tell whether Parliament is in session—if it is, by day the Union Jack (British
flag) flies from the Victoria Tower, and by night a bright light
shines about the clock.

Entering the MAIN HALL, you are in the only surviving part
of the medieval Palace of Westminster. Notice the magnificent
oak ceiling, dating from 1399. This was the site of the Great
Council which came before Parliament.

The Hall has been the scene of many famous trials. A brass
marker on the south steps shows the spot where Charles I was
condemned to death. Oliver Cromwell, who followed Charles,
became Protector in Westminster Hall in 1653. For a few years
England had no king, as Cromwell declared himself Head of
State. His statue stands outside on Parliament Square.

Parliament is made up of two houses, the House of Lords and the House of Commons. The original meaning of the word "parliament" is talk or discussion. In the beginning, the crown as head of the nation was supported by the great barons or landowners, who paid the state expenses. Special council meetings had to be held to get agreement on larger contributions. As the crown's requests grew, the smaller landowners (usually knights) were also asked to pay. They decided to meet separately and agree on the amount they could provide. The small landowners, feeling they had common interests, agreed to continue working together, and so the House of Commons was formed apart from the House of Lords. The main difference between the members is that the Commons are elected by the people (at least once every five years), while the Lords are born to their positions or are chosen for a life term.

The elected chairman of the Commons is the Speaker. He presides over the sessions and represents the members at all official ceremonies. The order of business begins with roll call on the motions or questions of the day. If two people disagree one member directs his argument to "Mr. Speaker" and not to the man with whom he disagrees. When Mr. Speaker rises from his chair members must stop talking. He has the authority to dismiss anyone out of order.

When the Gentleman-Usher of the Black Rod requests that the members of Commons join their colleagues in the House of Lords, Mr. Speaker leads the members. Wearing his wig and robes and bringing the great silver mace (staff), the symbol of his authority, he enters the House of Lords and places the mace on a table rack. The ancient custom helps remind the people of the prestige of Mr. Speaker's position. In former days this was particularly important when he reported to a king that the crown would not receive the money it requested. At that moment Mr. Speaker's life was in grave danger.

When Mr. Speaker leaves in the evening, the policemen in the passage cry out "Who goes home?" Everyone knows the House of Commons is closed for the day. The strange cry recalls that once there were no lampposts or street lights in London. The streets were dangerous and often filled with thieves. When members of Parliament finished their evening meetings they would collect in little groups and were lighted to their homes by "link-boys" carrying lanterns.

The House of Commons. Lots of activity here. Sit in the Strangers' Gallery and watch the comings and goings of the members. Some may be fast asleep on the back benches during a debate. Somehow the work does get done. The present chamber cannot, in fact, seat all the members of Parliament, by intention. When a few members are present it doesn't look so empty. Important issues have a full house, with people sitting on the steps. The small size also allows the members to talk in quiet tones. The majority party sits on the left.

When the House is in session you can get one of the 150 seats by applying to the U. S. Embassy, Grosvenor Square, London W. 1, or to the Admission Order Office in the central lobby. You don't need a ticket after 4:15 P.M. Monday to Thursday, or after 11:30 A.M. on Friday. (Line up at St. Stephen's entrance.) Check the newspapers for a day when it is likely that a lively debate will take place.

The House of Lords. In contrast to the soft green of the Commons, the Lords' Chamber is scarlet and gold. The rather small room is dominated by the glittering, canopied throne. Royalty has always had a right to sit in the House of Lords. In front of the throne is the "woolsack," a term used to describe the position of the Lord Chancellor, who is the highest judge in the land. The woolsack is an actual sack filled with wool upon which the Lord Chancellor sits as Speaker of the House of Lords. Since Lords are chosen rather than elected, the members are not as concerned about the public opinion and can speak freely. The debates are sometimes wiser and more interesting than they may be in Commons.

You don't need tickets to visit the Strangers' Gallery. Line up at St. Stephen's entrance up to one hour earlier for admission at 2:40 P.M. on Tuesday and Wednesday and at 3:10 P.M. on Thursday.

CITY OF THE LORD MAYOR

Law and order, commerce, and mastery of the sea still play a vital part in the London of today.

The top position in the City is that of Lord Mayor. A different man is elected each year by the liverymen or City officials. The loser of the current election will probably be the Lord Mayor the following year.

The man selected is always of high standing and usually wealthy enough to meet his tremendous entertainment expenses during his term of office. Within the City he has absolute authority except over the Queen.

Much of London's struggle for power has been between the money of the City merchants and the kings and Parliament at Westminster. The merchants always held the purse strings.

The City's independence is still shown today. The Queen must ask permission to enter the City on state occasions. She and her company present themselves at Temple Bar on the Strand, the City's invisible limits, and the Lord Mayor performs the "passing ceremony." He presents to the Queen one of four swords of the City, with the tip face down. The Queen hands it back and he carries it away erect as a symbol of his authority. Honor is served.

The first election of the Lord Mayor was in 1192. The best known of the early mayors was Dick Whittington, who was chosen for the office four times. He is familiar from the popular, partially true children's story. The legend tells of a poor boy who came to London from the west of England to seek his fortune. He was told the capital city's streets were "paved with gold." He found a job as a kitchen boy for a rich merchant and loaned him his favorite cat to take on a trading ship. The cook treated Dick Whittington badly and he decided to run away. While resting on Highgate Hill he heard Bow bells, the bells of St. Mary-le-Bow, calling out "Turn again Whittington, thrice Mayor of London." Heeding the call, he returned to the merchant's house to find his cat had been sold for a fortune to a foreign king whose palace had been overrun by rats. Dick Whittington became a wealthy gentleman, married the merchant's daughter, and became "thrice Mayor of London."

The actual Dick Whittington was a tailor who lived in London at the end of the fourteenth and the beginning of the fifteenth century. He was Lord Mayor four, not three times. Today there is a stone by the side of the road at Highgate Hill known as Whittington Stone, where he rested and heard the bells. And at Christmastime the musical "pantomimes" retell the story of Dick Whittington in a traditional stage spectacle of song and dance.

Lord Mayor Show. Another event that links London to its past is the Lord Mayor Show, given each second Saturday in November. A mile-long procession starts at Guildhall about 11:30 A.M. The military bands, decorated floats, Household Cavalry, state trumpeters, and coaches carry city officials past the Mansion House, the Lord Mayor's official residence.

The Lord Mayor enters his ornate gilded coach and follows the procession on his way to the Law Courts to be sworn into office. The huge carriage, built in 1757, weighs nearly four tons and is drawn by six stupendous horses. Pikemen and musketeers, helmeted and plumed, carry long pikes to guard him. The final touch is a banquet in Guildhall two days later. The Prime Minister is the guest of honor and the menu always includes turtle soup.

Mansion House, Mansion House Street. The Lord Mayor's home is open every other Saturday, 2 to 4 P.M. Write for tickets to Secretary's Office, Mansion House Bank, London E.C. 4, or phone MAN 2500. Free.

You can see the official chain of office, the splendid chain the Lord Mayor wears around his neck. It dates back to the mid-sixteenth century and is made up of the letter "S" linked together twenty-eight times. The jewel cameo in the center has the City of London coat of arms. See the EGYPTIAN HALL with its glass chandelier of eight thousand crystals and the lovely stained-glass windows with scenes showing the signing of the Magna Carta and Elizabeth I's coronation procession on the river.

Here is the only private house in the world with its own court of justice, called the Justice Room. There is also a prison below. The Lord Mayor judges cases twice a week and can give sentences up to one year, although he is neither a judge nor a lawyer.

Guildhall, King Street. Open year round Monday to Saturday 10 A.M. to 5 P.M. Sundays 2 to 5 P.M. Free.

Notice the City coat of arms over the porch. The GREAT HALL is the setting for the elections of the sheriffs of the City on Midsummer Day and for the Lord Mayor's Show in November. You can attend the celebration by writing in advance to the Hall Keeper, Guildhall, Gresham Street, London E.C. 2.

Find Gog and Magog, the two grim giant figures that protect the building. There are several legends about them. One tells how Gog was wounded when he helped the Trojans to attack London after a quarrel with Magog. Londoners are said to have nursed him so well that he made friends with Magog and agreed to guard the city ever afterward. It is also rumored that the giants come down to dine at the stroke of midnight. Since they are made of wood and plaster, they couldn't enjoy the meal very much.

There is also an impressive statue of Winston Churchill. Use the free radio tour guide to learn about the guilds and trades. You'll hear the voices of Queen Elizabeth II and Churchill in speeches they gave in this historic building.

Barristers: Lawyers. The law profession is divided into two different branches. Members of the bar, or barristers, wear long, flowing robes, short wigs, and white ties called "banderelettes." They speak for their clients in the High Court and the County Court but are not permitted to seek business. Solicitors, the other half of the profession, approach people who wish to be defended and bring cases to the barristers. They also may advise clients on legal matters but appear in lower courts only.

The Temple and the Law Courts. The Strand leads you to the Temple, which few visitors see because it is tucked away. Just behind St. Clement Danes Church is the fine building of the Law Courts or Royal Courts of Justice. They are called "courts" because the kings at one time decided all cases themselves. As the work increased the kings appointed judges to assist them. The Queen's judges in their robes and wigs still preside over the Royal Court. You can go into the central hall of the Royal Courts of Justice building, open from 8 A.M. until dusk. Ask a guard if you can see one of the courts in session.

For hundreds of years the barristers have had their offices (called chambers), libraries, dining halls, and often apartments grouped together around courtyards and gardens. Their quarters are known as "Inns of Court." Between 12:30 and 1:30 you can see barristers passing by dressed in full robes and wigs.

Old Bailey or the Central Criminal Court. Old Bailey, a famous court named for the street it is on, was built in the early part of this century. Visitors can see a trial by jury at 10:15 A.M. and 1:45 P.M. from the public galleries. Get to the entrance in Newgate Street early. Between May and September, the judges carry bouquets of flowers and sweet herbs are spread about the courts. The custom started when the judges needed to get rid of the unpleasant odor of the old Newgate Prison that once stood on the site of the present courts.

Fleet Street's Newspaper World. The hurry and bustle of this "street that never sleeps" creates famous newspapers. By day it is full of traffic, newspaper reporters, and photographers getting news and pictures. At night the oversized machines are cranking out printed papers. Motor vans rush them to the suburbs or to the stations to catch early trains. It probably started four hundred years ago when Wynkyn de Worde brought printing to Fleet Street. His former employer was William Caxton, who was the first man in England to use a printing press.

See tomorrow's news in the making. The following newspapers will show you their plant but you must write in advance since most are booked several months ahead.

The Times—Monday to Friday 8:30 to 10:30 P.M.; Mr. Peter Clark, The Times, Printing House Square, London E.C. 4.

News of the World—Saturday 7 to 10 P.M., one hour tour. You receive miniature copies of the paper. Production Manager, News of the World, 30 Bouverie Street, London E.C. 4.

The Sun—Tuesday to Friday 8 to 11 P.M. Promotions and Publicity Department, Odhams Press, 96 Long Acre, London W.C. 2.

The "Bobby": London Police. Long ago a person in each village was appointed by the crown to be responsible for good order and to arrest wrongdoers. To this day Londoners have the power of arrest for certain crimes. Although the idea may have been good, it did not work too well. One hundred and fifty years ago crimes were widespread throughout London and people were terrified to leave their homes. Sir Robert Peel organized the modern police force in 1829. The men were known as Bow Street Runners (where their headquarters stood), Robin Redbreasts (the bright red waistcoats they wore), and finally "peelers" or "bobbies," after their founder. He had difficulty convincing people that policemen were there to help. Today the City has its own police, independent of Scotland Yard. The members wear Roman helmets, red and white stripes on their sleeves, and lots of brass buttons on their jackets. Every man must be five foot eleven or taller and carry a radio speaker, something true of no other police in the world. All the men are especially trained to be of assistance to young people.

Trafalgar Square: The Tiniest Police Station in the World. At one corner find the small booth. It is the smallest police station in the world, with a direct line to Scotland Yard. A policeman is always on duty.

The square is a memorial to Admiral Lord Nelson, famous for winning the sea battle of Trafalgar. His statue stands at the top of the 185-foot column. On the terrace wall at the north side of the square locate the markers which are the official standards for British measures of length. Two other statues of famous people are close by, King Charles I, who was executed, and George Washington. At Christmastime crowds meet to see a beautifully decorated giant tree sent from Norway and to listen to lovely carols. It is almost like a scene from a Charles Dickens story.

Costermongers: Pearly Kings and Queens and Marketing. A curious tradition is the wearing of suits, dresses, and hats completely covered by thousands of pearl buttons. These are worn on special occasions by cockney street vendors selling fruit, fish, and other products, and are called "Pearlies." They come from the east or south of London with their donkey-drawn wagons or handbarrows. They are sometimes called "barrow-boys" but before they were known as "costermongers" or "costers." The "coster" came from the costard or custard apples they sold and the "monger" from trader. Before the industrial revolution the biggest bully could push the vendors aside and get the best selling spot for his own stall. To safeguard themselves, the traders elected a king to fight their battles and be the lawmaker. When licenses were issued for set stalls the pearlies turned from fighting each other to collecting money for charities.

The cockney traders are high-spirited and enjoy a good party. Every year there is a special celebration at the August Bank Holiday Fair at Hampstead Heath, one of London's best-known fairgrounds. In 1951 a Pearly King and Queen were chosen. The family, with their clothes covered from head to foot with buttons, will rule until 2051. Their children are referred to as "Prince" and "Princess."

Today costers or pearlies can be seen in the West End collecting money or at the annual harness horse parade in Regent's Park. Also early mornings in Chelsea colorful carts go bumping along the roads laden with flowers and fruits. The drivers come over the Albert Bridge from Battersea to sell their wares from door to door in the little streets by the river.

Go to a market. The bustling activities of market life begin in the early hours of the morning. You can start about 7:30 A.M.

Billingsgate, Lower Thames Street. Open from 6 to 10 A.M. Monday to Saturday. (Most trading is over by 9 A.M.) Sunday only shellfish are sold.

"Turbot! Turbot! All alive turbot! Beautiful lobsters good and cheap! Skate-oh! Skate-oh! Ha-a-andsome cod. The best in the market."

These are some of the calls you can hear in the oldest market in London, over one thousand years old. The "gate" in the name probably refers to one of the two river gates in the wall of the old Roman city.

The most colorful sight is the four-hundred-odd porters carrying their fish on their heads from the wholesaler to the retailer. This carrying is called "bobbing." The flat cap a porter wears is a bobbing hat made of leather and wood. A skilled porter can carry about one hundred pounds. The hats are handed down from father to son and have been a part of the market for years. Although the men used to be thought of as rude, they are very polite and helpful now. They will answer your questions and perhaps invite you to sample their shellfish.

Club Row Market, Sclater Street off Bethnal Green Road. Open Sunday only. This market has a character of its own. Animals and birds have been sold here for over a hundred years. Dogs are the main item sold but there are booths of fishes and birds. Lots of young Londoners rush here to enjoy looking at different types of rabbits and pigeons.

Covent Garden. Best time to visit is 6 to 9 A.M., although the markets are open until 10 or 11 A.M. In this world-famous market, fruit, vegetables, and flowers are sold in an area which was once a convent garden and the burial grounds for the monks of Westminster Abbey. It is a blaze of color at 6 A.M., when the carts and drivers arrive to stock their shops for the day. Nearby are the Royal Opera House and the Drury Lane Theatre, first set up by Charles II.

Leadenhall Market, off Gracechurch Street. Open Monday to Friday 9 A.M. to 5 P.M. Centuries ago this was a poultry market but now you can bargain for anything. The old traders' names are still above the shops.

Petticoat Lane, Middlesex Street, Whitechapel. Open Sunday morning only. (Best time is 9 A.M. till noon.) Lots of everything is sold here. Listen to the bargaining chatter as you pass the stalls.

Portobello Road, Notting Hill. Open Saturday only, 9 A.M. to 6 P.M. Walk down the narrow, winding hill, which has shops and covered markets on one side and stalls on the other. You'll find odds and ends—music boxes, posters, toys, stamps—anything you can want, with a willing seller nearby. Choose very carefully.

Smithfield Market, Charterhouse Street. Open Monday to Thursday 5 A.M. to 1 P.M. Best times is 7 to 9 A.M. Famous for its meat and its porters.

MORE OF WORKING LONDON

J. Lyons & Co., Cadby Hall. Fourteen miles of Swiss rolls are prepared in front of you. Cake is laid out, filled with cream and jam and rolled and sliced automatically. Two million cakes are baked daily. In the ornamental department, craftsmen create beautiful wedding cakes and others shaped like automobiles, animals, or mountain scenes.

Tours begin at 10:30 A.M. and 2:30 P.M. and include sample. Write to: The Manager, J. Lyons & Co., Cadby Hall, London W. 4.

The Royal Mint, Tower Hill. Seeing the coining of money in large quantities is a fascinating sight. Parties of six taken around, Monday to Friday 9:30 A.M. and 2:30 P.M., also between 2:50 and 5 P.M. on Monday and Thursday. Tours take about thirty-five minutes. Apply at least six weeks in advance to the Deputy Master, The Royal Mint, Tower Hill, London E.C. 3, and write exact number in group.

The Stock Exchange, Throgmorton Street. You don't have to be a big-time spender to enjoy this tour. High above the "floor," you can see the busy activities of the day. As the results flash across the screen the brokers are busy buying and selling. A tour guide will answer all your questions. Telephone LON 2355, Ext. 110, to arrange for a visit. Open Monday to Friday 10 A.M. to 3:15 P.M.

Twinings, Ibex House, Minories. A complete tour showing how tea is blended and packed. Write ahead for a visit.

Whitefriars Glass Works, Tudor Road, Harrow. A red-hot glass glob is blown by a human being into a round ball. Then with a few tools it is changed into a vase or bowl. To see this spectacular show write ahead about four weeks or phone HAR 1527.

Whitechapel Bell Foundry, 34 White Chapel Road. Big Ben and other famous bells were cast here. The sight of white-hot metal being poured provides great excitement.

OF SHIPS AND THE RIVER

Great Britain's full name is the United Kingdom, which includes England, Wales, Scotland, and Northern Ireland. As islanders living close to the ocean, the British have sea fever in their blood. For centuries Britain depended on the waterways to bring food, paid for by exporting coal and other goods. The sea was vital to trade and a sturdy defense against invaders.

The Thames River was and still is London's greatest highway. London is the major port of the United Kingdom and after New York and Rotterdam, the largest in the world. But the Thames is now not often thought of as a source of great pleasure as it was in the past. For centuries thousands of small boats would stand ready to taxi passengers up to Chelsea or down to Greenwich. Taking a boat from the royal Palace of Whitehall at Westminster to the Tower of London was quicker and safer. Walking the narrow, filthy London streets you risked being soaked by slop thrown out of an upper window.

Sailing on the river, there was a chance to see the glittering red and gold royal barge taking the royal family to a dinner party with friends or on a state business mission. On warm evenings Londoners rowed to a good spot to see the hundreds of boats going by and to spread the latest stories about the vessels' owners. Or they could drift along listening to the tunes played by the musicians in passing barges. The big event was the "swearing in" of the Lord Mayor, marked by fantastic floats and splendid fireworks.

Winter was ice carnival time. The largest celebration in 1683 lasted two months and changed the river into a miniature town of shops, booths, and tents. It was a Frost Fair with horse races, puppet shows, bull baiting, concerts, and roasted oxen.

You can still take a pleasure steamer to Greenwich or a river taxi inside the city. To re-create the past, visit the Victoria and Albert Museum to see the last royal barge; or go to the London Museum to look at the diorama of the Frost Fair. Then you'll know what the Thames means to Londoners and what Londoners feel about the Thames.

Discovery, King's Reach, Victoria Embankment. Usually open daily 1 to 4:45 P.M. including Sunday. Free. Captain Robert Falcon Scott sailed this ship on the first expedition to the Antarctic in 1901–4. He planned to take her to the South Pole in 1910 but another ship, the *Terra Nova* was used instead. Captain Scott lost his life on that voyage. The *Discovery* was the first ship expecially built for polar research. Although made of wood, it successfully broke through the ice. In Captain Scott's cabin you can see an exhibit of articles he and his men had to drag across the frozen wastes. Traveling over the icecaps proved impossible for dogs and ponies. The Wardroom has metal plates with the names of the original crew of officers and scientists.

Science Museum, Exhibition Road. Open Monday to Saturday 10 A.M. to 6 P.M., Sunday 2:30 to 6 P.M. Free. The push-button models of all kinds are fun to operate. Tours are given at 3 P.M. Tuesday, Thursday, and Saturday. The second floor has an amazing sea exhibit. Full-sized models of a ship's bridge, lighthouses, buoys, and other equipment give you an idea of how to navigate a ship. The history of sailing is dramatized through ships as different as Christopher Columbus' *Santa María* and modern warships. Don't miss the models of yachts, fishing boats, traders, Chinese junks, and other small vessels. Going through this section you can almost feel the salt spray against your face.

Royal Geographical Museum, 1 Kensington Gore. Open 9:30
A.M. to 5:30 P.M., Saturday 9:30 A.M. to 1 P.M. Free. A small
museum with relics of famous explorers.

River and Dock Cruises. The Port of London Authority, Trinity Square (telephone ROY 2000, Ext. 92). Saturday, May 22
to July 17; Thursday and Saturday, July 21 to September 4.
Embark 2:30 P.M., returning 6:30 P.M. Fee: 10/- ($1.20),
half price for children under sixteen.

The motor launches *Abercorn* and *Viscountess* take you on a
ten-mile journey downriver through the busy industrial section
of the Thames and then into the Royal Docks. A commentary
is given on the first part of the trip. Write in advance for book-
ings to P. O. Box 242, Trinity Square, London E.C. 3.

Downriver to Greenwich. Thames boats leave Westminster
Pier (WHI 2074) from April to September every twenty minutes
starting at 10:20 A.M. The trip takes fifty minutes and the cost
is 4/- (48 cents), half price for children.

As you go downstream you'll pass some unusual places with
strange names. There is Execution Dock (where pirates and
other sea criminals were once executed), Galleons Reach, Wap-
ping Old Stairs, Cherry Garden Stairs, Elephant Stairs, and others. Rounding the cape of the "Isle of Dogs" (no one knows
where it got its name), you get a view of the area.

Greenwich was the setting for some of the most colorful and
romantic pages of English history. The buildings you visit, the
Royal Naval College and the National Maritime Museum, are
on the site of the royal Palace of Placentia, built in 1433 and
the favorite of the Tudor kings. In Greenwich Henry VIII and
Elizabeth I were born; here Sir Francis Drake was knighted on
board the *Golden Hind;* the famous story of Sir Walter Raleigh's
placing his cape across a puddle to assist Elizabeth I is said to
have taken place at the gatehouse; Oliver Cromwell turned the
palace into a prison; and Admiral Nelson sailed from here to
win many battles.

The Cutty Sark Ship. Open weekdays 11 A.M. to 5 P.M., Sunday 2:30 to 6 P.M. Fee: 2/- (24 cents), half price for children.

The first thing you see in dry dock by the Greenwich Pier is the last of the tea clipper ships. It was launched in 1869 by Captain John Welles, known as "Old White Hat." The name of the ship means "short chemise (slip)" and comes from a poem by Robert Burns, "Tam O'Shanter." In it a witch, Nannie, "lapped and flanged" in a cutty sark. The figurehead on the bow of the ship is a somewhat fierce-looking Nannie.

The *Cutty Sark* was intended to outsail her rivals in bringing home from China the first of each new season's tea. She proved herself the fastest ship that ever moved through the water by the power of sails alone. On the tween deck the story of the ship is told in paintings and photographs. The lower deck has a display of old figureheads, among them Abraham Lincoln, Disraeli, and Gladstone.

The Royal Naval College. Open May to September daily 2:30 to 5 P.M. except Thursday; October to April daily except Thursday and Sunday. Free.

Originally a hospital for disabled sailors, the College is now used for the higher education of naval officers. You can visit the PAINTED HALL with its fantastic ceiling. It took Sir James Thornhill nineteen years to complete these huge murals. You see William and Mary surrounded by a great flying cloud, Queen Anne and Prince George of Denmark accompanying the landing of William of Orange. In the corner you can find a self-portrait of the artist. The room is the elegant dining quarters of four hundred officers.

National Maritime Museum. Open weekdays 10 A.M. to 6 P.M., Sunday 2:30 to 6 P.M. Free.

Each room is devoted to a different part of seafaring life. The principal hero is Admiral Nelson, who was killed in the Battle of Trafalgar. Galleries IX and X show scenes from all his battles and the uniform coat he wore when a sniper from the French ship hit him. The coat indicates that he was not a very large man.

The Old Royal Observatory. Open weekdays 10 A.M. to 6 P.M., Sunday 2:30 to 6 P.M. Free.

Five minutes away, on the top of the hill, is this world-renowned onion-shaped dome. It is from this site that both time and the earth's distances are determined. The "Greenwich Meridian" is a simple line drawn across the observatory path that starts somewhere from inside the building and disappears mysteriously under one of the shrubs outside. From this line all longitudes east and west are measured on the surface of the earth.

Greenwich mean time is a little more impressive. There is a red time-ball on the top of the east turret of the observatory which drops exactly at 1 P.M. British Summer Time each day, marking the hour throughout England and the entire world. Greenwich mean time is shown on the twenty-four-hour clock on the gate at the entrance to the Old Royal Observatory.

In the United States there are four time zones, Eastern, Central, Mountain, and Pacific. They are five, six, seven, and eight hours behind Greenwich time.

From this high vantage point on the hill you can, on a clear day, follow the windings of the Thames back toward the City and St. Paul's. As you return to board the boat for your return trip, take a last look across the river at the Isle of Dogs. From here three tiny ships, the *Susan Constant,* the *Godspeed,* and the *Discovery,* set sail on December 19, 1606, for Virginia.

CITY WITH A SWINGING PRESENT

London is a rare place, a world all by itself. You've seen the city of age-old history; now go to the city filled with young ideas, young fashions—"swinging" London.

Young people from all over the world come here to find out what's happening. You'll hear the current slang talk "London is fab," "London is turned on," "London is where the action is."

Carnaby Street is in the center of the swinging city. Not so long ago it was a drab place hidden behind Regent Street. Now bright op art and pop music are part of the narrow pavements crowded with "mods"—young boys with lots of hair, and flocks of "dolly birds,"—pretty girls dressed in granny shoes, colorful stockings, shiny raincoats, and short, short miniskirts. Lunch hour's the best time to see "the scene."

From one end of the street to the other is no more than 250 paces, but it is crammed with stores. **Kids in Gear,** 35 Carnaby Street, has clothes for eight- to twelve-year-olds in wonderful wild colors. Everything from Tom Sawyer hats, pants, and caps to T-shirts with funny sayings. There is plenty to see in Carnaby, a shop for old dustbins; **Hat Gear,** for all shapes and colors; and **James Galt,** for way-out toys. If you are hungry and want to mix with the Carnaby crowd, try the **Cranks Salad Table,** which bakes crusty whole-meal bread.

Chelsea is the nearby area where artists, writers, and musicians live. You can easily reach it by the Underground (subway) or bus. It is one of London's places for way-ahead art and fashions. **King's Road** is its main thoroughfare. This long, straggling street, a hodgepodge of coffeehouses, shops, fruit stalls, crowded pavements, and Mary Poppins rooftops is at its liveliest on Saturday mornings. King's Road actually begins at Eaton Square but changes character at Sloane Square, where the action begins.

Next door to the Sloane Street station is the **Royal Court Theatre,** which is like New York's Off-Broadway. On a bench in the square sit Chelsea pensioners (old soldiers from the nearby royal hospital founded by Charles II). You will know them by their scarlet uniforms.

The most unusual spot for lunch is on the roof of the **Chelsea Antique Market.** Chelsea's main street is full of good antique shops, but the market is crammed full with hundreds of stalls. The barnlike building was once a picture framer's workshop. Move among the good-natured crowd of bargain hunters. Buy a badger trap for 1/- (12 cents). You will be the first in your neighborhood to have this rare item. How about a stuffed barn owl in a glass case? There are old clocks, old prints, ostrich feather boas, and clothes that great-grandmother wore. Don't miss the shop called **Granny Takes a Trip** at 488 King's Road. You peek through the lips of a huge figure in the window to see what's on display.

What else in and around King's Road besides shops? **Beaton's** for crusty homemade bread; side streets with Victorian cottages painted in white, blue, or sugary pink; the **Duke of York's Headquarters,** which adds a military flavor to "the scene"; the old **Town Hall** with its gilded clock; and the **Chelsea Art School.** To round off the day you might try the informal restaurant **235 King's Road,** which had wooden benches, rust-colored curtains, and the day's menu chalked up on a blackboard.

LITERARY LONDON

Charles Dickens House, 48 Doughty Street. Open weekdays 10 A.M. to 12:30 P.M. and 2 to 5 P.M. Fee: 2/6 (30 cents), children 6d (6 cents).

Dickens, more than any other writer, has created the picture of early Victorian London—the fog, the dirt, the narrow lamplit streets, and the extremely rich and poor people who lived at the time. Many of his stories use incidents from his life. He knew poverty at firsthand. When he was a boy of ten, small for his age, his father was put in a debtors' prison and he was put in a factory to paste labels on bottles. His days were wretched and his nights worse. The child was left entirely by himself and had to walk four miles each evening to his lonely bedroom.

The Dickens House is neat and trim. It was the first real

home Dickens rented after he married and became a reporter and then a novelist. He signed a three-year lease when he was twenty-five and moved in with his wife, their small infant, his wife's sister Mary, and his younger brother Fred. The little back room on the first floor is where Dickens wrote *Pickwick Papers, Oliver Twist, Nicholas Nickleby,* and part of *Barnaby Rudge.* The cases contain manuscript pages of some of the books written in the house, and first editions of almost all his works. Other rooms are full of letters and pictures, and one has a statue of the famous author. The top-floor attic was his model for Scrooge's room in *A Christmas Carol.* Be sure to see the basement. It has been made into a replica of the Dingley Dell kitchen where Mr. Pickwick played games with the servants at Christmastime. It is amazing to see a scene re-created which was merely an image in the writer's mind in the room above.

The Old Curiosity Shop, 13/14 Portsmouth Street, is supposed to be the one in Dickens' story. It is open daily 9 A.M. to 6 P.M., Sunday 9:30 A.M. to 5:30 P.M. You can buy special little odds and ends.

Dr. Samuel Johnson's House, 17 Gough Square. Open May to September Monday to Saturday 10:30 A.M. to 5 P.M.; until 4:30 the rest of the year. Fee: 2/- (24 cents), children half price.

In the attic of this house Johnson and his secretaries spent eight years writing his famous dictionary. He also wrote a play, essays, and poems. The rooms contain many exhibits, including a lock of his hair (if you ask to see it) and an ivory-headed Malacca walking cane. Dr. Johnson is often quoted as saying, "When a man is tired of London, he is tired of life."

MUSEUMS AND SPECIAL INTERESTS

London has more museums for every square foot than any other city in the world. For a special organization that can help you get the most out of your visits to the museums and places of interest, write to Mrs. Anne White, Junior Museum Club, 8 Queen's Ride, London S.W. 13, or phone 01-788-8903.

Two collections cover a wide range of subjects (a more complete listing follows under the heading "Special Interests").

British Museum, Great Russell Street. Open weekdays 10 A.M. to 5 P.M., Sunday 2:30 to 6 P.M. Free.

Here are highlights from the largest museum in the world. The Clocks Room has old clocks that chime out the hour, play tunes, and have shows of dancing figurines. In the Greek and Roman Life Room, statues of the gods and parts of an old temple put you in an ancient era. The shrunken heads from South America in the Ethnographical Room may not please you, but they are fascinating. In the Egyptian Rooms, learn the secrets of how mummies were wrapped to keep them preserved. You'll even see mummies of sacred animals (cats, crocodiles, calves) and their wooden coffins. There is so much to see here, you may decide to return a second time.

Victoria and Albert Museum, Cromwell Road, South Kensington. Open weekdays 10 A.M. to 6 P.M., Sunday 2:30 to 6 P.M. Free.

Lots of exciting things tucked away: Elizabethan miniatures painted on bits of postage-stamp-size playing cards; a costume gallery; model theater sets; and "Tipoo's Tiger," a clockwork tiger made for an Indian prince. This last item has a mechanical organ which makes the sound of tiger's growls and the shrieks of the top-hatted man he is attacking. Ask the guard the time of the demonstration. The Javanese shadow puppets move gracefully at the turn of a handle. And don't miss the full-size whale. If you want to draw pictures of the exhibits the guard will arrange to lend you a stool.

ANIMALS

Young Zoologist (XYZ Club), The London Zoo, Regent's Park. If you are interested in animals and natural history, and are between the ages of nine and eighteen, you will enjoy being a member. For your subscription of 15/- ($1.80) a year you receive a club badge and membership card, six free admission tickets to the London Zoo, the chance to go to special lectures and films about animals, and the use of a free Information Bureau. You also receive the Zoo magazine free. It contains illustrated articles on pets, natural history, zoo life, and wild animals. There are competitions to interest everyone—painting, photography, essays, and general knowledge of natural history.

Horniman Museum, London Road, Forest Hill. Open weekdays 10:30 A.M. to 6 P.M., Sunday 2 to 6 P.M. Free.

THE NORTH HALL GALLERY shows how animals developed from the earliest times, how they move, protect themselves, and live. Other areas show arts and crafts through the ages.

CHILDREN'S ROOM is open during all London school holidays and from 4 P.M. Monday to Saturday. Drawing material may be borrowed.

Natural History Museum, Cromwell Road. Open weekdays 10 A.M. to 6 P.M., Sunday 2:30 to 6 P.M. Free.

Models tracing 400 million years of plant and animal life, including an eighty-five-foot dinosaur and a ninety-foot blue whale, are on display. The BIRD GALLERY has everything from hummingbirds to ostriches.

CHILDREN'S CENTRE, for eight- to fourteen-year-olds, is open Saturday 2 to 4:30 P.M., daily during London school holidays (Christmas, Easter, and mid-July to early September) 10:30 A.M. to 12:30 P.M. and 2 to 4:30 P.M. (Closed Sunday and Monday.) You may borrow drawing materials to copy exhibits; reference books are available.

Public Lectures are held at 3 P.M. daily (except Sunday) in the Lecture Hall of the Museum.

ARCHITECTURE

Sir John Soane's Museum, 13 Lincoln's Inn Fields. Open Tuesday to Saturday 10 A.M. to 5 P.M. Free. A small but exciting collection housed in an unusual room, full of drawings and pictures, in which the wall panels can be opened out and folded back to reveal more and more exhibits. It's almost like a magic trick.

ART

National Gallery, Trafalgar Square. Open Monday to Saturday 10 A.M. to 6 P.M. (Tuesday and Thursday until 9 P.M. in the summer), Sunday 2 to 6 P.M. Free.

Many paintings are on display—Leonardo da Vinci's "Virgin of the Rocks," others by Titian, Bellini, and Van Dyck, including the horse portrait of Charles I. See the peep-show box of painted rooms in the Hall of the Flemish School (Room 10). Special talks are given. Check at the door for the times and dates.

Tate Gallery, Millbank. Open Monday to Saturday 10 A.M. to 6 P.M., Sunday 2 to 6 P.M. Free.

Especially interesting arrangement of British paintings and sculptures (Epstein and Moore). Talks for young people are given. Check times and dates.

COINS AND MEDALS

Spink & Sons, 5 King Street. Experts in coins and medals of every country and period.

BUTTERFLY COLLECTORS

Desmond North, 59 Hall Drive. You can buy butterflies mounted on silk in neat cases.

DOLLS

Barry Elder's Doll Museum and Hospital, 114/116 Glenthorne Road. Open weekdays 9 A.M. to 6 P.M., Sundays 10 A.M. to 6 P.M.

Here is a lifelike collection of more than five hundred Victorian and Edwardian dolls made from wax, wood, porcelain, leather, china, and other materials. The beauty and variety of the dolls' faces and bodies are enhanced by the charming settings in which they are presented. Many life-size china boys and girls sit or recline on full-size chairs and chaise longues. Other dolls are placed around tables set for meals or are arranged to seem as if they are playing quaint antique musical instruments such as a spinet or a dulcimer. Lovely baby dolls lie asleep in Victorian four-poster beds or doze in strollers. Don't be put off by the shabby outside appearance of the museum.

Bethnal Green Museum, Cambridge Heath Road. Open weekdays 10 A.M. to 6 P.M., Sunday 2:30 to 6 P.M. Free.

Period dolls and their houses, wooden animals, toy soldiers and sailors, tea sets, and Victorian nursery games are beautifully displayed; also costumes, textiles, pottery, porcelain, and silver.

EARTH STUDIES

Geological Museum, Exhibition Road. Open weekdays 10 A.M. to 6 P.M., Sunday 2:30 to 6 P.M. Free.

Subjects include rocks, volcanoes, earthquakes, caves, pebbles, and stones from outer space. Talks and films are given each Tuesday, Wednesday, Thursday, and Saturday; also on Monday and Friday July 22 to September 9; all at 3 P.M. in the Lecture Room; suitable for ages ten and over. Free.

EGG COLLECTORS

Janson & Sons, 44 Great Russell Street. Experts in this field, who are called by museums to do delicate repairs.

HISTORY

Geffrye Museum, Kingsland Road. Open Tuesday to Saturday and bank holidays 10 A.M. to 5 P.M., Sunday 1 to 5 P.M. Free.

Series of charming rooms from 1600 to the present day. Everything works—clocks tick, spinets and pianos play.

CHILDREN'S ROOM on Saturday is almost like a clubhouse—young people come to draw, paint, or play the special pencil game made up by the museum.

National Portrait Gallery, St. Martin's Place, near Trafalgar Square. Open Monday to Saturday 10 A.M. to 6 P.M. (Tuesday and Thursday until 9 P.M. in the summer), Sunday 2 to 6 P.M.

Here are pictures of Britain's best-known citizens: Elizabeth I, Oliver Cromwell, Dr. Johnson, and Florence Nightingale. If you have ever wondered what your favorite historical Englishmen looked like, you are bound to find the answers here.

Public Record Office, Chancery Lane. Open Monday to Friday 1 to 4 P.M. Free.

National records since Norman conquest, including Domesday Book and signatures of kings and queens from Richard II.

Sir Winston Churchill's Dugout, Whitehall. How would you like to sit in the chair Prime Minister Winston Churchill used for his famous "blood, sweat, and tears" speech? You can if you visit his World War II underground dugout. Everything has been left intact, the maps on the wall with pins showing where the ships, troops, and planes were, and Sir Winston's bedroom and study. The tour in Whitehall lasts one to one and a half hours Monday to Friday. To make arrangements for a visit, write the Chief Clerk, Cabinet Office, Whitehall, London S.W. 1, or call WHI 5422, Ext. 96 or 237.

Wellington Museum, Apsley House, Hyde Park Corner. Open weekdays 10 A.M. to 6 P.M., Sundays from 2:30 P.M. Fee: 1/- (12 cents), children under sixteen half price.

Originally the home of the Duke of Wellington (the Iron Duke) the building is still more or less as he left it. Amid the silver and golden splendor you will find beautiful pictures, including three superb Velázquez paintings which were part of his battle spoils; a table laid as it was for the Duke's annual "Waterloo Dinner"; and a collection of fascinating personal mementos, including an array of field marshals' batons, uniforms, medals, and decorations, handwritten orders from the battlefields and even pillboxes with pills still in them.

MEDICINE

Wellcome Institute for the History of Medicine, 183 Euston Road. Open Monday to Friday 10 A.M. to 5 P.M., Saturday 9:30 A.M. to 4:30 P.M. Free.

Covers every aspect of medicine and science from the earliest times to the nineteenth century.

Royal Society of Medicine, 1 Wimpole Street.

Royal College of Physicians, 11 St. Andrew's Place. Lectures for young people during school holidays. Write for tickets to the Assistant Secretary, stating the days you'll be in London.

MUSIC

Royal College of Music, Prince Consort Road. Open 9:30 A.M. to 6 P.M. when the college is open. Closed for five weeks in summer and ten days at both Christmas and Easter.

More than three hundred instruments, including Haydn's clavichord, Handel's spinet, and the guitar which supposedly belonged to David Rizzio, Mary Queen of Scots' musician, who was murdered while playing it.

SPORTS

Lord's Cricket Museum, Lord's Cricket Ground, St. John's Wood. Open on match day 10:30 A.M. to close of play. Fee: 6d (6 cents), children half price. In winter open Monday to Friday 10 A.M. to 4 P.M.

Pictures and other exhibits showing the history of the game.

STAMPS

H. K. Harmer, 41 New Bond Street. Well-known auctioneers. Sessions are exciting to watch Mondays, Tuesdays, Wednesdays.

Keep still, for the slightest movement may cost a fortune. Specializes in postmarks.

THEATER

British Theatre Museum, Leighton House, 12 Holland Park Road. Open Tuesday, Thursday, and Saturday 11 A.M. to 5 P.M. Free.

A selection from the British theater; personal items from actors, costumes, promptbooks, letters, playbills, etc.

Pollock's Toy Museum and Toy Theatre, 44 Monmouth Street. Open weekdays 10 A.M. to 5 P.M. Free.

Lilliputian world of toys, games, dolls, magic lanterns of all nationalities. There is also a shop where you can buy old-fashioned toy theaters, lighting sets, plays with scenery, dolls, books, etc. If you write ahead you can get invited to special performances of the "A penny plain, twopence coloured" paper theater that has entertained young people for over one hundred years.

TRAINS

Museum of British Transport, Clapham High Street. Open Monday to Saturday 10 A.M. to 5:30 P.M. Fee: 2/6 (30 cents), children 1/6 (18 cents).

Locomotives from early ones with great copper domes to retired greats of steam; carriages from the earliest railway passenger car and the first sleeper. There are "wanted" signs of train robbers, handcuffs, billy clubs for railway police, metal bottles used as foot warmers, and lots of other items to keep you occupied for hours.

Steam Age, 59 Cadogan Street. Working models of every type of locomotive. You can visit the workshop if you write in advance.

WEAPONS AND ARMOR

Imperial War Museum, Lambeth Road. Open weekdays 10 A.M. to 6 P.M., Sunday 2 to 6 P.M. Free.

Exhibits about World Wars I and II, including weapons, uniforms, aircraft, decorations, and models.

Wallace Collection, Manchester Square. Open weekdays 10 A.M. to 5 P.M., Sunday 2 to 5 P.M. Free.

Every possible type of weapon, from the early cowhide shield and crossbow used at Agincourt to eight-foot shotguns that need two people to operate them, one to hold the gun up and the other to pull the trigger. Many guns and pistols are made of pearls and precious metals.

MONUMENTS AND CHURCHES

Streets and squares are filled with monuments, statues of kings, queens, princes, heroes, and artists. Look at their likenesses and see if you recognize them before reading the inscriptions.

Eros, the winged statue in **Piccadilly Circus,** is the Greek god of love. The name "Piccadilly" comes from piccadills, a type of high collar popular in the seventeenth century.

Waterloo Place has the Duke of York's statue, which a day's pay from each soldier in the army helped finance.

On the **Embankment** is Cleopatra's Needle which has nothing to do with the Egyptian queen. It was in existence fourteen hundred years before she was born, a monument to the sun god by a Pharaoh living about 1500 B.C. The city received it as a gift from Mohammed Ali in 1878.

Statues of Americans can also be found. The memorial to President Franklin D. Roosevelt is in **Grosvenor Square;** George Washington stands **in front of the National Gallery** looking out over Trafalgar Square.

Churches in the Middle Ages were all clustered together around old St. Paul's and London Bridge. There were more than a hundred. The part they played in London life is indicated by the fact that they have remained part of the songs and games children still play today.

One of the favorites is:

> Gay go up and gay go down.
> To ring the bells of London town.

St. Clement Danes, the Strand, is remembered in:

> Orange and lemons
> Say the bells of St. Clement's.

Listen to them ring at nine, noon, three, and six. Every year in March there is a special service for young people after which each child receives an orange and lemon to take home.

St. Mary-le-Bow, Cheapside, has:

> I do not know,
> Says the great bell of Bow.

Notice the beautiful steeple by the great architect Christopher Wren. The church is also noted for the old saying that a true cockney, a real native-born Londoner, is a person born "within the sound of Bow bells."

St. Paul's Cathedral is to the average Londoner what Westminster Abbey is to royalty. Sir Christopher Wren's masterpiece was built to replace the cathedral burned to the ground during the Great Fire of 1666. Wren's granddaughter was the first to be buried here. Wren himself, Admiral Lord Nelson, and the Duke of Wellington are buried here too.

Climb up to the WHISPERING GALLERY in the dome, where the smallest sound can be heard on the opposite side. Go out onto the STONE GALLERY for a magnificent view across the whole city.

Madame Tussaud's Waxworks, Marylebone Road. Open April to September Monday to Friday 10 A.M. to 6:30 P.M. (October to March until 5:30 P.M.), Saturday and Sunday 10 A.M. to 6:30 P.M. Fee: 7/6 (90 cents), children 3/6 (42 cents).

Pardon me, are you for real? This may very well be the question you ask of some of the five hundred famous and infamous people made of wax. One figure actually breathes.

Keep a sharp lookout, for you may see someone coming in to have his portrait made in the studios just as Voltaire (the writer), Benjamin Franklin, or Lord Byron came to Madame Tussaud many years ago (the heads of Marie Antoinette and Robespierre had to be brought in a basket).

Pick out your favorite hero—from Churchill, Kennedy, or Lawrence of Arabia. See some of the famous people in public life: the Beatles, Audrey Hepburn, or space explorer John Glenn.

You can mingle with the mighty, stare hard at their waxen images without rebuff. Take careful note of their features. See how tall or how short they were. Study their clothes, often their own.

Entire historic scenes are re-created—Lord Nelson's death, the little princes in the Tower, the Battle of Trafalgar with its moving ships. You'll shudder at the Chamber of Horrors, where Lee Harvey Oswald stands next to the assassin of President Garfield, where the man in the iron mask is set among the terrors of Dickens' London. Before leaving, take a last look at a little old lady in a velvet bonnet and dark shawl, her steel-rimmed spectacles gently placed on her nose. It's Anne Marie, Madame Tussaud, at eighty-one, a self-portrait fashioned just before she went into waxen retirement.

You can buy a combined ticket for Madame Tussaud's, the Battle of Trafalgar, and the Planetarium next door for 10/- ($1.20), children half price. The Planetarium's presentation is every hour weekdays 11 A.M. to 6 P.M., Sunday 1 to 6 P.M. Telephone HUN 1121.

COUNTRY IN THE CITY—PARKS

If you want to get away from the city for a few hours, just stay in it. All you do is step into one of the parks—Hyde, Regent's, St. James's, Kensington Gardens. They are practically next door to each other. There is plenty to do and it's almost like country living.

Hyde Park. There are plenty of things to do close at hand. The park was once owned by Henry VIII, who enjoyed hunting deer in it. Sail, row, swim, or tan right in the center of the park in the Lido of the Serpentine, from the end of April to September. It costs 1/6 (18 cents) for the entire day starting 10 A.M. to one hour before dusk. It's very busy on weekends.

Bird-watch at the sanctuary north of the lake. Visit the sad cemetery for pets located between Victoria and Westbourne gates. Or you can stand up on a soapbox at SPEAKERS' CORNER (near Marble Arch) and speak your mind on any subject you choose. Real democracy works here but be prepared to argue. On second thought, maybe you'd better just listen to the hecklers.

Nearby ride a horse rented from **L. G. Blum's Riding School and Livery Stable,** 32a Grosvenor Crescent Mews, telephone BEL 6846. The horse path is called Rotten Row. View the splendid sculpture of Jacob Epstein, "Rima" and the playful Greek god "Pan" leading a sprightly group below Bowater House at the Knightsbridge entrance. By this time perhaps you're hungry or thirsty. Stop at the delightful new restaurant and snack bar at the bridge that crosses the Serpentine.

Regent's Park. There are many pleasures to try here. The OUTER CIRCLE has a huge lake, large enough for small yachts. Rent a rowboat at the northwest end and drift awhile. The field nearby is usually filled with cricket matches, the English national game played with two teams of eleven men. The idea is to knock down the top of your opponent's wooden sticks, called "wickets," by hitting a heavy ball with a flat bat. The game takes its name from the old English word "cricke," meaning stick or staff.

Within the INNER CIRCLE (Queen Mary's Garden) is a museum like no other in the world. Every type of rose is raised to perfection. The names are carefully labeled. Notice the charming statue fountain of a boy studying a frog. His hand is raised and the frog sprouts water, which strikes the boy's hand. The water fans out to catch the light. Stroll through the rock gardens on the island in the small lake. You'll feel like Gulliver walking among the miniature Alps in the land of tiny Lilliputians.

THE OPEN-AIR THEATRE is like a natural setting for Shakespeare's *Midsummer Night's Dream*. His plays are performed here, as well as ballets and concerts. Relax and have an English refreshment at the Ring Tea House or lunch at the restaurant in a tent next to the auditorium. Ready for your next move?

CHIMPANZEES' TEA PARTY—THE ZOOLOGICAL GARDENS in Regent's Park are open 10 A.M. till dusk or about 7 P.M. Fee differs according to day and hours (3/- to 7/-) (36 to 84 cents), children half price.

Rain or shine this is a perfect way to spend an afternoon. There are fifty-eight hundred animals from all over the world.

Feeding times are posted near the entrance. Generally, the Chimpanzees' Tea Party is on the lawn near the Clock Tower at 4 P.M. Special gallery seats (6d—6 cents) can be purchased for this monkeyshine show. The sea lions (except Friday) eat at noon and 3:30 P.M. at their pool; the pelicans (near the Monkey House) at 2:30 P.M.; the penguins (near the Lion House) at 4 P.M.; lions and tigers at 3 P.M.; eagles at 3:30

P.M. You can feed some of the animals but only with specially prepared "Animal Snacks" on sale at the kiosks.

ANIMAL RIDES are great fun! Camel, pony, and llama rides are available in the summer in the Main Garden near the Lion House every afternoon (except Sunday) 1:45 to 3:30 P.M., 6d (6 cents).

THE CHILDREN'S ZOO is open all year. Fee: 1/- (12 cents), children half price. Introduce yourself at delightfully close quarters to the sort of animals that make good pets: guinea pigs, mice, rabbits, and tortoises. Also in the exhibit hall are hamsters, hedgehogs, and chinchillas. See a chick come out of the egg in the CHICK HATCHING ROOM. They look bedraggled in their newborn state but soon dry out and stagger to their feet.

BUSHBABY HALL has small, attractive mammals that are active only at night. Night and day are turned around so you can see this rare group in action.

THE ELEPHANTS' BATH, 11:30 A.M. each day at the newly opened Elephant and Rhino Pavilion, is enormous fun to watch.

One way of traveling to the zoo is on the canal boat *Jason*. From April to September, water buses leave Little Venice, Delamere Terrace, Paddington, every hour. The trip costs 2/- (24 cents), children half price.

St. James's Park. Ideal for picnics after a visit to Westminster Abbey, the Houses of Parliament, or other interesting sights in this area. The park is really a memorial to Charles II. What a pleasant thing it is to be remembered for a park full of flowers and a lake full of ducks. It used to be swampland, but Henry VIII drained it and put deer here to hunt. Charles II lovingly developed it to what it looks like now.

The lake is really a bird sanctuary and one of London's most fascinating sights. About 4 P.M. is the best time to see the three different types of pelicans with their long beaks being fed a daily ration of fish. Twenty kinds of colorful wild ducks and geese also live here. You can feed them and identify the various species from the helpful pictures at the waterside. The view from Birdcage Walk (birdcages used to be hung in the trees) is one of the finest in Europe.

Crystal Palace Park, Upper Norwood. Go even further back in time by visiting the tidal lake in the south end of the palace grounds. The four small islands show you how the earth was formed. A spectacular link between the past and the present is shown at the island with some two dozen life-size prehistoric monsters, from the giant toad of 350 million years ago to the Irish elks who were hunted by earliest man. You see brutish forms that once stalked the earth. The dinosaur lurks among the sycamore trees. The flying reptiles are shaded by the bramble-bushes, a scene right from the primeval swamps.

For a lighter mood, you can enjoy the Children's Zoo, a boating and fishing lake, and a lovely rock and water garden. The park's name comes from the building used in the Great Exhibition of 1851 which originally stood in Hyde Park. The vast glass structure was brought over in pieces and proudly assembled. Unfortunately it burned down in 1936, but the grounds were converted into this outstanding playful and educational park.

Free Entertainment. There are always a series of concerts and shows in the parks during the summer. To find out the details, write for the booklet "Open-Air Entertainment" (1/- [14 cents] including postage by surface mail) to the Chief Officer, Parks Department, Cavell House, 2A Charing Cross Road, London W.C. 2.

Battersea Fun Park. Open daily from Easter Sunday to last Sunday in September. Usually open 2 to 10:30 P.M. Fee: 6d (6 cents).

Battersea has everything for a happy outing, from the Big Dipper, the Flying Saucer (the largest water chute in Europe), the underground Grotto of the Winds, to a miniature zoo and lake. Don't forget the unique Tree Walk, a fascinating aerial pathway fifteen to twenty-five feet in height which weaves its way among the boughs of the fine old trees. The trees themselves are lit with great artistry and hidden among their branches are fantastic castles and lively figures. Take time for the Festival Clock, a favorite attraction of the gardens, with a quarter-hour animated review. There is also an open-air circus and variety show during school holidays. For additional information, telephone BAT 2226. You can get to Battersea by bus or by river from Charing Cross, Westminster, and Waterloo piers, at a cost of 2/- to 3/- (24 to 36 cents).

OFF TO A SHOW OR CONCERT

Street Entertainers—The Busker. Londoners flock to vaudeville and music hall shows. From childhood, young people are used to seeing acts in the streets, in the gutters, on the corner, in fairs and markets. Buskers, cockney street entertainers, have continued to amuse people lined up to buy tickets to the movies or the theater. Dressed in funny clothes and usually a silly mask, the one-man band does "his turn," the comics their old routines, the escape artists wiggle through swords and chains, and the tap dancer makes dodging the automobiles part of his act. Each performer must get and hold his audience and pass the cap for coins in less than five minutes. The next group waits to work "the queue" while the people still have money to spend. Many buskers claim to have worked with Charlie Chaplin, the sad movie tramp. He was a member of this ragtail company of clowns a long time ago. The "jogars," as they call themselves, can be seen near Leicester Square, the Haymarket, Old Compton Street, and Lower Regent Street.

Theater and Ballet. There are fifty theaters in London, far more than any other city in the world. Tickets are plentiful, so you can make up your mind at the last minute. A good seat downstairs often costs no more than £1 ($2.40).

The gallery and the gallery stool are peculiarly English. You buy tickets (at certain theaters only) on the day of the performance. The box office will tell you when you come back, generally a half hour before show time. On returning you'll find outside the gallery entrance a small wooden stool with your ticket number on it. Prices are very cheap, 2/6 to 5/6 (30 to 66 cents).

In the theater most people arrive five minutes before "curtain up." Programs cost 1/- (12 cents) and are sold by the usherettes, who show you to your seat but do not expect a tip. If the programs are printed before an actor for a part is known, the name listed is Walter Plinge. The real Mr. Plinge, long since dead, was a popular pubkeeper in the theater area. Trays of tea, sandwiches, or ices are served between the acts if you order from the usherettes before the show begins. There is also a snack bar.

Choosing a show is difficult just from the name alone. Go to the desk of the ticket broker in your hotel and ask for suggestions. Top-notch Shakespeare and classical plays are done by the National Theatre Company at the **Old Vic,** Waterloo Road (WATerloo 7617). The Royal Shakespeare Company performs at the **Aldwych Theatre,** Aldwych (TEM 6406). Opera and ballet are given beautiful performances at **Sadler's Wells,** Rosebery Avenue (TER 1672).

Christmas shows include "pantomimes," a song and dance show roughly following a well-known story like *Treasure Island, Pinocchio* or *Cinderella.* They are usually at the **Mermaid Theatre** (CIT 7656), the **Criterion** (WHI 3216), and the **Palladium** (GER 7373).

Circuses are in town during the holiday seasons. Try CIRCUS ADVENTURE, Hampstead Theatre Club, 19 Avenue Road (PRI 9301) and BERTRAM MILLS' CIRCUS at the Olympia, Kensington (FUL 3333), which has the most in elephants, the spangliest of tights, and the bravest galloping horses.

Special theater companies for young people put on shows throughout the year.

Little Angel Marionette Theatre, 14 Dagmar Passage (CAN 1787). Now performing in a brand-new, delightful theater. It is the first company of its kind and originally opened over one hundred years ago. The enchanting puppets perform such stories as *Hans the Bell Ringer, The Wild Night of the Witches,* and *Hans Christian Andersen's Little Mermaid.* Performances are usually Saturday at 11 A.M. for three- to seven-year-olds, 3 and 5 P.M. for older groups. Admission: adults 5/6 (66 cents), children 4/- (48 cents). Sunday at 3 P.M. for members only; annual fee 5/- (60 cents). Additional shows are given on holidays. Call or write for more information.

Unicorn Theatre Club, Arts Theatre, Great Newport Street. A club for five- to twelve-year-olds. Annual dues 7/6 (90 cents) entitle members to buy tickets for shows (plays, films, or puppets), receive news bulletins, and join any of the other activities. The show tickets cost between 7/- and 5/- (84 and 60 cents). Recent productions were *The Land of Green Ginger* and James Thurber's *The Thirteen Clocks.*

Musical concerts especially for young people are held approximately once a month, October to March, at the **Royal Festival Hall,** South Bank. Details may be had from the **Ernest Read Music Association,** 151 King Henry's Road, N.W. 3 (PRI 3020). There is also a series of regular concerts throughout the year, with ballet during the summer. **Royal Albert Hall,** Kensington Gore, has a large variety of musical events.

YOUR LONDON LODGINGS—HOTELS

All prices are for double room with bath and include breakfast brought to you or served in the dining room.

The Waldorf, Aldwych, is in the center of the theaters and shopping district. It has an old English air about it. The dining room is a large court with potted palms. Rates from 150/- ($18).

Hyde Park, Knightsbridge, gives you a chance to enjoy all fun of the nearby park. The hotel is a bit "stiff upper lip," but that can add to your enjoyment. The lobby sitters would not turn an eye if the Prime Minister rode up on a horse, turned it over to the doorman and then started talking to him about the latest issue before Parliament. Rates from 190/- ($22.80).

St. James's Court Hotel, Buckingham Gate, gives you a chance to imagine you are guests at the palace, which you can see from your lodgings. Rates from 82/6 ($9.90).

Goring, Grosvenor Gardens, is a pleasant family-owned hotel also close to Buckingham Palace. Rates from 141/- ($17).

Eden House, 111 Old Church Street, is in the middle of all the colorful activities of Chelsea. The hotel people especially welcome families and have many services catering to their needs. Rates start at 75/- ($9).

YOUR FOOD IS SERVED!

In Britain breakfast is often the favorite meal. It starts with fruit, served as juice or stewed. An English baked apple with cream makes a happy start. The national dish—porridge (oatmeal)—follows, served piping hot with milk or cream and sugar or syrup. Great pride is taken in the preparation to avoid even the tiniest lump.

Next comes the main dish, eggs, with many choices to accompany it. You can choose bacon, ham, sausages, tomatoes, or fried potatoes. As another choice or in addition you can have kippers, a salted smoked herring which is really quite tasty. Finnan Haddie, a fish treat with poached eggs on top crowned with a pat of melting butter, is another treat. The meal is finished off with lots of buttered toast spread with honey and sweet or bitter marmalade. This must surely be a national favorite, so much of it is eaten. Many Britishers are cutting down on breakfast and having "elevenses," a snack in the mid-morning.

Tea about 4:30 or 5 in the afternoon is a classical English meal. In a restaurant it may consist of a cup of strong tea with a scone (rich, crusty biscuit), served hot with butter and jam, or a crumpet (flat, toasted dough cakes). Other teacakes are called: Chelsea buns (cinnamon buns with currants), maids-of-honor (small almond tarts), and Sally Lunns (hot yeast cakes).

Lunch is 12:30 to 1 P.M. and dinner at about 7 P.M. Scotch smoked salmon and potted shrimp (in butter) are good items to try as a start. Fresh fish is special, particularly Dover sole. Fish and chips (fried fish and French fried potatoes) is a great favorite. Some places serve them in newspapers shaped into a cone.

Roast beef is excellent. The British cut small, thin pieces rather than one big slice and serve them with Yorkshire pudding (a popover). Roast lamb is also good. It comes with mint sauce. There are lots of different meat pies: Melton Mowbray (pork with hard-boiled egg in the center); shepherd's (minced meat with mashed potato crust); steak and kidney; and Stargazy (rich with fish).

Dessert favorites are fruit tarts, "fools" (notably raspberry and gooseberry with milk and cream), and Marlborough pudding (apple-flavored sweet). Stilton cheese is worth a try.

A few suggested restaurants are:

Sherlock Holmes Pub and Restaurant, 10 Northumberland Street, off Trafalgar Square. Lunch 12 to 2:15 P.M., Monday to Saturday. Dinner 6 to 9:15 P.M. Most meals priced 7/6 to 18/6 (90 cents to $2.22). In the upstairs restaurant you'll find a complete replica of Sherlock Holmes's living room, including the wax dummy in the window, his chemistry lab, pipes, disguises, handcuffs, and brass knuckles. Be sure to spot a memento of his expert marksmanship, bullet holes above the door spelling out "VR" (Victoria Regina). On the mantelpiece is a dagger holding firm his daily mail. Although the author of these mystery stories, Sir Arthur Conan Doyle, is dead, hearsay has it that he still inspects the room. His ghost may even appear during your visit.

Elizabethan Room, 189 Queen's Gate (Gore Hotel). A fast return four hundred years to the time of Elizabeth I. Food of the time is served in candlelight by girls dressed in seventeenth-century wenches' costumes. Long wooden dining tables covered with wood plates hold such old favorites as boar's head, peacock's breast, young swan, and syllabub (a special cream dessert). Troubadours stroll about singing of colorful adventures of yesteryear. You join in the fun for 42/- (about $5).

Tiddy Dol, 4 Hertford Street, is in Shepherd Market and very "ye olde." The building is filled with history and the food is traditional and good. Prices are reasonable.

Stone's Chop House, Panton Street, off the Haymarket, is where roast beef, saddle of lamb, and heavenly shepherd's pie are making British cookery hold up its head again.

Veeraswamy's, on the Corner of Regent and Swallow streets, is one of the leading Indian restaurants in London. A bright atmosphere prevails, with waiters dressed in tunics of scarlet, black, and yellow. The dishes are, of course, hot curries of all kinds. The menu describes each type of curry. Moderately priced, about 18/6 for lunch ($2.22) and 21/- for dinner (2.52).

Especially for Lunch

Charing Cross Pier's glass-wall restaurant floats on a pontoon on the Thames and gives the best possible view of the river.

Guinea and Piggy, 20 Leicester Square, is a self-service, eat-as-much-as-you-can place. Lunch about 20/- ($2.40), dinner 28/6 ($3.42). A treat for hungry teen-agers.

Derry & Tom's Roof Garden, Kensington High Street, has a summer garden restaurant with trees, flowers, waterfalls, a pond with ducks, and a wonderful rooftop view of London.

The Sizzling Sausage, Charing Cross Road, caters particularly to teen-agers. On the menu is a delicious large sausage on a roll, 2/- (24 cents), and a Pepsi-Cola.

TUPPENCE AND THRUPPENCE—WHAT THEY WILL BUY

The basic unit is the pound (written "£" and called "quid" in slang). It is worth about $2.40, which is enough to get a Tam O'Shanter cap in your favorite plaid.

A pound is made up of 20 shillings (written "s" or "/" and called "bob"). Each shilling is worth 12 cents and can buy a delicious package of mixed English toffee or a chocolate bar.

There are 12 pence ("d") in each shilling. Pence is plural for penny and each one is worth 1 cent. It takes four to ride the Underground and six to make a local telephone call.

Paper money comes in ten-, five-, and one-pound notes, also ten-shilling notes. Coins are a half crown (2/6), a florin (2/-), a shilling, sixpence, threepence ("thruppence"), and penny.

Study the coins carefully. If you don't you may give away half crowns for florins and sixpence for an old silver threepence.

TO SHOP

Burlington Arcade

"Old fine pieces for your chessboard? You'll find them all here, sir." The answer came from the guard called a beadle dressed in his black doeskin frock coat with brass buttons and square crown top hat trimmed in gold braid. Beadles have been guarding the Burlington Arcade (between Piccadilly and Burlington Gardens) since it opened in 1819. Each day at six o'clock, closing time, the beadle rings a warning note on the century-old hand bell. You are not allowed to run, whistle or sing, carry a large parcel, open an umbrella, or wheel a carriage through this area, another example of living old customs. But you can window-shop or buy merchandise from the charming stores, which have kept the look of another era. They are quite expensive.

The N. Peal Company 37 and 54 has cashmere and Shetland woolens for young people of all ages, as well as ties and socks of fine quality. Look at the lovely old water color of the arcade entrance over one hundred years ago and also color prints of Burlington House dated 1680.

Hummel at 16 specializes in military models and toy soldiers, all perfect in every detail. They also have historical dolls in rich costumes.

Number 16–17 has an enchanting display of chessmen and boards, the finest collection in the world. For browsing try 52–53. It is the **House of Rood,** renowned for selection of jewels.

Other Suggestions
BOOKS

Foyles' Children's Department, Charing Cross Road.
Times Book Shop, 42 Wigmore Street.

TOYS

Bargain Centre, 234 Shaftesbury Avenue, has books, toys, and novelties at ridiculously low prices.

Charles Bolton, 23 Manor Drive, is the place for perfect miniature Victorian chairs, four-poster beds in Tudor style, or any tiny replica for your dollhouse or display case.

Paul and Marjorie Abbatt, 94 Wimpole Street, has out-of-the-ordinary things.

Hamley's, 200 Regent Street, is the world's largest toy store.

The Rocking Horse, 23 St. John's Wood High Street, has antique toys, dolls, and rocking horses. The delicate repairs are done right in the store.

CLOTHES

Daniel Neal, 278 Oxford Street—for both boys and girls.

Rowes Ltd., 120 New Bond Street. Good selection of riding clothes.

Scott Adie, 14a Clifford Street, and the **Scotch House,** 2 Brompton Road, Knightsbridge, have kilts, tartans, and other specialties.

DEPARTMENT STORES

Fortnum & Mason, 181 Piccadilly. (Don't miss the show of the chiming clock on the hour.)

Harrods, Knightsbridge.

Marks and Spencer, 458 Oxford St. and about thirty-six other locations in London.

GETTING AROUND IN LONDON

Buses provide a grandstand view of the city from the top of a double-decker. The red buses go for journeys up to twelve miles out of town; the green ones go for longer trips. You pay according to how far you're going. The conductor collects the money as you go along. If you are wildly keen on buses you can get a master ticket for £2 ($4.80) from London Transport Head Office, St. James's Park Station, London S.W. 1. It gives you unlimited travel on London buses and Underground trains for seven days. Call ABB 123 for information about bus trips. London buses are cheap and the conductors helpful. Get a bus map at the Underground station to be sure about the routes.

The Underground closes at midnight. The underground is clean and safe, and maps are easy to follow. The lighted board tells you which trains are going to arrive at which platform and in what order. If you're going to return to the same station you start from, buy a round-trip ticket and tear it in half. Save the part with the "R" for the trip back.

Taxis are all over the city. If you see the "For Hire" sign lighted up just hail them. The fare starts at 2/- (24 cents) and increases every three quarters of a mile by 6d (6 cents). The average tip is 6d to 1/- for fares up to 5/- (60 cents).

Water buses are described in various parts of this chapter.

HELLO, CHUM!

To make contact with a friend ahead of time write to: International Friendship League, Correspondence Bureau, Peace Haven, Creswick Road, London W. 3, which caters to all ages.

Or write to Pen Friends Division, 16 East 69 Street, New York, New York 10021—ages nine to sixteen.

CHEERIO

Much of the old city will change, more and more new glass buildings will provide airier and lighter offices, wider tree-lined streets will help the traffic move faster, and many of the old houses will be spruced up and whitened.

Still much will remain; the bridges will stand in the same

spot and the dark, muddy Thames will have its white swans, barges, and tugs.

To visit London merely for the buildings, monuments, and history is to see only part of the city. For the greatness of London is in the people. If you've taken time to get acquainted with a chum or two you won't really want to say cheerio when you leave. More likely it will be "Keep your chin up till we meet again."

ENGLISHMAN'S ENGLISH

AMERICAN	BRITISH
To reserve seats	To book seats
Lodgings	"Digs"
Lobby	Entrance Hall
Second floor	First floor
Apartment	Flat
Elevator	Lift
Bell captain	Head porter
Closet	Cupboard
Comfort station	Public convenience
Line	Queue
Vaudeville	Music hall
Tavern	"Pub" or public house
Bill	Note/banknote
Check (in restaurant)	Bill
Can	Tin
Toilet	W.C., Lavatory
Truck	Lorry
Phonograph	Gramophone
Baby carriage/baby buggy	Perambulator/pram
"Cop"	"Bobby"
Laborer	Navvy
Patrol wagon	Black Maria
Station wagon	Estate car
Mailbox	Pillar box
The mail	The post

AMERICAN	BRITISH
Mailman	Postman
Flashlight	Torch
Radio	Wireless
Telephone booth	Call box
Call	Ring up
Pay telephone	Public call box
Long-distance call	Trunk call
Two weeks	Fortnight
Vacation	Holiday
Rubber boots	Wellingtons
Windbreaker	Windcheater
Bobby pins	Kirby grips
Raincoat	Mackintosh
Custom-built/-made	Made to measure
Haberdasher	Men's outfitter
Collar button	Stud, front or back
Garters	Suspenders
Pants	Trousers
Shorts	Pants
Vest	Waistcoat
Eraser	Rubber

EYE ON THE CALENDAR

End of March	**University Boat Race.** Oxford vs. Cambridge, River Thames, Putney to Mortlake.
Palm Sunday	**Blessing the Palms.** Impressive ceremony in Westminster Cathedral. Service begins at 10 A.M.
Easter Sunday	**Sunday Easter Parade.** Battersea Park. Great procession starts at 3 P.M. Floats and music center on theme. Jersey float carries Princess and attendants.
Easter Monday	**Harness Horse Parade.** Inner Circle Regent's Park. Wide variety of horses, ponies, and vehicles.
April (Ascension Day)	**Beating the Bounds.** Once every three years at the Tower of London (1969 and 1972). Ancient Middle Ages custom enacted after service at 11 A.M.—

striking of the boundary marks to recall time when maps were non-existent.

Late May   **Chelsea Flower Show.** Chelsea Founders' Day and The Chelsea Pensioners' Oak Apple Day, Royal Hospital Grounds. Pensioners parade in colorful uniforms for inspection.

June (usually   **Trooping the Color.**
  second
  Saturday)

July   **The Royal Tournament.** Earl's Court, 2:30 P.M. and 7:30 P.M. Bands, mock battles, gymnastics, marching. Thousands take part. Book in advance. Royal family attends event.

September 28   **Admission of Sheriffs.** Outside Guildhall. Pageantry
  (or previous   presentation of chains of office. Limited number can
  day if a   attend inside ceremonies by writing Keeper of the
  Sunday)   Guildhall, Guildhall Houses, Gresham Street, London E.C. 2.

September 29 (or   **Electing London's Lord Mayor.**
  previous day if
  a Sunday)

October 26   **Quit Rent Ceremony.** Law Courts between Fleet Street and the Strand at 3 P.M. Custom of presenting hatchet, two pieces of wood, and six ancient horseshoes with sixty-one nails to the Queen, recalling that the courts have only borrowed the land.

November   **The State Opening of Parliament.**

November 5   **Guy Fawkes Day.**

First Sunday in   **Antique Car Run.** Hyde Park. Race at 8 A.M. with
  November   all cars dating pre-1906 to 1895 all as near as possible to their original form.

Second Saturday   **The Lord Mayor's Show.**
  in November

6. MUNICH

Plätze, Puppets, and Pretzels

"Willkommen!" Welcome to the city of München (Munich). The sound of the name conjures up the past: wandering monks, fearless knights, robber barons, colorful kings and beautiful queens, rococo buildings, and alpine yodeling. Munich is the capital of Bavaria, the largest state in Germany, and is located on the Isar River. As you get acquainted, you'll discover its Plätze (squares), puppets, and pretzels.

EIGHT HUNDRED YEARS AGO

The city owes its beginnings eight centuries ago to a tough-minded businessman. Henry the Lion, Duke of Bavaria, was angry at the cleverness of the Bishop from the town of Freising. The Bishop realized he was on a road vital to salt traders coming from the mines in the south and the west. He insisted they pay a stiff tax every time they crossed his bridge over the Isar River. Duke Henry put a stop to this at once. He burned down the Bishop's bridge and built a new one a few miles south at the tiny settlement called Munichen—"at the monks"—which got its name from a group of wandering monks who decided to settle on the peaceful Isar River, where they could easily get water. Soon a market and a mint were added. Traders flocked to the village and it began to prosper. And, of course, the Duke imposed his own tax for using the bridge.

Until this day the city's coat of arms shows a monk with a Bible in his raised hand. The more popular symbol of the city is the Münchner Kindl, the "monk-child," in his black and yellow robes with a beer stein in one hand and a prayer book in the other.

EXPLORING THE CITY THROUGH ITS PLÄTZE (SQUARES)

Munich is a happy city. But it is also a city that was bombed so much that the pre-World War II city has almost disappeared. As you walk through the streets you may hardly notice this because of the many new buildings reconstructed almost as they were hundreds of years ago.

Marienplatz is the heart of the old town. All four main roads pass through the center of the square. Originally it was called Marktplatz (Market Place). Its present name is only one hundred years old.

You can still see the outline of the former fortification by looking at the original gates (the Isar, Sendling, and Karls gates). In medieval times people streamed through the gates to trade grain or salt, using the products to barter, as you would money. Soon smaller markets sprang up, and with them the offices of craftsmen and merchants, from whom the streets leading to the square got their names.

This was also the scene of celebrations and festivals. Apprentice knights in flashing armor held formal contests of skill—tournaments—to train for real battles and warfare. The place of combat, called the list, was this open space, usually with galleries for spectators. Knights from many parts of Europe attended, identified by their own special emblems. Trumpets blared, brilliant banners waved, and the pageantry continued until the combat began. The tournaments were hardly less dangerous than real battles, and many men were killed or wounded until judges awarded the victory to one of the sides.

The Glockenspiel (musical mechanical clock) in the tower of the Neues Rathaus (New Town Hall) comes to life at exactly 11 A.M. daily, depicting just such a tournament. It took place in this square four hundred years ago. Duke Wilhelm V and his bride celebrated their wedding. In their honor the tournament was held. The re-enactment of the tournament by the clock's figures ends in the second round with the victory of the Bavarian knight.

In the lower section of the clock the coopers, barrelmakers in the red frocks, perform a round dance to a centuries-old tune. The custom goes back to 1515–17, the time of the plague. The barrelmakers were the first men to venture in the streets and announce the end of the epidemic to the citizens with music and dancing in this square. The holiday is still celebrated with real live coopers once every seven years in the month of January. Don't turn away until you see the final act of the Glockenspiel— the golden rooster crowing at the top.

The steeple of the Rathaus (278 feet high) offers a good view of the city. You can get to the top by elevator.

The Mariensäule is the beautiful statue of the Madonna in the middle of the square. She looks down from her tall stand probably puzzled by all the cars whizzing around her. The figures of heroes at the foot of the column are supposed to save the city from sickness, war, famine, and heresy. The Blessed Virgin has been looked upon for so long as protectress of the city that one hundred years ago the square was named after her.

The Frauenkirche, (Our Dear Lady Cathedral) around the

corner is distinguished by its enormous pair of steeples (329 feet high). The cathedral is a landmark of the city and has many fascinating stories connected with it. Built in 1468 by the people, not the princes, it was the pride of the entire town. For some reason the lane around the cathedral walls acts as a wind trap. Standing in the main door, you are caught in a huge draft even on windless days. The legend goes that the devil came to visit when the church first opened. He tied up to the doorpost the four winds which helped him make his journey. Only partially entering the church, he saw total darkness and thought the builder had forgotten the windows. He was so overjoyed he stamped his foot so hard that to this day you can see marks of a print in the flagstone at the point where you can't see a single window. The devil was so pleased he rushed away to tell his fellow devils the good news. He left in such a hurry that he forgot to untie the winds, which are still blowing around the building. An elevator in the south tower will carry you up to the top, where in clear weather you can see the Alps.

The Viktualienmarkt (Food Market), a few streets away, has kiosks, booths, and stands that sell everything from chunks of meat to spices and fish to flowers. "What'll you have today?" asks the market woman, a special Munich type of person known for her humor, shrewdness, and knowledge of her wares. One corner of the square has a fish market with live fish swimming in a huge tank. The prices for the eels, trout, etc. are marked on a blackboard. This is a real country market and many of the vendors are farmers. If seeing all the food is making you hungry, stop at *Nürnberger Bratwurstglöckl* and have a "Münchner Weisswurst" (white sausage), a specialty of the city. Münchners tell you it must be eaten before noon since they are made after midnight and are particularly fresh for twelve hours. Before you leave be sure to notice the Maypole in the center of the market and the two small fountains with statues of Munich's most famous comedian, Karl Valentin, and the folk actress Lisl Karlstadt.

The Karl Valentin Museum in Isartorturm, in the south tower of the Isar gate, is really known as the nonsense museum. Here you can chuckle at a fur toothpick (for winter use); a glass nail; a plain brick which was Miss Muffet's tuffet; a painting, "Chimney Sweep by Night" (solid black); the apple that tempted Adam (black by now); and other amusing exhibits. Open 11:01 A.M. to 5:29 P.M. Fee: 99 pf. (24½ cents).

Odeonsplatz was made possible by an overly romantic king, Ludwig I (1825–48). When he ascended the throne he promised "to make a city that will do Germany so much honor that no one can claim to know Germany if he has not seen Munich." This he actually did, since he had begun his work while he was still a Crown Prince and brought his enthusiasm for Italy and Greece to the city's streets, squares, palaces, and museums even after he was forced to leave the throne.

His downfall began one night in the theater when he saw the wild, fiery dance performance of a young woman, Lola Montez. Soon she took over Ludwig's life, presiding at royal functions, firing employees, and spending large sums of the people's money. The church, the cabinet, the court, and the citizens all warned the King that she was destroying everything. Finally, when fist fights broke out in the streets over Miss Montez's control over the city, the King decided to banish her to a little cottage near Castle Nymphenburg and turn over the rule to his son.

The magnificent square of Odeonsplatz was designed after a piazza in Florence, Italy. **The Feldherrnhalle** (Hall of Generals) at one end of the square is a copy of the arcaded gallery the Loggia dei Lanci in Florence. It was built over 150 years ago in honor of heroic generals in the Bavarian army. In the middle of the square in front of a palace is a statue of King Ludwig dressed in royal robes and riding his favorite horse.

The Hofgarten, the former court garden, at the side of the palace is a popular place to enjoy a cool lemonade, feed the pigeons, or quietly promenade under the trees. When it rains you can take a long walk through the arcades.

The square is, in fact, the starting point of a wide road named after the King, Ludwigstrasse, which originally led into the open country. Today it ends in the village of Schwabing, an artists' center.

The Residenz (Royal Palace) nearby was modeled after the Pitti Palace in Florence, Italy, and has a rich collection of rare jewels, classic busts, and a magnificent little theater. The large group of buildings made up of three sections and more than fifty rooms was the home of the rulers of Bavaria—dukes at first, then electors and kings. During World War II it was almost totally destroyed. Recently it was completely restored and furnished with movable items that were saved.

THE SCHATZKAMMER (Treasury) is open 9 A.M. to 5 P.M. daily, Sunday 10 A.M. to 1 P.M. Fee: 1 DM (25 cents) or 1.50 DM (38 cents) for same ticket Residenz Museum. Crowns, diadems, illuminated prayer books, and lots of old relics are neatly displayed. A statue of St. George studded with 2291 diamonds, 209 pearls, and 406 rubies makes a most dazzling sight. THE RESIDENZMUSEUM (Palace Museum) is open April to September 30, 9 A.M. to 5 P.M., 10 A.M. to 4 P.M. the rest of the year. Sunday 10 A.M. to 1 P.M. Closed Monday. Fee: 50 pf. (13 cents). The gallery of the Wittelsbach family, the rulers of Bavaria for 750 years before 1918, has a place of honor for Charlemagne, Charles the Great, who was Emperor of most of Europe in the year 800. THE ANTIQUARIUM walls are decorated with over one hundred scenes of Bavarian towns and castles. THE GROTTO COURT gets its name from its cavelike atmosphere. The eighteenth-century HOFKAPELLE (Court Chapel) also has an unusual ceiling. On the first floor a strong room contains old treasures.

THE ALTE RESIDENZTHEATER (Palace Theater) is last and special. Open daily 2 to 5 P.M., Sunday 10 A.M. to 5 P.M. Fee: 50 pf. (13 cents). The designer, François Cuvilliés, began his career in a strange way. An elector of Bavaria, Max Emanuel, found himself ousted from his own country after a battle and exiled to France. His French hosts thought they would cheer him up with a huge feast. At the banquet an enormous pie was set on the table. The lid was lifted and out jumped a small boy dressed in a hussar's uniform. He solemnly marched around the table, careful not to step on the plates, and stood at attention before the Elector, who laughed until he had to gasp for air. The little hussar, François Cuvilliés, then eleven, was the size of a six-year-old. The Elector decided to keep him at court, for dwarfs were in fashion at the time. When the Elector was allowed to return to Bavaria ten years later it struck him that the country lacked the splendid architecture of the rest of Europe. He had an idea that François should become a designer. Off he went to Paris to study the art.

François returned to Munich and brought with him the knowledge and technique of a new style that was all the rage in France—rococo. The word means "rock and shell," images of which you can see in many of the overfancy designs. The courtiers were delighted and François was flooded with orders —country houses, interior decorations, and town houses.

Many of the buildings of the Residenz were rebuilt in this breath-taking style. The most magnificent is the Palace Theater. Built in 1753, it was originally never seen by the citizens of Munich, but reserved for the electors and the ladies and gentlemen of the court. Here Mozart produced two of his operas for the first time. Note the boxes on each of the four floors, which are different in shape and decoration. The Prince-Elector's box is the most elegant. Fortunately this gem of European theatrical architecture survived the bombs of the Second World War, and has been restored to its original eighteen-century splendor. Now it is not only a place to admire but also a setting to enjoy opera. There is no theatrical experience as enchanting as a performance of Mozart amid the gilt and plush, the pink plaster angels and mellow candles, where time seems to have stood still for two centuries.

PUPPETS ON SHOW

The puppet show itself is so old that it is impossible to tell when it began. Jointed dolls were used as idols in the early days of Egypt, Greece, Rome, and India, and such dolls have been found in ancient tombs. Later mathematicians and engineers built elaborate puppet theaters.

In the Middle Ages puppets were first used to enact religious scenes. Since at Christmas nativity plays centered around the Virgin Mary, the name Little Mary, or Marionette, was given to all puppets in the presentation and eventually to string puppets in general. When the puppets were banished from the church, the shows were forced out on the streets, where the puppeteer would wander the countryside telling amusing stories. In many countries the same puppet characters kept reappearing and the townspeople would look forward to learning the next adventure of their dear friends. Punch of Punch and Judy has been a favorite English puppet since the seventeenth century. In Russia Petrushka is a national hero. Turkey's favorite is Karagoz, and France's Guignol. Munich's special charmer is a sad but funny hobo named Casper or Kasperle, whom you will meet.

Münchner Stadtmuseum (Historical Museum of the City), St. Jakobsplatz 1. Open 9 A.M. to 4 P.M. every day except Monday. Fee: 50 pf. (13 cents), children under fourteen 20 pf. (5 cents).

You can't help but take a fancy to the little wooden or parchment puppet actors. There are more than forty thousand from all over the world for you to see. There are mysterious east Asian stick puppets, which take their name from the wood pieces used to move their limbs. There are fragile shadow puppets from the same part of the world. Their stage is a light-colored cloth on which they appear as delicate outlines. Armored Sicilian puppets with sweeping swords chop off their enemy's head or leg as they re-enact a historic moment in an ancient battle. Life-size and lifelike puppets swing on bars to do intricate balancing acts. And best of all there's lovable Kasperle with his sad face, who just can't keep out of trouble taking from the rich to help the poor. The attendant will be glad to show you how all the puppets work, and you'll have a chance to try one for yourself.

Another amazing group of puppets in a different part of the museum is the morris dancers. The ten carved wooden figures seem to be moving in comic, graceful dance positions. Possibly they are doing an old popular Polish dance called "Maruska." Or the word "Morisco" may have come from the people named Moors. As you watch, you can just about hear the music and see the dancers begin their lively performance.

Bayerisches Nationalmuseum (Bavarian National Museum), Prinzregentenstrasse. Open daily except Monday 9:30 A.M. to 4:30 P.M. Fee: 50 pf. (13 cents), children 10 pf. (3 cents).

THE KRIPPENSCHAU, (Christmas Crib Collection) on the ground floor is unsurpassed anywhere in the world—more than eight thousand crèches from Bavaria, Italy, and the Tyrol, the mountain region in southern Germany, northern Italy, and Austria. These marvelous miniature tableaus are built like tiny stages with changing figures and scenery. Each tableau illustrates the story of the events leading up to the birth of Jesus. The figures were created as far back as the Middle Ages. All the details are so vivid you can almost think the small figurines will begin to act out their special version of how Christmas began.

It was customary in the early days for families to devote an entire room to just one of these crèches. Each figure, carefully handmade of wax or wood, represented actual people in the village. As new townsfolk came to live in the village, they would be added to the scene. So you may very well recognize the miller, the candlemaker, or the town gossip placed in a splendid setting with extraordinarily handsome horses and exotic animals prancing about. Be sure also to see the ingenious wax cribs delicately placed in glass bottles.

The rest of the museum is equally special, from pieces of jewelry, ivory carvings, stone sculptures, and wooden tablets that were made in the fourth to seventh centuries (over one thousand years ago) to the amazing two weapons halls, where rows of complete suits of armor, some even pleated, are displayed. These were worn by knights and dukes more than four hundred years ago.

Deutsches Museum (German Museum), located on an island, Isarinsel. Open daily 9 A.M. to 5 P.M. Fee: 50 pf. for children, 1 DM for adults (13 and 25 cents).

Anyone fascinated by technical things will find this museum irresistible. Be prepared for a long walk, eight miles, if you want to see it all, from the life-size coal mine and a sixteenth-century alchemist's shop to the original early flying machines and the first motor car. The museum's special features are its do-it-yourself models and instruments; you merely push a button and you can X-ray your hand or walk the planks of an old sea vessel.

As for puppets, stop for a while in the Musical Instruments and Music Salon. A knowledgeable and friendly attendant will make the delicate dancers and animals housed in antique music boxes come alive. He will also play all the rare instruments in the room and show you how the automatic trumpets and pianos work.

The Münchner Marionettentheater (Marionette Theater) at Blumenstrasse 29 is a delightful small auditorium where you can see a full performance of the bungling misadventures of the hobo Kasperle. There are also familiar classic stories such as *Hänsel and Gretel, Tom Thumb, The Tinder Box.* Even if you don't understand the language, the stage effects alone are worth seeing.

Evening performers feature complete operas (Mozart's *Magic Flute, Don Giovanni*) and classic plays (*Midsummer Night's Dream* by Shakespeare, *Androcles and the Lion* by George Bernard Shaw). Ticket prices are 1.50 to 2.80 DM (38 to 71 cents) for afternoon shows and 3.50 to 5.70 DM (85 cents to $1.42) for the evening ones. Telephone 59 14 14 for the exact programs and times.

MORE THINGS TO SEE AND DO

Hellabrunn Zoo, south of town, has a population of over eleven thousand inhabitants, not counting the keepers. Animals of all species from snakes to seals, from antelopes to elephants, and all kinds of exotic birds live in open spaces separated by watered moats and arranged according to different parts of the world. Especially fascinating is the successful breeding of bison, called aurochs, and wild horses, which seemed to have died out about the year 1630 but were revived right here. But it is the "Ape Station" and its comic characters that draw the largest crowds. THE KINDER TIERPARK (Children's Zoo) is another attraction where you can spend many enjoyable hours. From the main restaurant there is a magnificent view over the animal-filled park.

The Bavaria on the west side of the Theresienwiese is a colossal statue of a woman. To give you an idea of exactly how big it is, here are some of the measurements: from bottom to top 98 feet (almost a ten-story building); face 5 feet; nose 14 inches; and width of one eye 11 inches. The entire figure is hollow, with 130 steps which can take you as far up as the eyes. Inside the head there is room for five people. Climb to the top and peek out via small shutters through the ringlets of the hair to get a splendid view. Behind the Bavaria is the Hall of Fame, made up of eighty-six life-size busts of famous Bavarians, and behind this extends the Exhibition Park. When the leaves of autumn fall in late September the grounds at the foot of the Bavaria turn into a gigantic fun fair. It's "Oktoberfest" time and the sounds of jingling merry-go-rounds, rattling scooters, sizzling chickens, and blaring brass bands fill the air. A special event is the SEIFENKISTLRENNEN, soapbox derby, which takes place on a track built especially for this race. The Oktoberfest opens with a parade of marksmen and people in native costume from Upper Bavaria and half of Europe. For sixteen days Munich is in a whirl of hilarity.

The Englische Garten (English Garden) on the east side of Schwabing, the artists' village, is one of the most attractive natural parks in Europe. Walk the middle path along the canal. Go for a boat ride on the lake or stop at the Chinese pagoda for a snack—a bratwurst (foot-long pork hot dog), a pretzel, and an orange drink, all for 1.50 DM (38 cents). This lovely park is a perfect place for meandering.

Schwabing, a short distance from the center of Munich, does not look too unusual in the daytime. There are a lot of windows in the roof studios where young students and painters live and work. By evening the town takes on a life of its own. Leopoldstrasse, the main street, has long lines of people parading back and forth. Clotheslines are stretched between poles and pictures hung on them, lit by lamps and guarded by their creators, bearded and sandaled young fellows or shaggy girls. Wobbly tables are set out to display knickknacks and trinkets for sale. Farther on, the streets are taken up by café tables and chairs. It's interesting to sit awhile and "people-watch" as you enjoy Italian ice cream.

Rafting on the Isar River is a splendid way to spend an after-noon. At Wolfratshausen, about eighteen miles south of Munich, the adventure begins as you climb aboard a bargelike vessel to take off for the rapids, the steepest featuring a drop of sixty feet in a distance of two hundred yards. It's perfectly safe. At Munich-Thalkirchen you get off and head back by bus, delighting in the triple attraction of a raft ride, an oom-pah band, and a stop for food—with even the possibility of taking a swim. The cost varies up to $5 for the one-way raft trip, which takes four to five hours. Contact Fremdenverkehrsamt, Bahnhofplatz 2 (phone 5558-81) for details, or Riedmayr-Reisebüro, Königsdorfer Str. 16, 819 Wolfratshausen, or telephone 0817-505.

Nymphenburg Palace is truly fit for a king, the largest and most important example in Germany of a palace and gardens of the baroque age. Actually it was a thank-you gift from Elector Ferdinand to his wife for the birth of their heir Max Emanuel. Construction went on for more than one hundred years before the palace reached its present form. The splendid castle, park, and pavilions are only fifteen minutes from town by streetcar lines 3, 21, and 30.

The castle is open 9 A.M. to 6 P.M. (in the summer); 10 A.M. to 4 P.M. in the winter. Fee: 1.50 DM (38 cents), which includes entrance to other buildings.

In July and August concerts are given by candlelight in the great FESTSAAL (Festival Hall). The wall paintings, frescoes, depict playful gods of Greek and Roman myths with the nympth Flora, goddess of flowers and spring, in the center. In the decoration around the pictures you can clearly see the cockleshell forms of the rococo style. The north gallery has painted panels showing the castle and park at the beginning of the eighteenth century. The south wing has an attractive Chinese room with many delicately painted oriental scenes, including some of children playing various games.

In the SUDTRAKT (South Pavilion), the apartment of Queen
Caroline has the "Gallery of Beauties," portraits of the most
beautiful women in the court of King Ludwig I. The best-
known is Lola Montez, the Spanish dancer for whom Ludwig
left his throne. THE MARSTALLMUSEUM (Carriage Museum) in
the south wing has splendid golden coronation coaches, carts,
and even a sedan chair.

The park has several smaller castles and pavilions. THE
AMALIENBURG, built as a hunting lodge for a princess, has a
charming kitchen made entirely from colored Dutch tiles and an
elegant room for dogs. No doubt the dachshunds who lived
in this fanciest of doghouses barked at the other dogs shown
in the pictures decorating the room. THE BADENBURG was a
princely whim with a white and blue swimming pool, with a
curious mural and a crystal chandelier on the ceiling. THE
PAGODENBURG, a dreamlike eight-sided building, is decorated in
a Chinese theme. Before leaving, stop by the workshops of the
famous STAATLICHE PORZELLANMANUFAKTUR (Porcelain Factory), where you can see how delicate figurines have been made
for some two hundred years. It is open daily 8 A.M. to noon
and 2 to 6 P.M., Saturday 8 A.M. to noon.

BLEIBEN: TO STAY

All three places listed are close to the center of town.

Vier Jahreszeiten, Maximilianstrasse 17. Here is elegant turn-
of-the-century charm with a little up-to-date convenience besides.
You might bump into a king or queen here. Doubles with bath
start at about 80 DM ($20).

Regina Palast, Maximiliansplatz 5, is another quaint hotel
with a chance for a huge room with your own balcony. The
summer garden has music in the afternoon and evening. Double
rooms with bath about 66 DM ($16.50).

Platzl, Münzstrasse (am Platze), gets its name from the square in which it is located, in one of the older parts of Munich. The Hofbräuhaus and the Platzl Music Hall are just around the corner. The rooms are smaller and more modern than those of the other hotels listed. Doubles with bath 48 DM ($12).

GELD: MONEY

The letters DM stand for Deutsche Mark. One is presently worth 25 cents and will buy a huge pretzel to munch on. Four marks make up one U.S. dollar and will pay for a trip to the zoo including refreshments. There are 100 Pfennige (pf.) in one DM, or about 4 pf. to 1 cent.

EINKAUFEN: TO SHOP

Hours are standard: 9 A.M. to 6:30 P.M. daily, Saturday closing at 2 P.M.

CLOCKS

Huber Uhren, Weinstrasse 8, has every variety and shape of clock. Four-hundred-day clocks start at about 75 DM ($18.75). Cuckoos from the Black Forest have not changed in style over two hundred years but the detail in each hand-carved clock is different. Each one has a happy little bird call out the time. Other clocks have figurines dance to a lovely melody or even re-create a rustic Alpine scene. The clocks are 38 DM to 110 DM ($9.50 to $27.50).

TOYS

Obletter, Karlplatz 11-12, has an amazing selection of electric trains, Steiff stuffed animals, and automatic toys. Two other stores to try are Schmidt, Neuhauserstrasse 20, and Teddy, am Marienplatz, Weinstrasse 3.

WOOD CARVINGS

Dehm, Bayerstrasse 2, claims to be the oldest shop of its kind in the city. The secrets of shaping these delightful figures have been handed down from generation to generation. The prices start at about 16 DM ($4).

BAVARIAN CLOTHING

Wallach, Residenzstrasse 3, has dirndls (folk dresses) lederhosen (short leather pants), hats, and every other article of clothing you could want. They also sell small objects of folk art, which make the store an interesting place to browse.

SUPERDUPER MARKET AND DELUXE DELICATESSEN

Dallmayrs, Dienerstrasse 14-15, should not be missed if you have a food-loving friend back home whom you want to present with a treat. The three-storied building is filled with goodies: eighty-two different sausages, eleven varieties of liverwurst, chocolate truffles that grow under marzipan trees, ninety-seven types of cheese, and twenty-one teas from all over the world. The second-floor boutique sells delightful surprises such as candies made up as a bunch of violet flowers or a candy tree. Everything can be shipped if you wish. Prices in the boutique start at about 16 DM ($4) and can go up very high. For people who like food this place is a dream come true.

ESSEN: TO EAT

Pretzels. As the monk-child is everywhere to be seen when you explore the Plätze, so is the pretzel as you enjoy good

German food. With lunch, dinner, or snacks, you'll be served a delicious crisp biscuit, some large, others small, made from slender rolls of dough heavily sprinkled with salt and baked in the form of a loose knot. Pretzels were first invented right here in Bavaria by an order of monks who wanted to reward young people for saying their prayers. That is why the shape of the pretzel resembles two arms crossed. If you would like to see a present-day pretzelmaker in action go to the shop of **Anton Seidl** at Marsstrasse 18-24 near the train station, or to **Karl Baekere,** Platzl 2, near the Hofbräuhaus. The owner, Franz Karl, will be happy to show you his establishment. The best time to see the nimble fingers in action is as early in the morning as possible.

Other Bavarian Food Specialties. Snacks: "Leberkäs" (a meat loaf with liver, pork, and beef), "Weisswurst" (a small white veal sausage). Main meals: "Brathendl" (chicken roasted on a spit), "Steckerlfisch" (river fish grilled on sticks), "Kalbshaxe" (veal), "Schweinshaxe" (pork). Most of the dishes are served with "Knödeln" (a type of dumpling) made with either potatoes or rolls. Particularly tasty desserts are: "Strudel," a type of pastry made from a thin dough and filled with whipped cream, apples, and raisins; and the "Zwetschgendatschi," a yummy plum pastry not equaled anywhere in the world.

RESTAURANTS

Peterhof, Marienplatz 22. It is here the famous veal sausage of Munich, "Weisswurst," was first served, more than two centuries ago. The dining room on the second floor offers a splendid view of the Glockenspiel.

Donisl, Weinstrassel 1, on Marienplatz. About five centuries ago this was the headquarters of the King's Guards. Today it is the headquarters for Bavarian heartiness and especially "Leberkäs," the puffed meat loaf eaten with sweet mustard. Zither music, dirndled waitresses, and quaint decoration complete the picture of coziness.

Platzl, am Platzl. This place is devoted to song, fun, and frolic. It features Bavarian shows with yodeling music and Bavarian food. It will give you the feeling of an old-fashioned German music hall. Entrance fee is 60 cents, with dinner about 8 DM ($2).

Hofbräuhaus, am Platzl, is directly across the street from the Platzl restaurant. Famed in story and song, this place can seat several thousand people and look only half full. Try the dining room on the second floor or the Festival Hall on the top floor. Both are open for lunch. "Sauerbraten" (soured roast beef) is always good and available—served with Knödeln. The waitresses' smiles are as big as the beers they carry, sometimes fifteen steins at one time. Friday, Saturday, and Sunday nights everybody joins in the singing.

DIE FREUNDE: FRIENDS

There are two ways to arrange for introductions before your visit. Contact one of the two newspapers which will print your letter. The names and address of the papers are **Süddeutsche Zeitung,** Sendlingerstrasse 80, and **Münchner Merkur,** Bayerstrasse 57-59, both München 2.

An organization to write to is: Jugendkulturwerk der Landeshauptstadt, Gewürzmühlstrasse 5/11, München 22. The telephone number is 2 29 97/461. The youth center has many different recreation and cultural groups. Be sure to state your particular interest and age since there are many different clubs: theater, music, dance, art, sports, and others.

Another contact is: Mrs. Elizabeth Lemmerz, German-American Club, Farbergraben 35-6, 8 München 2.

If reading and books are your special interest, visit the International Youth Library, Kaulbachstrasse 11A, Gartenhaus, 8 München 22. Young people from all over the world visit this leading library center, which now contains over 125,000 books from practically every country. Activities range from book discussions and English and French language classes to children's art studios.

AUF WIEDERSEHEN: FAREWELL

After you've explored Plätze, munched pretzels, and giggled at puppets, don't overlook another important part of the city, Munich's very own dog—the Dackel or dachshund. Smooth-, long-, or rough-haired, you'll find him in all sizes and shapes romping with children, spreading good cheer and warmth in homes, comforting the old and lonely. Bavaria's heraldic beast is the lion, but if Munich had one, it would be without a doubt the Dackel. This popularity is due to the fact that he has qualities of character that the German people admire—intelligence, good humor, and heartiness.

In the early days of the dachshund's history he was bred chiefly by noblemen to protect the forests from being overrun by badgers. This took keen senses and quickness of mind. Soon his loving nature made countless friends and he was sent all over the world.

If dachshunds are your favorite, just a hundred miles northeast of Munich is the town of Gergweis. Here dachshunds outnumber humans (six hundred to five hundred). Gergweis has been going to the dogs ever since Frau Katie Dorfmeister brought along thirty-one of the pets as a dowry when she married her hunter husband over thirty-two years ago. Today the silver-haired grandmother has a luxurious kennel. Gourmet meals of liver, hearts, and spleens are cooked in a gleaming kitchen. There is a canine hospital, a maternity center for expectant mothers,

and a home for the elderly. After a visit to Gergweis you may
begin to ask yourself, "What's so bad about a dog's life?"

SPRECHEN: TO SPEAK

ENGLISH	GERMAN	PRONUNCIATION
Good morning	Guten Morgen	Goo-ten more-gen
Good day	Guten Tag	Goo-ten tahg
Good evening	Guten Abend	Goo-ten ah-bend
What is your name?	Wie heissen Sie?	Vee hi-sen zee
My name is	Ich heisse	Isch hi-sah
How are you?	Wie geht es Ihnen?	Vee gate s ee-nen
I am fine	Es geht mir gut	S gate meer goot
Thank you very much	Danke sehr	Dunk-a sehr
Speak slowly, please	Sprechen Sie bitte langsam	Sprech-ken zee bit-a lahng-sam
You speak too fast	Sie sprechen zu schnell	Zee sprech-ken tsoo schnell
You're welcome	Bitte sehr	Bit-a zerh
Please	Bitte	Bit-a
Goodbye	Auf Wiedersehen	Off vee-dehr-zehn
Pardon me, please	Verzeihen Sie, bitte	Fehr-tsi-en zee, bit-a
What is that?	Was ist das?	Vas ist das
Where is	Wo ist	Vo ist
How do I get to	Wie komme ich zu	Vee kom-a isch tsoo
Right	Rechts	Reschts
Left	Links	Links
Right around the corner	Gleich um die Ecke	Gleisch uhm dee ek-ka
Straight ahead	Geradeaus	Ger-ad-a-aus
Can you tell me where	Konnen sie mir sagen wo	Kur-nen zee meer sah-gen vo
I can't speak German	Ich kann kein Deutsch sprechen	Isch kan kein Deutsch sprech-ken

ENGLISH	GERMAN	PRONUNCIATION
Do you speak English?	Sprechen Sie Englisch?	Sprech-ken zee ehng-lisch
Will you help me, please?	Wollen Sie mir helfen, bitte?	Vol-len zee meer hel-fen, bit-a
I am looking for the hotel	Ich suche das Hotel	Isch soo-ka das ho-tel
Excuse me, please	Entschuldigen Sie, bitte	Ehn-schul-dee-gen zee, bit-a
How do you say	Wie sagt man	Vee sockt mahn
How much does it cost?	Wieviel kostet das?	Vee-ful cos-ta das
What time is it?	Wieviel Uhr ist es?	Vee-feel oohr ist
Men/Women	Männer/Frauen	Men-ner/Fraw-en
Entrance	Eingang	Eyn-gahng
Exit	Ausgang	Aus-gahng
Drugstore	Drogerie	Drug-erie
Barbershop	Friseur (Herren)	Free-seur
Toilet	Toiletten	Toil-let-ten
1	eins	eynz
2	zwei	tswhy
3	drei	dry
4	vier	fear
5	fünf	fuhnf
6	sechs	sex
7	sieben	see-ben
8	acht	acht
9	neun	nawyn
10	zehn	tschn
11	elf	elf
12	zwölf	tswolf
13	dreizehn	dry-tsehn
14	vierzehn	fear-tsehn
15	fünfzehn	fuhnf-tsehn
20	zwanzig	tswan-sich
50	fünfzig	fuhnf-sich
100	hundert	hoon-dert

FEIERTAGE: HOLIDAYS

January to Shrove Tuesday (late February or early March)	**Fasching** (Carnival Time). Great processions, crowning of king and queen, floats, costumes, dancing, and plenty of merriment.
Middle of March	**International Handicraft Fair.** Exhibition Hall filled with ingenious displays.
Easter	**Celebrations.** Lighting of bonfires and raising of Easter flag.
End of April–beginning of May	**Mai Dult Fair** (Farmers' and Antique Market). Mariahilfsplatz. Huge rummage sale—great fun. Punch and Judy shows, rides, and lots of things to look at or buy.
Early June through September	**Music Festival.** Throughout the city.
End of July–August	**Sommer Dult Fair** (Farmers' Market).
Late September (last week)–first week in October	**Oktoberfest.** Fun fair, rides, parades, and lots of food.
Middle or end of October	**Herbst Dult Fair** (Farmers' and Antique Market).
December through Christmas	**Arrival of St. Nikolaus.** Carrying his bag and switch, he punishes or praises children and brings first gingerbread. **Christkindlmarkt.** Opens with goodies of all kinds—toys, decorations, gifts. Carol singing by star-carrying children, splendid trees, some lit by real candles.

7. PARIS

But the Echo Remains

"Bienvenue!" Welcome to Paris, for centuries the center of enlightenment, art, and learning. That is why it is called "la ville lumière," the city of light.

And it does seem full of light. On clear days a slight haze softens the sunlight and gives the city a delicate glow. Handsome buildings of weathered stone look out on tree-shaded avenues, open squares, or green parks. Few buildings are taller than six or seven stories and only the church towers and spires rise above the level of chimney tops. Light flows freely through the narrowest of winding streets right into the oldest quarters. Follow the well-worn paths and hear the echoes of centuries past.

"I am innocent," pleaded the trembling, sweet shepherdess Joan of Arc in 1431. "My voices are from God and commanded me to halt the horror of war." Her story will take you to the place where she was wounded and to the river where she was finally laid to rest.

"The King must die that the country may live!" raged Robespierre to the angered revolutionary mob of 1789. The razor-sharp guillotine dropped like a flash. Your journey into torture chambers, dark dungeons, and bloodstained squares will show you what all revolutions are like.

"If I had succeeded I should have been the greatest man the world has ever known." Napoleon Bonaparte was brilliant in victory, bitter at his 1815 defeat at Waterloo. Yet you will discover he did succeed in reorganizing almost everything— roads, factories, harbors, and the schools which had been destroyed by the Revolution. He was also responsible for a code of law still used today in many countries.

Paris offers a colorful pageant of famous men and women, saints and sinners, emperors, kings and queens, wending their way through the pages of history. Many of them need little introduction since their names and faces are well known. Others may be new to you.

Get to know the city through its artists. Each has tried to define the spell Paris weaves, to catch one of its many moods. There is the Paris of Manet, of Monet, of Renoir, of Utrillo. Each is quite different.

Meet modern Parisians in the student quarter of the Left Bank, in a bistro, in one of the cool parks or gardens. The shopkeepers, the subway ticket puncher, the bus conductor, the gendarme directing traffic, the concierge in the hotel, the garçon in the restaurant are only a few of the Parisians you will encounter. They are proud of the city and are ready to share its many moods with you.

THE BEGINNING: A SEEDLING FLOWERS

It happened many thousands of years ago. Almost as if in an eerie dream, the city rose out of the ocean of water. The entire area on which Paris stands today was completely covered with water. Slowly numerous islets emerged from the water. It was one of these tiny islands located in the middle of the Seine, known now as the "Ile de la Cité" (the Island City), that was the seedling that grew to present-day Paris.

Years later, says legend, navigators appeared on the marsh-laden wet banks, exhausted from traveling on their frail skiffs, probably searching for a good fishing place. The oval-shaped land seemed an ideal place for a settlement. The Seine divided its two arms around the island, leaving it lonely and set apart with a natural moat isolating it from the surrounding land, a good place for defense. So the Parisii, the name of the Gallic tribe, gathered there among the rushes and willows, built round thatched huts on the western part, and dedicated the eastern side to the worship of their pagan gods. Since the river was deep and the current slow, the Parisii, dressed in cloaks made of skins, became boatmen and fishing traders. They built a wooden bridge across to the north bank, where they could hunt game in the woods or prey on the water birds in the marshlands or defend themselves against the tribes living beyond the hills.

The Ile de la Cité was usually peaceful and quiet except for the occasional steps of the hunter or the cries of the waterfowl. The island is shaped like a boat with its bow headed downstream, and the figure of a boat has become the symbol of the city. The seal on the coat of arms includes a picture of a ship with the Latin motto "Fluctuat nec imergitur"—It rocks but it does not sink. Parisians believe in the deeper meaning of the saying—although the city may undergo misfortune it will never be destroyed.

Despite a heroic battle, the Parisii were conquered in 52 B.C. by Romans encamped on the mountains opposite the island (Mont St. Geneviève and Montmartre). With Caesar's victory, the Romans built the first permanent city with homes, roads, aqueducts, and arenas, all constructed from stone quarried near the Seine. The limestone was so nearly white that the Romans called their city Lutetia, (White City). In A.D. 307 the name was changed to Paris, honoring the original settlers, the Parisii.

During the long rule of the Romans two saints played a dazzling part of the city's history. It is said that around A.D. 252 Bishop Denis (Dionysius) was sent to convert more people to Christianity. The Romans were gravely displeased. They preferred that people pray at the temple built to the gods Mercury and Mars, located on the high and holy peak where the Parisii once had their sacred grove. St. Denis was ordered by the Romans to stop holding secret meetings for Christians. He would not obey. One day Roman soldiers discovered St. Denis' hiding place in a cave under the Left Bank. He and his two most loyal followers were captured, brought to trial, and sentenced to death. About halfway up the hill to the Roman temple, all three were swiftly beheaded. Then a strange thing happened. As soon as the head of St. Denis was struck off, he stooped and picked it up. With his severed head tucked under his arm, he walked for two miles, until he sank lifeless at the spot where he was to be buried. Over his tomb rose the Abbey of St. Denis, where kings and queens of France have been laid to rest. St. Denis became one of the city's patron saints, and the hill where he died is no longer the Mount of Mercury and Mars but the Mount of Martyrs, named Montmartre.

Another patron saint with a fantastic legend is Geneviève. While still in her twenties in the year A.D. 450 she was brave enough to defy the terrible Attila, King of the Huns, as he was laying waste all of Europe. He came sweeping across France with his squat horsemen, ravaging, murdering, and boasting that grass would not grow again where his horses had galloped. The Parisians were terrified as Attila approached the city. Geneviève calmed the people, organized the city's defense, housing, and food supply, and then began to pray. Attila did not enter the city but rerouted his men to Châlons-sur-Marne, one hundred miles from Paris, where he suffered his worst defeat. Over 1 million men were killed. More men died in this one battle than in any other in history.

On another occasion when Paris was besieged Geneviève came to its aid. Enemy tribes controlled the Seine both above and below Paris. Since the river was the main highway for food and supplies, the people of Paris were starving. Boats had made several attempts to get out but were captured. One dark night clever Geneviève along with several strong men muffled the oars of a boat and set out to row up the river. Suddenly a heavy mist descended and cloaked the boat from enemy eyes. After what seemed like hours, the boat arrived safely at the city of Troyes, loaded its cargo of food, and set sail for its return voyage. Once again the darkness, the mist, and Geneviève's prayers brought the boat through, and the famished city was saved.

The people of Paris named the hill on the Left Bank Mont St. Geneviève in her honor. On Pont de la Tournelle, a beautiful bridge crossing from the Left Bank to the Ile St. Louis, on the left side of the central arch, facing east, is the tall, gracious statue of Geneviève. The figure is perched high, almost as if Geneviève's spirit is ready to spring forth and defeat invasion, epidemic, drought, flood, and frost, which she has been summoned to do for hundreds of years.

EXPLORING WHAT REMAINS OF THE BEGINNING

The places to see history come alive are not listed by areas of the city. They are arranged in chronological order.

Musée de Cluny (Cluny Museum), 6 Place Paul-Painlevé. Open daily except Tuesday 10 A.M. to 12:45 P.M. and 2 to 5 P.M. Fee: 3 F (54 cents); Sunday 1.50 F (27 cents).

First proceed to the end of the passage to the vast, silent halls of the ancient Roman baths built in 200 B.C. You descend the steps over what were once tile and mosaic floors. All at once you are standing in the frigidarium, a huge room with a high-vaulted ceiling. It is silent. The six-and-a-half-foot-thick stone walls and the small red Roman bricks shut out all noises of today. Feel the silence of twenty-one centuries around you. Romans came here for peace and quiet and for cold baths to cool off. Look at the ribs of the vaults in the ceiling. The supports are sculptured to resemble the prows of boats, probably because the first citizens of Lutetia were men of the river, sailors and traders between the winding Seine banks. Now notice the fragmented column and the half-broken stones displayed by the eastern wall. These are the oldest relics in Paris and perhaps the most wonderful. They were the pillars and pagan altar built by the Nautae, Lutetia's guild of boatmen, in praise of Jupiter, the Roman god who was believed to be ruler of the heavens and gatherer of the clouds.

This rare find was discovered two and a half centuries ago beneath Notre Dame. The writing on the pillar shows it was standing in place when Jesus Christ was crucified. It reads, "To Jove the Great and the Good, we, the Guild of Boatmen, founded this altar when Tiberius was Caesar."

After leaving the ancient ruins, see the rest of the museum. It is a perfect preview to the medieval period, the next part of your walk through history. Here is the best example of craftsman-ship of the time: silver, enamels, wood carving, ironwork, furni-ture, jewelry, even some seventh-century crowns. Above all, see the six glorious tapestry hangings of the "Dame à la Licorne" ("Lady and the Unicorn"). Displayed in a special circular room, the graceful lady with her legendary unicorn steps lightly among the flowers, animals, and trees in the magic circle of a meadow against a rose-red background decorated with flowers and birds. The description by ancient Greek writers of the unicorn, possibly a rhinoceros or an antelope, inspired medieval storytellers to create many myths about it. The red, black, and white horn was said to be an antidote for poisons; learned men seriously talked about its curative value. According to legend, the unicorn could be captured and subdued only by a maiden. Five of the tapestries are believed to represent the five senses, touch, smell, hearing, taste, and sight. The sixth pictures a wedding uniting the two families for which the tapestries were woven.

Les Arènes de Lutèce, an old amphitheater at 49 Rue Monge on the hill of St. Geneviève, is another remnant of the Romans. It is not as easy to find as the Cluny Museum because it is hidden behind a clifflike house-block. When you get to the Rue Monge ask the first Parisian you see for directions. He will help you to the main archway. Pass through it onto the arena floor of a great circus. The thirty-six tiers of seats sloping behind and around you held sixteen thousand spectators, almost the entire population of Lutetia. In bad weather an immense tent covered the entire theater. A notice at one of the two main entrances where the happy people swarmed through announced the main event of the day—a mock sea battle, a fierce gladiator contest, exciting exhibits of wild beasts, or a Christian martyr thrown to the lions. Immediately in front is the stage and the actors' dressing rooms on the level of the lowest tier. Here plays of comedy and tragedy were presented. Some historians think that St. Denis may have been executed at this very spot.

The Panthéon, Place du Panthéon, off the Boulevard St. Michel, was built in honor of St. Geneviève. All her life she devoted herself to the care of the sick and the poor. Until her death at age eighty-nine she performed many miracles. She made the blind see, cured fevers, and lighted candles by passing her hand over them. When Louis XV was seriously ill in 1774, he vowed that if he recovered he would build St. Geneviève a magnificent new temple to replace her decaying church (the original was almost six hundred years old). He kept his promise by constructing this building with the help of funds he received from a lottery. The walls of the Panthéon are decorated with lovely paintings showing the history of the city. The most beautiful scenes comes from the soft and gentle brush of the artist

Puvis de Chavannes: St. Geneviève feeding the people of Paris; St. Geneviève watching over her city while it sleeps. The staircase at the end of the choir loft leads to the crypt, where famous people have been buried. You'll find the tombs of the philosopher and writer Voltaire, the essayist Rousseau, the dramatist and novelist Victor Hugo (*The Hunchback of Notre Dame* and *Les Misérables*), and the writer Zola.

The Old Abbey of St. Geneviève (part of the Lycée Henri IV), at the side of the Panthéon, is worth looking at for the steeple named the Tower of Clovis and its unusual place in history. The Franks, meaning freemen, a group of North German tribes, assisted the Romans in defeating Attila the Hun at the fateful battle of Châlons. They then proceeded to invade the country, even giving it their name, France. It was St. Geneviève watching over her city who advised her people to surrender to Clovis, the crowned King of the Franks. Clovis, though no saint, having few scruples and less pity, was nonetheless a churchman. One day, after declaring Paris the capital of France, he rushed out to the hillside and flung his battle-ax this way and that to mark the spot where a great church would be built worthy of the capital and the memory of St. Geneviève. The Tower of Clovis steeple is the only thing that remains of the basilica he built. Now let's go to the Ile de la Cité for a closer look at where it all began.

Ile de la Cité was and still is the center of Paris. Although it is not the home of big business, famous shops, main banks, or renowned theaters, it is the gem of France because of what remains here. It has two masterpieces of Gothic architecture (Notre Dame and St. Chapelle), with stories of pious kings; the principal courts of law (Palais de Justice), with grim dungeons overly active during the bloody Revolution; and the remains of an antique palace.

The travels of the early Parisii tribe had been over field tracks and trestle bridges. The Romans built long, well-paved roads.

The original road which ran across Lutetia coming from Orléans in the south and going to Rouen in the north is still there. Follow in the footsteps of the Roman legions as they parade to the center of the island. Coming from the Left Bank off the St. Germain turn onto Rue St. Jacques and continue on Rue du Petit Pont. On the Right Bank go ahead on the Rue St. Martin through the Pont Notre Dame. Either way you will arrive on the Rue de la Cité, then allow the Roman legions to march past you. Looking at your map, you see this road runs right through Paris as straight as a taut rope.

The Romans found the island an excellent and safe place for holding their assemblies; and Caesar summoned the tribes to meet there. The Préfecture de Police (Police Headquarters) stands upon the approximate site of the gracious Forum, where Roman forces were based. The Palais de Justice (Palace of Justice), once the palace of kings, rests on a still earlier palace. From it Julian Caesar—soon to be acclaimed the Emperor Julian —issued the laws of Rome to the island city and the dark forests of France.

But the best place to get a feeling for the island's past is in the square of the cathedral of Notre Dame (Place du Parvis-Notre Dame). The name "Parvis" originated when the mystery and miracle plays were performed here and the space in front of the church represented Paradise. In this area the old gods of the forest were worshiped by the native Parisii. Later a Roman temple stood there. Then eight hundred years ago loving hands produced Notre Dame (Our Lady of Paris). Right in front of the cathedral is a huge hole about sixty-five yards long and twenty-seven yards wide, and inside the eighteen-hundred-year-old remains of Lutetia. They were uncovered in 1965 during the construction of an underground garage. In the two and one half years of digging, twenty-seven thousand ancient items were found. They range in size from coins no bigger than a dime to huge blocks of stone that formed part of the defense wall around the city. Also discovered were remains traced to the second and third centuries, with the tile floors of public buildings showing the use of central heating, furnaces carrying hot air in ducts under the floors. Lutetia proved to be a very well-planned city. A hole in Paradise is an amazing place to discover the origins of a city.

OLD PARIS, MEDIEVAL TIMES (476–1400s)

After Clovis, King of the Franks, died, his sons and grandsons ruled the country. But they were so busy fighting among themselves for control that looting, killing, and many other crimes were widespread in the countryside and city. Finding themselves in mortal danger, the people turned for protection to their richer and stronger neighbors, and the "feudal system" began. "Lords" became responsible for "vassals" who swore allegiance to them. In time the vassals became totally dependent on the lords for food and shelter and were treated like slaves.

As the lords became powerful they declared war on each other. When the army of an enemy lord approached, the people scurried behind the thick walls of their protector's castle. Gradually the people moved as close to the castle as they could. These clusters of houses grew into bigger and bigger towns and the walls around them became thicker and thicker.

Medieval Paris attracted more people than other towns, but the city was neither spacious nor comfortable. The streets were narrow, crooked, dark, and filthy. The buildings were so close that the houses often shut out the sunlight. Not more than two horsemen could ride abreast even down the royal highways. The streets were not paved but dotted with mudholes. Adding to the filth, people threw their garbage out the windows onto the street. The city was a breeding ground for disease.

Police protection was unknown. A citizen venturing out on

the street took his servant along to help fight off the robbers. With no street lights available, torches and lanterns had to be carried. The wooden buildings were so clustered together that fire was an ever-present danger. A severe one could wipe out the entire city.

In 870 Paris was threatened once again, this time from the sea in beautiful boats with high bows manned by Danes called "Norsemen"; they came from the north. They tried to but could not capture the city. Instead, they settled for rich farmland on the river between Paris and the sea in what became the province of Normandy.

After the Norse siege, the nobles decided to band together. They elected Hugh Capet, the Count of Paris, as their king. Combining his lands to the south with the property of the noblemen, he had what was referred to as "Royal Domain." Later kings added their property to the Domain and the city grew.

In 1066 Duke William of Normandy, who was as ambitious and tough as his Norse ancestors, hurried across the English Channel with an army of sixty thousand, defeated Harold at the Battle of Hastings, and became William the Conqueror, King of England. The news did not please the King of the small Royal Domain, since the Duke of Normandy was supposed to be his vassal. It was the beginning of long years of wars.

Shortly afterward another event shook not only Paris but the world. Peter the Hermit, a French monk, became one of the leaders of the First Crusade. He rode about on a mule preaching of the duty of Christians to free Jerusalem from the Moslems. Men, women, and children, most of them poor peasants, flocked to Peter and donned their cross of red cloth, the symbol of the departing crusaders. A great wave of religious excitement brought thousands of people of all ranks from all over Europe to continue these journeys for over two hundred years.

One tragic expedition was made by bands of French and

German children, who marched to Mediterranean ports, convinced that the sea would dry up and permit them to reach the Holy Land. No such miracle occurred and several shiploads of children were carried into slavery in Turkish territories. Others perished, straggled home, or wandered aimlessly around Europe. The pathetic story may have inspired Robert Browning's famous poem "The Pied Piper of Hamelin."

The Crusades altered the entire way of life in Europe. Learning about the East and being in contact with various people of Europe led to the exchange of ideas, customs, and techniques. Interest in geography and navigation was stimulated; better maps were drawn; and more and more sea captains adopted the Arabs' crude compass.

Trade and commerce flourished as the growing middle class of merchants and craftsmen demanded such new foods as cane sugar, rice, and garlic and textiles like silk, muslin, and satin. Goods brought to Europe had to be distributed. As trade increased so did the towns and cities along the inland routes. Finance and business practices were changed. Gold coins were minted and letters of credit came into use for the convenience of the crusaders. To finance the expeditions, the wealthy were taxed and the serfs allowed to buy their freedom and sometimes the land on which they worked. So the number of small landowners increased and the feudal system weakened.

The people of Paris were also on the move, pushing out far beyond the city walls, eating better, dressing smarter, and breaking the bonds of feudalism completely. The citizens pledged their allegiance only to their work guilds and the King and asked for a "Charter of Liberties" to run their own city. The King gladly agreed, since he needed the people's support against the nobles. Along with the charter, the King established the city's own police force to try to control thievery and murders. The citizens promised money and soldiers and were known as "bourgeois" now that the city was an independent burg. The landowners (burgesses) in turn formed a "commune," a joint pact to stand together to maintain and defend their rights and liberties.

Paris at this time was deeply religious. The Ile de la Cité counted no less than twenty churches crowded together. In times of great danger such as floods, the relics of St. Geneviève were carried in procession through the streets of the city. In 1163 the Bishop of Paris, Maurice de Sully, wishing to show his great devotion, began to build a great new cathedral over the stones of the ancient Parisii altars. The two high towers and flying buttresses of Notre Dame dominate the island and the city today, as they did then.

In addition to places of worship, the cathedral and the neighboring cloisters served as schools of learning. The only education in those days was offered by the church and mainly to young men who were to become priests or monks. Books were rare, since the manuscripts were handwritten by monks in cloisters. The only way knowledge could be passed on was through lectures. Paris had attracted many scholars. They spoke before crowds of boys and young men, some rich in fine clothes, but many more poor in thin rags covered by the students' short sack gowns. The students who were determined to have an education worked at any kind of odd job they could get. With inkpot and feathered quill, they transcribed texts for the rich boys. Stationing themselves with little stools by the bridges, they wrote love notes and letters for illiterate businessmen and sweethearts. Some carried pails of water or slop pots up and down many flights of stairs.

In 1200 King Philippe Auguste handed over to the city the deed to found the University of Paris. It was not long before learned men and students from all parts of Europe thronged its benches. The city was bulging at the seams. The students and teachers moved to the narrow, muddy old streets of the Left Bank, then called the "Pays Latin" because everybody there had to speak Latin. Whoever ventured to enter any of the students' inns without knowing Latin was regarded as an intruder and given a sound beating.

The King himself paid for a new great square building with a central tower and corner turrets, built on the Right Bank on ruins of the old fortress called the Louver, which later was spelled "Louvre." He also ordered the streets to be paved.

Years later Louis IX, known as St. Louis, ordered all old records and manuscripts copied and kept. They became the basis for the vast National Library of today. He founded the College of Sorbonne and established the rule of justice by law, in the Roman tradition. While leading a crusade to the Holy Land, he died of the plague. He is particularly remembered for building the St. Chapelle, where you will see his story told in dazzling glass.

By the end of the thirteenth century Paris had grown to a population of 250,000. Cobbled stone wharves along the river west of the city island were crowded with loaded boats. And the crowds in the streets were greater, more exciting than before. The end of the Middle Ages was marked by bitter wars and confusion. The assembly of nobles chose as king Philip IV of the Valois family, who was related by blood to the early king Hugh Capet. Bad times followed. The English king, Philip's nephew, demanded the lands of the old dukes of Normandy. For over one hundred years a terrible war raged, killing thousands of people.

In 1415, after a decisive battle at Agincourt, Henry V of England was proclaimed ruler of northern France. But that was not the end of death. The plague, the Black Death, swept Europe, claiming one third of the people. Havoc reigned in the city and the country. Bands of soldiers wandered about, plundering and killing in the name of one king or another. Paris, filled with filth and disease, was the scene of riots.

During the eight-year occupation by the English, three kings vied for power. The weakest was Crown Prince Charles, or the Dauphin as he was called. His father disinherited him and agreed that Henry VI of England was the rightful heir to the throne of France. Where would a leader be found who would rouse the hearts of the people to return France to its countrymen?

From the little town of Domrémy in Lorraine, a peasant girl of sixteen insisted on presenting herself to the Dauphin, claiming that angels told her to deliver France from the enemy. At first the Dauphin refused to see Joan of Arc, but her energy and faith finally moved him. He consented to meet her but to test her power he hid among his courtiers in disguise. Although she had never seen him before, she immediately recognized him and knelt at his feet. Charles gave her four thousand men to regain the vital city of Orléans, then surrounded by the English. Clad in full armor and holding her own white standard embroidered with lilies of France, she rode at the head of the army. The troops, happy to find an inspiring leader after years of disastrous warfare, followed her with enthusiasm. They even gave up cursing when she ordered it. It was a miracle to everyone that she won battles and had Charles crowned King. Joan was determined to take Paris. She was wounded in the assault on the Port St. Honoré outside of Paris, and was forced to retreat. Later she was betrayed to the English, tried and condemned as a witch, and ordered to be burned at the stake.

King Charles had gained courage for the first time in his life. He crushed a revolt of the barons, organized a regular army, and by 1453 succeeded in ridding his country of the English. Joan of Arc had won her victory. France was back in the hands of the French.

Jeanne d'Arc's statue is at the Place des Pyramides on the Right Bank. The bronze-gilt figure of gallant Joan of Arc on horseback stands a few yards from the spot where she fell wounded in her attack on English-occupied Paris. She was just about to measure the depth of the moat with her spear when a traitor stole up behind her. Parisians make a pilgrimage to the statue on May 30, the date of her death.

Now let's return to the Ile de la Cité and our visit to medieval Paris.

Notre Dame (Cathedral of Our Lady), Ile de la Cité, open 7 A.M. to 5:30 P.M.

Imagine that it is the year A.D. 1248. The cathedral square is much smaller then. The three- and four-story houses of wood and plaster lean heavily against the cathedral building. Knights, serfs, monks, men-at-arms, artisans, and shopkeepers pass, talking loudly in old Latin and other foreign tongues ranging from English to Syrian.

This historic day the minstrels of the Petit Pont, the ancient little bridge, have heard that King Louis IX, St. Louis, is coming to the cathedral to say his final prayer before embarking on his second crusade. Quickly the square fills up. A great audience lodged on the lofty walls and roofs and towers of the cathedral gazes down on the royal scene. Musicians tune up. Tumblers limber up. Jugglers get out their multicolored balls. The knife thrower boasts he can shave the down off a cheek without drawing blood. And a small-fry minstrel sings about his father selling his lute for a loaf of bread. And not to let the merry mood die, a swift change of acts takes place. Two contortionists with a monkey mount a table and stand on their heads, while folding their legs around their necks. Looking through their legs they wink at the King. For a clown can wink at a king, if the King happens to be St. Louis. So these wanderers do their turns before the door of the church depicting the Last Judgment, the building carved with saints and gargoyles, devils and angels. The whole scene seems right, for it is all part of heaven and earth.

The approach to the cathedral is full of wonders. First the two strong, solid towers, then the long line of statues of the kings of France, and lastly the three doorways. The center portal is the largest, showing the angel sounding his trumpet for the Last Judgment. The left one has the Virgin and Child, and the right, St. Anne with statues of Louis VII and the Bishop of Paris, founders of the church.

Inside, the high, soaring ceilings are overwhelming, as are the tall, slim columns and pointed arches. The architectural style is Gothic. The style originated in northern France and spread over Europe in the last part of the twelfth century. Italians thought these tall, grand buildings were barbaric and scornfully named the form after a primitive tribe that had once conquered them, the Goths. The builders discovered that a buttress supporting a side wall need not be solid. If it were shaped like half an arch, it would provide support where it was needed. This type of support became known as a flying buttress, giving the impression of oars almost dipping into the Seine. With such light and strong support, Gothic cathedrals could be built very high and quite large. Ample space was a necessity since thousands of worshipers crowded into the building. The architects learned that a pointed arch carried the weight of a wall better than a round one. And if slender columns were carefully placed for support of the roof, the main aisle (nave) could be widened. A cross aisle (transept) completed the shape of the cross. Light roofs made of ribs of stone were introduced. The great skill of the builders in putting each part exactly where it would carry weight without being bulky left a great deal of open space which could be used for windows. The art of stained glass was developed to bring color as well as light to the interior.

The great rose window on the left inside is magnificent. It is as it was in the thirteenth century. The petals picture Bible characters, with Mary and the Child enthroned in the middle. Eighteen kings of Judah, ancestors of Mary appear in the row below. During World War II the French took this and two other windows apart and hid them in the cellar of a distant castle.

A glassworker must be both an artist and a sculptor. He

first draws his design full size on his workbench, placing heavy lines for the iron bars that will support the glass pieces. He must make sure the window will withstand the severest storms. At hand he has sheets of glass, colored by bits of metal added while the glass is in a melted state. He cuts tiny pieces, often not more than one inch, a separate piece for each color or shade. He puts them together with strips of lead, mindful of what the colors will look like when placed on top or next to each other. In designing the prodigal son feeding the swine, he may make one pig green and two blue, and one red for a certain effect. When he wants purple, he may place red and blue side by side and allow the eye to mix them. The result is a glass flower of fiery light.

The cathedral has witnessed many great and moving events. Only twice, however, have kings been crowned there. The first was a nine-year-old, the English King Henry VI, and the other was Napoleon when he became Emperor in 1804.

For one of the loveliest and most interesting views climb to either the north or south tower. The entrance along the Rue du Cloître-Notre Dame is open 10 A.M. to 4 P.M. (closed on Tuesday). Fee: 2 F (36 cents). From this excellent vantage point get a close look at the gargoyles, the gruesome-looking creatures sticking out from the sides of the building. Actually, the word in old French means "throat," which their function of draining the rain water from the roof resembles. In the Middle Ages they were carved into grotesque birds, beasts, and devils, perhaps to keep the builder's imagination alive or to frighten evil spirits away. From the south tower the entire island can be seen in a glance, with the other islet, Ile St. Louis, pulling behind almost like a barge tugging the bigger ship into harbor.

Stroll through the **Old Quarter** of the city, which runs alongside the cathedral. It consists of some half-dozen interlaced streets still winding their way to the Quai (pier) aux Fleurs (where no flowers are sold). Before the quay was built the river came up to the houses on the Rue des Ursins and was the Port St. Landry, the very first harbor in Paris. Many of the houses date from the 1400s and several doorways and court-yards are decorated with remains of far earlier structures.

St. Chapelle, part of the group of Palais de Justice buildings (off the Boulevard du Palais), is open daily except Tuesday 10 A.M. to noon and 1:30 to 5 or 6 P.M. Fee: 2 F (36 cents).

After the departure of the Romans, the kings of France used the royal palace as their home. The oldest portion of the palace still remaining intact is the glorious chapel. Built by the Crusader King Louis IX, St. Louis, it was erected as a shrine for relics of Christ's death—the crown of thorns he wore, two pieces of the cross, a portion of the spear that stabbed him, shreds of cloths, and the branch the Romans thrust on Jesus as a scepter. The King did not win these sacred objects on the Crusades. The crown of thorns was rescued from Venice. The owner, Baldwin, Emperor of Constantinople, had sold it to earn some quick money. The second group of objects was purchased di-rectly from Baldwin, whose poverty was more pressing than his religious beliefs. These relics are now housed in the Treasury of Notre Dame but displayed only on special holidays (Lent and Easter week).

The building is two chapels in one. You may see the story, illustrated in brilliant glass, of how the sacred objects were brought to Paris when you visit the UPPER CHAPEL, the St. Chapelle. The LOWER CHAPEL was made for the King's servants. Go to the second level by a winding stone stairway, past stone walls and arrow-slit windows that tell us the chapel was built in the age of castles. From the barren little tower walk into a blaze of gilt and color and into the heart of the Middle Ages. The slender columns sweep up like water jets; the walls between have tall stained-glass windows of gleaming blue, ruby red, and deep green showing fifteen hundred scenes from the Bible. There also, if you can find it in the profusion of color, is the account of the voyage of the sacred items—the two friars weighing out gold in Constantinople, where St. Louis had sent his ambassadors to make the final purchase of the precious relics; St. Louis and his brothers walking barefoot carrying the articles on their shoulders to Notre Dame; and Queen Blanche, his mother, following behind with a tall candle in her hand. At first you may think the colors are too brilliant, especially the blues. But remember this is the Middle Ages and there was a great love of brightness. Religious items were particularly colorful. In the fourth bay, on the right, note the small grated window through which the altar could be watched from an unseen place outside. The King would sometimes prefer to worship there alone. The St. Chapelle was finished just about the time St. Louis was about to embark on another crusade, his seventh. Perhaps his courtiers attended the farewell service dressed in their cloaks with the emblem of the Crusades, *the cross on the shoulder.*

Tour de l'Horloge (The Clock Tower), around the corner from the chapel, is one of the other remnants of the Middle Ages. It was the first clock in Paris and was added to the tower in 1370.

The Conciergerie, down the street, is the noted prison of the Revolution and is still in use. All of the tragedy and horror associated with it will be described in the section "Rumbles of the Revolution."

Lunch or dinner? The QUASIMODO is an excellent restaurant with a fine view of the entire island and particularly Notre Dame. It's located on the tip of the neighboring Ile St. Louis at 42 Quai d'Orléans. The name comes from Victor Hugo's book *The Hunchback of Notre Dame* and the poor, one-eyed dwarf bell-ringer of Notre Dame, who stood and watched the dancing of Esmeralda, the gypsy girl. From the northern tower of the cathedral he hurled an evil priest to the ground to protect his lovely gypsy idol. The restaurant serves, among other specialties, mussel soup, and the average meal is 30 to 35 F ($5.40 to $6.30). It is closed on Monday.

THE LATIN QUARTER (WHERE THE STUDENTS DWELL)

Although there are no visible walls, the Latin Quarter on the Left Bank is as separate from the rest of Paris as a moated medieval city. The Boulevard St. Michel, "Boul Mich," has been a favorite gathering place of college and university students since the thirteenth century, when teachers were given permission to cross the Petit Pont to teach outside the confines of Notre Dame. To house poor students who came from everywhere to sit at the feet of the great teachers, colleges were constructed by wealthy patrons. (Students did "sit at the feet" of the professors on the ground or on straw spread for that purpose.) The first, the Collège des Dix-Huit, was founded in 1180 by an Englishman on his way home from the Crusades; the next in 1204, the Collège de Constantinople, for Greek and Byzantine students. Within thirty-two years there were more than sixty colleges in the Quarter. By 1257 the renowned Collège de Sorbonne was established by a gift of houses from King St. Louis to Robert de Sorbon. When it began it was a dormitory for ten or twelve poor students. It is still expanding.

Many students still live in the same area, the Rue St. Jacques, which once was a Roman highway. They buy books in the Quarter's musty bookstores, eat in the crowded bistros, and linger in the cafés arguing. Latin is no longer the only language spoken. You will hear all the languages of Europe along with Arabic, Chinese, and African languages. A walk through the Latin Quarter is a stroll through a great learning center, centuries old. It is also the starting point of the famous "monôme" parade through the streets in single file. On these occasions, students, singing and gesturing, are often on their way to boo a severe professor or government official whose political opinions are not to their liking.

Start at the **Place St. Michel** and turn from the boulevard into the Rue de la Huchette, where a nest of short intertwined streets date from the twelfth and thirteenth centuries and have seen the worst and best of Paris. At Number 10, a thin, unemployed young man stayed for 3 francs a week. He was a brigadier general who was finally summoned to fight. Three months later he commanded the Italian war and was on his way to glory. His name, Napoleon. The Théâtre de la Huchette is the smallest one in Paris. Do look into the famous old Rue du Chat-qui-Pêche (Street of the Fishing Cat), the shortest street in Paris. Retrace your steps to the Rue de la Harpe and walk by the students' church, St. Severin. At the outer corner of the chapel is a statue to the protector of travelers on horseback. It used to be customary to nail a horseshoe on the panels of the door to ensure safe journeys. Around these streets were the parchment makers, copyists, and booksellers—all under university control and world-famous. The streets take their names from the names of whatever tradesman had his business at the corner—Rue de la Parcheminerie (Parchment Maker Street), for example. Continue your tour past the Cluny Museum, which was described in an earlier section, and on to the Rue de la Sorbonne and the college.

The Sorbonne's handsome Court of Honor is off 17 Rue de la Sorbonne, where upon request the concierge will show you in one of the open courts the outline of the original tiny school. The markers are like small gravestones bordering the resting place of something vanished and yet marvelously alive. Wander through the many large vestibules and galleries lined by statues of famous persons. Take a few minutes to go into the CHURCH OF THE SORBONNE to see the tomb of the famous Cardinal Richelieu, the rebuilder of the university. It is open daily 9 A.M. to noon and 1 to 4 P.M.

Richelieu (1585–1642) plays an active part in our next venture into the past. As a forceful French statesman and chief minister of King Louis XIII, he believed the nobles were danger-ous, since they often used their power to lead rebellions against the King and start civil wars. He ordered all castles not near the borders of the country destroyed and forbade dueling, which often led to private warfare. When the nobles continued to plot against both Richelieu and the King, the revolts were quickly crushed and the leaders executed. Inside the church to the right is the white marble tomb, a reclining statue of the Cardinal with a figure of Science in tears. Above the tomb hangs the Cardinal's hat.

Want a snack? The "Boul Mich" is just a few streets away. The many cafés are crowded with students. **The Edelweiss** at 31 Boulevard St. Michel or **La Source** at 35 are both popular. Try a "croque monsieur," an open-faced sandwich with cheese and fried ham, or a "croque madame," chicken instead of ham. The regular sandwiches on French bread are also delicious. While you munch and sip a drink (2.50 to 3 F—45 to 54 cents), you'll have a chance for some student-watching, close up.

The next leg of the walk is a bit far but well worth the effort. You'll be going to one of the oldest street markets in Paris, Mouffetard. Go back to the Sorbonne and walk along Rue Victor-Cousin to Rue Soufflot, which leads to the Panthéon, described earlier. Behind it on the Rue Clotilde stands the Lycée Henri IV, school of some of the greatest men of France. Turn left on the Rue de l'Estrapade, which runs into Rue Blainville. It ends at the Place de la Contrescarpe, a rather dilapidated square, the meeting place for younger artists who dress in the fanciful clothes of tomorrow, not always spotlessly clean. **The Requin Chagrin** (Sad Shark) restaurant is now popular with the

Bohemian set. It specializes in food of the French island of Réunion in the Indian Ocean.

Off the square is the **Rue Mouffetard,** a lively open-air market dating from the thirteenth century. The street twists down a steep slope to the right and is jammed with working people of the quarter dashing in and out of many shops—the greengrocer's heaped with vegetables including huge cucumbers, the "charcuterie" with beautifully displayed meat cuts, and the bakery with long, crusty baguettes and other inviting shapes of breads and "pâtisseries" (cakes, tarts). Nearby the bearded student plays his guitar in a wineshop-and-bar.

In the streets at the end of the market, you see a few of the shop signs of the Middle Ages, and the old and sometimes crumbling houses still have hidden treasures. Recently a delighted householder discovered a hoard of gold hidden for over three hundred years.

The Rue Mouffetard is rich in local color and movement, almost like an Eastern bazaar. During November through December there are many folk festivals. If you or your companion speaks French, M. Jean Guyon, the President of the Street Association at number 132, will be pleased to give you a personal tour of the markets. Write ahead of time or go by to see him afternoons in his office, located at the end of a delightful garden. The market is particularly crowded at 11 A.M. The shops are usually closed 2 to 4 P.M. for lunch.

RUMBLES OF THE REVOLUTION (1460–1800)

Wars were over, the English driven out, and the strife of Frenchmen fighting Frenchmen finished. The people were exhausted, hungry, and without property, yet anticipating a new era. For the rest of Europe it was an exciting time—the age of discovery. Christopher Columbus found the New World for

Spain. Vasco da Gama explored a route around Africa to India, opening up a vast, wealthy source of trade. The invention of the printing press by Johann Gutenberg produced a flow of books reflecting man's new desire for freedom of thought.

In France the kings and noblemen returning from the wars were filled with enthusiasm for what they had seen in Italy and brought famous Italian artists, painters, and architects, to the French court. King Francis I, "the most beautiful man in France," was careless, bold, extravagant, and unwise, but a lover of the arts and beautiful things. Under him, old, dingy, worn Paris was redone in the Italian manner. His nobles built huge châteaux on their country estates, which Francis I visited for balls and hunts. He then remade the old fortress of the Louvre into a palace, all windows and shining halls, courtyards, and gardens. The nobles flocked to Paris to live in the lavish apartments of the Louvre to be near the King and take part in the extravagant entertainments. Paris began to prosper and became a major art center.

Then a period of bloody wars began again. This time the main cause was religion. On one side were the French Catholics supported by Spain. On the other were French Protestants called Huguenots, helped by the English. The split was due partially to the leaders of the Catholic Church. They lived in luxury and fought wars with their own armies as if they were kings. They had angered the people by demanding heavy taxes. There were so many scandals that many Catholic priests preached against luxury and corruption evident in the churches everywhere.

When Charles IX came to the throne in 1560, he was a boy of ten and the real power was wielded by his mother, Catherine de Médicis. Both the Catholics and the Protestants were trying to seize political control of France. Trying to keep peace by playing one faction against the other, Catherine hoped to prevent either one from becoming a threat to the throne. Her plan did not succeed. She was forced to act. Catherine con-

vinced her son that the Protestants were conspiring to murder
him. Charles ordered all Protestants to be killed on the twenty-
fourth of August 1572. The bloodshed began in Paris at two
o'clock in the morning. Men were hunted and dragged out of
their houses and killed in the gutters. By noon more than two
thousand people had been slaughtered. The violence spread to
other towns and before it ended there were at least twenty
thousand victims. It was called "The Massacre of St. Bartholo-
mew's Day."

Peace was finally won when Henry of Bourbon, a Protestant,
fought the great battle of Ivry in 1590 to claim his throne, and
with his white-plumed hat shining laid siege to Paris. Catholic
Paris held out against him. He knew he could not win, and as
a way of getting the people to find him acceptable, he joined
the Catholic Church and took his vows in the old church of
St. Denis outside the gates. Then as the newly crowned King
Henry IV, under the Bourbon banner, among the shouting crowds
and clanging bells he rode into Paris as its ruler. It was a dismal
time to reign. Even the King was poor. But he and his minister,
Sully, began at once to improve conditions. One of the early acts
was the Edict of Nantes, a famous law granting to all men the
right to worship as they pleased. They lowered the farmers'
taxes and helped the people to improve their farms. They
brought silkworms and the silk industry to Paris, also lacemakers,
glass blowers, papermakers, and weavers. New roads and canals
were built. Henry enlarged the palace of the Louvre beyond
the city wall by the river, connecting it with Catherine de Médicis' palace of the Tuileries. The first new bridge in several
years, the Pont Neuf, was constructed over the Seine to the Island City. It had several innovations. No houses lined the sides
of the bridge and the road was covered with pavement. Not a
single street had achieved this yet. Henry's bronze statue still
stands at the center of the bridge, where crowds gathered to
see jugglers and tightrope walkers perform in a fairlike at-

mosphere. He achieved what he set out to do—free France and restore it to its proper place in the world. Tragedy struck when the King was murdered by the Catholic fanatic Ravaillac in 1610.

Henry IV was one of five Bourbon kings characterized by their rather large noses. They ruled for the next two hundred years and guided Paris into becoming one of Europe's most magnificent cities. Art, drama, sculpture, architecture, poetry, and music, as well as the brilliant writings of philosophers and scientists, became the basis of a new French civilization that influenced all of Europe.

The next four Bourbon kings were named Louis after Clovis, the Frank who was the first King of France. After Henry was assassinated, his nine-year-old son, Louis XIII, became king. The nobles tried to take advantage of the child-king to regain their power. Their plans were upset by a remarkable and clever man, Cardinal Richelieu. As adviser to the King, he weakened the power of the nobles by placing the middle class in a position of authority. He broke the power of the Protestants and united France under one ruler. But Richelieu was a tyrant, and even the King had little to say about running the government. Taxes were increased and many liberties were taken away.

THE DRUMBEAT SOUNDS

The four Louis' succeeded in getting absolute power in their own hands by setting each class of people against the other. They provided special privileges and few taxes to the rich and the clergy, while the farmers were paying more than 80 percent of their income and given little opportunity to protest. The farmers paid taxes on income, on land, on property, and on their crops. They even paid a tax for the privilege of being born. Further, they had to provide free labor for the crown and for the local lord, usually ten days a year. They were forbidden to kill game animals, even ones destroying their crops, and the army took their sons for six years just when they reached manhood. For the peasant, France had barely moved out of the Middle Ages.

Then the successful American Revolution made a tremendous impression on France. Why could not the French free themselves? At the time of the Revolution, Louis XVI was on the throne. He was an honest and easygoing man whose greatest difficulty was making up his mind. Painfully shy and grossly fat, his clownish delight in practical jokes made him the laughingstock of his court. His principal wish was to be in his workshop repairing locks or in his library dabbling in mathematics. Harmless as these qualities are, they were fatal shortcomings during this seething period.

The people were not bitter against the King, for they took it for granted that they should be ruled by him. It was the Queen, the young and beautiful Austrian-born Marie Antoinette, whom they hated. For Louis was a weak, simple man, and it was the Queen and her favorites who controlled the government. Vicious stories circulated about the Queen. She was supposed to have taken money from the French treasury and sent it secretly to her brother, the Emperor of Austria. So accustomed to luxury was she that when told her people were without bread, in her ignorance she said, "Well, let them eat cake."

These stories may not be true. But the people were right about the Queen and her favorites being selfish, thoughtless, and arrogant. Although people starved in the streets, courtiers haughtily strolled about the gilded rooms of the palace, idling their time flirting and gambling. The court's main concerns of the day were which man had the right to visit the King's bedchamber or what women would be allowed to dress the Queen. To satisfy as many as possible, the Queen's clothes would be passed through the hands of a dozen noblewomen outside her door. Time was frittered away in fancy-dress balls, elaborate parties, and ornate theatrical performances presented in the Queen's summerhouse at Versailles. All of this was paid for by the ordinary people in taxes. They supported the court, the noblemen in their manor houses, and the bishops and cardinals. Any minister who tried to cut down the royal extravagance was dismissed, for the King controlled the ministers, and the Queen controlled the King.

The country was constantly in debt. Louis was forced to levy a new tax that even the wealthy had to pay, although he had no legal right to do so. It was called "the twentieth," since it represented that portion of a man's income. On top of this, the spring of 1789 saw a harvest failure, and as a result, wheat flour was scarce for bread. It was the wrong time to propose anything.

The nobles objected to the new tax. Blocked at every turn, Louis called a meeting of the most notable aristocrats. He appealed to them for help. The answer was firm: No taxes without change. The young Marquis de Lafayette, recently returned hero of the American Revolution, suggested summoning an Assembly of the inactive Estates-General, the elected representatives of the people. The Assembly was divided into three groups called "estates." The nobility and the clery made up the first two estates. The farmers (peasants) formed a part of what was called the third estate. This class also included merchants, lawyers, and professional men, some of the most able and best-informed people in France. They paid almost all the taxes but had almost no rights.

The Estates-General met for the first time in 175 years. There were over ninety elected representatives of the peasants, many more than there were for the nobles or the clergy. The first two estates insisted that each group be given only one vote. The enraged third estate shouted "No." The King immediately dismissed the Assembly. The third estate refused to leave. They gathered in the handball court at Versailles and established their own government, the National Assembly, composed of members from all three estates. The King promised to reform the taxes and the courts if everyone would "just go home." It was too late. Count de Mirabeau, elected leader of the National Assembly, replied to the King's messenger, "Go tell your master that we are here by the will of the people and nothing but bayonets shall drive us out."

Writers and poets were stirred by the new ideas and made fiery speeches on street corners. Discontent men out of work, hungry, bitter, and landless, came out of the working quarters and slums to join the mobs that started roaring in the streets. They seized some weapons and rushed to overtake the old prison of the Bastille. Here men were kept prisoners without trial by the King's order for years. The raging mob sent the garrison up in smoke and released the bewildered prisoners. A court official woke the King and told him what had happened, but Louis did not understand. "It is a revolt," he said. "No, sir," was the reply. "It is a revolution." News of the destroyed Bastille gave full strength to the movement as it spread to other cities and towns. The army joined the uncontrolled mob. The nobles, fearing they would be murdered, fled the country, leaving their flaming estates behind them. Tax collectors were brutally beaten. The mob stormed the National Assembly and insisted the members vote that all special privileges be dispensed with.

After finding no bread in the bakers' shops, a crowd of women collected at the city hall. Getting little satisfaction, the seven or eight thousand women decided to march to Versailles and make their demands known to the royal family. After killing two of the guards, they captured King Louis, his wife Marie Antoinette, and their little son and won a promise that both grain and their prisoners would return to Paris with them. The unkempt and ragged gang of women accompanied the triumphant procession back to Paris, shouting, "Here comes the baker, the baker's wife, and the baker's boy." What a strange homecoming for a king.

Later, the royal family attempted to escape to Austria. Disguised as a governess and servants, the fugitives sneaked out of the palace. Through a series of unlucky events and Louis' own weakness, they were recognized. Word spread like wildfire. A humorous notice was placed on the wall: "Citizens are warned that a fat man has escaped the Tuileries. Those who find him are asked to bring him back to his lodgings." But most Parisians were far from amused. They were shocked and outraged that Louis had broken his promise to support the Revolution. He was returned to Paris, never to leave again.

Outside France, terrified kings and aristocrats feared that the changes signaled by the Revolution would spread to their own countries. Prussia joined Austria, the Queen's country, to declare war on France. Lafayette commanded the French troops and soon found the soldiers lacked loyalty. Five hundred specially picked National Guards came from Marseilles and the provinces to aid in the Revolution. They marched into Paris singing their new war song, "La Marseillaise." Frenchmen in later years would never forget it, for "La Marseillaise" would become the national anthem of France.

Led by Jean Paul Marat and leaders of a political group, the Jacobin Club, the people of Paris were shouting to put an end to the monarchy. Marat was a strange creature. He was a tiny man who suffered from a horrible skin disease, which some people say he had developed when hiding from the police in the sewers. He dressed in rags and seemed never to wash, so that his foul-smelling body was caked in filth. He was consumed with hatred and envy for everyone. He spread venom through his influential newspaper "The Friend of the People." But violence brings more violence and he was killed when Charlotte

Corday, a young girl, stabbed him with a butcher's knife to ensure what she thought would be France's survival.

Because the royal family was suspected of dealing with the enemies of the Revolution, Parisians, now calling themselves by their old name, "The Commune of Paris," sacked the royal palace and killed the King's Swiss guards. The royal family appealed to the Assembly for assistance, but it was too late. They took away the King's power and put him in prison. The Assembly declared that all males over twenty-one had the right to vote and ordered the election of a new government, the National Convention. Lafayette tried to rescue the King, but in vain. The King was condemned to death.

The months that followed are known as the "Reign of Terror." Thousands of people suspected of treason against the Revolution were imprisoned and then carried in farm carts, tumbrels, to the open Place de la Révolution (Place de la Concorde), where the razor-sharp guillotine stood. Here the window-shaped instrument would do its swift deed, killing the King and Queen, famous scientists, poets, and innocent victims who just seemed to have gotten in the way.

There were two political parties in the Convention vying for power. One was the moderates, led by Georges Jacques Danton, a big man in size as well as spirit. His huge frame with its brutally battered prize-fighter's face towered above everyone. He was the Convention's elected chairman until he was replaced by the radical party's Maximilien Robespierre, who saw to it that Danton was executed. Robespierre sent about twelve hundred people to the guillotine within six weeks to enforce his ideas of morality. He felt fear was the best way to keep everyone under his control. Everyone became suspect of treason. The Convention finally rose up against him. He attempted to escape, but was recaptured and executed by the same guillotine to which he had condemned so many.

By 1794 France was exhausted with bloodshed. The Revolution was over. It had changed everything, even the calendar. The year one was 1790. The names of the months were different. Everyone was equal and only the titles "Citizen" and "Citizeness" were used.

FOLLOWING THE REVOLUTION'S PATH

Now let's be on our way to the sections of the city that repeatedly sent French men and women storming along the streets to change history. During the eighteenth century the Rue St. Honoré ran on and out beyond the old strong gate to the new ramparts, passing on the way the old convent hall of the Jacobins, where Robespierre and his fanatical followers in the Jacobin Club inspired and guided the Reign of Terror. It came to a dusty, unfinished, and empty road which crossed it (the Rue Royale) and ended in an enormous open space, the Bastille at one end, the Place de la Révolution (Place de la Concorde) at the other.

Eastward along St. Antoine the revolutionaries rushed to the prison stronghold and overthrew it. Westward along St. Honoré they came day after day, evening after evening, month in and month out, those wooden farm wagons or dumpcarts called tumbrels, not bearing vegetables from the field but men and women, princesses, a King and a Queen, Charlotte Corday, Danton, and Robespierre to feed the Revolution with their blood from the guillotine set up in the Place de la Concorde. Some twenty-eight hundred persons must have come in their tumbrels along this way.

Here are the places where the major events of the Revolution took place. You may wish to change the sequence so that you do not have to double back to see the various places located in the same area. Look at a map and make your plans.

The Palais Royal (Royal Palace) is on the Rue St. Honoré near the Tuileries. Although Louis XIV is said to have fallen into one of the fountains as a boy, this somber series of buildings with echoing galleries, formal gardens, and ghostly statues has been closer to the Revolution than to royalty. Cardinal Richelieu had it built in 1635 and placed in it his priceless art, his household of some twelve hundred people, and a theater (Comédie Française) where the playwright Molière later appeared. After Richelieu died, the palace fell to a series of royal relatives, who made it into a fashionable meeting place for rakes, dancing girls, and duchesses. One noble added the three vast wings that seal off the gardens and, to make ends meet, rented space to gambling houses (the best-known at number 13) and to small shops (jewelers, cafés, gunsmiths, and a waxworks).

Today it is a court. The inside of the building cannot be visited, but the charming gardens can be seen. It was once enlivened by money-changers, artists, circuses, orchestras, and balloon ascensions. It was also a gathering place of the revolutionaries and the scene of explosive debates and demonstrations. Now it is a quiet spot in a busy city, a place to re-create the past. Who is that attractive twenty-four-year-old girl with chestnut brown hair weaving in and out of the crowd searching for a particular shop? It is Charlotte Corday. She has spotted number 177 and after pausing a second, walks in. It is a cutlery store and she carefully selects the implement to do her bidding, a sheath knife. She has paid 2 francs (36 cents) for it and quickly, among all these people, hides it in the folds of her dress. Her mission is to drive the deadly instrument this evening or tomorrow into the heart of Jean Paul Marat, who is hounding her friends, the Girondists, a political party, toward prison and death. Having killed him, she will accept her fate calmly, for she is prepared to do anything to rid the world of Marat. The cutlery shop still stands at the eastern arcade, now occupied by the Ministère des Affaires Culturelles.

But let's go further back in the past, four years earlier,

to the explosive moments that cause the storming of the Bastille—the date, July 14, 1789, in this very garden!

It is midday and the little "toy" cannon sounds its noonday signal as the sun's rays fire the cap. The cannon is still at the south end of one of the flower beds, but it has long been silent and ivy-covered. At the appointed signal, the action begins. A young lawyer rushes out of the Café de Foy, leaps upon a table under the trees, and shouts as he waves a pistol, "Citizens, I come from Versailles." He stutters and his fury makes him stammer more. "The Swiss troops are advancing on Paris. To arms! Our hour is now." The crowd echoes his ire, for they have been ready to charge ahead for several months.

"But wait. We must have some way of identifying one another," stutters the lawyer, whose name is Camille Desmoulins. The crowd rushes to the trees and grabs green chestnut leaves, which become the tricolored cockade worn as the emblem of the Revolution. Some from the mob snatch Desmoulins from the table to embraced him and weep while others yell "To arms! To arms!" as they rush off to the gunshops in the arcades. These they ransack and then push on to the arsenals where they steal thirty thousand muskets and a few cannons. And then, swept up by the urgency of their cause, they march along St. Honoré and St. Antoine to capture the Bastille, their ranks swelling as from every house and street more people join in.

The Place de la Bastille is where for many centuries the famous fortress stood. Built in 1369, it had eight towers, a moat, and drawbridges, and during its existence held many famous captives.

The Colonne de Juillet (Column of July) in the center is 170 feet high. The figure at the top is the god of liberty. You can climb a narrow, winding staircase and stand on the little balcony directly under the winged statue. It is open daily except Tuesday 10 A.M. to 5 P.M., admission 2 F (36 cents). The names of 615 patriots who died during the three-day battle signaling the beginning of the Revolution are inscribed in gilt letters.

From your high vantage point you are in about the same place where one of the towers stood. Hereabouts the governor of the prison, the Marquis de Launay, listened as you are listening and peered as you are peering. He was waiting and ready for the anticipated trouble. No one was spoiling for a fight less than De Launay. All his thoughts were turned to how to give in to the mob without too much indignity. Suddenly at about eleven o'clock the sound of wild cheering came from the outer courtyard. A few daring men clambered over the roofs of the little houses nestling against the walls and fixed themselves on the hauled-up drawbridge. Soon they cut its chains, and down it came. A group of the leaders went inside to confer with the governor on the terms of surrender. Not wanting to seem too eager, De Launay invited them to breakfast.

Outside, the huge and excited crowds were impatient to see the flag lowered. As this did not happen, suspicions of treachery arose. Shouts of "They have murdered our brothers!" rang out. Muskets went off, cannons boomed. Nervous soldiers from the fortress parapets fired back. Men fell dead and wounded. When De Launay saw what was happening, he panicked. A porthole opened in the drawbridge and a hand waved a slip of paper. It read: "We have more than twenty tons of gunpowder, and we will blow up the fortress and the whole neighborhood unless you allow us to surrender." The Bastille was captured and the symbol of the King's tyranny finished.

The crowds rampaged through the building, breaking down doors, shattering windows, and smashing furniture. The captives were marched off to the city hall, where three of the men were strung up on the lamppost before their guards could come to the rescue. The governor suffered the cruelest fate of all. His head was chopped off and paraded through the streets on a pitchfork.

Late in the evening someone remembered that there were prisoners in the dungeon of the Bastille. The keys were still being carried in the victory parade so the cells had to be forced open. Four forgers, two madmen, and a count shut up at the request of his family were released. The following day, July 15, workers started tearing down the fortress and continued doing so through the year, ending with a dance on the bare Place de la Bastille. A re-enactment of the battle and celebration are held every year on Bastille Day.

Having relived the Revolution from the top of the Colonne de Juillet, return to the square itself. You can trace the outline of the original old fortress walls on the Boulevard Henri IV. They are marked by a line of white stones.

The Conciergerie, part of the Palais de Justice on the Ile de la Cité, was the most notorious prison in the world. No other building in France is more closely associated with the Revolution. It is open 10 A.M. to noon and 1:30 to 5 P.M. every day except Tuesday. Fee is 2 F (36 cents), 1 F (18 cents) on Sunday. The entrance stands next to the twin towers which once guarded the main entrance of the palace on the Quai de l'Horloge.

The prison is named for the "Concierge," the Master of the King's Household. Whoever held the office had a healthy income from the shops and stalls rented in the palace. Go through the gloomy passageway into a small courtyard. Once inside look for the winding staircase in front of the kitchen. It led to the Revolutionary Tribunal courtroom, which tried Marie Antoinette. The men met in a long, bare room with the judge sitting on a raised platform and the jury opposite him. But the judges were not "judges" as we understand the word. They had no training in the law and no duty to conduct fair trials. They and the jury were chosen to find all accused prisoners guilty and condemn them to death.

When you pass through the Rue de Paris, you will see a hall of horror where prisoners were taken to spend the last days of their lives. Most of the men and women were heaped together in this stone corridor, known as the MOUSETRAP. Hundreds of prisoners lay or squatted on filthy mattresses cursing, shrieking, or mumbling prayers in the sweltering air. They were packed so close that there was no room to step by and any prisoner wanting to walk had to tread on the bodies of his fellow prisoners. On either side of the Mousetrap were dozens of little cells divided from each other by thin wooden partitions. These were cells where prisoners with money could have a shred of privacy.

THE PRISONERS' GALLERY, a dark, dank corridor at the far end, got that name because it was there that prisoners entered and left the prison. In the left end of the corridor is a narrow recess about four feet deep with a low bench running along its length. This cagelike area is where condemned women had their hair cut off and were made ready for the executioner.

One of the dungeon cells in the gallery was the last home of Queen Marie Antoinette. She was kept in this small, square room with its low ceiling, its single barred window her only contact with the outside world. All she could see was the legs of women prisoners as they walked in the courtyard. She was not allowed even a candle to read by. The damp stone floor was cold. Only four years earlier she had hundreds of servants anxious to satisfy her smallest whim. Now a young girl, Rosalie Lamorlière, was the only one to tend to her daily needs. And on the farther side of a wooden screen which stretched across the cell lived two guards who ate and slept always in close sight of her. Soon her eyesight began to fail and her auburn hair, always carefully tended, turned snow-white. She looked more than twice her thirty-eight years.

A doorway on the far side leads to a larger room used for the overflow of twelve hundred prisoners. To this room, for their last night alive, came twenty-one deputies of the Gironde, the onetime powerful political group, singing the "Marseillaise."

They spent the night here singing and jesting and, as far as might be possible, feasting and carousing. Among the objects on display here is a picture, "L'Appel des Girondins," of their last banquet. The room looked then exactly as it does now. Other exhibits are a facsimile of a letter to the Queen a would-be rescuer pricked out with a pin, the door of her cell, a guillotine knife, and paintings of the Revolution.

From here you pass into the COUR DES FEMMES (THE WOMEN'S COURTYARD), where the female prisoners took their exercise and washed their linen at a fountain still there. The bell on the wall between two dark arches announced to the prisoners that their tumbrel was ready.

As you walk past this gate now, so did the Queen, known here simply as "the Widow Capet," the family name, walk past it. The previous night she had written a farewell letter to her sister-in-law, Madame Elizabeth. At five in the morning, while she was still at her desk, drummers all over Paris began pounding the funeral roll. Later the foot soldiers and cavalry lined the streets to ensure that any attempt to save the former Queen could be halted immediately. Pale from lack of sunlight, Marie Antoinette smoothed her white muslin dress and put on her one good pair of shoes. Covering her head with a cap, she left the prison and went to her waiting tumbrel. Louis, her husband, had ridden to his death in a closed carriage, but now all people were equal and she rode to the guillotine like all other prisoners. However, from the soldiers and the crowds that followed behind, it was evident that the people of Paris did not regard this as an ordinary execution.

The Place de la Concorde was the final destination for the roaring, curious crowds and the slow-moving tumbrels. They came along the Rue St. Honoré, which met the Rue Royale, the end of the road. In the rolling carts were young and old, men and women, tiny children and sometimes whole families including grandchildren sitting on the planks side by side.

Two years before, a mild-mannered doctor, Joseph Guillotin, had invented what he called a decapitating machine. Before, Frenchmen condemned to death were hung. Now the new instrument was an improvement in speed and efficiency. The victim lay on a slab of wood with his head clamped into position inside a wooden vise. From above, a razor blade dropped like a flash between two wooden supports and crisply cut off the victim's head, which dropped neatly into a basket. The new instrument, the guillotine, named for its creator, was set up in the center of this tremendous square. It was placed on a high platform, so that the grim symbol of death would stand out against the sky. Here on the morning of January 21, 1793, the King paid for his crimes against the Revolution.

One of the first to follow was Charlotte Corday. A picture shows her standing in the cart alone with the executioner behind her. The jeering crowd cannot get at her because of the mounted soldiers who rode by her side. It is almost a triumphal procession. After a while she leans forward to study the guillotine as it comes into view. The executioner tries to stop her, but she rebuffs him with "I have a right to be curious."

Three months later the Queen made her final journey. An artist, Jacques Louis David, did a hasty sketch showing her sitting bolt upright, her mouth turned down as if in scorn of the screaming crowds.

And the victims kept coming until guillotining was such a familiar occurrence that Sanson, the executioner, didn't bother to wave the heads around to satisfy the bloodthirsty mob.

Despite the grisly events in the Place de la Concorde, social life in salons and drawing rooms was back to its original brilliance. Cafés and terraces were filled with laughter, gossip, and talk about art, music, and literature. Children didn't bother to look up from their games. Carriages and coaches passed along the narrow streets, the gentlemen wearing powdered wigs and the ladies their silks and jewels. "Even though heads are falling like roofing slates," one man wrote, "we are calm."

Today the square is still so large that it seems to open and air the whole city. Louis XV in 1755 ordered the building of it to house a statue of himself. During the Revolution the statue was ripped down. In the center is the **Obelisk** from Luxor, the site of the ancient town of Thebes. It was a gift from an Egyptian viceroy. The ninety-foot structure weighs 230 tons. The story of how it was erected is drawn on two sides of the pedestal. The hieroglyphics tell of the singlehanded victories of Rameses II, "son of the sun, king all-powerful who by sword and strength has become master of the earth." Around the square are stone figures honoring various cities and towns in France.

On the north side are two buildings from the square as it originally appeared—the Hotel Crillon and the Marine Ministry. It is particularly beautiful here at night, all lighted up, but a peril to pedestrians and riders in rush-hour traffic. There are twelve lanes for traffic each way, no lights, just police.

Between numbers 398 and 400 Rue St. Honoré is one of the many hidden sights of Paris. As the trumbrels drew near the Rue Royale, they passed here, the door of Robespierre's home. To get to it, find the narrow passage with a pâtisserie on one side and a coiffeur on the other. Go between them into a small court and there in the far corner is an oddly paneled door, La Porte de Robespierre. Maurice Duplay, the cabinetmaker who owned the house, had it installed when Robespierre, the masterman of the Reign of Terror, rose to greatness. The door led to a separate, guarded entrance to a new stairway to his bedroom. It was fitted with massive locks and bolts. Out of this door he came on that 9th Thermidor (the revolutionary renaming of part of July and August), unaware that he would never return, for in less than twenty hours his head would fall and his revolution die.

For a complete feeling of the revolutionary period, visit a section called the **"Marais,"** meaning marsh. During the Middle Ages this entire quarter was often flooded when the Seine rose. It was transformed into a lavish place to live during the seventeenth and eighteenth centuries. In the grimy streets and blind alleys rise scores of magnificent "hotels" (grand, noble mansions); many have fallen to ruin, but some have been restored to their former elegance and are floodlighted in July and August.

Begin your stroll at the Place de la Bastille and end at the Musée Carnavalet, where lively displays in seventy-nine rooms will trace the history of Paris, with models of old Paris showing how the streets you have just passed have changed, wrought-iron shop and tavern signs, and a rare collection of costumes. Follow the Rue St. Antoine and turn right into the Rue des Tournelles. Number 28 contains a charming courtyard. Continue left on the Pas de la Mule (the Mule's Step) to reach your next stop.

The Place des Vosges, a square, is a fit jewel box for the gems of the glittering seventeenth century. Henry IV ordered it built as a model low-rent development with shops and a place where people could promenade. Paris at the time had few areas for strolling. The narrow streets were deep in stinking mud and jammed with carts, horses, barrows, and people. Through the thick of this, servants beat and shoved a clearing for their employers. The square, originally known as the Place Royale, was to have two pavilions, one in the south for the King and one in the north for the Queen. Two years before completion, Henry was assassinated. His son, Louis XIII, presided over the opening ceremonies, which could only be matched by the celebrations of the double wedding to follow, a horse ballet backed by 150 musicians climaxed with rockets bursting from the towers of the Bastille to shower multicolored stars over the ten thousand spectators.

The square immediately became the meeting place for Paris society. It was also fashionable to fight duels there until Cardinal Richelieu put an end to that practice. The name changed from Royale after the Revolution to Place des Vosges to honor the citizens of the Vosges, who were the first to pay taxes to the new government. In the center of the park is the statue of Louis XIII. Nearly every address in the square recalls an illustrious name. Cardinal Richelieu lived at number 21; Victor Hugo at number 6, which you can visit since it is a museum.

Leaving the Place des Vosges, follow Rue des Francs-Bourgeois to reach another point of special interest.

Musée Carnavalet, 23 Rue de Sévigné, is open 10 A.M. to noon and 2 to 5 P.M. every day except Tuesday. Fee: 1 F (18 cents), free on Sunday.

Constructed in 1550, the building was owned by Madame de Sévigné, famous for the hundreds of letters she wrote her children. Her correspondence is one of the best chronicles of social life between 1669 and 1695. Her drawing room can still be seen on the second floor.

The ground floor contains interesting inn and shop signs, clothing, models of the old streets and quarters of Paris, and an old apothecary store with an odd display of stuffed dressed mice busily engaged in mixing a chemical formula. The courtyard has a statue of Louis XIV, the only royal statue that survived the Revolution. The others were completely destroyed by the raging mob.

This museum has the best collection on the Revolution: models of both the Bastille and the guillotine, historical panoramas made like stage sets, complete in every detail; souvenirs of the imprisoned royal family (the chessmen with which Louis XVI whiled away his last hours, clothing of Marie Antoinette, and the copybook of their son, the Dauphin, who was to disappear at the age of ten, written in his childish hand).

In the wide collection of paintings take a close look at Danton on his way to the scaffold still looking wild, Paris on the eve of the Revolution with its narrow, winding streets and jumbled buildings, and the National Guardsmen returning the royal family from Versailles. Note that although the carriage is completely surrounded by soldiers the pickpockets in the crowd continue to practice their profession. Another interesting painting is the "Liberty Tree" planting scene, a ceremony popular throughout France during the Revolution. In this picture the mayor holding the shovel is backed by the National Guardsmen and serenaded by singers and musicians. The men planting the trees are wearing a typical revolutionary costume of long pants called sans-culottes (without elegant knee breeches) and pointed red hats.

Checking your lists of things not to miss, locate the peculiar inkstand showing a sans-culotte bonnet, the typical hat worn by revolutionists, squashing a writhing priest. The top of the bonnet is hinged to make a lid. Another rare item is a wooden statue of a National Guardsman, which was used to indicate the location of an enrollment center.

NAPOLEON'S STORY: THE RISE AND FALL OF AN EMPEROR

Amid shouts of "Death to the tyrant!" shots rang out and ripped into a uniformed hanging dummy. The cursing mob pushed and shoved against a long row of dusty carriages. The largest carriage held a short, rather fat man, cowering behind one of his companions.

"Leave him alone," the Russian officer accompanying him

called out. "Look at him! Can't you see that contempt is the only weapon you ought to use on this man? He is dangerous no longer." The words had their effect. The excited crowd broke out cheering.

The little man who had nearly been lynched was one of the remarkable conquerors and military leaders of modern times. Just a few days earlier his titles were Napoleon I, Emperor of France, King of Italy, and Protector of the Rhine. For fifteen years Napoleon Bonaparte was the most talked-about and feared man in Europe. His ambition was to rule the world. He almost succeeded. Now he was on his way to a tiny Mediterranean island, Elba, off Italy, reduced to ruling eighty-six square miles of rocky land and a handful of peasants and fishermen.

Napoleon's rise to power was made possible because he lived during an extraordinary time. Born into a poor family on the island of Corsica, the second of eight children, he entered a military school at the age of ten. By fifteen he advanced to the Military Academy in Paris, determined to free Corsica, which France had taken by force. In 1789 Napoleon, now twenty, joined the Jacobin Club with its revolutionary rally cry of "Liberty, equality, fraternity."

If the Revolution had not completely shaken France and all Europe, Napoleon might never have gone higher in rank than captain or major. Once given an opportunity, he seized it. He beat the Austrians so badly they were glad to sue for peace and gave France all of Belgium and the territory bordering the left bank of the Rhine. Spain, Prussia, and Holland had already withdrawn from the war. Only Britain continued the struggle.

Then twenty-eight, General Bonaparte sailed in a colossal convoy to Egypt and successfully dodged the British fleet under the command of Admiral Lord Horatio Nelson. In three weeks of brilliant combat Napoleon conquered the whole of Egypt, but the British ships destroyed the French fleet in the Mediterranean. Next Napoleon took his army to Syria and beat the Turks.

When Napoleon returned to Paris, the government was headed by five directors with two councils called "the Directory." Napoleon's brother Lucien was appointed president in honor of the General's conquests. The members were deeply worried about Napoleon's tremendous influence over the army and the people, tired of confusion and bloodshed.

One morning Napoleon walked into the Council Hall and started to make a speech. From all sides came shouts of "Down with the tyrant! Outlaw him! Outlaw him!" A handful of Napoleon's soldiers with fixed bayonets good-humoredly evicted the members from the hall. Later that night a few came back and under Lucien's direction helped write a new constitution. The executive power was to be held by three consuls, of which Napoleon was the first.

Using his dictatorial powers and driving energy, Napoleon immediately set out to solve the problems facing France from within and without. He set up the "Code Napoléon," laws he felt were excellent, just, and exact. The value of the franc was definitely fixed, and taxes were regularly collected. Some of the money was used to begin a system of schools for everyone. Other social reforms were put into effect, including the protection of all children under fifteen having a legal claim to their father's support. Napoleon then signed an agreement with the Pope that the Catholic Church was to be the official church of France. The people settled down fairly happily with their strong-minded master.

Still to be reckoned with were the enemies the Revolution had made for France. In 1801 Napoleon beat the Austrians again, waging an astonishing battle. He led his troops over the treacherous snowy Alps, and his men made huge sledges from pine trees and tugged, heaved, dug, and sweated until somehow they reached the other side of the mountains and achieved a successful surprise attack. He dared not invade England because of the impossibility of defeating the British fleet, so he made temporary peace with that country.

At home, a few royalist nobles who had escaped the Reign of Terror had returned to oppose Napoleon. Quickly he had their leaders seized and killed. To make sure of his absolute control, he had himself elected First Consul for life.

But this was not enough. He was concerned about not having an heir. By unanimous vote he had himself proclaimed Emperor of the French, a title that could be passed on to his family. He brought the Pope to Paris to crown him Emperor in Notre Dame. Then as his wife Josephine knelt before him, Napoleon crowned her Empress of the French. He had married the attractive Creole widow Josephine de Beauharnais, six years his senior, early in his career; so that the gap in their ages should not be recorded at their wedding, each claimed to be twenty-eight. The coronation ceremony is brilliantly recorded in a painting that hangs in the Louvre.

The French Empire now included half of Europe—France, Belgium, Holland, parts of Switzerland, Germany, and Italy—and 100 million people. In France Napoleon restricted all the liberties of the people, had absolute control over the press, and imposed new and heavier taxes. But he also made France rich with new industries and secured the position of Paris as one of the greatest and wealthiest cities in the world. He added new buildings, such as the Invalides, a home for soldiers. To celebrate his victories, he had the avenue of the Champs Elysées widened and planted with trees and the ridge to which it leads crowned with the Arc de Triomphe. As he captured each country, he brought its paintings and statues to the museums of Paris.

Napoleon's court at the Tuileries, filled with people to whom he gave titles, was dazzling, with a new style of furniture and a new mode of clothing—"Empire style." The furnishings used the Emperor's initials and his emblem, the bee; military trophies; and after the successful winning of Egypt, Egyptian motifs.

Tables with claw feet became all the rage and a most popular piece was a bed shaped like a gondola or sleigh.

Marie Antoinette's dressmaker, who had fled to England during the Revolution, now returned with a Grecian-type dress similar to those worn by the English peasants. The thin chemise gowns were decorated with flowers and ribbons. The long, straight skirts sometimes had waistlines only four inches below the neck, leaving much of a lady's upper body exposed. Empress Josephine introduced the long train to the court dress. Men stopped wearing powdered wigs and began to wear full-length trousers and polished top hats. Going out to dine, to see and be seen, was the order of the day.

Napoleon reached the height of his power between 1808 and 1812. Whenever he saw a throne, he said he had to sit on it. During this time he divorced Josephine because no heir to the throne had been born. He married into an old and proud royal family, choosing Marie Louise, daughter of Francis I of Austria. To Napoleon's joy, a son was born the following year and he crowned him King of Rome.

Napoleon's fatal battle was in 1812. He invaded Russia with an army of 450,000 men. When he marched on Moscow, the Russians burned it. For four days the capital city raged in flames. Napoleon's forces were reduced to 100,000 starving, tired soldiers. A painting in the Musée de l'Armée depicts the remnants of the Grand Army following Napoleon's carriage on the dismal retreat, while stragglers butcher a horse amid dead and dying comrades.

Now no longer victorious, Napoleon's enemies gained courage to attack. He lost battles in Germany. Then France was invaded by armies of Prussians, of Germans and Russians. By 1814 Napoleon was crushed and forced to abdicate in favor, he thought, of his infant son.

But Charles Maurice de Talleyrand, his former Foreign Minister, had other plans. Able, ambitious, and totally scheming, he had foreseen the overthrow of his master. He succeeded in persuading Czar Alexander of Russia that Louis XVIII, the Bourbon King living in exile, should claim the throne. The Emperor's hopes of passing his title to his son were futile. Marie Louise and the child went to Austria and Napoleon was never to see either of them again.

In the courtyard of the palace of Fontainebleau, Napoleon took leave of his beloved Old Guard. He said a few simple words and embraced the Guard's commander. As he turned to enter the carriage that would take him to exile on the island of Elba, his comrades in battle sobbed.

A last chapter to Napoleon's amazing story took place during a period of one hundred days. Early in March 1815 he set sail for Cannes, France, with a thousand men in seven little frigates. The peasants who had shouted insults now cheered him, for the reigning King Louis XVIII proved to be totally incompetent—more concerned with eating than ruling. When the King's troops arrived to intercept Napoleon, he greeted them as old friends who had fought at his side. Dismounting from his horse, he threw open his cloak and stood before them, saying, "If there is one among you who wishes to kill his Emperor, let him come forward and do so. Here I am." It was a daring act but it worked. The troops joined him.

Napoleon did manage to overtake Paris and then march on Prussia. But in Belgium the British Duke of Wellington defeated him at the Battle of Waterloo. That was the end of Napoleon Bonaparte. As a last gesture of power, he proclaimed his son, Napoleon II, Emperor of France. But his wishes were ignored. The unhappy King of Rome, then in Austria, died before he was twenty-one without ever gaining a throne.

The fallen Emperor lived out his six remaining years on St. Helena, a British island off the west coast of Africa. There, surrounded by a few companions and servants, he spent his time bitterly arguing with the governor, writing his life story and growing fatter and fatter. Boredom and illness gradually killed him.

THE WAY OF GLORY

After nineteen years the British Government agreed to release the Emperor's remains so he could be brought back to Paris for the long-awaited grandiose state funeral. Carefully the precious cargo was loaded onto the ship *Belle Poule* on St. Helena. The Prince of Joinville, son of the Citizen King Louis Philippe, and five hundred officials accompanied the body back to Paris. There a hearse "high as a golden mountain," as described by Victor Hugo, and drawn by sixteen white horses—four abreast—carried the Little Corporal through the Arc de Triomphe, the gateway Napoleon had given his capital, down the Champs-Elysées and over the Seine to the Church of the Invalides.

The Arc de Triomphe at the Place de l'Etoile was commissioned by Napoleon in 1806 to celebrate the victories of the French armies. Under the arch a flame burns in the simple slab in the ground that serves as a Tomb of the Unknown Soldier. There are several carved reliefs but the best is the one on the right as seen facing the Champs-Elysées. The militant glory and the unbridled terror of the French Revolution are captured in this dramatic sculpture, "The Marseillaise." It portrays the goddess of war calling Frenchmen to arms to defend the nation.

Ascend the Arc by either stairs or elevator for a superb view 165 feet above the ground. It is open 10 A.M. to 5 P.M. daily except Tuesday. Fee: 1 F (18 cents).

The Etoile, below, focal point of twelve avenues, is called "the Star" because of its shape. The broad avenues were part of one of history's most ambitious pieces of town planning, conceived by Napoleon III and completed by Baron Haussmann, who had been chosen Prefect of Paris for this purpose. The Emperor was determined to make Paris the finest capital in the world. To accomplish his purpose, many beautiful and historic streets and houses in the old quarters had to be destroyed.

The Invalides. The best way to approach the buildings is over the Pont Alexandre III. You will spot Napoleon's tomb easily. It is under the building with the golden dome. Beyond the garden, pass through the gateway leading to the Court of Honor. At the far end in a second-story niche is the statue "Le Petit Caporal" (the Little Corporal), the soldiers' nickname for Napoleon. For years it crowned the Vendôme Column in the square of the same name. The entrance to the church, the first stop, is from the gallery, where old guns can be seen. At the foot of one of the steps is a "taxi of the Marne," one of the unusual vehicles that saved France by carrying troops from Paris to the Marne during World War I.

The Church of St. Louis des Invalides, open 10 A.M. to 5 P.M. daily except Tuesday, free, has in Napoleon's chapel (St. Nicolas) an interesting display of souvenirs from his last exile to St. Helena: the death mask of the Emperor; the stone slabs covering his tomb; and at the back, the copper coffin and velvet covering used to bring back his body.

Turn left when you leave the church, and go to the Western Gallery for the next visit.

The Musée de l'Armée is open 10 A.M. to noon and 1:30 to 5 P.M. except Tuesday. Admission: 1 F (18 cents).

With military displays ranging from ancient armor to the Armistice bugle of World War I, the splendid collection is the greatest of its kind in the world. It is divided into two galleries.

The ground floor of the GALERIE DE L'OCCIDENT has every type of armor from sober decorative pieces to warlike ones, all worn by famous historical figures. In the Francis I room are three beautiful examples of equestrian armor (1400–1500); note particularly the one owned by Elector Palatine Othon Henri.

What a huge man he was at the age of thirty. Henry II's armor, made in 1545, was decorated with his monogram, and Catherine de Médicis' and Diane de Poitiers' with emblems of Diana the Huntress (the bow and the quiver). By their side is the half-armor of Henry's two sons (Francis II and Charles IX). The Rufin and Accory rooms contain the famous suit known as the "armor of the lions," one of the most richly decorated pieces of the museum, designed for Francis I in 1540. The turned-up ties on the shoes of some of the suits may have been a substitute for built-in spurs, made in reverse. The Oriental Room has the strange war attire worn by the Emperor of China, along with Japanese armor made of blackened blades or lacquered skin.

Exhibits on the second level (first floor) feature paintings and mementos of World War I, including the Armistice bugle on which Corporal Sellier sounded the cease-fire in 1918 (1914–18 Room), the last dispatch, and uniforms worn by the French army. The third floor has additional mementos from this war.

On the other side, GALERIE DE L'ORIENT, are displays more closely connected with Napoleon. The SALLE TURENNE contains Napoleon's uniform, a gray frock coat (showing how short he was); the hat he wore at St. Helena; and his personal weapons. The VAUBAN ROOM is probably one of the most impressive in the museum. A succession of eighteen models traces the history of soldiers on horseback. Each is completely restored, re-creating the uniforms, equipment, harnesses, and arms of the French mounted troops through 1940.

The most brilliant, glittering uniforms belong to the cavalry during Napoleon's reign. Boys, sometimes under seventeen, longed to be part of the adventure of the cavalry. Promotions came so fast to men so young, who knew what the future held? The uniforms for each division were the same. But each group tried to outshine the other in color, gold braids, brass buttons, and flair.

The 1st Hussars' standard was "lovelocks" (as the curls on

the temples were called), mustaches, and two pigtails. For the fresh young trooper still not old enough to shave, a barber would be enlisted to provide the missing parts until they grew in. The lack of a mustache was remedied by a pot of blacking. With two strokes of a finger, a fine, sweeping mustache was created.

When Napoleon took charge of the army, the cavalry was composed of the "heavies," the "light" cavalry, and the dragoons. He kept the same divisions but changed the number of each, cutting down the heavies, the cuirassiers and carbineers. (Their uniforms are seen in one of the cases.) It was difficult to find horses that could carry large men in heavy armor. They wore both breastplate and backplate, but instead of the cocked hat, they had a steel helmet topped by a long horsehair plume. The heavy cavalry was kept in reserve to strike decisive blows at crucial moments.

A few more exhibits are particularly noteworthy. In the second-floor NAPOLEON ROOM is the Emperor's favorite bench at St. Helena, the bed in which he died, and a case with mounted figures of his horse Vizir and the dog he had in exile on Elba. The third floor has a tremendous collection of model soldiers made of tin, pewter, and cardboard, presented in every conceivable size against the background of historical scenes. The war uniforms date from ancient times to the nineteenth century.

After you leave the museum, follow the Metz corridor to Napoleon's tomb.

The Church of the Dome is open 10 A.M. to 5:30 P.M. daily. Fee: 1 F (18 cents), includes guided tour of Napoleon's tomb.

In the center of the church is a sunken vault. Below is the crypt carved of red porphyry, the funeral stone of Roman emperors. Napoleon's body was placed in six coffins, each one inside the other. The first is of sheet iron, the second of mahogany, the next two of lead, the fifth of ebony, and the last of oak.

The scenes on the walls around the crypt depict the Emperor's accomplishments—among them the "Code Napoléon," which forms the basis of French law today. Above the entrance to the tomb are engraved Napoleon's own words, "I wish my body to rest near the banks of the Seine, in the midst of the French people I love so well." The colossal figures surrounding the tomb represent his major victories.

Recently, a French historian has made the shocking charge that the real remains of Napoleon are not in the tomb. To support his case, he states that when the French authorities in 1840 went to claim the body, they asked to see it before signing a receipt. The British reluctantly agreed, but set an odd hour for the meeting—midnight, when only flickering torches could be used. He cites evidence of the differences in how Napoleon was supposed to be dressed according to the records and what the French authorities actually encountered. The final claim is that Cipriani, Napoleon's look-alike butler, is buried in the tomb and Napoleon is buried in Westminster Abbey in a crypt marked "Undercroft." Whether there is any truth to the claim remains to be proven.

The final resting places of Napoleon's relatives are in the chapels on the floor level. Joseph and Jerome Bonaparte, his brothers, and the King of Rome, his son, lie here.

The front of the Church of the Dome is on the Avenue de Tourville. Go to your right past the Ecole Militaire, the academy Napoleon attended, to the Place Joffre on the left. As you turn the corner, your next adventure is in full sight.

The Tour Eiffel has all platforms open daily at 10 A.M. July 1 to September 15. First and second platforms open to midnight May 1 to September 30. Top platform closes 6:30 P.M. Fee: depends on level of platform.

Cries of outrage greeted Gustave Eiffel's tower being built on the Seine to advertise France's new steel industry and to attract visitors to the Paris Exhibition of 1889. From three hundred noted Parisians came a bitter attack on "that loathsome tin construction." Author Guy de Maupassant went into exile in protest against "this tall, lanky pyramid, this assemblage of iron ladders."

But the tower kept growing, defying predictions that it would collapse. Engineer Eiffel knew steel. He had used it in a great Paris department store and had spun it into bridges on three continents. He also built the inner steel framework of the Statue of Liberty in New York harbor and constructed the first iron bridge, which took half as long to complete and cost only half as much as one of stone. Experience had taught him so well that in March 1889 he brought the tower to its full 984 feet without altering one of the 2.5 million rivets. At the time, it was the tallest structure in the world.

The tower's cost was over 1 million dollars. The French Government had given Eiffel only $292,000, so they let him keep all the admission fees for twenty years. In the first year, Eiffel was able to earn back almost the whole cost of the tower.

At sixty Eiffel experimented with effects of air currents on buildings and airplanes. He set aside a room at the top of his tower as a laboratory where scientists still study winds and weather.

Whether or not you're an aspiring astronomer (stars), nephologist (clouds), anamologer (wind), or physiogeologer (earth), the panoramic sight from the top is like "a stairway leading to infinity." On a clear day you can see a distance of over forty miles. Paris looks as if it is an immense map. It is particularly radiant at sunset.

IMPRESSIONS OF MODERN PARIS

Another Napoleon was destined to leave his mark. A new constitution said the government should consist of one legislative assembly and a president of the republic, elected by the people.

Napoleon's nephew, Prince Louis Napoleon, a dapper little man with a moustache like knitting needles, was waiting in exile for his chance. In 1848 his opportunity came through a series of lucky situations. France was exhausted. The middle class wanted peace. The Catholics were for him and the followers of his uncle voted in his favor out of respect for his great name. He was elected by over 5.5 million votes. Gradually he changed the laws, giving himself more power. Finally, in 1852, he became the Emperor Napoleon III, and France had its Second Empire.

Haunted by the memory of former street riots, Napoleon III had Baron Haussmann, his prefect, make a new plan for the worn and shabby, overcrowded city. He drew a large ring of wide new boulevards where the walls had enclosed the small old city. Other new boulevards radiated across it. The city was opened up to light and air. Miles of streets were planted with trees. New parks and gardens were built, with ponds, statues, wide walks, and fountains of water in rushing cascades. But to be on the safe side, the open spaces where the boulevards came together could, if necessary, be used as sites for cannons to shoot down advancing mobs.

In spite of many more surface political turmoils and wars, the period that followed came to be known as the "Century of Progress." Queen Marie Amélie bravely stepped onto the first passenger train, which took her from Paris to St. Germain. Too dangerous a venture for her husband, Louis Philippe, she reported to him, "It travels at a terrific speed without discomfort to the passengers." The inaugural test of a steamboat in the Seine by the American inventor Robert Fulton was a resounding success, but the Emperor shook his head skeptically.

It was a time of enterprise everywhere. Scientists were uncovering new inventions: gas for factories, gas for lighting, electric telegraph, and photography were modernizing the world. In Paris talented writers were creating poetry, novels, and books that brought new ideas to enrich people's minds—Victor Hugo, Alexandre Dumas, Honoré de Balzac, and George Sand.

It was also the golden age of the Latin Quarter, or Left Bank. Struggling students jammed the revived schools of the university to learn from men such as the scientist Louis Pasteur. Aspiring artists flocked to study at the schools. Both groups had one thing in common—very little money. Necessity made them instant close companions. The cafés and cramped studios were the settings where they could share whatever small income they had. This atmosphere became the background for a best-selling book, *La Vie de Bohème* (*Life of a Bohemian*). The novel was adapted into a play and then an opera, *La Bohème,* which is still popular. So the term Bohemian, from an old gypsy word meaning careless of money, dedicated to art and being different, became the name for a person living in this part of the city. As the Left Bank became overcrowded and the cost of living got higher, the Bohemians started a rival district in Montmartre across the Seine.

AN ART REVOLUTION

Six men banded together defiantly to launch their own revolution. Armed with rainbow colors and canvases, they were fighting for the right to picture the actual world, to show more truly what they saw with their eyes at that particular moment. Artists before them were content to paint scenes of past history, legends, and portraits. These young revolutionists wanted to capture a world at a glance and translate it into color for everyone to enjoy.

The first thing they did was to go out into the open air and get to work. All painting had been done indoors until then. They selected the strongest contrasts of light and shadow in order to use the brightest colors—the orange rays of the setting sun, trees and grass at high noon, flowers and snow in every degree of light. These were vivid, dancing colors of nature which had never before been seen on canvas.

And with what zeal these men worked. They stared at the sun till their eyes ached and peered endlessly at the leaves to see the many tiny blotches of color that blended together to make green. Shadows were not merely darker shades of the same color, but different colors often reflected from other objects. The revolutionists soon discovered that sunlight was composed of three basic colors—red, yellow, and blue. The rest are combinations: red and yellow make orange, blue and yellow become green, and red and blue blend into violet. Some of these sitting side by side have merely to be mixed by the eye.

Try an experiment. Look at the yellow sun set in the blue sky for a short time and then close your tired eyes. With your eyes shut, you'll see greenish disks everywhere. Light plays tricks. Looking at these artists' works closely, you might see flat spots and splashes of bright color; but step back and what a sight meets the eye. Brilliant light fills the scene as it never before had in paintings.

The year was 1874. When the six men—Renoir, Degas, Cézanne, Sisley, Pissarro, and Monet—were constantly refused showings by the official galleries, they decided to have their own exhibit in what they called "The Gallery of the Rejected." The opening was greeted with jeers and looks of horror. Lunatics! Disasters! One of Monet's paintings was listed as "Sunrise, An Impression." A smart reporter, picking up the title, jokingly called all the painters in the show "Impressionists." The word caught on, at first as a mark of ridicule, but as the men refused to be put down and they began to become popular, it became an honorable title for all painters recording sensations of light and color.

EDOUARD MANET (1832–83) was one of the early painters to break away from tradition. Born wealthy, he convinced his parents when he reached his sixteenth birthday that only in art could he hope to achieve fame. His training and studies were based on the work of the classic painters—Hals, Rembrandt, Velázquez, and Goya. Carefully copying each picture, he analyzed how the colors were put together. His own style had more lively brushwork and use of color. When Manet broke loose with his startling shades of light, the critics and general public were shocked and angry. Who would dare create a scene with a nude feminine bather and her escorts like "Luncheon on the Grass"? There followed another canvas of a nude young woman, this time reclining on a bed, "Olympia." Standing behind the woman is a maid offering some flowers, while a black cat with arched back watches. How dare the painter pose and paint his models in bright sunlight, out of doors? This was a radical departure from the colorless kind of studio painting the Parisian art lover was accustomed to. Until he died, Manet remained the center of violent controversy.

CLAUDE MONET (1840–1926), a close friend of Manet's, was the leader of the Impressionists. He was a poor young man with the strong belief that a painter *must* work out of doors. One summer he had a trench dug in his garden into which he lowered a huge canvas by means of a pulley. From this underground spot he painted a huge picture, "Women in the Garden," showing ladies at leisure against the sunlight streaming through leafy trees. Monet wanted so much to be an observer of life that he turned a tiny houseboat into a studio and traveled along the Seine in search of scenes to paint. Totally possessed with his desire to know a subject fully, he often painted the same object several times, since it appeared different to him at each different time of day. The Rouen cathedral is done in several pictures, shown in gray morning mist to full sunshine.

Do not think, though, that the Impressionists were interested only in landscapes and the effect of light on the surfaces of things. AUGUSTE RENOIR (1841–1919) and EDGAR DE-GAS (1834–1917) used their techniques to paint charming portraits and studies of people. Renoir loved to paint scenes of dancing and revelry and beautiful women and children, fresh and healthy, with pink cheeks and large eyes. "The Swing" depicts a fine summer day. Two young men in straw hats are talking to a girl in a swing, as a little child gazes up in wonder. The park is the garden of the Rue Cortot in Montmartre, and the girl, Jeanne, Renoir's favorite model.

Degas' ambition was "to observe his models through a keyhole," to catch them off guard in unusual lifelike poses. An admirer of photography, he painted horse races, ballet dancers, and women in bathtubs with a camera's eye, with the realism of a snapshot. He was marvelously skillful with pastels (dry crayons), making study after study of women. These pictures offended French taste and he was accused of depicting only ugliness. Degas stopped showing his pictures and lived as a recluse for thirty years, avoided by all because of his rages and sarcasm.

All of the paintings described were done at the beginning of the art revolution. They can be seen in one of Paris' most delightful museums, the Jeu de Paume, along with hundreds of other Impressionist canvases in dazzling fairy-tale colors.

The greatest sculptor of the nineteenth century, AUGUSTE RODIN (1840–1917) was also what might be called an Impressionist. He fashioned his figures to look as if they were told to freeze in mid-action. How does a man actually look when he is walking? We know that when one foot is on the ground, the other is slightly raised, but do we see this with our eyes? Or is the motion too fast for our eyes to catch? In his group of walking figures "Burghers of Calais," Rodin began the practice of showing only the parts of the body that seemed important to him. He also planned that the statues could be seen from any angle with equal interest.

Now let's get a close-up look at the artists' masterpieces, the places that inspired them, and what remains of where they worked, lived, and spent their more trouble-free hours.

LIGHT, CANVAS, AND CREATIVE PAINTERS

Musée du Jeu de Paume, Place de la Concorde. Open daily 10 A.M. to 5 P.M. except Tuesday and holidays. Fee: 3 F (54 cents), Sunday 1 F (18 cents).

A nineteenth-century indoor tennis court now houses this part of the Louvre, which displays the Impressionists' paintings. Diagrams, dates, and important parts of the art movement are clearly shown.

EDOUARD MANET—"The Fifer" was another reject by the judges of the galleries. The sad-eyed little boy seems almost separated from the background, entirely surrounded by air. There is a difference of opinion about the model's identity. One source says it is a band boy sent over by a friend of Manet. Another account points out the strong resemblance to the artist's model, Victorine Meurend. This would explain how the young woman posing would be wearing a costume much too big for her slight body.

CLAUDE MONET—"The Gare St. Lazare" is a reminder that the railway was still a novelty. Artists who did their work out of doors, almost always in the suburbs of Paris, often traveled to their destination by train. They studied with immense interest the play of steam and smoke constantly changing with the wind and light. For them catching the passing moment—such as the smoke of the locomotivelike clouds reflected in a pond—was part of something their eyes had just discovered, which was constantly seen differently.

"The Asparagus" has an unusual story. Monet was requested to do a still life of a large bunch of vegetables. When he delivered it and received his money, the price he received was much more than he expected. To show his appreciation, Monet painted another picture, this time with only one asparagus in it.

EDGAR DEGAS—"The Dancing Class" started a new trend of painting from a high angle. The lines on the floor and the smaller figures in the background give the feeling of a long room with plenty of space in the center for the dancers to practice. But now the ballet master, who stands with his cane, is in full command. The girls in the foreground do not seem too pleased. One stands heavily on her feet awaiting her chance to turn into a graceful swan. The other, seated on the piano, is twisting in order to scratch her back. Only the small, bushy dog seems unaffected by the rehearsal. Soon the future ballerinas will adopt queenly airs as they take flight. Right now they are nicknamed "petits rats" (little rats), possibly because they sound like mice squeaking as they rush about backstage.

AUGUSTE RENOIR—"Le Moulin de la Galette" derived its name from one of several windmills in Montmartre. Inside, one could sit and eat a griddlecake, the specialty of the area. Around it was an open-air café where on Sunday students and artists came to dance. Renoir was intrigued by the cheerful crowd and found a lodging nearby at 78 Rue Corot, so that he could return every day and paint the people and the setting. He lived in the same studio for over four years and the mill became the background for several portraits.

PAUL CÉZANNE—"Apples and Oranges" displays the artist's concern to correct the mistakes he believed the other Impressionists were making. The outlines of the objects in the paintings were being overwhelmed by the brightly colored brush strokes. Carefully Cézanne set out each item in his still-life pictures and painted over and over each one until the simple bowls of fruit seemed solid and firm. To strengthen the composition further, he would distort the shapes—a bowl became not quite round, a table tilted forward. By emphasizing shapes, he made design more important than it had ever been before.

VINCENT VAN GOGH—"Vincent's Room at Arles" looks like such a peaceful setting. So it was when he arrived. The climate and sky enchanted him. "Here I see everything in a new way." Then an extremely bad bout of hard work and sitting for long hours in the hot sun seemed to have a dreadful effect on him. In an attack of madness, he tried to kill himself; then to punish himself, he cut off a piece of his own ear. This is the room Van Gogh was living in at the time of the drama. He stayed for only a few months before his nervous attacks got worse and he was admitted to an asylum, where he stayed for a year. All of his paintings with bold, swirling lines cry out in a desperate effort to transfer his anguish to canvas. His pictures of houses almost shake and topple over, all to express the agony of the man himself—the intense feelings, the faith, the suffering that went into each painting.

PAUL GAUGUIN—"Women of Tahiti" is part of a series sometimes called "On the Beach." The artist, a close friend of Van Gogh's, was a French businessman whose great interest in painting drove him to seek the simple life. And so Gauguin went to the South Seas to live with the natives as one of them and to paint their way of life. The picture, painted during Gauguin's first visit, accents the squat bodies of his sitters and makes them fatter by giving them thick wrists and necks. The figures may seem drawn in a childish way, primitive, but this is not important, for it is done as part of a pattern, just as men in the jungle seem to be part of nature.

HENRI DE TOULOUSE-LAUTREC—"Jane Avril Dancing" almost tells the entire bitter, sad story of the artist's life. Afflicted from birth with a weakness of the bones, in his childhood he twice stumbled and fell, breaking both thighs. His torso developed normally, but his legs shriveled into those of a midget and he was a strange figure indeed when standing.

Degas suggested he study and paint dancers. While Degas chose the ballet, Lautrec picked the sinners and denizens of the underworld. This portrait of Jane Avril was done at the Moulin Rouge, a celebrated café-concert hall. She was a dancing sensation and went under the name of La Mélenite. Lautrec was enchanted by her movements. "She turned to and fro, graceful, light on her feet, a trifle mad, pale, thin and aristocratic. Her dance steps were always sideways. She always danced alone. She always wore appropriate colorful costumes to go with her movements." He was even more attracted to her face, "wan, nervous, ailing," and always lonely. She came from a noble background and was somehow worthy of a better setting. Like Lautrec she seemed abandoned. He painted her many times: dancing, arriving at the Moulin Rouge, putting on her gloves; and views of her from the front and back.

"Cha-U-Kao, the Female Clown" is a portrait of another performer at the Moulin Rouge, showing her comic yellow tutu skirt spiraling around her large frame and ending at the top of the white tufted wig. The scene is apparently a private room in a restaurant. A cloth is on the corner of the table with a napkin just about visible, while above, a mirror reflects the figure of an old man in evening dress.

GEORGES SEURAT—"The Circus" is composed of countless tiny circular dots, every single one set down with a view to its exact effect on the other dots. Seurat and others who painted like him were named Pointillists. The picture is hard to see, and unless looked at from exactly the right distance it appears like a shower of confetti.

Parisians loved the excitement of the circus in the nineteenth century. The artist spent long hours in the Cirque Medrano, which just recently stopped giving performances. He attempted to pin down movement on canvas. Of all the acts, he favored the bareback rider. Probably no painter has ever created a lighter equestrienne. She floats, weightless. There is sharp contrast between the elegant performer and the motionless audience.

The Tuileries Gardens next to the Jeu de Paume is the perfect place to relax and recall for a moment the splendid array of canvases. Here is an Eden in a historic park. On a sultry day in 1792 the King and Queen and the little Dauphin came with some loyal friends, hurrying to refuge with the Assembly in the Riding School. The armed mob was storming their palace of the Tuileries.

You can follow their path and discover a secret door. Walk along the eastern side by the terrace wall just where it turns into the Quai des Tuileries, and there you'll see a stone lion standing on a high base. Just beyond is a small door. Out of it in 1848 rushed the last Bourbon king, Louis Philippe, with Queen Amélie, to a waiting carriage. A revolution was stirring and they wanted no part of it. The mob almost stopped them, but at the last minute shouted, "Oh well, we are no assassins; let him go." And the royal couple ran.

Choose from a variety of activities: Rent a chair (.25 F or 4 cents) and bask in the sun; ride a prancing charger on the portable merry-go-round; watch puppets—Guignol, a ridiculous policeman, and his plotting pal Gnafron battle away (once or twice a day in the afternoon during the summer); rent a miniature sailboat to try your skill in steering it to all corners of the world in the pools; or go roller skating. It's a good way to get to know French young people. One other pastime is watching a game of boules, a sort of bowling with the rules of horseshoe tossing. In just a few minutes you'll catch on to how it's played.

The Louvre Museum, Palais du Louvre, is open daily 10 A.M. to 5 P.M. except Tuesday and holidays. Fee: 3 F (54 cents), Sunday free.

The problem here is how to tackle such a splendid and immense collection of works of art in the time available. If time is really short, see the five world-famous statues and paintings:

the Venus de Milo, whose noble beauty is the subject of continued debate (some feel the statue is finer because the arms are missing); the Winged Victory, discovered on Samothrace, a Greek island, which stands ready to fly from the stone base atop the grand staircase; the Seated Scribe, an ageless Egyptian statue whose unknown creator was asked to make a lifelike portrait (parts of the eyes are inlaid with glass to make the expression seem real); the "Mona Lisa" or "Gioconda," the Leonardo da Vinci painting named after the noblewoman with the puzzling expression (the most expensive face in the world); and "The Marriage at Cana," the Louvre's largest canvas, by Paolo Veronese, depicts a Bible feast crowded with 132 figures (the artist plays the viola surrounded by his friends).

It is very difficult to spend more than about an hour in a museum without getting exhausted. If you have a chance for a second visit, divide your time between the different schools of paintings, but decide beforehand which is your main interest. As you go through the rooms, make a note about which one you might like to return to. A tour of the French School of the nineteenth century will offer glorious visual echoes of the past.

Outstanding pictorial moments are: David's "The Coronation of Napoleon I by Pope Pius VII," which shows the Emperor refusing to entrust the supreme moment of the crowning ceremony to anyone but himself. The artist's first version showed him rudely turning his back on the Pope and crowning himself. The last rendering shows the more gracious act of crowning the Empress. Napoleon also insisted that the artist paint the Pope's hand raised as if in blessing. Ingres' "Joan of Arc at the Coronation of Charles VII"; Delacroix's "The 28th of July 1820," showing the goddess of liberty leading her men onward; and Courbet's "The Artist's Studio," portraying at work the artist who strongly influenced Manet to develop Impressionist art.

A third visit might include some time in the GALERIE D'APOL-

LON to see the crown jewels of France and a half hour in the Egyptian-Etruscan section. By this time you'll be thoroughly familiar with the layout—perhaps making later visits more interesting.

MONTMARTRE'S LINGERING MAGIC

Let the old-fashioned funicular take you up the steep slope. The cable car station is located where Place St. Pierre and Rue Tardieu meet. As you rise 238 feet above the Seine, picture the hill as it was. Here centuries ago the Parisii had their temple to the pagan gods Mercury and Mars. St. Denis stooped, picked up his severed head, and carried it over the hilltop for a mile or two before he fell dead. It became popularly known as the "Butte" (French for "hill") in the fifteenth century after the Battle of Agincourt, when English archers used it for shooting butts (ranges). The shape of the hill was changed when people started to dig into it to extract the ingredients of plaster from it. Plaster is a quick-setting paste. If you break your arm or leg it is set in a cast known everywhere as "plaster of Paris."

By the seventeenth century a series of windmills dotted the hillside, nestled between farms, vineyards, woods, and grazing fields for sheep and cattle. The wayside village was considered the far outskirts of Paris and became notorious for its secret dives and dark cellars where hardened criminals met to plot their next job. For nearly two centuries Parisians were terrified to come anywhere near until writers and painters rediscovered the countrified atmosphere and wonderful views. Rent and food were cheap and the artists enjoyed painting the old, winding streets, the squares, the taverns, and the windmills. Quickly they established cheerful cafés, restaurants, and dance halls similar to the ones they had frequented on the Left Bank. Groups of men and women, many shabbily but colorfully dressed, met in inexpensive bars and cafés, sat at wooden tables on rough chairs, and talked their ideas way into the night. Soon the elite of Paris followed to see the new Bohemian quarter.

Now that you've arrived at the terrace in front of the white **Basilica of Sacré Coeur** (Sacred Heart), climb the steps for the wonderful panorama that unfolds. Straight ahead is Notre Dame and the Panthéon, while on the right is the Eiffel Tower. (You are about level with the second landing.) Over the main door of the basilica are equestrian statues of St. Louis and Joan of Arc. The interior is richly decorated with mosaics. On the right is the Army Chapel, with another statue of St. Joan. One of the largest bells in the world, the Savoyarde, hangs in the steeple. It weighs nineteen tons.

The Church of St. Pierre, one of the oldest in Paris, is next to the Sacré Coeur. Inside are the remains of a still older church; the four columns of the choir are the original Roman pillars.

The Place du Tertre (hilltop) looks like a small village square of a tiny French town, certainly not like one in the city of Paris. The narrow cobblestone street is usually crowded with visitors watching the artists at work dressed in beret, colorful blue jeans, and a gray sweater, applying paint with a palette knife. The artist Francisque Poulbot (1879–1946) lived nearby. His paintings of sad-eyed children became so famous that all children from Montmartre are lovingly nicknamed "Poulbot's kids." At number 3 in the square is the first town hall (1790) and next to it the post office, with a single employee pleased to stamp your postcards. In front of La Mère Catherine, the square's famous restaurant, you get another special look at the Sacré Coeur.

The Musée Historial de Montmartre, off the narrow Passage Trainee, is open 10 A.M. to noon and 2 to 7 P.M. Fee: 3 F (54 cents).

The wax museum's fourteen tableaux depict different periods in the history of Montmartre. Some scenes show artists like Toulouse-Lautrec, others the period of the Revolution with Danton and Lafayette, still others more recent people—Georges Clemenceau, Montmartre's earliest mayor (1871) and France's noted premier in World War I. Tours are conducted in English.

Find the Rue du Mont Cenis on the right and then the tiny street or passageway, the Rue Rustique. Here are the scenes that intrigued the painters, old-fashioned lampposts and window boxes overhanging the alley. On to the Rue Cortot and a look at the kind of dives the artists lived in. At number 12 lived Renoir, Maurice Utrillo (1883–1955) (whose scenes of Montmartre are world-famous), and Raoul Dufy (1877–1953). Right again on the Rue des Saules to the **Clos Montmartre,** the only vineyard in Paris recalling the old farm days. Each fall there is a joyous harvest celebration with girls dressed in cancan costumes.

The Musée du Vieux Montmartre along the Rue St. Vincent is open 2 to 5 P.M. every day except Tuesday. Fee: 2 F (36 cents). The models, pictures, and posters will give you a good idea of the quality of Montmartre's history.

Le Lapin Agile at the corner of Rue St. Vincent and Rue des Saules was a little wayside inn, the popular meeting place of such artists as Picasso and Utrillo. The weather-beaten sign near the door shows an agile rabbit leaping into a saucepan with a bottle of wine in its paw. The joke of the sign painter became the tavern's name. Artists who could not pay their bills often gave the inn's owner their canvases. Now the masterpieces are worth millions of dollars.

The Moulin de la Galette (Griddlecake Windmill) is farther along St. Vincent toward the Rue Girardon, past run-down cottages with old chimney pots. On the corner of the Rue Lepic stands the celebrated windmill turned dance hall, the scene of Renoir's great paintings. This mill is the last of several that used to stand on La Butte a hundred years ago.

The Place Emile Goudeau is the next stop. Go to the right on the Rue Lepic and ask for directions to Rue Ravignan. In the square look for a poor cracked, ramshackle building at number 13, "Le Bateau-Lavoir." Here lived Pablo Picasso, perhaps the greatest painter of our time, and Amedeo Modigliani (1884–1920), working on his superb portraits known for their extremely long oval-shaped heads and elongated necks. Many others lived here too, never winning great fame, but dreaming of it all the same. Peek in at the narrow wooden passages and you'll see the artists' calling cards tacked on the cracking doors of their studios. The building is named Le Bateau-Lavoir (Laundry Boat) because some of the painters thought it was shaped like the boats from which washerwomen laundered linen in the Seine. Perhaps a bottle of wine at the café helped their imaginations along.

The rest of your walk, on Rue des Martyrs toward the main Boulevard de Clichy, will take you along streets that St. Denis tread centuries ago.

ARTISTS' STUDIOS (THE LEFT BANK)

Musée Rodin, 77 Rue de Varenne, is open 1 to 6 P.M. daily except Tuesday, Sunday till 5 P.M. Fee: 3 F (54 cents), 1.50 F (27 cents) Sunday.

Auguste Rodin lived and sculpted here for many years before his death in 1917. The home has the largest collection of his world-famous statues.

He was so successful that when his first full-scale figure was exhibited, "The Age of Bronze," a life-size naked man, he was accused of making the statue with a plastic cast of the model. To show the charge was false, Rodin at his own expense had photographs and casts made of his model, the Belgian soldier Auguste Neyt, who had posed for eighteen months. It took three years to prove the statue was a work of art, although some critics never accepted it. As his other works appeared, however, Rodin proved that the realism of his figures was due to his skill.

Rodin developed Impressionism in sculpture. He used broken surfaces to make the statues appear to be in a flickering light. This is done by making parts of the stone highly polished and shiny, while the rest is roughly chiseled.

In "The Centauress," a marble monster with a woman's head, trunk, and arms and a horse's body and legs, the figure seems to be growing or racing out of the rough stone, a style the sculptor had learned from study of Michelangelo. Rodin was the first to make unfinished statues accepted artistically.

For his last twenty years, he worked on the gigantic design of two doors, "The Gates of Hell." These were commissioned by the French Government for a museum, but were never used for that purpose. The masterpiece, located in the front of the building, is a glorious summation of the artist's works. Many of the figures on the door were enlarged and made into individual statues. They are found throughout the museum.

The doors were inspired by Dante's poem *The Divine Comedy*.

"The Gates of Hell" has some 186 graceful figures, each moving in all phases of anguish or terror. The famous statue of "The Thinker," originally called "The Poet," is calmly seated just above the doors. At the very top is "The Three Shadows" with their look of peace and contentment. On the doors themselves the figures are tumbling downward, while around the sides there is a sense of floating up toward the heavens. Many of Rodin's most moving works were offsprings of the doors. See how many you can identify when you look at the statues on display inside.

"The Burghers of Calais" is another powerful group of figures, standing near "The Gates of Hell." Rodin's assignment was to re-create from medieval books the heroic sacrifice of six leading citizens of Calais who in 1347 put on sackcloth and gave them-

selves up as hostages to the English in return for the lifting of
an eleven-month siege of the city. The citizens were not pleased
with Rodin's work. They were offended because the figures
looked so forlorn. Walk around the group and see how many
different angles you can find to view. One of the faces resembles
"The Man with the Broken Nose."

While inside notice the turntable easels used for displaying
the statues. These are the actual stands sculptors work on. Take
a few minutes before you leave for a stroll through the garden
behind the museum. It is delightful with its view across to the
gilded dome of the Invalides and the Eiffel Tower.

Refreshments and artist-watching? Head for the Boulevard
St. Germain on the way to the next artist's studio. Window-
shopping is fun, for the shops have the newest mod look, with
light shows and other clever eye-catching devices. Find one of
two cafés—**Les Deux Magôts** (Two Monkeys), number 170, or
the **Café de Flore,** number 172—and try a "tarte au fromage
grand-mére" (cheese and mushroom tart). These two cafés are
the meeting places of artists and writers.

The Place de Fürstenberg is right off the Rue de l'Abbaye.
Here is one of Paris' most enchanting old miniature squares,
shaded by four magnolia trees. Ferdinand Delacroix (1798–
1863) had his studio at number 6, now a museum open daily
10 A.M. noon and 2 to 6 P.M. (closed November 1 to May 1).
For 1 F (18 cents) you see the drawings, the water colors, and
the paintings. But most memorable is the charm of the studio
setting.

The Luxembourg Palace and Gardens are just a few minutes
away. They have kept a few features from their earliest days.
The flower beds, the fountain, and the central walk are part of
the classic 1615 French gardens of Marie de Médicis. There
are unexpected surprises of statues of famous people (George
Sand, Delacroix). The center water basin has sailboats and next
to it the celebrated puppet theater, the Théâtre des Marionnettes

au Jardin Luxembourg (July to October daily at 4 P.M., January to December 31 Thursday and Sunday, also holidays, at 2:30 and 3:30 P.M.). A seat is 1 to 2 F (18 to 36 cents).

A-MARKETING WE WILL GO

Marché aux Puces, (the Flea Market) originally named after the bugs in its cut-rate bedding, is open for business or haggling from 7 A.M. to 7 P.M. on Saturday, Sunday, and Monday. It's a thirty-minute Métro ride from the center of Paris. The stop is Porte de Clignancourt.

Beginning about 1892 the police herded the peddlers into the prairie of St. Ouen, just north of the city. This mishmash beginning grew into a greater mishmash of flimsy shops, covered stalls, and sidewalk displays that extend over four miles. There are individual sections for specific items, from mod clothes on the main street to the side alleys with bric-a-brac, antique coins, and toy soldiers. The market, one of the best in Europe, is fun to explore, but short on bargains.

Marché aux Fleurs, Oiseaux (Bird and Flower Market), Place Louis Lépine on the Ile de la Cité, is open from 9 A.M. till 7 P.M. on Sunday for the birds and every other day 9 A.M. to noon and 2 to 6 P.M. for flowers. The open-air market is always filled with vivid colors or a chorus of peeping sounds. The flowers are inexpensive, and strolling through the market is one of the Parisians' pleasant pastimes.

Marché aux Chiens (Dog Market), Rue Brancion 106, is open Sunday 1 to 4 P.M. Donkeys and mules are sold at the same place Monday, Wednesday, and Friday.

Food Markets (in addition to the Mouffetard, described earlier) are all over the city on different days from 7 A.M. to 1 P.M. Some of the most interesting are Belleville, Buci, Lepic, and Ménilmontant. Maybe your hotel chef or one of his assistants would consent to take you with him some early morning. They are worth visiting, for they tell you a great deal about the people of the country, what they eat, and what they must pay for each item.

Country bread and fruit tarts at Rue du Cherche-Midi 8 off Rue des Sts. Péres—open all day and night.

M. Pierre Poilâné is one of the most beloved and well-known bakery owners in Paris. He or his sons will take you below to the eleventh-century cave where one of the last wood-burning ovens is located. Young boys, working in shifts around the clock, measure exact portions of round balls of natural dough (no chemicals are used). They mold the form and place it on long-handled palettes which are shoved into the heated ovens; the bread and tarts are all prepared by hand. More than one thousand loafs are bought every twenty-four hours.

M. Poilâné, a delightful man, started making a particular bread called "pain de campagne" (country bread) at the urging of a doctor who was worried about the lack of food value in ordinary bread. With the help of several doctors, he developed a special formula made from stone-ground whole wheat flour. His customers come from miles around to sample his delicious creation. Among the famous people who purchase their loaves here are movie stars, dukes and duchesses, and the French premier and his cabinet members.

But his special clients are the artists. After taking a close look at the shop with its rustic atmosphere and picture tiles, ask M. Poilâné if you can visit his gallery of paintings. What a surprise when he opens the door to the adjoining room. The walls are completely covered with artists' versions of his beloved country bread done in every possible style (Impressionistic, realistic, and abstract). Many of the painters are well known. When they leave the city, they show their appreciation for the delectable bread by sending M. Poilâné water-color paintings done on envelopes from the places they travel to around the world. Instead of writing out his name and address the artists interpret both. His name means "hair of the donkey." Somehow, the postman knows where to deliver letters for M. Poilâné.

The Catacombs tour meets at Place Denfert-Rochereau 2 the first and third Saturdays of the month and every Saturday July 1 to October 15. The tour begins at 2 P.M.

In quarries dug by the Romans into the hills lie several million skeletons moved from overcrowded cemeteries in the eighteenth and nineteenth centuries. The eerie galleries are decorated with skulls and bones.

Egout (sewer) tours gather at Place de la Concorde, near the Statue de Lille, the second and fourth Thursdays of May and June, every Thursday July 1 to October 15, and the last Saturday May through September. Tours are at 2, 3, 4, and 5 P.M. Fee: .30 F (6 cents) by boat. Paris sewers are quite clean and a descent into them can be fascinating. You can sail on one main tunnel from the Concorde to the Madeleine.

HOBBIES OR SPECIAL INTERESTS, ANYONE?

If you have a hobby or special interest, you can have lots of fun in Paris. If you don't, here is the perfect place to acquire one. Here are some suggestions.

AQUARIUMS

Palais de Chaillot (Métro stop Trocadéro) is open 10 A.M. to 5:30 P.M. Fee: .75 F (12 cents).

A very fine grotto with fresh-water fish is located in the garden.

Musée des Arts Africains et Océaniens, Avenue Daumesnil

293, is open 10 A.M. to 5 P.M. daily except Tuesday. Fee: 1 F (18 cents), Sunday .50 F (9 cents).

ANIMALS

Guided tours to **Zoos and Stables of the Republican Guard.** Fourth Thursday of every month from May to October. Write or call: Animal Protection Society, Boulevard Berthier 39. Fee: 1 F (18 cents) for young people under eighteen.

ART AND SCULPTURING

L'Atelier, Rue de Vaugirard 130. Classes every Thursday 10 A.M. to noon and 2:30 to 4:30 P.M. in painting, sculpture, and art history. Fee varies.
and wood sculpture. Fee varies.

ASTRONOMY

Les Apprentis Sculpteurs, Rue Ducouëdic 36, clay modeling
Musée du Palais de la Découverte, Grand Palais des Champs-Elysées, Avenue Franklin Roosevelt. Open 10 A.M. to noon and 2 to 6 P.M. daily except Friday. Fee: 1 F (18 cents).

Highlights: planetarium; exhibits of latest achievements; push buttons to set things in motion.

BALLET

Musée de l'Opéra, Place Charles Garnier (inside opera building). Open 10 A.M. to 5 P.M. daily except Sunday. Fee: 1 F (18 cents).

Highlights: miniature opera and ballet scenes; costumes of famous singers; Pavlova's ballet slippers.

CAVE EXPLORING (SPELEOLOGIST)

Spéléo-Club de Paris, Rue La Boetie, ANJou 54-45. Open

daily (except Sunday, Monday, and holidays); closed August and September. Fee: 10 F ($1.80).

Visits can be arranged to some of the most famous caves, caverns, and grottoes.

CIRCUS FAN

Club du Cirque, Rue Bonaparte 31. DAN 87-36. (Closed during July and August).

COINS

Musée Monétaire, Quai de Conti 11. Open daily 11 A.M. to 5 P.M. except Sunday and holidays. Free.

Highlights: history of French currency; workshop and mint where coins are made as you watch (open Tuesday and Thursday afternoon 2 to 3:30 P.M.).

COSTUMES AND FASHION

Musée du Costume, Avenue du Président Wilson 11. Open 10 A.M. to noon daily.

Highlight: five thousand gowns offer French history of fashion designing.

FOLKLORE

Musée des Arts et Traditions Populaires and **Musée de l'Homme Palais de Chaillot,** Place du Trocadéro (East Wing one section of four part museum). Open 10 A.M. to 6 P.M. except Tuesday. Fee: 1.70 F (30 cents). Exhibit keeps changing.

HISTORY

Musée de l'Histoire de France, Rue des Francs-Bourgeois. Open 2 to 5 P.M. daily except Tuesday. Fee: .50 F (19 cents).

Highlights: French history from Middle Ages up to 1848; private diary of Louis XVI, whose sole entry for the fateful date of the siege of the Bastille (July 14, 1789) was "nothing."

MAGIC

Association Française des Artistes Prestigitateurs, Rue de Béarn 13, 887-92-69.

NATURAL HISTORY

Musée National d'Histoire Naturelle, Rue Geoffroy-St. Hilaire (Jardin des Plantes). Gardens open daily 7 A.M. till sunset (summers), 8 A.M. to sunset (winters). Menageries open daily 9 A.M. to 5 P.M. Fee: 2 F (36 cents). Galleries (mineralogy, zoology) open daily except Tuesday.

Highlights: exotic flowers; fossils; zoos; aquariums; mushroom exhibit in October.

PHOTOGRAPHY

Two Frenchmen (Daguerre and Niepce) invented photography. Many other scientists played an important role in its development.

Société Française de la Photographie, Rue Montalembert 9, BAB 37-13. Open 2 to 8 P.M.

Musée du Conservatoire National des Arts et Métiers, 2 Rue St. Martin 292. TUR 64-40. Open daily 1:30 to 5:30 P.M., 10 A.M. to 5 P.M. Sunday, closed Monday. Fee: 2 F (36 cents). Free on Sunday.

Highlight: excellent photographic exhibit. Also the airplane in which Blériot first flew the Channel in 1909 and splendid mechanical exhibits that tell the history of clockworks.

SHIPS

Musée de la Marine, Palais de Chaillot, Place du Trocadéro (West Wing—one section of four-part museum). Open 10 A.M. to 6 P.M. (5 P.M. during winter), closed Tuesday. Fee: 2 F (36 cents).

Highlights: traces development of ships from oar through sail to steam. Dozens of scale models include ancient galleys; Columbus' *Santa María;* a three-decker man of war; *Gloire,* considered first steam-driven battleship; chance to buy plans for making models of some of the world's famous historical ships.

STAMP COLLECTING

Musée Postal, Rue St. Romain 4. Open daily 2 to 6 P.M. except Tuesday and holidays. Fee: 1 F (18 cents), Sunday .50 F (9 cents).

Highlights: first mailbox; earliest stamps; current issues of stamps sold with special cancellation; illustrated lesson on how stamps are made.

Stamp Market, Avenues Marignan and Gabriel. Open 8 A.M. to 7 P.M. Thursday, Saturday, and Sunday.

TIN OR LEAD SOLDIERS

Société des Collectionneurs de Figurines Historiques, Rue de Lubeck 38. PAS 43-76.

Société des Amis du Musée de la Figurine Historique, Rue de la Muette 3. AUT 55-00.

TRAINS

The Association Française des Amis des Chemins de Fer, at Gare de l'Est, Place de Strasbourg, meets every Thursday 8:30 to 11 P.M. and Saturday 3 to 7 P.M.; closed in August.

GETTING AROUND

Paris is divided into twenty "Arrondissements" (quarters). Each has a mayor, town hall, police station, and central post office. The Seine separates the two sections—the Rive Droite (Right Bank), the north shore, and the Rive Gauche (Left Bank), the south. The quarters are numbered starting on the

Right Bank next to the river and go around like a snail in circles
(numbers 1–4, 8–12, 16–20, *right,* and 5–6, 13–15, *left*). The
house numbers begin from the end nearest to the river.

The subways (Métro) are the easiest way to get around the
city. They run from 5:30 in the morning until 1:15 at night.
Small plans of the Métro network are handed out free in most
stations and hotels. The lines are named after the trains' last
stop. Maps are shown at all stations, on the platforms and in
cars, with routes and transfer points. At about every third station there is an electric route indicator. Press the button next
to your destination and your entire route, including transfer
points (called "correspondances"), lights up. You buy tickets
at a booth one flight down from the street level and then these
tickets are punched at the entrance to the train platform. There
are first-class and second-class tickets—first class is a little nicer
and less crowded. Keep your tickets on the train to show the
fare inspectors, who check from time to time.

The fares are uniform—1.50 F (27 cents) first class and 1 F
(18 cents) second. If you're going to stay in Paris for several
days, you could buy a booklet of ten tickets (carnet) at 9 F
($1.62) first class and 6 F ($1.08) second.

A gate prevents people from reaching the platform when a
train is coming into or is already in the station. If you are first
by the train door, lift the latch and slide the double doors open.

Buses usually run from 6 A.M. to 9:15 P.M., some until
12:30 A.M. Fares are .50 F (9 cents) for each stage or section
you're going to travel, or a book of twenty tickets for 6 F
($1.08). The sections are marked on a map inside the bus. In
rush hours, tear off a numbered ticket at the bus stop so you'll
have a place in the line. The conductor will call "priorities" and
the disabled, the blind, and the pregnant ladies will board first.

The fiacre (horse-drawn carriage) is a delightful but expensive way to see Paris. It costs about 11 F ($1.98) an hour. Car-
riages can be found around the Eiffel Tower, the Opéra, the

Tuileries, and along the Champs-Elysées. The drivers will take you on a lovely drive through the Bois de Boulogne (woods) for a few extra francs.

Pleasure steamers (bateaux-mouches) are comfortable enclosed boats offering one- to two-and-a-half-hour rides along the Seine. They depart every half hour 10 A.M. to 9 P.M. from the Right Bank between Pont des Invalides and Pont de l' Alma. Tickets cost 5 F (90 cents). The boats are ideal places to have a picnic of French bread, cheese, and fruit, although they usually have restaurants aboard. For more information call BAL 96-10.

JUST FOR FUN

The Vincennes Zoo, Avenue de St. Maurice, is reached by Métro (get off at Porte Dorée). Fee: 2 F (36 cents).

Ride a camel through the garden or just look at the six hundred animals and over seven hundred birds that wander more or less freely in the park's enclosures. Ice cream and cold drinks are sold at kiosks on the grounds.

Jardin d'Acclimation, in the Bois de Boulogne, is by the Métro stop Sablons. But Porte Maillot, a little farther, has the added advantage of linking up with a miniature train shuttling through the leafy trees to the gates (about .25 F—4 cents—one way and .50 F—9 cents—round trip). Gardens are open 9 A.M. to sunset in winter and until 7 P.M. in summer. Fee: 1 F (18 cents).

Parisians call the park their enchanted forest. It was once the hunting preserve of kings and is a trip to the country completely within the city limits. There are open fields for soccer players ("le football" to the French); paths for hikers, cyclists, and horseback riders; lakes for boaters; grassy banks by the Seine for sunning; and quiet, shaded places for doing just nothing.

And several restaurants to choose from: **Le Pre-Catelan** under the trees by the pond, or **La Grande Cascade** on a terrace near the waterfall.

In the park there is a new surprise waiting around every corner: the zoo, with nearly five hundred animals; a puppet theater; pedal cars; swings; slides (all free). There are all sorts of beautifully tended rare plants to admire and a floral clock. For .50 to 1 F (9 to 18 cents), there is the "Enchanted River" to explore, a mini golf course, a bowling and shooting gallery, and all kinds of exciting rides. And if you tire of all these, join the other young people flying kites in the neighboring field.

The circus, housed in its own building, has one ring. It is usually closed in July and August. **Cirque d'Hiver,** Rue Amelot, ROQ 12-25. Matinees Monday, Thursday, and Saturday at 3 P.M., Sunday at 2:15 and 5 P.M., daily (except Friday), evening performances at 9 P.M. Tickets cost about 8 to 15 F ($1.44 to $2.70).

Theater for Young People. Although all the plays are presented in French, the stories are familiar classics such as *Alice In Wonderland* or *Robinson Crusoe*. Check the newspapers or call the theater for times and dates of performances. **Le Théâtre Des Enfants,** Théâtre de la Porte St. Martin, 16 Boulevard St. Denis. 607-37-53; **Théâtre Le Kaléidoscope,** 5 Rue Frédérique Sauton, 633-26-96.

A show in addition to those already mentioned in the various parks is the **Théâtre du Vrai Guignolet** in the Champs-Elysées gardens (the oldest puppet show in Paris). In the winter months: **André Blin Marionnettes,** Rue Emile Boutroux, at 2 P.M. Thursday only; and CLAUDE AND DANIEL BAZILIER, Rue Mouffetard 76. Shows include *Gulliver's Travels* and *Pinocchio*.

Musée Grévin, Boulevard Montmartre 10. Open 2 to 7 P.M. weekdays, 1:30 to 8 P.M. Saturday and Sunday. Fee: 6 F ($1.08), 3 F (54 cents) for children up to fifteen.

Highlights: famous figures such as Napoleon and Josephine and Queen Elizabeth II and the Duke of Edinburgh.

Theater is difficult if you don't know French, but the plays at the **Comédie Française,** Place du Théâtre Français, are so well done that if you understand the story, it is well worth a visit. Ask the concierge to recommend a play you will enjoy.

The Châtelet, Place du Châtelet, turns the entire theater into an operetta setting. There are many special effects like waterfalls, trains and horse races, and a cast of hundreds. Knowing French is not essential to enjoying the show since most of the show is music, dance, and spectacle.

The Olympia, Boulevard des Capucines 28, RIC 25-49, features fast-moving variety acts: pop singers, movie stars, animals, comedians. The show changes almost weekly.

RESTER: TO STAY

As part of what you pay for your room, a continental breakfast, "petit déjeuner" (petie dayj'nay) is served—hot chocolate, tea, and the most delicious croissants, half-moon-shaped rolls, you have ever tasted.

RIGHT BANK

Hotel Vendôme, 1 Place Vendôme, is everything a small French hotel should be. A tiny open elevator hoists you to your room, decorated with the same color carpet, draperies, and bedspread, usually red. A shiny brass headstead and footstead grace a bed with a fluffy coverlet and huge, downy pillows. The big bathroom, almost the size of the bedroom, has a clean terrycloth robe for you to use after your bath. The hotel is near the Opéra, shopping, the Louvre and Jeu de Paume galleries, and the Tuileries. Price for a double room with bath is about 100 F ($18). Juice, sausages, and eggs cost extra.

Family, Rue Cambon 34, is just that—a small hotel run by the same family for years. They take a personal interest in everyone who stays here. It has its own special French charm. Price for a double room with bath is 100 F ($18).

LEFT BANK

The Scandinavia, Rue de Tournon 27, two blocks from the Sorbonne, is a historic inn, completely redone but still keeping the beamed ceilings, period furniture, and old paintings, enough to give you a feeling of medieval lore. It is a short stroll to the Luxembourg Gardens. Double room with bath is about 55 F ($9.90).

Saints Pères, Rue des Sts. Pères 65, is in the heart of the artists' section, near cafés, bookshops, galleries, and shops filled with the latest clothes. Double room with bath is 70 F ($12.60).

MANGER: TO EAT

The French did not invent the word "gastronomy" (from the Greek word for the belly), but they take such delight in food preparation and eating that you'd think they did. On the other hand, many dining customs actually did begin in France.

In the fourteenth century a child generally turned the spit for roasting fowl and meat. Later dogs were trained to do the same chore. Young boys were also given the task of acting as bellows by blowing into long copper tubes leading to ovens. It was the first step in learning to bake pies.

Before plates had been thought of, meat was placed on slices of bread. Afterward the bread was tossed to the dogs, who were always scrounging under the table. During the meal, fingers were wiped on the tablecloth, for napkins had never been heard of.

By the sixteenth century Catherine de Médicis had come to

France to wed the Dauphin, and she brought a new concept of table manners. Earthenware plates and knives and forks were introduced. It was not uncommon to have a banquet with more than two hundred different dishes with fancy decorations. Elaborate and wonderful desserts were popular; a gigantic pie crust holding a complete orchestra was the hit of one party. The nursery rhyme with the line "four and twenty blackbirds" may very well have been composed for this occasion.

Up to the seventeenth century the word "restaurant" was used for a warming drink, generally very spiced soup. A Parisian, M. Boulanger, sold soup in cups on bare tables. M. Boulanger became the founder of the "restaurant."

Snacks? There are lots of possibilities. In shops marked "Pâtisserie" you can buy a "quiche Lorraine" (incrusted omelet with ham, bacon, or mushrooms) or a fruit "tarte" (a pie). These are not expensive and are fun to try. **A l'Alsacienne,** 54 Boulevard St. Michel (Left Bank), is one of the best snack shops. Try "tarte amande cerises" (almond paste and cherries) at 1.50 F (27 cents). Buy to go or eat at the table with hot chocolate.

Crêpes are extra-thin pancakes sometimes filled with goodies (jam or jelly). These heavenly French treats, "crêpe au beurre" (butter) or "crêpe au miel" (honey), are sold at stands throughout the city or at regular restaurants. Crêpe suzettes are for dessert and are served with flaming brandy sauce. **Crêperie Saint André,** 59 Rue St. André des Arts (Left Bank), has every type of crêpe possible. Many young Parisians come here with friends. Ice cream and soft drinks are also served.

Still on the run? The best ice cream is at **Berthillon,** 31 Rue St. Louis en l'Ile, or **Fauchon,** 26 Place de la Madeleine (Right Bank). If you want a hamburger or milkshake, try **Le Drugstore,** 133 Avenue des Champs-Elysées (Right Bank). The chocolate rock is the biggest dessert you've ever had, 4.50 F (81 cents). Your dish comes with the flag of your country;

see if you can fool the waitress. **Pam Pam** and **Wimpey** luncheon-
ettes are dotted around Paris.

Real Dining out. Lunch at noon and dinner 7 to 8 P.M.
are usually large meals. Look at the menu or bill of fare. The
French call "prix fixe" a whole meal at a set price. A la carte
dishes are bought separately. The first section on the menu is
usually the hors d'oeuvres, the appetizers, which ordinarily begin
the noonday meal. Then come the soups, which you have at
supper instead of the appetizers. The fish, poultry, meats, salads,
and dessert follow. Items marked in red are dishes the restaurant
is particularly proud of preparing, not something left over from
yesterday. Paris is a good place to try something you have not
tasted before, for the chef takes extra care to fix each dish
just right. Frenchmen love their food, so they describe things
they like in terms of a particular dish. "My little chou" (cabbage
with smoked meat)—"Your tears are salty like marennes" (a
special type of oyster).

RIGHT BANK

Rôtisserie Reine Pédauque, Rue de la Pépinière 6 (in the
Opéra area), is open every day. Country inn setting with colored
windowpanes has very good food from the province of Burgundy.
Cost is about 30 F ($5.40).

Caveau Montpensier, Rue de Montpensier 15, is open every
day. A candlelit seventeenth-century cellar with ancient armor
and modern paintings. Music in the evening. Specialty is escargots
(snails). They're good! Price about 20 F ($3.60).

Coconnas, 2 bis Place des Vosges (overlooking the square),
closed on Tuesdays. Situated in an ancient flower market that
became a king's pavilion. Long, narrow room with wooden
tables. Specialties: hors d'oeuvres—"Merlan en colère" (a whiting biting his own tail); "Poule au pot" (chicken in the pot);

"Merlan coconnas" (ask the waiter to describe this); and "Tarte des demoiselles taten." Price about 25 F ($4.50).

LEFT BANK

Le Procope, 13 Rue de l'Ancienne Comédie (off Boulevard St. Germain), closed on Monday. It is one of the world's oldest cafés (1686) and some parts of it are just as they were hundreds of years ago. Ben Franklin, Victor Hugo, and Voltaire were among its notable guests. Robespierre, Danton, and Marat used the café as a meeting place to plan the Revolution, and the young lieutenant Napoleon Bonaparte left his hat here as a pledge to his country. On the second floor in the hallway Voltaire's original table is set aside. Price about 20 F ($3.60).

La Méditerranée, 2 Place de l'Odéon, is open every day and has bright, map-lined tablecloths and charming atmosphere. Specialties: real bouillabaisse (fish soup) and frog legs. Price about 25 F ($4.50).

Can Camaou, 14 Rue Pascal (near Mouffetard market), is open daily. Delightful for lunch. The food and rustic setting are country-style, from Catalogne province. The self-service hors d'oeuvres are on a long table and are a meal in themselves. The roasted meat dishes are delicious. Price about 25 F ($4.50).

ARGENT MONNAIE: MONEY AND WHAT IT WILL BUY

The franc is the basic unit of money and is worth about 18 cents. Each franc is divided into 100 centimes; 50 centimes is worth about 9 cents.

One centime will buy a caramel penny candy; 25 centimes, a croissant (roll). One franc is enough for a seat at the marionette show or a delicious plain crepe, and 5 francs, the latest hit record.

Shopping hours are usually 9:30 A.M. till noon and 2:30 to 7 P.M. Many stores are closed on Monday and during the month of August.

TOYS

Baby Train, 9 Rue du Petit Pont. Don't be fooled by the name. The store has fantastic miniature trains. Adults enjoy looking and playing too.

Au Nain Bleu, 406-410 Rue St. Honoré. Large selection of dolls in regional costumes, doll houses, and stuffed animals. Other toys from all over the world.

Farandole, 48 Avenue Victor Hugo.

Le Monde en March, 54 Rue Mazarine.

CLOTHES

Virginie, 168 Faubourg St. Honoré. Elegant clothes for young girls.

Jones, 39 Avenue Victor Hugo. Fine collection for both boys and girls.

Mod clothes for girls: All along the Boulevard St. Germain and the side streets.

La Gamineric, number 137, Boulevard St. Germain, is one of the newest shops. Prices: Hats 29 F ($5.22); blouses 65 F $11.70).

Chez Tinker, 7 Rue St. Jacques.

RECORDS

Chanteclair, 61 Boulevard St. Michel. Specializes in shelf after shelf of latest hits. 45 RPMs 9 F ($1.62), albums from 8 to 30 F ($1.44 to $5.40). Also nonsense toys.

La Cave aux Disques, 24 Place St. André des Arts.

DEPARTMENT STORES

They sell everything at a lower price, including toys.

Au Printemps, 64 Boulevard Haussmann. Information Service, on the ground floor, has a hostess who speaks English.

Au Trois Quartiers, 21 Boulevard de la Madeleine.

Galeries Lafayette, Boulevard Haussmann.

GROWING UP IN PARIS

In addition to having a long school day, young people six to sixteen take a great deal of work home. Parents are usually requested to sign homework as proof that it has been done by their children. Schools encourage sports. They arrange for popular vacation camps. Many are holiday centers where teen-agers do public work but also have plenty of time for their own pleasure. Most schools are not closed for the weekend, but have a holiday in the middle of the week, Thursday, for religious instruction. The normal week is Monday to Wednesday, Friday and Saturday. Summer vacation is from the middle of July to the end of September. Families ordinarily go away for the entire month of August. The favorite sport is cycle racing over long distances. Each French town has its own club and on any summer Sunday a rural road will be disturbed by a loudspeaker in a car: "Look out! The cycle race is coming!" A few minutes later the road is filled with cycles, pedaled by young men in gaily colored shirts and shorts.

Mon Cher Ami. There are several clubs you can write to, to meet people your own age with similar interests:

Information Office for Youth (BIJ)
7 Rue Balzac. Tel: 225-91-88

Amitié Internationale des Jeunes
123 Rue de la Tour. Tel: 870-18-10

Club des Quatre-Vents (young girls)
1 Rue Gozlin. Tel: 033-70-25

Club France-États-Unis
6 Boulevard de Grenelle or 23 Rue du Cherche-Midi. Tel:
   222-50-34

Le Scoutisme Français (boys and girls)
92 Avenue d'Iéna. Tel: 727-88-22

Éclaireurs de France (boys and girls)
66 Rue de la Chaussée d'Antin. Tel: 874-51-40

AU REVOIR

So long to the sight of young people kissing on the sidewalk,
everybody shaking hands even if it holds up traffic, French
gentlemen kissing married ladies' hands upon greeting them,
lunch that lasts two hours, cafés where people talk and talk
and talk and look and look and look.

So long to the people who helped. "Le porteur," carrying
the bags. "Un flic," the Paris policemen, leading chaotic traffic
and saluting when he gives helpful directions, sometimes in
English. "Le concierge," the indispensable man in the hotel,
changing money, selling stamps, arranging for cabs, telling you
the bus or train to take, telling you anything else you needed,
even where to find a dentist for a toothache. "L'ouvreuse," the
usherette, courteously showing you to your seat as you give her
a modest tip. "Le garçon," the waiter, with a flourish serving all
your fine French meals.

So long to the history of the city that never stands still. New
paintings, new music, new foods, new clothes, and new people
to enjoy it all. By seeing and hearing the echoes of the past,
you've gotten to know the present, for the never-ending wind-

ing streets are filled with markets and fairs where people shopped, joked, quarreled, always living with zest. You've gotten to know the lives of rich and poor, statesmen, students, café waiters, taxi drivers, and that special friend. The French people old and young love their city and are proud of it. If you were willing to get to know their home, they were agreeable and fun and anxious to hear you say "Au revoir," I will see you soon.

PARLER: TO SPEAK

ENGLISH	FRENCH	PRONUNCIATION
Good day	Bonjour	Bohn-joor
Good evening	Bonsoir	Bohn-swah
Goodbye	Au revoir	Oh revwar
My name is	Je m'appelle	J'mapell
How do you do?	Comment allez-vous?	Ki-mont al-ly voo
I am fine	Bien merci	B'yehn mair-see
Thank you	Merci	Mair-see
Excuse me	Excusez-moi	Ex-ku-zay mwa
Speak more slowly	Parlez plus lentement	Par-lay plu lahnte-mahn
Please	S'il vous plaît	Sea voo play
Do you understand?	Comprenez-vous?	Kom-pren-ay voo?
Where is the toilet?	Où sont les toilettes?	Oo sohn lay twah-let
Go	Allez	Ah-lay
How do I get to	Quelle direction pour aller à	Kel di-rec-yohn poor ah-lay ah
Right	A droite	Ah dwat
Left	A gauche	Ah goch
Straight ahead	Tout droit	Too dwah
Around the corner	Au coin	Oh kwehn
How much is this?	C'est combien?	Say cohm-byehn
Men	Messieurs	M's-yur
Ladies	Dames	Dahm

ENGLISH	FRENCH	PRONUNCIATION
Shut	Fermé	Fair-may
Open	Ouvert	Oo-vair
Warm	Chaud	Show
Cold	Froid	Frwah
Yes	Oui	Wee
No	Non	Nohn
1	un	uh
2	deux	d
3	trois	twah
4	quatre	catr
5	cinq	sank
6	six	seess
7	sept	set
8	huit	weet
9	neuf	nuhf
10	dix	deess
11	onze	ohnz
12	douze	dooz
13	treize	trehz
14	quatorze	kat-torz
15	quinze	kanz
20	vingt	van
50	cinquante	sank-ahnt
100	cent	sahn

FETES: DATES TO REMEMBER

January 1   **New Year's Day.** Young people give parents handmade articles and wish them "Bonne année." Trade folk give gifts to patrons (baker—brioche, fish merchant—oyster, butcher—chicken). Families have large dinner parties.

January 6   **Day of Three Kings.** Youngest members of family hunt for tiny bean or gift baked in a cake ("la galette"); finder becomes king or queen for a day.

February-March (Tuesday before Ash Wednesday)	**Mardi Gras.** Three days of confetti, flowers, tooting of tin horns, and parades. Butchers celebrate Boeuf Gras (Fat Ox) decked with garlands and ribbons and led through streets by little boy known as "King of the Butchers."
April 1	**April Fish.** Similar to April Fool's, with candymakers displaying chocolate fish. Friends send fake gifts and humorous cards.
April (fourth Sunday in Lent)	**Laundress Day.** Washerwomen compete to be chosen "Queen of Queens," who chooses her king. Both attend colorful ball in their honor.
March or early April	**Easter.** Small children hunt chocolate eggs in parks, listening for "bells returning from Rome." Candlelight processions. Young people receive small gifts. Egg omelet traditional breakfast.
April-May (one month after Easter)	**Gingerbread Fair.** Near Place de la Nation. Lots of goodies, rides, and street entertainment.
May 1	**May Day.** Everyone wears "muguets" (lilies of the valley) and wishes each other good fortune. Many celebrate with picnic in the country.
July 14	**Bastille Day.** Big parades, fireworks, and dancing in the streets.
September-October	**Montmartre Harvest Festival.** Singing, dancing, and lots of colorful costumes.
November 25	**St. Catherine's Day.** Unmarried seamstresses wearing weird hats parade the Avenue Montaigne and surround men for a kiss.
December 6	**St. Nicholas' Eve.** Christmas activities begin. Young people place shoes near fire. Small gifts are left along with birch twigs as reminder to behave.
December 24	**Christmas Eve.** After midnight mass, family walks home for "le réveillon," dinner of oysters, foie gras, sausages, cakes, candies, and pancakes. Youngsters sent to bed to wait for Père Noël, hoping for gifts left in their shoes.

8. ROME

Ancient and Modern

"Benvenuti a Roma!" Welcome to Rome, a city whose sunlight sparkles against orange and yellow buildings, stately green umbrella trees, splashing fountains, impressive squares, winding side streets, shuttered houses, and huge doors with shiny knockers. Try to imagine ancient Rome as you live and enjoy the fun of modern Rome.

THE ROMAN STORY

According to legend, Rome first came into being over 2700 years ago, founded by a pair of male twins, Romulus and Remus. They were the sons of Mars, the Roman war god. The twins were left by their mother on the banks of the Tiber River and were raised by an old she-wolf, whose likeness you can see in statues and on postage stamps, bookends, and posters all over Rome. As a reminder of the legend, a live she-wolf is still caged beside the Campidoglio (Capitoline Hill), once the center of ancient Rome.

Romulus, the story goes, killed his brother shortly after Remus told him the site of the new city. Eventually Romulus too was whisked away by the gods, but not until he had ruled the country for many years.

The city was actually a fortified market. Sheepherders, farmers, traders, and merchants crowded the area, partly for business but also to protect themselves from warring tribes. The city of walls and deep moats sat on the Palatine Hill, one of the famous seven hills of Rome. Early settlers named the city "Roma" from the ancient word "ruman," meaning river.

From its humble beginnings, Rome gradually prospered, and by the time of the emperors Julius Caesar and Augustus, who lived during the first centuries B.C. and A.D., had become the seat of a mighty empire extending throughout Europe and well into the Near East and northern Africa. Its very size contributed to its eventual downfall, and shortly after the Emperor Constantine made Christianity the official state religion (A.D. 313), a formal breach between the Eastern and Western parts of the empire occurred, and Rome lost its eminence as the principal city in the empire. The population of the city shrank drastically to only a few thousand people, whereas in the greatest days of the empire more than a million persons had lived there.

Several centuries passed before Rome regained its former important position, but not as the center of a mighty military empire, but as the recognized center of the Christian religion, the home of popes. Church leaders and wealthy patrons invited the finest artists to design palaces and churches, fashion beautiful fountains, and paint vivid blue and deep red canvases. All the artists were furnished with food, shelter, and financial support. The city flowered and became a lovely gem. This was only about five hundred years ago and the period was called the Renaissance, which comes from a word meaning "to be born again." As you visit museums, churches, and art galleries, you'll encounter the works of many Renaissance artists such as Michelangelo, Bernini, and Raphael.

In more recent times, and with the help of people like the patriot Garibaldi, the Italian people united into one country, with Rome as its capital. This occurred only one hundred years ago.

Modern young Italian people, like their parents, enjoy life to its fullest. Don't be afraid to join in and you'll find the language will not stand in your way.

EXPLORING THE CITY

More than two million people live and work in this capital, but few can truly call themselves real Romans. Most have come from different parts of Italy to find their fortunes and live the good life. The northerner brings his enormous drive and bustling energy, the southerner, a more leisurely attitude toward work. This may be one explanation of what happens in Rome each noon hour.

Suddenly, as if the floodgates have been opened, people stream onto the streets. With enormous determination, they crowd onto trolleys and race through the back doors of the green buses. Be very cautious not to exit from the rear door or you'll be thrown down. People leap into tiny automobiles and jump onto motorcycles or scooters which wiggle in and around larger vehicles. In the center of all this activity is the calm police-man waving his white gloves as gracefully as if he were con-ducting a symphony orchestra.

Then, within a half hour, all is quiet. Practically everyone has disappeared into a restaurant or has reached home to have a leisurely lunch with his family. Three hours later the same frantic activity occurs as everyone returns to work. The people will probably finish work about 7:30 P.M.

For the three-hour lunch time Rome seems half asleep. Even the famous cats snooze in some doorway or alley. If you look closely at the people left scurrying about during this time, you'll notice they are not Italians. They are Japanese, French, English, Indians, Americans, and people from all parts of the world. Some are priests in black cassocks, or violet if the priest is from Scotland and red if from Germany. Many are students who have come to Rome as part of their education. And then, of course, there are a number of people like yourself, who have come to discover a city that for a long time was the most important in the Western world.

Because there are so many visitors, taking care of them has become an important part of the city's life. Thousands of professional guides give you firsthand information about the glories of the city. These guides have studied for many years and have passed difficult tests to qualify for their jobs. You will also find many young boys who aspire to be guides and know the names of the emperors and piazzas (squares), but are not able to show you the city as the trained guides can.

Rome's streets and avenues seem to wander in and out aimlessly. Many narrow alleyways lead into grand piazzas. On the tiny side streets are shops of all kinds, selling everything from rare coins to old furniture. Suddenly you may come upon an old palace. Through it all winds the Tiber River, which the Romans call "Tevere." It cuts modern Rome in two; the eastern side has the low hills—the seven hills of Rome—with their government buildings, hotels, shops, and theaters. This is probably where you will spend most of your time in Rome.

Notice the high red brick wall that goes around the seven hills. It was built in 275 by a Roman emperor fearful of an attack from the north. All the streets running from the center of the city have to cross a bridge or go through the wall's big, turreted gates.

The other side of the river is called **Trastévere** or "across the

Tiber." This part of the city was settled in the fifth century by a group of refugees fleeing from invading northern warriors. It was very flat, marshy, and uncomfortable, but through great effort was built into winding alleys, charming buildings, and lovely piazzas. The people of Trastévere are particularly proud of their portion of the city.

No one can possibly see all or most of Rome in a few days, but you can see the highlights. Just as in New York visitors measure attractions according to their proximity to Times Square, or in Washington, D.C., to the White House, or in Chicago to the Loop, so is there a favored place in Rome which serves as a reference point for travelers. It is the Piazza Venezia (Venice Square). Even Romans tell you how far places are from the Piazza Venezia, with its monument to King Victor Emanuel II. People call the monument the "Wedding Cake." It was built in 1911. Inside is the Tomb of the Unknown Soldier from World War I. Take a city map and climb the stairs to the top for a full view of the city and to identify all of the places you are about to visit.

ANCIENT ROME

Roman Forum, Via dei Fori Imperiali. Open daily except Tuesday, winter 9 A.M. to 5 P.M., summer 9 A.M. to 7 P.M. Fee: 200 lire (32 cents), Sunday half price.

The largest public square in ancient times had about 1 million people streaming through its marble and gold palaces, temples, and markets. More people lived in this one area than had ever lived together before. At noontime musicians, jesters, masked slaves, tradesmen, and rich and poor of all kinds were out to buy or sell something or to wander about to be seen. It was a great festival repeated daily. Then earthquakes and floods destroyed and buried the columns, the arches, and the temples. To finish the job, thieves stole the marble and gold. Today only ruins remain.

Along the outer edge are columns which were actually parts of the temples and monuments built to honor a hero or a tremendous victory. The temples were as important in politics as in religion. All the major events affecting the daily lives of the people took place on the temples' steps. Senators campaigned for office and within five days of election were sworn in and pledged to uphold the laws. From these same steps the man called the censor announced which people could not vote in the next election. Eventually many of the temples became government offices.

Toward the end of the Roman Forum is the Curia, the square brick building Julius Caesar began in 44 B.C. which became the meeting place for the Senate. Climb the stairway and picture the Senate in action. From the benches where they sat, the senators moved to the right side if they agreed, and to the left if they disagreed. A pull of the beard meant a violent protest against the idea proposed. This would trigger a tremendous argument between the two sides. It was all part of the great show in which everyone participated, including the observers. To get a more complete feeling of the Forum's history attend the "Sound and Light" spectacles performed June through October at 9 and 10:30 P.M. With music, sounds, lights, and a storyteller, the entire tale comes to life.

Mamertine Prison. Ready for something scary and gloomy but fascinating? To the right of the Temple of Concord in the Forum is the Church of San Giuseppe; underneath the Church is the Mamertine Prison. Very few people in ancient times ever came out of the two-celled dungeon alive. It is said that St. Peter spent a few uncomfortable days here. The guide will show you a spring of water which St. Peter created to baptize the guards.

Palatine Hill, Piazzale del Colosseo. Open every day except Tuesday, winter 9 A.M. to 5 P.M., summer 9 A.M. to 7 P.M. Fee: 200 lire (32 cents), Sunday half price.

At the top of the Forum is the Palatine, the spot where Romulus and Remus are said to have founded the city. Later, noblemen and rich Romans built their villas and palaces here. And it was the birthplace in the year 63 B.C. of the first emperor, Octavius. A walk among the cool umbrella pine trees gives you another view of the ruins.

Colosseum, Piazzale del Colosseo. Open every day, winter 9 A.M. to 5 P.M., summer 9 A.M. to 7:30 P.M. Fee: 150 lire (24 cents), Sunday free.

Fires and earthquakes have not destroyed the most important of Rome's treasures, the Colosseum, the symbol of the city. An English monk of the Middle Ages once wrote, "While the Colosseum stands, so will Rome; when the Colosseum falls, so will Rome; but when Rome falls, the world will end." The Romans are worried, for the rumbling of the cars, buses, and motor scooters is causing the stones of the foundation to crumble.

The name "Colosseum" comes from the word "colossus," which means "huge." It is as high as a modern twelve-storied building and was built in A.D. 80. Fifty thousand people could be seated in its six levels. The ancient Romans were so clever that they even built a huge sunshade to protect the spectators.

The Colosseum is at its best at sunset. Walk up the staircase to the highest gallery and look down. The arena stage was sometimes flooded with water and mock naval battles were performed. The most popular show was the gladiators fighting in pairs against wild beasts. The word gladiator comes from "gladius" (short sword), which the men carried with them into the arena. These men were slaves or criminals who could free themselves by fighting in the arena. When one of them was badly hurt, he asked to be spared by raising his finger. The final answer came from the people watching; if they waved their togas the gladiator was set free; a closed fist with the thumb down meant the fighting had to continue.

Today the floor of the arena has disappeared. Only the cells for the animals and gladiators remain. The only animals visible are cats wandering through the ruins and one stone lion proudly standing guard.

Baths of Caracalla, Parco di Porta Capena. Open 9 A.M. until one hour before sunset. Fee: 100 lire (16 cents), Sunday half price.

The most impressive baths of their time (A.D. 217) were named for the son of the man who began its construction. They had an artificial lake used by people wishing to learn to swim but not risk the currents of the Tiber River. The baths accommodated about sixteen hundred people, who chose between hot or cold baths, curative waters, or showers of steam. The decorations were so rich with marble, rare mosaics, and every kind of art work that the baths were compared to an oriental palace.

Now part of the ruins has become a stage for opera in July and August. Everyone dresses informally and a lot of young people attend the performances. One of the most impressive operas is *Aida,* with a cast of hundreds of people, camels, elephants, and white horses. Find out the basic story of the opera and then sit back and watch everyone enjoy the show. The Italians really let you know how much they like it; some laugh, cry, or just hum the melodies. There are many interesting snacks you can eat during the performance and between acts, from lemonade and popcorn to little ham sandwiches called "panino con prosciutto."

Pantheon, Piazza della Rotonda. Open every day 9 A.M. until one hour before sunset.

The temple is one of the best-preserved monuments in Rome. You go through the original ancient bronze doors. The only light inside comes from the round hole in the domed ceiling. There are numerous tombs of former kings and queens. Be sure to find the tomb of the great Renaissance painter Raphael.

Campidoglio (Capitoline Hill). The most famous of the Roman hills is still the headquarters of the city council. A terrible legend is connected with it. It seems a Roman girl, Tarpeia, showed the tribes attacking Rome, the Sabines, a secret way onto the hill. In revenge the Romans hurled the beautiful but deceitful girl from that very place to her death.

Another story is that she was buried on the rock and covered with the gold and jewels she had received from the Sabines, as a warning to anyone who thought he could succeed in betraying the Romans.

Michelangelo designed the piazza (square). At the far end is the palace of the Senate with its impressive clock tower. On either side are two palaces: Palazzo Nuovo (New Palace) and Palazzo dei Conservatori (Palace of the Conservators), both with important museums and galleries. The Palazzo dei Conservatori has the original bronze statue of Romulus and Remus and the she-wolf, the symbol of Rome.

The piazza has a pattern of stars. In the center is a large statue of a man on horseback, Marcus Aurelius, considered one of the noblest and most peace-loving emperors of his time (A.D. 121–80). The traces of glitter sparkling on the statue are the remains of the pure gold that once covered the entire figure. The hill is also the place where President John F. Kennedy spoke to the Italian people in 1963.

Tiber Island. After visiting the Capitoline Hill, go down to the Tiber River and look at the unusual island in the center. It is the scene of a curious story of the beginnings of the city.

The island was formed in ancient times when the people were celebrating the end of the reign of a disliked ruler. Marching down to the river's edge, they dumped the harvest gathered from the ruler's property. The river was at its lowest point and the vast amount of grain piled up and became a little island. Actually, the island formed at a natural point where the river had widened and the current was weakest, connecting the rich farm lands of the south and the mineral wealth of the north. The formation of the island is probably one of the reasons that the city of Rome began on the Capitoline Hill.

The wall around the island had the shape of a boat and the great column in the center looked like its mast. A temple to the god of medicine was built on the island. It served as a shelter for sick pilgrims who came to be cured of their illnesses. Today it still serves the same purpose. A modern hospital has replaced the ancient temple.

Castel Sant'Angelo (St. Angel's Castle), Largo Castelli. Open every day except Monday 9 A.M. to 4 P.M.; summer until 6:30 P.M. Fee: 200 lire (32 cents), holidays 100 lire (16 cents).

On the other side of the Tiber River is a building that has been a fort, a torture chamber, a prison, and the home of a pope. The building's purpose changed every time a new leader took over. Walk across the spiral ramps and through its many grand halls and secret passages.

On the first floor in ROOM NUMBER 1 are models of the most important alterations in the castle over the years. The castle was first built in A.D. 135 as a tomb for Emperor Hadrian. According to legend, it got its current name from an event that took place 450 years later. The Pope was in a procession crossing the bridge leading toward the castle, praying that the plague which had spread throughout Rome would disappear. Suddenly an angel appeared over the top of the castle and was seen placing his sword back into its holder. This told the Pope that the anger of God had been soothed. Ever since, the monument has had the name of Castel Sant'Angelo (St. Angel's Castle).

A ramp leads to a drawbridge and then into a courtyard

where there are piles of stone balls used as ammunition for cannons. In the rooms is the original armor of ancient soldiers. Other rooms offer a glimpse into settings just as they were in the past—for instance, a guard room as it was over three hundred years ago.

For a special bit of a spy thriller explore the prison cells. Proceed through Hall 19 into a courtyard and find DOOR 29. It is marked "Ingresso alle Prigioni Storiche" (Entrance to the Historical Prisons). Climb down the narrow stairs and you will see four doors opening into tiny cells. The last one held for awhile a colorful prisoner, Benvenuto Cellini. Though at the time he lived (1500–71) he was best known as the world's greatest goldsmith and an outstanding sculptor, he was later more widely famed for his exciting spy adventures. According to his own words, he was "a man of great excellence," whether on the battlefield or in his workshop. At the siege of Rome in 1527, he saved the city and slew the leaders of the invading army—at least that is what he recorded. During this period he found his way in and out of this cell. One attempted escape through the secret underground vaults was stopped due to mistaken identity. The guard on duty thought Cellini in his disguise was an ally. Cellini was so shook up by the guard's cordiality that he forgot for a moment whom he was impersonating. The guard then recognized Cellini and returned him to his cell. During another escape attempt he tied sheets together into a long rope, tossed them out of his window, and scaled the castle walls. At the bottom the guards were waiting. This time his imprisonment was short. He was freed by order of a cardinal. Looking carefully at the left cell wall, you can see the vague outline of a charcoal sketch Cellini drew of a Christ figure.

Hungry? There is a pleasant place for lunch on the next level, Ristorante Caffè le Terrazze. While enjoying the beautiful view ask for a "timballo," a kind of pasta pie with salami as the bottom and top layers and pasta, cheese, and meat sauce in the middle. The price: 350 lire (a little more than 50 cents).

The Vatican: A Country within the City. Vatican City is the smallest independent country in the world, 108 acres spread over a hill on the other side of the Tiber River in Trastévere. It is a tiny walled city inside the big city of Rome. The ruler is the Pope of the Roman Catholic Church.

When Victor Emanuel II, the King of Italy, made Rome the capital of his new kingdom, the Pope's governing power was weakened and he shut himself inside the Vatican. He told the people he was being held a prisoner by the Italian King. For nearly sixty years no Pope ever went outside the Vatican.

Finally, an agreement called the Lateran Treaty was signed in 1929. The Vatican was recognized as a separate country and the Pope agreed not to try to increase its land beyond the Vatican walls. Today a thousand people live inside Vatican City. Some are priests and church officers; others take care of the wonderful museum and outstanding library. There are shopkeepers, engineers, gardeners, cooks, cleaners, and so on. The little state has its own flag, newspaper, radio station, model railway station, and post office. The people print their own money and issue their own stamps. You can even find a glass-making factory, an observatory, and a power plant. The cars from the Vatican have special license plates. The plate number "1" is the Pope's. His automobile has a glass roof with only one seat in the back, set like a throne in the center. All the telephones in the Vatican begin with the letters VC. The telephone on the Pope's desk is VC 101.

The Pope lives in a simple apartment on the top floor of his palace. His rooms used to be servants' quarters. As the ruler of the Vatican he owns some of the world's greatest treasures— art, rare books, and priceless jewels.

The entire city is protected by 137 Catholic young men from Switzerland. They are called the Swiss Guard. Their bright uniforms of red, yellow, and blue were designed by Michelangelo more than four hundred years ago.

St. Peter's is the largest and probably most magnificent church in the world. The dome rises 404 feet in the air. The church is said to be where St. Peter is buried.

To give you an idea of how large the building is, go over to one of the tiny angels attached to the columns. Place your arm across the sole of one of the angel's feet and you will discover that it is probably longer than the tip of your finger to your elbow. It is because all parts of the giant building are so perfectly matched that the vastness escapes you. Also, look at the markers in the marble floor running down the center aisle. Each mark shows the size of different churches throughout the world.

Walking up and down the aisles, you are passing some of the world's finest works of art, by Bernini, Michelangelo, Canova, and Della Porta. Keep score to see how many of these famous artists' works you can find.

Stop at the first chapel on the right. It contains the marble statue named "Pietà" by Michelangelo. Looking carefully, you can see the artist's signature in the upper part of the folds of the Virgin Mother's dress. This is the only time the artist ever signed his name to one of his works. He was twenty-five years old when he completed the statue.

Nearby is the statue of St. Peter, whose toe has been worn smooth by the kisses of the people who have come to pray.

Before leaving St. Peter's take the elevator up to the dome. At the top only sixteen people can stand at one time. The view is magnificent.

The Vatican Museum, Viale Vaticano. Open every day except holidays, summer and winter 9 A.M. to 2 P.M. Fee: 500 lire (80 cents).

A series of fifteen museums, galleries, and rooms, with two sections of particular interest.

THE PIUS CLEMENTINUS MUSEUM has many statues of Greek and Koman gods and goddesses. Remember Apollo? His chariot pulled the sun around the earth. Diana, his sister, ruled the moon and was a queen and famous huntress. Zeus, the father of all gods, was the keeper of thunder and lightning. Hercules, the strong man, defeated lions and beasts of all kinds. How about Venus, the goddess of love? On Valentine's Day her son Cupid is in full view. These are just a few of many familiar figures.

THE SISTINE CHAPEL ceiling has some of the richest colors you will ever see. This masterpiece was painted by Michelangelo using a particularly difficult technique called fresco. The artist painted on a lime base right on the ceiling while it was still wet. If the ceiling was allowed to dry while Michelangelo was still at work, a thin, moldy crust would have formed. Fresco painting calls for a swift, skillful hand and, most of all, sound judgment since the colors when applied on the wet base appear very different when they are dry.

Michelangelo did not want to paint the chapel ceiling, for he considered himself a sculptor, yet this creation has become his best-known work. Lying on his back on a huge scaffolding, he painted 343 figures covering 10,000 square feet. The ceiling illustrates his version of the Book of Genesis from the story of creation to the story of the flood. Working backward, Michelangelo started with Noah and ended with the Creator. After four years of extraordinary labor, the work was completed and all Rome was filled with admiration.

Find the Deluge, one of the most unusual scenes. Most paintings depict this story with stormy seas, pouring rain, and lightning. Michelangelo chose instead to concentrate on the frenzied flight of people; the raging elements do not appear. The victims carry their possessions on their backs or on their heads, painfully climbing a bank to dry land. Other panels portray the struggles of various people. A woman of Herculean stature balances on her head an upside down kitchen stool on which is placed a jar, loaves of bread, a plate, and knives. Other people are in a desperate state of anguish. A mother clasps one child in her massive embrace, while another child seeks protection clinging to her leg. Her face and especially her jaw express the mother's determination to protect her children at all cost. In other panels are scenes of the struggle for existence. In an overladen tublike boat, which is on the point of upsetting, two men—one with a club and the other with his fists—try to drive another from climbing in. Outside the ark in the background a man is about to bring down an ax on someone struggling to save himself. Although this spectacular painting is on a flat surface the genius of Michelangelo has made the entire scene have a spectacular sense of movement.

Seeing the Pope. About 1000 people are received by the Pope privately each year. More than 900,000 have a public audience with him either in the Vatican Palace or at Castel Gandolfo. You have to get special permission in order to attend a public audience. Write ahead to: Pontifical North American College, Via dell'Umiltà 30, Vatican City, Italy; or tell the guard at the front entrance to the Vatican that you would like an "udienza" (oo-dee-en-sa), audience. He will give you a form to fill out and the tickets should arrive at your hotel in two or three days. The Pope also appears in St. Peter's Square at the open window of his attic room every Sunday at twelve noon. It is a wonderful experience to see him even if you are not Catholic. Everyone anticipates the arrival of the Pope. Excitement seems to be a part of the air around you. The second he appears, there is a burst of cheers, people wave their handkerchiefs wildly, and everyone is together for a few seconds. You too will find yourself shouting "Viva il Papa!" (Long live the Pope!).

OTHER CHURCHES AND THE CATACOMBS

Santa Maria in Cosmedin, Piazza della Bocca della Verità. One of the most ancient and beautiful churches in Rome also tests your honesty. Go over to the great stone disc known as the "Bocca della Verità" (Mouth of Truth). It gives its name to the piazza outside. Find the old carved mask. The superstition says anyone who puts his hand in the mouth and tells a lie will have his hand bitten. In ancient times, to give the legend a little help, a guard would stand beside the mask and poke his sword at an offending hand.

San Pietro in Vincoli (St. Peter in Chains), Piazza San Pietro in Vincoli. The wonderful statue of Moses by Michelangelo is here, and part of the unfinished tomb of Julius II. See if you can find a tiny sculptured head of Michelangelo turned upside down, neatly placed in the beard of Moses.

Catacombs of Priscilla, Via Salaria 430. Autobuses 35, 56. Open every day; winter 8:30 to noon, 2:30 to 5 P.M.; summer till 7 P.M. Fee: 100 lire (16 cents).

These are long underground passages where early Christians hid in order to pray and bury their dead. Although dark and eerie, you will enjoy recognizing paintings of familiar scenes from both the Old and the New Testament, such as Noah in the ark, Daniel in the lions' den, and many others.

WELL-KNOWN LANDMARKS

Piazza di Spagna. Sunset is the perfect time for the Spanish Steps, in the piazza. There are 137 steps. Before the climb pause for a drink of water from the Barcaccia Fountain at the foot of the stairs. It was designed to resemble a leaking war vessel as a reminder of a boat washed ashore during a flood of the

Tiber River. Before you go up, stop at the red and yellow house on the right. The English poet John Keats lived and died here. On one of the upper floors is the **Keats-Shelley Memorial.** Percy B. Shelley, another English poet, was Keats's close friend. The tiny rooms are open 9 A.M. to noon and 3 to 5 P.M., except Saturday and Sunday afternoon, and have the original handwritten copies of their poems.

At the top of the steps, you'll be facing the church, **Trinità dei Monti,** built three years after Columbus discovered America. In the 1700s the steps were the central meeting place for young artists who lived nearby on the streets of Via Margutta. At this time of the day, artists' models would dress in bright-colored peasant costumes and stroll the steps selling violets. The steps themselves wore a fine covering of flowers. Even today many fashion models pose against the background, and each spring the steps are still covered with a show of more than five thousand azalea plants in bloom.

After returning to the bottom of the stairs, relax for a few minutes at the **Caffè Greco,** the famous meeting spot for the composers Wagner, Chopin, Lizst, and Bizet and for many other people from Buffalo Bill to Casanova. It is right on the main street leading down from the Spanish Steps on the Via Condotti. Have a refreshing orange ice. This café is also famous for a particularly good blend of coffee. Walk around and locate the picture of Hans Christian Andersen. He wrote two of his famous children's stories at one of these tables. After your pause, you might like to window-shop. The area has some of the best shops in Rome, such familiar names as Gucci (leather), Richard Ginori (ceramics), Perugina (candy).

SPLENDID FOUNTAINS

Everywhere you wander in Rome there are different and unusual fountains. Here are two that are truly outstanding.

Fountain of the Rivers. Set in the center of the Piazza Navona, the fountain is by the sculptor and artist Bernini. From the middle of the round base rises an enormous rock pierced with caves. Water streams from the sides, where a lion and other fantastic animals drink. Four figures sit atop the rock to represent the major rivers from the four parts of the world known in Bernini's time (The Nile of Africa, the Río de la Plata of South America, the Ganges of India, and the Danube of Europe). In the center is a tall needle or obelisk.

An amusing story is told about the fountain. Notice that all the statues are making horrible faces and the figure representing the Río de la Plata has his arm raised to protect himself from something terrible. Designer Bernini was telling the world what he thought of his great rival Borromini, the man who made the church in front of the fountain. Borromini, however, had his answer. High on the base of the bell tower of the church, he had a statue of St. Agnes built with her hand on her chest, promising that the church will stand longer than the fountain. People who side with Borromini still say that the obelisk (needle) in the fountain will one night fall and break into pieces.

The story may not have any truth, but it is fun to think about as you have a snack nearby at the **Tre Scalini** (Three Steps), a restaurant and sidewalk café next to the fountain. Try the "gelato tartufo," an unusual mixture of delicious chocolate ice cream with chocolate chips and a cherry in the center and whipped cream on top—all for 300 lire (less than 50 cents).

The square is typically Roman and a favorite of artists. Generally at least one is working at an easel with a crowd of children watching him critically. Mothers with their babies sit around to talk about important matters, idling the day away.

Long ago the square was an amphitheater, and chariots would race for prize trophies. It was even flooded for mock sea battles. A waiter at Tre Scalini has said crocodiles were placed in the water. In later times the square was used at festival time for a parade of carriages of princes and nobility.

Festivities are still carried on today. Prior to Christmas, the great oval becomes an open market. Hundreds of wooden booths are built to sell everything from sweets to tiny crèche figures for manger scenes—the Holy Family, cows, sheep, camels—an endless variety of figures. The shepherds come down from the Alban Hills in sheepskin jackets, to play their bagpipes. And the old witch "Befana," who takes the place of Santa Claus, walks around promising gifts to the good or pieces of coal to the bad.

Speaking Statues. Can a statue keep a secret? Before leaving the Piazza Navona, visit an unusual curiosity of Rome. Ask someone for directions to Palazzo (Palace) Braschi. To the right is the Piazza di Pasquino and a statue that looks fairly worn out. Ancient Romans stood behind the figure and used the statue as a mouthpiece to get back at their rivals or to criticize the authorities. Many times they would compose long poems called "pasquinate," meaning "lampoons," to tell people their real thoughts. This is another side of the Italian personality. There is a particularly good speaking statue in the Piazzetta San Marco near the Piazza Venezia, opposite the Victor Emanuel statue. It is a statue of Lucrezia Borgia. Climb behind it and speak your mind.

Fontana di Trevi (Fountain of Trevi). Appearing so often in motion pictures, this is probably one of the best-known fountains in the world. In the center, Neptune, powerful god of the sea, rides the tumbling waves, braced against the wind. After throwing your coin into the fountain to ensure your return to Rome, look at the church on the opposite side and the sculptured head of a young woman. It is said the artist who designed the fountain was the rejected sweetheart of the girl. He insisted that she or her spirit look at his work of art for the rest of her time whether she liked it or not.

MUSEUMS TO LEARN ABOUT THE ITALIANS

Burcardo Theatrical Museum, Casa del Burcardo, Via del Sudario 44, off the Largo di Torre Argentina. Open daily 9 A.M. to 2 P.M., closed holidays. Free.

Let the curtain rise! It's the early Italian theater, and a period that greatly affected modern theater. The commedia dell'arte, as it is called, comes alive in this small but charming museum. Outside, the building sign reads "Società Italiana degli Editori." Go to the second level where the collection begins.

The play starts as you look at the hundreds of clay figures of characters that make up the members of the comic troupe. Masks, funny faces, silly poses, colorful costumes are all part of the story. Imagine it is the year 1600. You are in a public square in Italy. The prosperous merchants, haughty noblemen, eager countryfolk, wiggling children, and vendors selling medical cure-alls, love potions, and sweets are all milling about. You are watching jugglers toss plates and balls into the air. The performance is on a crude six-foot platform in the middle of the square. The act ends as one man leaps to another's shoulders and continues juggling. The crowd buzzes with approval and the jugglers leave. Behind the jugglers is a ragged curtain with a rough charcoal sketch of a street scene. The dramatic actors enter.

The audience immediately roars with laughter. And why not? They know every character from his mask and his standard costume. Here is Pantaloon, a silly, easily fooled old man, and his learned friend, the Doctor, full of long words he can't understand. There is tricky Harlequin in his patched suit ready to give the bragging Captain a fierce beating. The adoring lovers appear with their servants, scheming and schemed against. All of the players wear half masks that tell the audience at once who they are. Only the romantic leads are allowed to show their real faces.

The audience knows what part each actor will play but it does not know what sidesplitting comic situation will happen. Neither do the actors. Only a few minutes earlier the company manager gave them the plot outline (scenario), posted on a hook. They know the main line of action and when to enter and leave. The rest they will make up as they go along. In music, dance, song, poetry, and sight gags, they will create a play as the audience watches.

This could be the story. The sly Harlequin has told Pantaloon that a rich noble lady has fallen in love with him. To protect the lady's reputation Pantaloon disguises himself as a woman to go and meet her. Harlequin tells the same story to the Doctor and now the silly old men are dressed in ridiculous ladies' clothes, each sure the other is the woman madly in love with him. The actors perform to perfection and the crowd is on the ground roaring with laughter.

This was the commedia dell'arte, a troupe of strolling players whose fame spread to France and England. The same stories and situations they created on the spot are the very ones you enjoy in the theater and the movies and on television.

Examine the facial expressions of the figurines in the case and note the names of the comedy characters on a piece of paper. The case in the center of the room contains Harlequin's costume and his slapsticks, made with two pieces of wood attached at one end by a strip of leather. When slapped together they make a loud cracking noise. The actors used these to indicate they were comically beating each other up. The boards would not touch the actors, but the sound would be ear-shattering.

On the floor above, toward the back of the room, along with old theater posters, are several portraits of one of Italy's most famous vaudeville comedians, Petrolini. Back in the 1920s and

'30s, Petrolini's appearance on a stage assured success for any play. He too was best-known for his imitations and on-the-spot plots.

As you look at each picture, which commedia dell'arte character does he remind you of? Try your skill at the funny faces. Or better still, attempt an improvised play, after you've decided on the main plot line.

When you leave the museum, walk to the old ruins in the center of the LARGO DI TORRE ARGENTINA. These were uncovered when work on a new apartment building had begun. Although the building was never completed, a whole community of Roman cats moved in. It has become the official meeting place for hundreds of these feline citizens. The cats wander about, doze in the shade, and get fed quite regularly by devoted ladies. At night, they roam through the back alleys of the city.

Carabinieri Museum (Il Museo Storico dell'arme dei Carabinieri), Piazza del Risorgimento 46 (near the Castel Sant'Angelo and Vatican City). Open Tuesday, Thursday 10 A.M. to 1:30 P.M., Sunday 10 A.M. to 12:30 P.M. Free.

Touring the city you can see men dressed in black, wearing high, stiff, half-moon-shaped hats and long-tailed coats with a red stripe running down the side of the trousers. These policemen are called "carabinieri." The word actually means a soldier on foot or horseback armed with a special type of rifle known as a carbine. The use of the gun goes back to the sixteenth century. Regiments of these soldiers were used throughout Europe.

The Italian carabinieri were originally part of a select group set up by Victor Emanuel I, King of Sardinia, to watch over his territories. After Italy became one nation they acquired other special police duties. One squadron still guards the President. When they are patrolling, they always walk in pairs and keep an exact slow pace. The men wearing capes ride horses.

The museum illustrates the full history of these unique men, including their adventures in Africa. Starting in Room V on the second level, you can examine models wearing uniforms that go back to around 1830. The models may seem a bit short to you. Perhaps the guard can tell you the required height of a carabinieri.

Museum of the Mint, Via XX Settembre (inside the center of the Treasury Building courtyard). Open every day 9:30 A.M. to noon, except Sunday. Free.

An ideal place to learn about Italian money as well as see a rare collection of old coins from all over the world. What nations did the square and porcelain coins come from?

VILLA BORGHESE: A PLEASURE PARK AND GARDEN

The largest and most beautiful park in Rome has green fields, old, shady trees, and many statues. There are lots of activities to choose from.

Bicycle Riding. Rental places are everywhere. One in particular is very close to the arched wall leading into the park. The price is about 300 lire (48 cents) an hour. While riding through the park, stop for a few minutes and watch a soccer game. This version of football has a round ball that is never touched by arms or hands. The two teams of eleven men move on a field with a goal at either end; the ball is moved chiefly by kicking or by bunting with the head. Soccer is the most important sport in Italy. During the major league soccer season, September through May, thousands of fans jam the stadiums all over the country. Each town has its own team. If you watch the young people playing long enough, you may be invited to join.

Horseback Riding. Ask for the section called the "Galoppatoio" (Riding Track) to rent a horse. The fee is rather inexpensive. Watch the riders practicing jumps.

If you are in Rome during the spring, you can attend the horse show in the Piazza di Siena, right near where you rent the horse. It is one of the most beautiful natural amphitheaters in the world. The show brings international teams from all over the world and many of the finest horsemen, including Olympic team winners. The jumping competition is filled with exciting moments. A lot of young Italians are horse enthusiasts and perform in the finale. On the last day the "Carabinieri Carrousel" (policemen on horseback) do a dazzling display accompanied by their own special band. This horse show is the only public performance given by the carabinieri throughout the year.

Boat Rides. The Giardino del Lago (Lake Garden) is open from 7 A.M. until sundown and is near the Piazza di Siena amphitheater. Choose between a rowboat, pedalboat, or motorboat to go among the ducks and swans as you glide by an old temple.

Zoological Gardens. Open 7 A.M. until sundown and near the Giardino del Lago, it houses more than thirty-five hundred animals. The animals are kept in open areas rather than in cages but are separated from you by a long ditch which they can't cross. The zoo is famous for being the birthplace of the first twin elephants born in captivity. Of course, they were named Roma and Remus.

Puppet Shows. There are two central places where the Punch and Judy shows are performed—the Giardino del Lago and the Pincio. The stories or acts go back to the beginning of the commedia dell'arte. Yet you can probably see their similarity to old movies on television with Laurel and Hardy, Abbott and Costello, or more modern comedians.

The interesting moment to watch is at the very end when Pulcinella, the servant, whose name means "buffoon," lowers a small bucket to collect coins for his show. Many very young people, after giving their offering, say "Arrivederci" (See you soon).

Cartoon Theater. If you like cartoons or have a younger brother or sister, the Cinema dei Piccoli near the park entrance has a treat for you. This small movie theater shows forty-five minutes of continuous cartoons. It is open Friday through Sunday 10 A.M. to 12:30 P.M. and 3 to 8 P.M. and costs 150 lire, less than 25 cents. The movies seen included *Miao, Miao, Arriba*. Even though you don't understand the Italian language, the humor is quite easy to follow.

The Villa Borghese is a wonderful change of pace from sight-seeing. It's perfectly safe because the Italian people enjoy young people and really protect them. Make sure you know how to explain where your hotel is located and where you want to go. As a reminder of this lovely garden, you may want to buy something to recall your visit. Odd-shaped balloons sell for 200 lire (32 cents) and unusual pinwheels are the same price.

A LITTLE OUTSIDE OF ROME

BEACHES

The Lido. The best way to go is by car, so that you can go to one of the farthest beaches, Castel Fusano. It is the least crowded. You can also get there by the subway. It leaves from the "Stazione Termini" (train station) and takes about thirty minutes.

You don't have to wear your swimsuit on the way. Little wooden rooms called "cabanas" can be rented right on the beach. The entrance fee includes the use of the dressing room, 1000 lire ($1.60). It is important to get there early, particularly on the weekend. The cabanas rent quickly. Italian families eat their lunches and play cards on the little cabana porches.

They have volleyball nets up and there is always a game going. Here is another chance for you to join in the fun.

The more central beaches have cafés, snack bars, and playing areas for children; some have pools for small children. Lunch at the Vecchia Pineta by the sea is especially delightful. For dessert the boy at the ice cream bar will make you a great "gelato misto," giving you every one of the twelve flavors of delicious ice cream shown in his glass-covered counter; only 50 lire (8 cents).

The sand at this beach is a gray color and looks black when it is wet. Be careful, for this kind of sand absorbs the sun's rays and you can burn easily.

Fregene. Fifteen minutes away is Fregene, a less crowded beach with green pine woods and golden sand. Many movie stars have beautiful villas in this area. If a policeman is nearby, ask him to point out the different homes. You can get to Fregene by bus, which leaves from Via Alessandria 200, in the center of the city.

Ostia Antica: An Antique City. Open 9 A.M. till one hour before sunset. Fee: 150 lire (24 cents), half price on holidays. Parking: 100 lire (16 cents).

On the way back from the beach, stop to see these amazing ruins of an entire ancient city, the port of Rome two thousand years ago. Now only the outlines of homes, gardens, stores, pools, and doorways remain. No terrible disaster hit Ostia Antica; it just died when people left. The entire area became overrun with undergrowth and dust. It was rediscovered when someone was digging up the road.

Wander through the lanes among gardens and ghosts of grand temples and full markets. The museum has all kinds of interesting masks and statues. In July and August the amphitheater has live shows. In back of the amphitheater is a mosaic floor covered with pictures of different animals. It was here that the animal traders had their stores. The Romans were and still are very fond of animals, but at that time to have rare pets was a sign of wealth. So people would contact these merchants to arrange their purchases.

E.U.R.: Modern Rome. Here is a full day of activity but a different kind of experience. The initials stand for "Esposizione Universale di Roma" (Universal Exposition of Rome). This part of the city was built by Mussolini as a permanent world's fair. Now it has carefully planned special centers with parks and shopping. Numerous business and government buildings have moved here from the center of Rome, making this area a complete modern community. It is a short drive by car or a fifteen-minute ride by the underground train, Metropolitana. Trains leave from the Stazione Termini quite frequently. Ask for one going in the direction of the Lido. After nine stations, get off at the Esposizione. The fare is 50 lire (8 cents) and is well worth it. To start your tour, go to a delightful folk museum. Turn right as you leave the station.

Museo Nazionale delle Arti e Tradizioni Popolari (Folklore Museum), Piazza Marconi 8, Quartiere dell'Esposizione. Open daily 9 A.M. to 2 P.M., closed Monday. Free.

Knowing how people live, work, and play is the best way to understand them. The museum has an amazing exhibit of the folkways of the Italian people covering all parts of the country. You will find old Italian mangers; masks from one of the oldest traveling comedy troupes (commedia dell'arte); cone-shaped houses from southern Italy called trulli cottages; and elaborate costumes, handicrafts, armored Sicilian puppets, carts, instruments, and hundreds of displays of old city and country life. Ask the guard where you can hear a special folk song performed just for you during your visit.

The Pigornini Prehistoric and Ethnographical Museum (at the opposite side of this square) has an excellent collection of ancient items dug up from the ground. These will give you an idea of how the ancient Romans lived. There are cases filled with unusual jewelry, looking amazingly similar to those sold today. The rarest exhibit contains metal spearlike items that were used for money. Carrying large amounts of these peculiarly shaped pieces to buy something expensive at the market must have been quite a chore.

Lunch? Eat at one of many nice restaurant cafés right near the museums or go to the charming park near the train station and enjoy a light meal sitting next to the cool lake. The park has several features: paddle boating, 450 lire (72 cents) an hour; motorboating 1000 lire ($1.60) an hour for three people; Gustav the talking parrot (Italian only); and miniature golf. Nearby you can swim in a huge pool for 240 lire (40 cents).

Automobile fans can begin their driving lessons in the Parco Scuola del Traffico. This driving school is specially designed for young people. The cars are very slow, but you have an entire miniature village to cover. The school is open every day from 3:30 to 9 P.M. and is located close to Luna Park in front of the Campo delle Tre Fontane (Field of the Three Fountains). The price is 315 lire (50 cents) for the car and 365 lire (58 cents) for a lesson. Ten lessons cost 2006 lire ($3.20).

If you still have time, energy, and money you can go to Luna Park, an amusement area next to the driving school, with plenty of rides to keep you busy for hours.

Tivoli: Villa d'Este's Enchanted Gardens. About thirty-two kilometers away (twenty miles) by Rome-Avezzano Railway; bus lines from Via Gaeta; by car on Via Tiburtina; or regularly conducted tours. Open 9 A.M. till sunset. Fountains work from 10:30 A.M. to 12:30 P.M., 3 P.M. till sunset. Fee: 200 lire (32 cents). Evening lighting: May, June, September—Tuesday, Thursday, Saturday, and Sunday; July and August—nightly 8:30 to 11:30 P.M. Fee: 400 lire (64 cents).

Just inside the entrance is a "growing calendar" right in the shrubbery directly below the palace. You'll find today's date all spelled out. Ask the guard to show you how he changes the numbers and the names of the months.

Inside the gardens, duck under the Round Fountain, chase colorful rainbows, or listen to the music of the Organ Fountain. There are over fifteen hundred fountains to look at.

Cross the garden and find the Rometta, a small model of the Tiber Island, and other miniatures of places in Rome. Look for all the odd names of the fountains like Peacock, Deluge, and Dragons. Don't miss the Fountain of the Owl, which cries out like a real bird. Make notes of the funny names and then, on the way home, see who can tell the most fantastic story using the names as part of your amazing tale.

If you can stay till dark, the gardens become a wonderland. The fountains, greenery, and palace light up and you are in a faraway land.

Hotels, restaurants, shopping, vocabulary, and events for Rome are listed following the section on Venice.

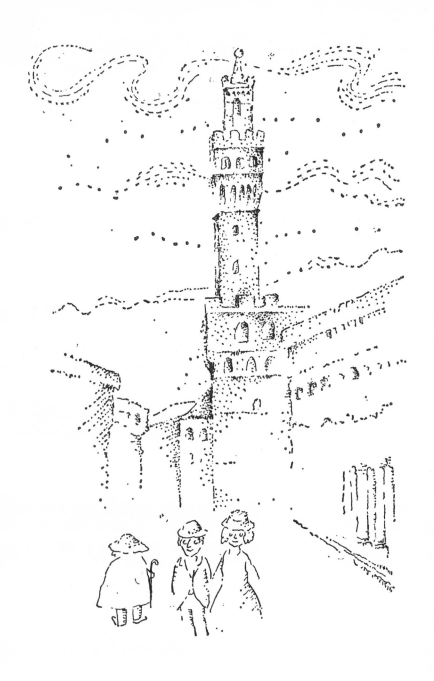

9. FLORENCE

Living Museum

There are two parts of the city, separated by the Arno River and connected by several bridges. The **Ponte Vecchio** is the most famous bridge, mostly because it has many shops on it, selling leather, jewelry, and other items. The two streets along each side of the river are called Lungarno.

After World War II when the people of Florence were ready to rebuild the Holy Trinity Bridge, they waited a long time until they had enough money to put it together stone by stone so that it would appear to be the exact same bridge all of Florence remembered from before the war. First they tried to find all the original stones. When they found that some of the stones were too crushed to use, they hunted in old records to locate where the stones had come from four hundred years ago. The rebuilding of the bridge took thirteen years, but to the people of Florence it was worth it.

In November of 1966, during the terrible floods, the water from the overflowing river went as high as twenty-six feet. With great determination, the people cleared out and rebuilt the affected parts of the city in a matter of a few months. Not for one moment did they lose their sense of humor. The day after the tide went down, stores were ready for business with signs that read "Open—but nervous," or "Mudbaths, cheap." Today the only reminder of the floods are black marks on buildings to show how high the water reached or pictures in restaurants and hotels to give you an idea of the terrible things the water had done.

There are two reasons why the Florentines keep their city looking as it did five hundred years ago. In the first place, they're proud of the black and white churches, the stone palaces, the arched bridges and tall towers. And most Florentines earn their living assisting the thousands of travelers who have come to their city. Visitors come to admire the paintings and statues created by some of the greatest artists and to see how they lived during the amazing time called the Renaissance, the rebirth of knowledge.

During this period, the thirteenth to sixteenth centuries, modern capitalism established itself. Rich Florentine families became bankers. Until that time the church forbade the lending of money for interest. And for the first time, it became possible to get credit by showing a letter.

At the same time two important Florentine writers became very popular throughout Italy, Dante for his long poem *The Divine Comedy,* and Boccaccio for witty, naughty stories. The Italians so enjoyed these two writers that the Florentine dialect became the standard for educated people. Before then everyone spoke his own dialect, each of which sounded like a different language. Florence blossomed because the banking, great writing, and great artists came at the same time. Get to know the city through some of the people who made this time possible.

The Medici were a rich and powerful family who ruled Florence for three hundred years. The Medici helped support many of the painters, sculptors, architects, and poets of the time.

They built magnificent palaces and churches. Their collection of paintings and statues is the basis for two museums, the Uffizi and the Pitti.

The Medici Chapel, Piazza Madonna degli Aldobrandini (opposite the Palazzo Medici Riccardi). Open summer 9:30 A.M. to 4:30 P.M., winter 9:30 A.M. to 4 P.M.; Sunday to 7:00 P.M. Holidays 9:30 A.M. to 1 P.M. Closed Tuesday. Fee: 150 lire (24 cents), Sunday free.

Inside the Church of San Lorenzo, the oldest Christian church in existence (A.D. 390), is the chapel. Here will be found the elaborate tombs of the Medici grand dukes. The church, in the form of a cross, has a very elaborate altar. Go behind the altar to the Chapel of Princes. Right inside the door is the Medici family crest. Some say the origin of the name comes from the five gold balls ("dieci" in Italian is the number ten and "me" means half). Another story is that the early members of the family were doctors (medici) and their patron saints were Cosmas and Damian, two martyred doctors. Perhaps the balls on the coat of arms are in reality pills. In any case, since the family were known to be bankers, it is thought the three balls used as a sign for pawnshops originally came from the Medici crest. The meaning of the sixth ball (blue) also is in dispute. Some historians feel it was for Catherine de Médicis, who became Queen of France.

After you leave the chapel, ask where the New Sacristy is. It was worked on by Michelangelo and holds several marble statues. All have interesting names. Count the number of statues Michelangelo carved. Ask the guard if you have the correct number.

RAPHAEL was one of the greatest painters of his time (1483–1520). He is famous for his fifty canvases of Madonnas, his works in the Pope's palace, and the restoring of ancient Rome.

Uffizi Gallery, Loggiato degli Uffizi 6. Open daily 9:30 A.M.

to 4 P.M., Sunday and holidays 9 A.M. to 1 P.M.; closed Monday. Fee: 200 lire (32 cents), Sunday free.

Go to the Raphael Room to see the "Madonna del Cardellino" (goldfinch). Look closely at the faces in the picture. Each tells an entire story. Notice the deep red colors. No other painter has ever been able to come close to these shades.

An unusual feature in Raphael's paintings is his horses. You'll find they are much shorter and heavier and have more muscles than our modern horses. Probably they were bred for battle rather than for speed.

MICHELANGELO (1475–1564) was the son of a poor Florentine gentleman. At the age of thirteen, against his parents' wishes, he became an artist's apprentice. His master sent him to meet Lorenzo dei Medici, who was so impressed with the young boy's work that he invited him to stay at his home.

As the years passed, he created some of the world's greatest masterpieces—the Sistine Chapel ceiling, the "Pietà," and "David." In addition to his sculpture and painting, he was a powerful poet, architect, and military engineer. Michelangelo's enormous versatility and superiority in so many arts have led to his being referred to frequently as a model "Renaissance man," a term which has come to mean a person who excels in a wide range of cultural activities.

Accademia di Belle Arti (Academy of Art), Via Ricasoli 60. Open daily 9:30 A.M. to 4 P.M., Sunday and holidays to 1 P.M.; closed Monday. Fee: 150 lire (24 cents), Sunday free.

A block of marble worked on and then left in a courtyard became one of the best-known statues in the world. "David" by Michelangelo is the marble statue you see at the end of the hall when you enter this building. The Old Testament story of the young boy and the huge giant Goliath inspired many artists of this time to create statues and paintings showing how they thought the event happened. Perhaps they thought the ancient legend meant that they too could overcome their worst enemies.

In any case, "David" was carved when Michelangelo was quite young, twenty-five years old, but already a great master. The sculptor's task is to look at a piece of marble and decide what beautiful form is hidden inside. Perhaps the different shades of marble give him the idea or the size and shape of the piece do. With hammer and chisel the artist works away until he has freed the figure he wants to show.

"David" is a shining example of this, with its fine form, its head and its strong hands telling us many things. Here is a young boy preparing himself for a life-or-death fight to save his people.

Piazza della Signoria. The people of Florence so loved the original "David" that a copy was made and placed in this square when the original had to be moved indoors. The square and its palaces were the setting for an important power fight between the noblemen (emperors, dukes) and the working guild people (goldsmiths, butchers, doctors). The working guild people sat on the marble seats in the open building called the Loggia (gallery) dei Lanzi, to hold their elections or have important meetings, while the Signoria (noblemen) met in the nearby palace. The first statue placed in the square was the crouching lion, the symbol of the strength of Florence. The enemies of Florence, mainly prisoners defeated in wars, were forced to kiss the lion's paw. There are so many statues in this square it almost appears as if a museum has been moved out of doors.

Casa Buonarroti (The House of Michelangelo), Via Ghibellina 70. Open daily 9:30 A.M. to 4 P.M., Sunday and holidays to 1 P.M.; closed Tuesday. Fee: 100 lire (16 cents), Sunday free.

You'll find many art pieces by Michelangelo everywhere you go in Florence, but here you'll see his early work. The

house was bought by him for his family and has many personal
items. It also has some interesting models of his famous statues.

TITIAN was one of the last and greatest of the Renaissance
artists and lived to the age of ninety-nine (1477–1576). When
he was a young boy of ten, he was brought to Venice from his
home in the Alps to study art. As time passed, his works became
known in Florence for their rich tones of red, white, and black.
Titian put the paint on his canvases with both a brush and his
hands. So many of his pictures have women with yellow-red hair
that people today call that hair color titian.

Palazzo Pitti (Pitti Palace), Piazza Pitti. Open daily 9:30
A.M. to 4 P.M., Sunday and holidays till 1 P.M.; closed Tuesday.
Fee: 200 lire (32 cents), Sunday free.

Rich merchants and bankers tried to build palaces which
would outdo each other in size and grandness. This one was
built by the Pittis, one of the wealthiest banking families and
the closest rivals of the Medicis. The people of Florence were
forced to say which family they most favored. Matters became
so tense that two separate groups were formed. One side called
themselves the Party of the Mountain—the Pitti Palace is on
a slight hill; the other side named itself the Party of the Plain—
the Medici Palace is in a flat place.

From the outside the palace looks forbidding, but inside it is
quite different. The rooms are grand but bright and cheerful.
You will walk past furniture and works of art which were part
of the lives of grand dukes for more than three hundred years.

In the ROOMS OF VENUS are three of Titian's paintings. "La
Bella" is a portrait of a lady the artist thought was one of the
most beautiful women in the world. She has titian-colored hair.
Many of the pictures in the gallery show the women a bit
plump, a sign of beauty in that time.

The painting "Pietro Aretino" is of Titian's very close friend.
When the two met, it was a turning point in the artist's life.
Pietro Aretino was a clever writer interested in politics. The two

friends became the center of all the plots going on in the city of Venice.

The third picture, "The Concert," tells a story. The man in the center is playing a harpsichord, the forerunner of the piano. The other man, looking out of the corner of his eye, is holding an unusual instrument. The lady standing nearby may very well be trying to say, "You're not supposed to be looking," or is she? Many of Titian's paintings seem to be part of an exciting tale. He painted people he really knew and tried to comment on the life and times in which he lived.

Before leaving the palace, stop at the Boboli Gardens in the back. The lovely fountains, statues, and greenery will give you an idea of a typical Renaissance garden. It is still used as the setting for concerts, comedies, and masques.

DONATELLO (1386–1466). Very early in life Donatello was able to sculpt pieces made of every kind of material. He would shape metal, wood, stone, and even terra cotta (a hard brown-red clay). As you look at his figures they almost seem to be moving or singing, or dancing. When Michelangelo first saw Donatello's statue of "St. George" he cried, "March!"

Palazzo del Bargello (National Museum), Via del Proconsole 4. Open daily 9:30 A.M. to 4 P.M., Sunday and holidays 9 A.M. to 1 P.M.; closed Tuesday. Fee: 150 lire (24 cents), Sunday free.

The building is strong and rugged. It was built as a small fort to defend the people against warring tribes. Climb one flight up to the GENERAL COUNCIL HALL (Salone del Consiglio Generale) for a view of several of Donatello's statues. In the center of the back wall is "St. George," one of Donatello's most famous figures. See the way St. George is standing. He is ready to defend himself and attack. His face shows worry, but at any moment he will spring forward. Donatello was asked to make the statue by the men of the armor guild.

Directly below the statue is a bas-relief, a sculpture in which the figures stand out from the background. The scene tells the story of St. George and the dragon. Here is the tale. Near a town in Libya, Africa, there was a pond in which a dragon, sometimes called a serpent, lived. He would approach the walls of the city breathing fire and killing all who lived nearby. The dragon promised to stop if the citizens would feed him their sons and daughters. Finally it was the King's turn to give up his daughter. He pleaded with the dragon and offered gold, silver, and half of his kingdom. The dragon refused. Just at that moment, St. George, who was in the army of a Roman emperor, happened to be passing on horseback. With sword in hand, he subdued the dragon and saved the princess. The princess tied her belt around the beast's neck and led him through the streets like a terrified dog on a leash.

Though St. George is the patron saint of England, the English say that he never slew a dragon. It doesn't matter. The bas-relief showing the ugly serpent and St. George on his magnificent horse is interesting even without the story. Don't overlook the sad princess hoping her hero will save her.

Also in this room are two statues of David, one in marble and the other in bronze. How do they differ from Michelangelo's?

LEONARDO DA VINCI (1452–1519). Leonardo's last name came from the small town Vinci outside Florence where he was born. Florence was a busy, bustling place with 100,000 people. The streets were lined with churches, fine shops, and stone houses. At the age of sixteen, Leonardo left his tiny country village and came to Florence, the center of a new and beautiful world filled with music and color. He had a curious mind and wanted to find out about everything.

As a young boy, Leonardo had little time to go to school. He taught himself enough Latin so that he could read books on the many subjects of interest to him. His one bad subject was arithmetic, but he learned enough about adding and multiplying to invent new measuring systems later.

Luckily, Leonardo lived at a time when he could make the most of his studies. During the fifteenth century artists like Leonardo often worked for important princes and dukes, who were their patrons. Leonardo's painting of "The Last Supper," on the wall of a Milan church, was commissioned by his patron. Painting was only one of his duties. Artists were asked to plan and give pageants, and to do the costumes, properties, and scenery. He was also called on to find a way to heat a duchess' bath water.

Leonardo worked in different fields. Although he lived long ago, his notebooks show he had ideas about things made many years later—the helicopter, the horseless wagon (automobile), the telescope, the parachute, maps that show hills and valleys, and much more. Because he was so inventive, people thought he was a magician. He wrote his notes backward. To read his writing you have to hold the paper up to a mirror.

Leonardo, more than any other person, is the Renaissance. This one man, who lived very much alone, saw everything, thought about it, and wrote so much that we marvel at how he did it. Today in the Uffizi Gallery Room XV has his unfinished painting "Adoration of the Magi." See how many objects you can find in the background—horsemen, trees, old buildings. Some paintings have several layers. Here in the background you can clearly see the underpainting, which is in deep brown.

Vinci Museum, near Il Castello. Open 8 A.M. to noon and 3 to 6 P.M. in winter, 8 A.M. to noon and 4 to 7 P.M. in summer; Sunday and holidays 10 A.M. to noon. Fee: 50 lire (8 cents).

If you are going by car outside of Florence, stop in the little village of Vinci. The Vinci Museum is in an old castle. The view from the top is worth the trip, but better still are the show-cases inside. Around the huge room is an exhibit that will help you understand the different aspects of Leonardo. His wide, varied accomplishments and interests in technology, medicine, music, military science, anatomy, and other areas are represented in the museum.

A few more renaissance discoveries to admire are at the **Baptistery of St. John the Baptist,** Piazza del Duomo, is the world-famous GATES OF PARADISE, a name used by Michelangelo when he first saw it. It took the sculptor, Lorenzo Ghiberti, almost thirty-five years to complete these panels. Count the number of panels you can find. The answer should be fourteen. You may have to look closely for the last four. The panels show scenes from the Old Testament—Adam and Eve sent from the Garden of Eden, Cain and Abel, Noah and the Ark, the story of Moses, Saul and David (including David slaying the giant Goliath), the Queen of Sheba's visit to King Solomon, and several more.

LEAVING THE RENAISSANCE

Collodi: Pinocchio's Home Town. Thirty-nine miles west of Florence, you come to a small village set on a hill, Collodi. It is now a special place for all the fans of the wooden puppet Pinocchio. He, of course, is the mischievous storybook character with a pointed nose and bottle-green suit who has several adventures with Geppetto, the woodcarver who made him, the talking cricket, the cat, the beautiful fairy with the blue hair, and others.

Few people remember the name of Pinocchio's creator, Collodi, which was not his real name but one he used for his books. He took his pen name from the town his mother was born in. His real name was Carlo Lorenzini.

Now you can see the bronze statue made in Pinocchio's honor. Money sent by children all over the world paid for it. Next to the statue is MAGIC SQUARE, where the puppet's adventures are shown in colored tiles. There is also a copy of THE RED CRAWFISH INN, where the cat ate much too much and became quite ill. In the nearby Villa Garzoni Gardens, don't be surprised to find the keeper looking very much like an adult Pinocchio.

Hotels, restaurants, shopping, vocabulary, and events in Florence are listed following the section on Venice.

10. VENICE

Mirror City

Have you ever heard of a city built on water without any streets? Instead there are canals, or waterways, going around the more than one hundred islands which make up the city. Many of the canals are so small that boats can't even get through. The main waterway, called the Grand Canal, is two miles long. All 177 smaller canals stem from this main street and are connected by four hundred tiny bridges.

The only wheels in Venice are on children's toys or baby carriages. If you arrive in an automobile, you leave it in an enormous garage outside the city. Every kind of boat sails the canals. Some are unique to Venice. Early in the morning, scows line up to carry the vegetables, fresh meat, and other goods to the city markets. To get from one place to another, you can use the "vaporetto" (steamboat), a large power boat that looks like a small ferry and takes the place of a public water bus. It is the least expensive way to get around. For faster but more expensive service, go in a "motoscafo," a motor launch which acts as a private water taxi.

But the most famous boats in Venice are the gondolas, which

look like sleek black canoes with curved ends. The craft is said to be from Turkey. No one is sure what the word "gondola" actually means. Some scholars say it comes from the Greek word for cup or, of all things, mussel shell. It does have the shape of both items.

The gondola is built in the boat yards of Venice, tucked away in the back canals of the city. If you ask one of the workmen he may even make you a miniature craft. Find out how much it will cost first.

The boats are made of several different woods—oak, walnut, cherry, elm, or pine—and are immensely strong and fast. The modern gondola does not often have the "felze," the little black cabin, but it still is thickly carpeted and fitted with a brass sea horse at the front. All of them are the same, except some are a little bigger for ferry runs or are toylike models for racing. They are slightly lopsided, with one side somewhat bigger than the other for the oarsman to have a place to row.

A new gondola costs about $900 and is usually paid for a little bit at a time. Every three weeks or so in the summer it must go back to the yards to be scraped of weeds and tarred again. In the 1700s there were ten thousand. Today there are about four hundred.

It is not at all easy to row a gondola. The blade must be kept in the water going either backward or forward. This must be done to keep the front (bow) straight. The gondolier in his colorful sailorlike costume and flat straw hat has his feet firmly placed almost in a balletlike position, toes a little out. The oar is raised to waist height, the body twisted in the opposite position; the gondolier turns with a graceful swing, and you're off and gliding gently through the water in a very steady movement. Occasionally the quiet sound of the oar will be broken by the gondolier singing or giving warning cries to the other boats. Prices for the ride differ according to where you're going but the average is 1500 lire ($2.40), which will take you from the station to the main part of town. A half-hour ride in a gondola with as many as four people costs about $6 to $8. There are some extra charges. It is important to fix the price of your ride ahead of time.

Venetian life is ruled by the water. The businessman cannot hop into his car and rush off to work. The housewife has to take a boat to go to the store to buy groceries. To get to school, young people must leave very early, even though the distance is short. They have to walk across a variety of bridges and through a maze of alleyways to be there on time. Luckily, some people go to school near a water bus stop. Parents who are nervous about their children getting to school watch their progress through a telescope on the terrace, for some must go halfway across the city. Water makes life move more slowly.

Waterways have their own activity. Early in the morning food is delivered on barges as the day begins. Hundreds of boats go about their chores—parcel post boats, milk boats, ambulance boats, garbage boats, fire boats. The canals are always patrolled by police boats, which make sure the five-mile-an-hour speed limit is observed and that all boatmen obey the traffic lights at important crossings.

The few people who don't rely on boats for their work are the road repair men. First they drain a small part of a canal by blocking it off, then they walk around in the deep mud to fix the pipes or mooring poles and carry away the silt to clear the canal. When everything is repaired, they fill the canal and traffic begins again.

Venice was settled more than fifteen hundred years ago by Italians escaping from tribes coming down into Italy from the north. They took refuge on an island since their enemies did not have boats.

Venetians became sea traders. One of the most famous is Marco Polo. He searched for new places to buy and sell things and brought oriental fineries and rare articles from Arabia,

China, and the Indies back to Venice—silks, marble, cloth of gold, ivory, spices, rubies. People flocked into the city from all over the world to trade and also to admire the rich palaces and churches that seem to float on the top of the water.

As you arrive in Venice by boat, you'll pass houses and shops that come right to the edge of the canal, with stairs leading into the water. You'll tie up at a colorful mooring pole and enter the mirror city. Its reflection is always in the water; in an unusual way, and because the city "sees" itself, perhaps you will see two cities—the real one and its image.

ON LAND, TO LEARN ABOUT THE SEA

No traffic noises will bother you, only the sound of people moving along the street, neighbors shouting from the top floors, and the water slapping against the stone houses.

Piazza San Marco (St. Mark's Square). Perhaps the best place to start is at the center of Venetian life, the Piazza San Marco. Sit outdoors at the Caffè Quadri, on the north side, where a small orchestra plays pleasant music three times a day. You can get an over-all feeling for the square here.

The Legend of St. Mark. What did St. Mark have to do with Venice? The traditional story goes back to 829. The Caliph of Egypt, supreme ruler of the Moslem state, was hostile toward Christianity. When he decided to build a splendid new palace he instructed his men to steal treasured objects from Christian temples.

Two men from Venice, Buono and Rustico, heard about the Caliph's plan while they were moored in the port of Alexandria. Fearing that the city's Tomb of the Apostle St. Mark would be destroyed, the Venetians devised a plan to save the saint's remains. Convincing the official priest of the temple to assist them, they quickly removed St. Mark from the tomb and replaced him with another shroud-covered figure. They placed St. Mark in a deep basket and covered him with herbs and pork. Slowly walking through the streets of the city, the Venetians shouted "Khanzir! Khanzir!" "Pork! Pork!" Since pork is repulsive to Mohammedans, and most Egyptians are Mohammedans, no one would come near. When the men finally reached the boat, the delicate cargo was placed between two slabs of pork.

As soon as the Venetians had opened St. Mark's tomb a sweet, spicy odor crept through the city. The Moslems traced the smell to the tomb. Even though the tomb contained a body, they were suspicious and quickly went to the port, where they had been told Venetians had a ship. They searched the boat completely but dared not touch the pork. Seeing nothing, the Moslems allowed the ship to sail.

A fresh wind rapidly sent the ship out onto the high seas. Two days later the water became so rough that the Venetians feared they would sink with their sacred treasure. All at once one of the passengers, a priest, had a vision that St. Mark had told him to furl the sails and he would lead everyone safely out of the storm.

Days later the ship sailed into the port of Venice. Everyone there rejoiced when they heard about the miracle.

Legend has it that the event was the turning point in Venetian history. Trade with other nations flourished, since it was felt among mariners that the port was especially blessed. Coins were minted, banners were woven, and a church was built to honor St. Mark, who was declared patron saint of the city. When Venetian men went to battle the cry was "Viva San Marco!"

The Square. In ancient times, this square was a meadow and in the middle flowed a river. It was filled in, but during the late fall and early spring the water gushes back and people have to walk on boards laid over the water to get around.

Nowadays the square is a favorite meeting place for both Venetians and visitors from all over the world. It is also the home of other most honored citizens—the pigeons, protected because when Doge Dandolo stormed Constantinople, he sent word of the victory by carrier pigeon. They are fed twice a day, once at about 9 A.M. and again at 2 P.M. High above you can hear the nervous flutter of wings as the bird feeder steps onto the square with two bins of corn. He does not move. The pigeons seem to know that the grain will not be distributed until the bells of St. Mark's Campanile strike the hour. No other clock will do. At precisely the first stroke there is a loud rustle and a deluge of birds descends onto the square with a deafening whooshing sound of wings. The struggle to get the most corn off the pavement begins.

All of the pigeons are very tame and enjoy eating out of your hand. They seem to rush after visitors only, while remaining indifferent to Venetians.

Basilica di San Marco (St. Mark's Church). The outside looks oriental, recalling the trading ties with the East. If you counted the marble columns, you would find there are more than five hundred.

Above the main door are four bronze horses which Doge Enrico Dandolo brought back from his battle at Constantinople. They were carried to Paris in 1797 by Napoleon Bonaparte but were returned to Venice in 1815. You can see the horses best by climbing the porch by the stairs inside the church. Can you guess their size? Actually they are over five feet high.

Inside, St. Mark's is filled with wonderful mosaics and rare marble. Look at the gold altar screen (pala d'oro) and take a wild guess as to how many jewels it might have. If you said six thousand, you were close.

Find the door leading to the Treasure Rooms. It has an Arabic arch overhead. Here you find interesting paintings and objects having to do with St. Mark and other religious figures.

Crossing the church you reach the small door leading to the museum. Go to the last room and find the painting "Scene from St. Mark's Life." In full, rich colors you see the entire scene of St. Mark leading the people through the troubled waters from Alexandria to his resting place in Venice. There seems to be a woman in the boat and a man almost springing from the mountain painted in the background.

Torre dell'Orologio (Clock Tower). Open 9 A.M. to noon and 3 to 6 P.M. in summer, 9 A.M. to noon and 2 to 4 P.M. in winter. Fee: 100 lire (16 cents).

The tower is right below the Merceria, the main shopping avenue. Climb the tower from the entrance on this street. Examine the great gold and enamel face on the clock and find your birthday sign. Notice the Arabic and Roman numerals that indicate the hours and minutes.

On the second floor, there is a statue of the Virgin and Child. At her side two small doors open to show the hours and the minutes.

At the top of the tower, the two giant bronze figures, called the Moors, have been striking the hours with their hammer for five hundred years. During Christmas and Whitsuntide, the three wise men and a trumpeting angel are added to the Watch Tower.

Campanile (Bell Tower). Open 9 A.M. to midnight in summer, 9:20 A.M. to noon and 2 P.M. to sunset in winter. Fee: 200 lire (32 cents). Take the elevator up to the top for a splendid view of the sea all around Venice. Do you have any idea how high you are? One clue—it is a little bit higher than a football field is long.

The Piazzetta is a few yards from the square beyond the Bell Tower. It has several places of interest. The two columns close to the water are famous landmarks. Both were brought all the way from Constantinople. One is topped by the symbol of Venice, the lion of St. Mark. He is one of many symbols of the king of beasts you will find in Venice. They are all over the city. Those who carry open Bibles are peaceful. Closed books usually mean war. The winged lion is really St. Mark. On the companion column sits the statue of St. Theodore and his crocodile. He was the patron saint of Venice before St. Mark.

Palazzo Ducale (Doges' Palace). Open 9 A.M. to 6 P.M. in summer, till 5 P.M. in winter. Fee: 300 lire (48 cents), Sunday and holidays half price.

After the Room of the Civil Court (Maranta Civile Nuova), you come to the Polling Room (Sala dello Scrutinio). Here the Great Council votes were counted to elect the Doge and other officers of the Republic.

Two paintings in particular give you a full idea of what naval battles were like. Above the window is Vicentino's "Battle of Lepanto," and nearby Liberi's "Defeat of the Turks in the Dardanelles." Often the Venetian artists liked to show their devilish sense of humor by hiding a portrait of themselves somewhere in a painting. Look hard at the naval Battle of Lepanto, the first painting, and you'll find among all the bodies a tidy little gentleman, calm and neatly bearded, with a lace collar, up to his neck in the water. That is the artist. In the other picture the painter has included himself as a fat, naked slave holding a dagger. While you're near the window enjoy a wonderful view of the St. Mark basin and the other parts of the city.

From the second floor of the Doges' Palace you go down a narrow staircase to the prison called *The Wells.* The cells are a bit dark and gloomy but you can still see where the prisoners wrote on the walls. Next to the Wells were the torture rooms.

From here you go to the prison called **The Leads,** so named because they were just under the palace roof, which was covered by sheets of lead.

Now go through the door marked "Prisons" and you are on the **Bridge of Sighs.** Prisoners passing over the bridge on their way to the judge lamented their fate in such pitiful tones that the bridge took its name from their sighs.

LEARNING ABOUT THE SEA AT MUSEUMS

Museo Correr, Piazza San Marco. Open 9:30 A.M. to 12:30 P.M. and 3 to 6:30 P.M. in summer, till 5 P.M. in winter; Sunday and holidays 9 A.M. to 1 P.M. Fee: 100 lire (16 cents), Sunday and holidays free.

Room XIV is devoted to naval history. In the middle you will see a large ship's lantern which belonged to a wealthy family. At the end of their careers, naval captains would hang the lantern to the mooring poles of their palaces. One of the museum's principal attractions is bits and pieces from the last bucentaur. These were floating royal palaces. How magnificent to sail down the Grand Canal on one.

Museo Storico Navale (Historical Naval Museum), Campo Angelo Emo 2148. Open summer 9:30 A.M. to 12:30 P.M. and 4:30 to 6:30 P.M. (Sunday and holidays 9 A.M. to noon); winter 9:30 A.M. to 12:30 P.M. and 2:30 to 4:30 P.M. (Sunday and holidays 9 A.M. to noon); closed Tuesday. Fee: 50 lire (8 cents).

Here are classical ships along with the only eighteenth-century freight gondola still in existence. Look for the remains of royal boats used by the Doge and noblemen attending the most important ceremonies. And take careful note of the richly decorated model by Antonio Corrandini. Remember that each oar had a man rowing it.

Museo Civico di Storia Naturale (Natural History Museum), Fontego dei Turchi. Open summer 9:30 A.M. to 12:30 P.M. and 3 to 6:30 P.M. (Sunday and holidays 9 A.M. to 12:30 P.M.); winter 9 A.M. to 5 P.M. (Sunday and holidays 9 A.M. to 12:30 P.M.). Fee: 100 lire (16 cents).

The courtyard is part boathouse and part gallery with pictures of admirals, painters, scholars, poets, and architects.

A curious feature of this area is the tiny living creatures who temporarily make their home here—baby seagulls, ducks, salamanders.

TO MARKET FOR FISH AND THINGS

You are about to set out on an adventure into one of the busiest corners of Venice.

Rialto Bridge. This bridge was once the important meeting place in Venice. It was here that men swapped currencies, invested money, rented ships, talked politics, and learned news from the East. Two or three times a year fashion designers from all over Europe would build high platforms and place huge dolls on them dressed in their latest creations. These periodic events were the forerunner of modern-day fashion showings where designers unveil next year's styles. The bridge became the most celebrated place in the world for all kinds of commercial exchange between the East and West and is referred to in the phrase "What's new on the Rialto?"

Food Market. Just across the bridge you'll find yourself in a street crowded with shoppers. During weekdays people gather in front of one open stall after another choosing from displays of fruits, vegetables, flowers, meat, and cheese of every kind. Wander from one shop to the next and learn firsthand the art of bargaining. Italians have been masters of it for centuries. Watch how the scene mounts in excitement as the vendor, who is usually already prepared to lower his price, carries on as though he is being insulted into giving his products away, while the buyer maintains the offended air of one who is being taken advantage of.

Fish Market. Turn right under the arch and then zigzag your way to the city's fish market. Walking along you'll find the street merchants not only shouting but perhaps singing about their wares in order to attract a customer's attention in this crowded area (probably a forerunner of singing commercials).

On numerous open tables are every type of seafood. Look for the mussels, snails, and octopi.

TO SEA, TO SEE THE ISLANDS

Set sail! Go to some colorful islands off the mainland— Torcello, Burano, and Murano. The people who first came to these islands were not adventurers but outcasts. Many disagreed with the government and were told to leave Venice at once. Some climbed the city watchtower to see where else they might live, and seeing where the boats and ships were going, chose a new island home. Taking everything possible with them, they started a new life.

You can reach these islands by taking the vaporetto, water bus, at either St. Mark's Square pier or at the train station. Be sure someone checks the schedule after you get off the boat, to see how you can get to the next island. Two daily guided tours of all three islands are conducted by the CIT company at 9:30 A.M. and 2:30 P.M. from April through October. It costs about 1200 lire ($1.92) and takes three and a half hours.

Torcello. In old times the island was rich with temples and palaces. Today it is planted with fields of vegetables, artichokes, and scrubby orchards. Go for an interesting walk along the shore to the middle of the main square. All around are the remains of a once elegant city: the Council House (from the twelfth century), the Archives Palace, the Provincial Museum (where you will see a wonderful silver-gilded altar piece one

Get Ready! Get Set! Go!

thousand years old), and most of all, the cathedral and the Church of St. Fosca.

The cathedral, begun in A.D. 640, combines building styles: Gothic, high-pointed arches and Byzantine, very round domes. This gives it an Eastern as well as Western feeling. The seemingly confused mixture of styles was the result of the builders' being in a great hurry to finish the construction. They were forewarned that the end of the world would come in the year 1000.

Take particular notice of the mosaics, the lovely pictures and designs made by fitting small bits of stone together. Find the one called "Teotoca Madonna." The tall, slender figure is terribly sad but beautiful. There are tears on her cheeks as she looks down on the church, lovingly holding the Child. Ask the young man in the cathedral to explain how mosaics are made.

Before leaving the island, pose for your picture at Attila's throne, a great stone chair. Attila was the ruler of the Huns, fierce, warlike wanderers in A.D. 400. He gathered together countless tribes from northern and eastern Europe and conquered most of the Western world up to the very gates of Rome itself.

Burano. You will remember this town as a sheer splash of color. Its small toylike houses look like an adobe village surrounded by a desert. The homes are painted red and blue, yellow and orange, white and purple. Rising from this miniature village is a campanile (bell tower), which leans at a funny angle.

Burano lives by fishing and lacemaking, a Venetian craft which goes back centuries. At one time Venetian lace was considered the best and most delicate in the world. You can see the lace made in the SCUOLA DI MERLETTI upstairs on the second floor. Young girls in smocks sit on benches and busily engage themselves in making the most intricate patterns, much as their mothers and grandmothers before them did.

Along the streets of Burano you can see groups of old, black-shawled ladies sitting on chairs in the sun in front of low houses, making lace. Bead-making is also a specialty with women, who like to have you watch them as they stand in their open kitchens poking a wire into a dish of colored glass beads and, with a whish, string them as fast as they can.

Fishermen sail their boats right up to the door to deposit their daily catch. They look a little different from Venetians, who have more delicate features. Looking almost like strong men in the circus, the men are brawny with dark complexions, and always have a smile.

For young people who enjoy painting or sketching, this is an ideal setting. Bring your rainbow-colored paints and plan to spend a few extra hours letting your imagination soar.

Murano. This big island was once the playground for wealthy gentlemen who would stroll under the vines and fruit trees talking about poetry and politics. It was like a large private club. The island became a glass foundry when Venetians became the most expert fashioners of glass. They were the only ones who knew how to make mirrors. After a series of terrible fires in Venice all the furnaces were moved to Murano. By the sixteenth century, thirty thousand people were working on the island. Besides having a particular quality of sand and important vegetation in the water, it was believed the air helped form jewel-like glass.

The real secret, of course, was the men who worked at shaping the glass. The government began to recognize this fact and started doing all it could to keep the glass-men of Murano happy. Nothing was too good for them. Some craftsmen were almost thought of as noblemen. Their portraits were hung in the Museum of Glass, and coins were minted with their pictures. If someone left the island to set up his own business the government followed closely and tried to stop him. In some instances, unco-operative craftsmen were actually killed by the government.

Glassmaking is still the only industry on the island and there are numerous small factories. Learning the mystery of making glass can be fascinating. The artist stands holding a long tube almost like a magic wand. He blows a gentle breath into one end and a round glass bubble appears. With a snip of the iron rod, off the bubble goes. A twist, a chip, another turn, and a prancing horse, a devilish clown, or a masked harlequin appears. Think of your favorite animal and ask these amazing artisans to create it before your eyes.

ALLOGGIARE: TO STAY

ROME

The Hotel Eliseo, Via di Porta Pinciana 30, is directly opposite the entrance to the Villa Borghese gardens, the largest park in Rome. The hotel is small but comfortable and all rooms have private baths. It is fairly inexpensive—10,000 lire ($16). Best of all is the roof garden where you can see for miles around —particularly the cupola of St. Peter's and all of the Villa Borghese.

The Hotel Forum, Via Tor di Conti 25-30, sits alongside the Roman Forum. From your window or from the lovely roof garden conjure up the image of this area two thousand years ago when it was the very heart of Rome. Rooms are about 10,000 lire ($16) for a double with a private bath.

FLORENCE

Villa Villoresi, Via delle Torri, 63/67. This inn goes back to before the Renaissance, seven hundred years ago. It is owned and run by a real countess. Staying here can give you the feeling of living in an ancient villa just as it was lived in centuries ago. It looks out on a garden overrun with flowers. The courtyard inside is filled with orange and lemon trees. All around, antiques fill your room, but you can still enjoy a modern bath. The very old and the new are side by side. You eat from a thirteenth-century table and swim in a twentieth-century pool. The price is about 8000 lire ($12.80) for a double room with breakfast and dinner included.

VENICE

Two places are suggested. The first is in the center of the city and the other a little farther away, to give you the feeling of being an islander.

Danieli Royal Excelsior, St. Mark's basin. Between the eleventh and sixteenth centuries in Venice and Genoa, the name given to the ruling magistrate was "doge." Chosen by the people for life, he was considered the most important man of his day. He called all the meetings and proposed solutions to Venice's problems. The wealthy people would then vote to indicate if they agreed with the Doge.

The Danieli Hotel gives you a chance to live like a doge in a palace. It was originally owned by one of the most adventurous doges, Enrico Dandolo (1108–1205). As a forceful crusader, he conquered new lands for Venice and extended the border much beyond the present city limits. Though very old and blind as well, he commanded a fleet of ships to Constantinople and won valuable Greek territories.

The rooms have a special old-Venice feeling about them, but have modern bathrooms. A double room is approximately 8000 to 15,000 lire ($12.80 to $24). The roof terrace restaurant has a wonderful view of the city, especially when the canals light up with fireworks. As each great flare goes up you get a different, more enchanting view of the city, while hundreds of gondolas bob about in the water.

Hotel Cipriani. Here is island living. The hotel is on Giudecca Island in a quiet garden overlooking the lagoon. All the bedrooms in the Hotel Cipriani are air-conditioned and have private bathrooms. A double room is about 8000 to 10,000 lire ($12.80 to $16). A free motor launch runs day and night between the hotel and the center of St. Mark's Square.

Two unusual places on the island will tell you a little bit about sea life. At the very eastern end of Giudecca, find the old boat yards making motor launches or private water cabs. They are quite a sight.

Another special place near the hotel is a market right off the Rio della Croce. With the arrival of the steamboats (water buses) the gondoliers and ferrymen were sure their jobs had ended and immediately went on strike. Of course, Venice would not be the same without gondoliers or ferrymen, and they did not lose their jobs. The statue in this spot was erected by the ferrymen to thank the Holy Mother for ensuring their livelihood.

MANGIARE: TO EAT

When in Italy eat like an Italian. Breakfast is usually very light, with merely hot chocolate, tea, or coffee and a roll with butter. You can get eggs, cereal, and other items if you ask for them, but save some room for tasty snacks before lunch.

The midday meal at about one o'clock is the big one for most people. You can begin with an "antipasto" (a variety of appetizers). Sometimes there is a huge choice of different dishes, sometimes the choice is very limited. Then comes "pasta," any of several types of noodles (including spaghetti), and here you can choose from hundreds of different kinds. Try "maccheroni" (round, short, tubular-shaped), really invented by an Englishman in the 1700s because he found spaghetti impossible to handle, "fettucine" (thick noodles), "linguine" (very thin noodles), or "tortellini" (a meat-filled miniature doughnut-shaped noodle), just to name a few.

If not pasta, how about soup? Soups here are almost a whole meal in themselves.

Next is the main course. Some of the words you'll find on the menu are: "vitello" (veal), "fegato" (liver); "pollo" (chicken). Veal is the most popular meat and is used in many different dishes like "saltimbocca," a veal with ham—something well worth trying.

Dessert can be cake, fruit tart, or "gelato" (ice cream). Try the Italian favorite, fruit or cheese or both. Ask the waiter to cut an "arancio" (orange) for you and to place a few cherries on the dish for variety. Watch the waiter perform his work of art. Skillfully he will unwind the orange peel as if he were carving a statue. Most waiters learned their jobs from their fathers. Each time they serve you they do it with a great deal of pride.

Dinner is much like lunch but less food is served. Italians eat out of doors, or "all'aperto" as much as possible. If the weather permits, why not, while in Italy, enjoy your meals "all'aperto"?

Rome

As you decide where you are going to eat, you will find different signs. Here are some of the names and what they mean.

The "ristorante" is the fanciest type of restaurant and costs the most money. You will find a few less expensive ones listed a little later in this section.

The "trattoria" or "osteria" is small, patronized by lots of families. They usually go back to the same one every day. The atmosphere is informal or rustic. A fairly new one is Osteria di Charlie Brown, Via Margutta 82. It is very close to the Piazza di Spagna. While you eat in a colorful setting, you can enjoy the funny huge cartoons of Peanuts displayed on the walls.

The "tavola calda" (hot table) serves hot meals but you can usually sit at a counter and eat quickly.

The "pasticceria" has delicious snacks of pastry or little sandwiches. Snack times are 11 A.M. and 5 P.M. First look at the choices. You'll have a difficult time making a selection, so just sample a few this time and try others the next snack time. After you have made up your mind, pay the cashier and give the serving person your receipt with 10 lire (1.6 cents) for his tip. Two particularly good "pasticcerie" are: **Alemagna,** 181 Via del Corso, near Piazza Colonna (open from 9 A.M. to midnight) and **Motta,** Piazza Santa Maria Maggiore, near the railway station (open from 9 A.M. to midnight). Most sandwiches or pastry cost about 120 lire (18 cents).

The "latteria" serves cheese, cake, and ice cream.

Ristorante Casale, Via Flaminia 10 (about five miles outside of Rome). Closed Thursday. The name means "Country Inn" and that's exactly what it was and is. For two hundred years people have been coming here to eat and even to stay overnight on their way to or from Rome. Now you can still see the old barnyard (where you can eat outdoors), the haystacks, and even nesting ducks.

The entrance doesn't have a sign but you'll know when you arrive by the flaming torches that sit near the road. The setting inside has a huge open fireplace, hanging corn, peppers, garlic, a beamed ceiling, antique spinning wheels, and many other things to make you feel as though you are in an old farmhouse.

One special item is a fabulous antipasto, a variety of almost fifty different foods. You can choose the dish you want to try and go back for as many helpings as you like. It doesn't cost extra. This is a good place to sample all the different Italian specialties. When you discover one you particularly like, ask the waiter to tell you the name. Later you can order it again in another restaurant. For dessert try chestnut or cherry jam cake. Price for complete meal about 2400 lire ($3.84). Don't be surprised if you find a movie star sitting right next to you.

Da Meo Patacco, Piazza dei Mercanti 93 (in Trastévere). Cost about $5. Closed for lunch. Dine outdoors or indoors. The piazza is lit with flaming torches; a man on a white horse watches the cars; a gypsy lady sells red roses at the door.

Inside, the walls are covered with horse harnesses and bridle bells of all kinds. Two or three bands of musicians dressed in costumes from all over Italy sing folk songs from Naples, Spain, Russia, Mexico, and America.

Sit near the open fireplace and watch the chicken or lamb you ordered turned on the spit over the fire. This is a very popular place for young people from all over the world.

After dinner, ask if you can ride in the old, brightly colored Sicilian horse-drawn cart.

Piccadilly, Via Barberini 8. Open 7 A.M. until 2 A.M. Choice of either the restaurant, self-service cafeteria, snack bar, or roof garden. Many Italian young people come here for a quick lunch. It is an easy place to find since it is right at the bottom of the Via Veneto.

Order American-style hamburgers, hot dogs, steak sandwiches, and banana splits or milk shakes. The Italian dishes are also very good. All of the food is very inexpensive. Since the idea of a self-service place is fairly new to Rome, you will find Italian parents taking their younger children here just to have a look.

Florence

Tredici Gobbi, Via Porcellana 9. One of the oldest restaurants in Florence. The name means "thirteen hunchbacks," for the Italian superstition that says it is good luck to touch a hunchback or dwarf. "Paglia e fieno" (straw and hay) is their famous dish, made from different sizes of green and white spaghetti covered with a delicious sauce and prepared exactly as it was centuries ago. Meals cost about 1250 lire ($2).

Venice

Al Padovani, Dorsoduro 2839. Fish food reigns supreme. Popular with students and artists, who often trade their paintings for food. The walls are covered with many of them. Lunch and dinner about 1200 lire ($2).

Trattoria alla Madonna, Riva del Vin (near the Rialto). Fish made to perfection. Try the "Risotto di pesce" (fish and rice). Customers are mainly Venetians and gondoliers. Lunch and dinner about 1800 lire ($3).

MONETA: MONEY, ITALIAN-STYLE

The basic unit is called the lira, or if there are many, lire (lee-ra). A 10-lire coin is worth about 1.6 cents. It is not used often except on some elevators to start the car. Fifty lire (8 cents) will buy you a ticket on the city bus. One hundred lire (16 cents) will fetch a Coke or lemonade; 500 lire (80 cents), the average ride in a taxi; 1000 lire ($1.60) a good lunch at a snack bar.

Study the coins so that you are familiar with them. Paper money is marked clearly. As an extra thing to notice, hold the paper money up to the light and famous faces will appear. These are called "water marks," to try to stop forgers from printing their own money.

COMPRARE: TO BUY OR NOT TO BUY

You will want to buy so many things here because Italy has a different store around every corner. Select things that are within your allowance and that you cannot get at home. Many of the items you'll want are exported to the United States. Most stores are open from 9 A.M. until 1 P.M. and then from 4 until 8 P.M. They are closed on Sunday and holidays.

Rome

TOYS

E. De Sanctis, Via Veneto 94. Set of ancient Roman armor (hat, shield, breastplate, sword), 2000 to 6500 lire ($3.20 to $10.40); Roman soldiers, Swiss Guardsmen, 400 to 600 lire (64 to 96 cents); Pinocchio and commedia dell'arte puppets (original Punch and Judy) 1200 to 4000 lire ($1.92 to $6.40). Other stores in the same price range: **Lenci,** Via Bissolati 33; **Girotondo,** Via Frattina 25; **Sonnino,** Via Due Macelli 23.

CLOTHES

Zigone, Via della Maddalena 27. This department store for young people has prices somewhat lower than most stores. Others are: **La Cicogna,** Via Frattina 136; **Leri,** Via del Corso 114.

Carnaby Street is on Via Margutta. The street has become so famous in London that Italians have introduced their own smaller version. It's worth a quick look. Older boys and girls may find some hip mod clothes they can't buy at home. All the shops are called Carnaby Street, but there is one that specializes in clothes for young girls. It is on Via Alibert 14/7. You can buy a silver lamé pants suit for 2900 lire ($4.64), or a mini chemise for 4500 lire ($7.20).

Department stores sell lots of Italian clothes very inexpensively. The quality is not as good as in the better shops, but you can get about everything you want. You can also buy gift items for very little money, everything from leather wallets and records to silk kerchiefs or mini sweaters. Prices range from 625 lire ($1) and up. Save the original wrappings. They give your gift a special Italian touch. The stores are: **CIM,** Via XX Settembre; **La Rinascente,** Piazza Colonna.

BOOKS

Lion Bookshop, Via del Babuino 181; **Anglo-American Bookshop,** Via delle Vite 57.

Most of the books are printed in England and are less expensive than books in North America.

ART GIFTS

Ditta Carlo Manetti, Via Due Macelli 63-65. This shop has models of all kinds of famous statues. The prices begin at about 625 lire ($1) and of course go very high. A special friend might like to have a copy of Michelangelo's "David" or "Moses." It's fun to go into this shop just to look. You'll feel as though you are in a mystery movie set.

Florence

Mercato Nuovo (the Straw Market). All kinds of old stalls are loaded with straw items to buy. Go to the life-size boar, dip your hand into his mouth, and then rub his shiny nose. Italians predict it ensures good things.

Another bargain tip is part of an old custom. It seems the merchants feel if they lose their first sale it will bring bad luck all day. Early birds arriving about 8 A.M. save money. You can buy hats, shopping bags, skirts, mats made of straw. Some of the better buys are Florentine gold trays, jewelry boxes, pepper mills—1250 to 4800 lire ($2 to $7.68). Don't forget to bargain —it's the accepted way to shop.

The Leather School. Run by the Monastery of Santa Croce, this school is worth a visit. Here you can watch young boys learning the art of gold tooling and leather works. You'll find finely made gift items, cuff link boxes, and eyeglass cases from 700 to 1400 lire ($1.12 to $2.24). In the same square you can also see silver, ceramics, and mosaics shaped and molded into wonderful forms and colors.

Venice

GLASS

Salviati, San Gregorio 195. Glassmaking is done in the back. A small inexpensive piece can make an attractive gift for a friend, about 1200 lire ($1.92).

TOYS

Navarra, Via Accademia 1056. Lots of stuffed toys and other items. About 1800 lire ($2.88).

CLOTHES

Roberta di Camerino, Ascensione 1259. All kinds of things to gape at from pop-art dresses to way-out watch straps and lovely scarves. It is expensive, so plan to look rather than buy.

LA SCUOLA (SCHOOL)

On certain days, throughout Italy you may see the streets filled with singing and dancing young people wearing brightly colored felt hats covered with charms and medals. The brim of the hat turns up at the sides and comes to a point in the front. It looks almost like a duck's beak. These are university students celebrating their vacation. They have taken over the city with their gaiety and for the most part the people watch, smile, and enjoy the noise.

Holidays are really the exception. Students are usually very serious. Italians consider education extremely important and think the title of "Professor" or "Doctor" a great honor. From the time young people start school, they look forward with great expectation to attending Italy's leading universities.

Italian children in the lower grades, one through five, "Scuola Elementare," usually go to school from 8:30 in the morning until 12:30, Monday through Saturday. They study many subjects and are given a great deal of homework. School is a very serious matter, with few social activities.

You can usually spot young students by the colored smock with a white collar and bow that they wear over their clothes. There are reasons for this—one person shouldn't look better dressed than the next and the clothes can be kept clean.

After the age of eleven, students enter the "Scuola Media," which is similar to our junior high school. They can, if they wish, go to a technical school where they will begin to learn a trade. Students completing the "Scuola Media" at about fourteen are not required to study further but may choose to go on to the "Liceo" (high school), where they can continue with their trade or prepare for the university. The school year starts in October and goes through the end of July. August 15 is "Ferragosto," the beginning of holiday time. Most families leave the cities for the mountains or the sea on their annual vacations.

AMICI ITALIANI: FRIENDS

On your visit you will want to get to know the best of Italy—the people. You'll find many of them have the same interests you do, but perhaps a different point of view or a special way of expressing themselves.

Here is a list of names of clubs that you can write to:

Rome

Cinema del Fronte della Famiglia, Piazza d'Aracoeli 6. Young people attend special movies and have discussions afterward.

Centro Educazione Artistica, Via Arioso 25. This organization can direct you to schools or clubs for acting, dancing, and athletics.

Young Italian Explorers, Via Teatro di Marcello 47.

Fondazione Marco Besso, Largo Argentina 11. You can also visit the foundation, which is dedicated to exchanging art experiences with children of the world.

Florence

British Institute of Florence, Via Tornabuoni 2.

Venice

ASCI, Esploratori d'Italia, Ponte della Paglia.

Centro Salesiano Arti e Mestieri, Isola di San Giorgio.

These last two organizations are educational and recreational, with daily meetings and many English-speaking members.

ARRIVEDERCI!

Why is Italy so special? Is it the delicious food, the dazzling colors, the significant history, the warm people? The answer is yes, it is all of these. But maybe it is really the Mediterranean light, which gives Italy its special glow. There is so much in this country that when you leave you will say, "Ritornerò presto," "I shall return soon."

PARLARE: TO SPEAK

ENGLISH	ITALIAN	PRONUNCIATION
Please	Per piacere	Pehr pyah-cheh-reh
	Per favore	Pehr fah-voh-reh
Thank you	Grazie	Grah-tsyeh
Thank you very much	Grazie mille	Grah-tsyeh meel-leh
Good morning	Buon giorno	Bwawn johr-noh
Good evening	Buona sera	Bwaw-nah seh-rah
Good night	Buona notte	Bwaw-nah nawt-teh
Excuse me	Scusi	Skoo-see
Hello (on telephone only)	Pronto!	Prohn-toh
Goodbye	Ciao	Chah-oh
	Arrivederci	Ahr-ree-veh-dehr-chee
How does one say	Come si dice	Koh-meh see dee-cheh
How much is it?	Quanto costa?	Kwahn-toh koh-stah?
I am sorry	Mi dispiace	Mee dees-pyah-cheh
Yes (no) sir, madam, miss	Si (no), signore, signora, signorina	See (naw) see-nyoh-reh see-nyoh-rah see-nyoh-reena
What time is it?	Che ora è?	Kay oh-rah eh?
I feel sick	Mi sento male	Mee sehn-toh mah-leh
I need a doctor	Ho bisogno di un medico	Aw bee-zaw-nyoh dee oon meh-dee-koh
To the right	A destra	Ah deh-strah
To the left	A sinistra	Ah see-nees-trah
Where is	Dov'è	Dohv-eh
Bring me	Mi porti	Mee pawr-tee
Speak slowly	Parli lentamente	Pahr-lee lehn-teh-mehn-teh
Ladies	Signore	See-nyo-ray

ENGLISH	ITALIAN	PRONUNCIATION
Women	Donne	Do-nay
Gentlemen	Signori	See-nyo-ree
Men	Uomini	Wo-mee-nee
Entrance	Entrata	Ain-trah-tah
Exit	Uscita	Oo-shee-tah
Drugstore	Farmacia	Far-mah-chiah
Barbershop	Barbiere	Bahr-by-a-re
Hotel	Albergo	Ahl-behr-go
Toilet	Toilette	Toh-lethe
1	uno	oon-oh
2	due	doo-ay
3	tre	tray
4	quattro	kwah-troh
5	cinque	chen-kway
6	sei	say
7	sette	set-tay
8	otto	aw-toh
9	nove	noh-vay
10	dieci	dee-ay-chee
11	undici	oon-dee-chee
12	dodici	doh-dee-chee
13	tredici	tray-dee-chee
14	quattordici	kwah-tohr-dee-chee
15	quindici	kween-dee-chee
20	venti	vayn-tee
50	cinquanta	cheen-kwahn-tah
100	cento	chayn-to

FESTE: EVENTS

Rome

January 5–6   **Befana Fair.** The befana is the old witch similar to Santa Claus. The Epiphany or Twelfth Night festivity is held in Piazza Navona. Children's gifts are given on this day rather than on Christmas. Wooden stalls

	sell toys, all kinds of sweets, and decorations. Toy trumpets and whistles can be heard.
February-March (week before Ash Wednesday)	**Carnevale Bambini.** Young people with masks and costumes parade in the streets.
Good Friday	**Via Crucis.** Way of the Cross procession from the Colosseum to the Palatine Hill.
Easter Sunday	**High Mass** at St. Peter's with special blessing by the Pope to the crowds in the square.
May	**International Riding Contest** at the Piazza di Siena in Villa Borghese.
May	**Sports Tournaments.** International water polo contests at Acqua Acetosa and the International Tennis Championships at Foro Italico. Foro Italico is a large, modern sports arena. Observe and participate in events: swimming, tennis, roller skating, and even marbles.
June 2	**Festival of the Republic.** Military parade in Via dei Fori Imperiali to mark Italy's national day.
June	**Open-Air Art Exhibit,** on Via Margutta. Rome's leading artists show current work.
June 24	**St. John's Day.** Fireworks display in Piazza Laterno in front of the Basilica of San Giovanni. Open-air concerts at the Basilica of Maxentius on Via dei Fori Imperiali.
Mid-July	**Festa de' Noantri** (*Festival for Ourselves*). Popular street festival sets up shop for one week in the old quarter of Trastévere. Different food stalls, amusements, and rides. Fun includes high-flying balloons, roasting pigs, colorful singing and dancing.
December	**Christmas Season.** Young people go to the Church of the S. Maria D'Aracoeli to present their Christmas poems and see lovely manger scenes.

Florence

Easter Sunday	**Explosion of the Cart,** in the Cathedral Square. A fuse shaped like a dove sets off a cart filled with firecrackers. Singing in the square of the cathedral.

	Successful explosion sign of a good harvest. Traditional ceremony celebrates return from the First Crusade.
March–May	Musical programs in the afternoon at the White Hall of Pitti Palace.
April–May	**Arts and Crafts Fair.** Exhibit at parterre in Piazza della Libertà from at least thirty-eight different countries from all continents.
Early May	**Festival of the Crickets.** A colorful folk festival in Cascine Park. Live crickets are sold in tiny cages.
May	**Maggio Musicale.** Annual music festival of opera, ballet, and concerts.
May 19, June 24, 28	**Il Gioco del Calcio.** Football games in sixteenth-century costumes. First played in 1530 to show the Florentines' fearlessness to army about to lay siege to the city. Drums, trumpets, banners, and historical costumes. May 19 played in the Boboli Gardens; June 24 and 28 (evening) it is held in Piazza della Signoria.
Mid-July	**High Fashion Show** at Pitti Palace for girls who enjoy seeing pretty clothes. To arrange for an invitation write to: Centro Nazionale della Moda Italiana, Piazza della Repubblica 59, Rome.
July–August	**Musical evenings.** Concerts and recitals in Pitti Palace courtyard.
September 7	**Festival of the Paper Lanterns.** Dates from olden days when ladies from the mountains carried little lamps of colored paper to light their way to the city on the eve of the birthday of the Virgin Mary. Festival features nighttime children's procession carrying lanterns shaped like animals. Orchestra accompanies the parade. Procession goes to Piazzale Michelangelo, then returns to Ponte San Niccolò and down to the Arno River. Boats with musicians and singers entertain.
September	**International Leatherwork and Footwear Fair.** Exhibition at parterre in Piazza della Libertà shows steps in making shoes. Interesting for various samples of leatherwork.

Venice

April	**Festival of St. Mark's.** Boating race for gondolas called a "regatta." The word originated in Venice.
June	**Palio of Ancient Maritime Republics.** Boating competition among teams from Amalfi, Genoa, Pisa, and Venice, the four old sea powers. Participants dress in historical costumes. Procession begins the contest.
June–October	**Biennale of Venice.** Biannual festival dealing with three different arts:

The International Art Exhibit. Even-numbered years, countries have own special exhibit halls in the Giardini Pubblici (Public Gardens).

International Film Festival. Every year, August through early September. Also, an exhibition of films for children.

Festival of Contemporary Music. Annually in September.

Mid-July	**Festival of the Redeemer.** Procession at night across a bridge of boats. Dates from 1575. Venetians vowed to build a church on the island of Giudecca to end the plague.
August	**Fresco Notturno.** Night scene created by the illumination of boats and buildings lining the Grand Canal. Venetians serenade from the boats.
First Sunday in September	**Historic Regatta.** A race of double-oared gondolas over a four-and-a-half-mile course. Beginning with procession of historical boats.

11. VIENNA

Music in the Air

"Willkommen!" Welcome to Vienna. What other people say with words the Austrians say in folk songs, operas, and symphonies. Great masters of music from Mozart and Beethoven to Strauss and Lehar told of Vienna's legendary woods, rushing rivers, and dreamy palaces. Find out what inspired the great musical geniuses of all time. Learn about the unique style called "baroque." Listen to and enjoy the city's many different melodies, rhythms, and sounds.

THE OVERTURE

In Austria, as in other countries, orders of monks were the center of musical activities. Monks sang many Gregorian chants, religious music still heard in Catholic churches today. Learning the theory of music was part of the training necessary to become a member of the monastery. Monks were careful to pass on their knowledge to young people, mainly in the form of boys' choirs, which rehearsed for long hours at a time. Today many boys' choirs trace their beginnings back eight hundred years.

By the twelfth century the monks had welcomed wandering minstrels called minnesingers into the monastery. Walther von der Vogelweide is considered the most famous traveling balladeer. His songs often contained news or gossip from a neighboring village or town. Eventually he was introduced to the royal court. His story of a nightingale who spied on everyone while perched in a lime tree on the slopes of the Vienna woods was an instant hit. From that moment on the royal court was enchanted with live concerts.

In the fifteenth century Emperor Maximilian I, himself a trained singer and musician, started the custom of having a special court orchestra. Soon other courts followed his example, each one trying for something a little bigger and better. Choirs were formed and personal composers were retained.

Just about this time the craftsmen had formed themselves into guilds, or unions, in order to safeguard their professions. Musicians formed their own association, whether they played in the church or in the court. The musicians' guild soon grew into a large organization. A member's social standing was judged by the instrument he played. The lower groups were lute players, pipers, cornet and trombone players, trumpeters, drummers, and instrument makers. The string players—violin, cello, and bass— were upper class because they were more in demand for concerts.

Music became a popular form of entertainment for everyone. In private homes a delightful evening consisted of folk tunes or imitation court songs either sung in harmony or played on instruments. A particular treat was a musical game called "Quodlibet" ("what you please"). It was a kind of joke. The fun was to find two or more melodies from different compositions and then play them at the same time. Try singing "Mary Had a Little Lamb" while someone else sings "Lullaby and Good Night" at the same time. Or a variation on the game would be to recite poetry against an unusual musical background, Shakespeare with the Tijuana Brass as accompaniment.

The eighteenth century was the wonderful time of the Viennese classical period, sometimes called the Golden Age of Music. The imperial rulers proved themselves staunch supporters of music and opera. Leopold I was not only a lover of music but also a composer. Among his compositions were 79 religious works, 155 dramatic shows with music, and 17 ballets. His son, Charles VI, was known as a violonist and conductor. He would often lead an opera or ballet to the delight of his family, who would play their instruments alongside professional musicians. Among those who took an active part in these evenings was his daughter Maria Theresa, who became Empress of Austria.

Here is where our adventure begins. During the reign of Maria Theresa and her husband Francis I, nearly half a million people lived in Vienna. Most of them were enthusiastic supporters of music and opera. The imperial couple helped to finance many of the composers and artists who came to the city. Nevertheless, the artists found it difficult to support themselves, because their works were so different from the then popular Italian operas and French Italian music.

THE CAST

WOLFGANG AMADEUS MOZART (1756–91) It was the autumn of 1762. A small boy of six, his sister Marianne or Nannerl, as she was called, and their father and mother had been commanded to perform before the Empress Maria Theresa and her family at Schönbrunn Palace. Word had gotten back that the boy was a "kleiner Hexenmeister" (little magician). As a joke, the Emperor made young Mozart perform with one finger and then with a covering placed over the keyboard. He amazed the court with his ability to play music on sight and to compose melodies spontaneously. At the end of the concert Mozart rushed to the Empress, leaped into her lap, threw his arms around her neck, and soundly kissed her.

Wolfgang and Nannerl lived up to their reputation as "Wunderkinder" (wonder children). For Wolfgang it started when he was three years old. Listening to his sister practice her music lesson, he started to play the pieces he had heard. Encouraged by this, his father taught him minuets on the harpsichord. At the age of five he started composing his own pieces. Even at an early age he had an eagerness to learn everything, especially arithmetic. His ear for music was so delicate that he could recall every melody he had ever heard. His sensitivity caused him such pain that he fainted after listening closely to the sound of a trumpet.

Mozart's father was ambitious. He took his two children throughout Europe to perform hundreds of concerts. When Mozart had grown to manhood he returned to Vienna to live. His life in the city was extremely difficult. Although Joseph II appointed him court composer, he was offered a meager salary which just about paid his rent. Mozart had wanted the post for so long he overlooked the question of money. Soon he was kept busy writing dances and minuets for court balls. It was the custom of patrons to use composers to their fullest capacities, locking them into rooms until they completed a selection to be presented at an evening gathering.

Mozart owed money for practically all his life. It was not until after his death that some of his more than six hundred operas, sonatas, symphonies, and other compositions were recognized as the finest music ever written. Most of these works were first completed in his head, then copied on paper as a purely mechanical task. Compositions which seem to have been created on the spur of the moment may have been stirring in his mind for months. His handwriting was beautifully clear and he rarely used an eraser.

Mozart particularly enjoyed writing operas. Among his best were *Don Giovanni, The Marriage of Figaro,* and *The Magic Flute.* The last was the first German opera buffa, a form started in Italy and characeried by two acts, lively humor, well-developed characters, and an extended finale with everyone participating. In spite of Mozart's genius, he died in poverty and was buried in an unmarked grave. His bad luck followed him to his resting place. The day of his funeral was so stormy that the mourners could not reach the cemetery. The coffin was thrown into a grave whose whereabouts are still unknown.

Certain places in Vienna today recall events in the great man's life.

Mozart "Figaro-Haus," Domgasse 5. Open daily 9 A.M. to 4 P.M., Sunday 9 A.M. to 1 P.M.; closed Monday. Fee: 10 schillings (40 cents).

A seventeenth-century burgher's house has a plaque under one of the windows which tells you Mozart lived in an apartment on one of the top floors from 1784 to 1787. It was here that he wrote *The Marriage of Figaro.* The stone stairs lead to the apartment called the Mozart Memorial Rooms. It's exciting to know that Mozart played chamber music here with Haydn and Beethoven. Can you imagine what glorious music could be heard outside these windows by the neighbors?

Here is the composer's study. Look closely at the pictures of him. Does he look at all as you imagined? Carefully examine the scores of his compositions on the walls. Do you recognize any of the titles?

Nearby is the Burggarten, a small, lovely park, where you can see an impressive statue of the great man right in the center. Several memorial markers throughout the city and a square named Mozartplatz honor the great composer.

The best way to enjoy and appreciate Mozart is to hear his music in a Viennese setting.

JOSEPH HAYDN (1732–1809) When they met, Haydn

was forty-nine and Mozart twenty-five. In other musicians Mozart encountered jealousy and treachery. Here, warm friendship and mutual admiration was the rule. Haydn, himself considered the world's greatest living composer, insisted that the title belonged to Mozart. This affectionate regard for people and in particular toward musicians gave him the nickname "Papa" Haydn.

As a small boy of eight he came to Vienna to become a member of the boys' choir of St. Stephen's Cathedral. For years he learned the music with a choirmaster who treated the boys like slaves. Then his voice started cracking as it began to change. After that the choirmaster watched Haydn closely and finally found a reason to dismiss him when he cut off another choirboy's pigtail. Penniless and cold, the boy wandered through the drafty streets of Vienna. Fortunately a fellow choir member offered him a room in his home.

In later years he became "Kapellmeister" (choirmaster and conductor) for Prince Esterházy. The Esterházy musicians were paid very well but there were no living quarters in the palace for their families. The men could visit their wives and children only when the Prince gave them leave. Once when they were long overdue to go, Haydn found a musical solution to their problem. He wrote a composition in which each part finished at a different time. As soon as his last note was played, each musician blew out his candle, took his instrument, and left. Finally Haydn was the only one left, with a brightly lit candle. The Prince got the idea, thought it was very clever, and gave the musicians a much needed vacation. The work Haydn composed for the occasion is called the "Farewell" Symphony.

Haydn's early training in singing influenced him greatly throughout his life. He said, "Singing is almost one of the forgotten arts, and that is why instruments are allowed to overpower the voice." His music has a strong melodic line that can be easily remembered.

Quartets were his natural way of expressing himself. These are compositions written for four instruments, usually strings, with the first violinist playing the melody. He also composed sonatas, operas, church music, choral works, dances, marches, folk songs, symphonies, the Austrian national anthem, and even tunes for mechanical clocks.

Haydn Museum, Haydngasse 19. Open daily 9 A.M. to 4 P.M., Sunday 9 A.M. to 1 P.M.; closed Monday.

Haydn lived the last part of his life in this quaint, old-fashioned two-story house, typically Viennese. Today, inside and out, it is kept exactly as it was when Haydn lived and died in it.

The original huge wooden doors open onto a charming courtyard. The spiral staircase leads to Haydn's small apartment. Medals, manuscripts, pictures, and furniture fill the rooms.

In one of the rooms locate the large bust of Haydn. It is so lifelike he seems to be present. Seated in one of these very chairs, he would look prim in his powdered wig and side locks, properly dressed from his high white collar and red embroidered waistcoat to his bold buckled shoes. Suddenly there might be a knock at the door and his old pupil Ludwig van Beethoven might come for a visit as he had done in these rooms many, many times. During the conversation Haydn would suggest that perhaps everyone would like to see the numerous gifts he had received from famous people during his travels. He was so proud of these souvenirs that he kept them in a special box. These are the very items on display.

Ask the attendant if you may sit by Haydn's very old small grand piano. The tinkling tone it makes is not at all like the sound a piano makes today. Notice the keyboard. The colors have been reversed. The white keys are where the black ones are today.

Stand by Haydn's writing desk. It was here that he wrote the popular *The Creation* and *The Seasons,* two oratorios, music inspired by dramatic poems, sung with solo and chorus voices and accompanied by a full orchestra. *The Creation* is from the Bible's Book of Genesis, how the world began, and a famous poem by John Milton, *Paradise Lost*. It was a tremendous success everywhere. Haydn composed it late in life and considered it one of his greatest achievements. At its first performance he said, "One moment I was as cold as ice, the next I seemed on fire; more than once I thought I should have a fit." Find the original sheet music for both *The Creation* and *The Seasons* in one of the museum rooms.

Gaze out of the picturesque casement windows opening onto the pretty Austrian court where in his last days Haydn loved to sit and look down.

Haydn Memorial Statue, Mariahilferstrasse 55 (near the Technical Museum).

In front of the Maria Hilf Church stands an impressive likeness of the composer. He has just completed an inspiring piece of music.

Throughout Vienna you will find plaques, items, and pictures to remind you of this amazing man's career.

The Society of Friends of Music (Gesellschaft der Musikfreunde), Bösendorferstrasse 12. Write in advance. Free.

A fine Haydn collection includes his square portable piano and the unusual instrument the baryton, which is like a viola. The right hand uses the bow across six strings while the left thumb plucks the sixteen wire strings behind the instrument's neck. It takes a great deal of co-ordination to play correctly. Haydn wrote 170 selections for this instrument for his patron Prince Esterházy, who enjoyed playing it.

About thirty-two miles southeast of Vienna is the peaceful town of Eisenstadt. Everything here is reminiscent of the composer. The castle of the Esterházy princes (Schloss Esterházy) has the Haydn Room (Haydn-Saal). In the noble setting of these huge, elegant halls, Haydn nearly every evening conducted the Prince's orchestra and had his own works performed. Imagine yourself listening to his majestic music or perhaps dancing a delightful minuet.

Haydn-Hause, Haydngasse 21, is the modest house where the composer lived from 1766 to 1778. Through the covered passage and a charming little court filled with flowers, you discover a museum with more reminders of the great musician.

Just a short distance from the house and you are at the **Kalvarienbergkirche** (Church of the Calvary), where you'll see Haydn's tomb.

LUDWIG VAN BEETHOVEN (1770–1827) Wild cheers filled the air as "Papa" Haydn made his farewell appearance after the first performance of his oratorio *The Creation*. Beethoven rushed forward, fell to his knees, and kissed the hands and forehead of the kindly old man. Tears of love filled everyone's eyes.

This act of affection was rare for Beethoven. Although one of the great giants of music, he never heard most of his works performed. From the age of twenty-six he started to become deaf and from year to year got worse until he was finally completely shut out from the world about him. Toward the end of his embittered life, while thousands had the pleasure of his music, he would only hear the sounds inside his own head.

At the age of four Beethoven began his musical training. His father thought that he would show the world he too had a child genius like Mozart. Beethoven had no childhood time of fun and play. Instead, his life consisted of endless hours of practice at the piano, violin, and viola. Occasional beatings were in order if he did not practice enough or made a mistake.

As he grew to manhood he swore he would always remain independent. By the age of sixteen his musical talent had impressed several musicians. In 1792 Haydn, passing through Beethoven's home in Bonn, Germany, heard him play and offered to become his teacher in Vienna. Beethoven eagerly accepted the invitation and hurried to the city which was to become his adopted home.

Beethoven studied with Haydn for a while but decided that he had different ideas about music as well as the world in which he lived. He would not accept the old relationship between musicians and patron. In many cases noblemen felt they owned the composers and musicians, treating them like servants.

Beethoven would not tolerate this attitude. He tried to support himself by giving concerts. He composed many of his selections. He was a magnificent pianist and his listeners regretted his decision to give up the concert stage to work on composing.

Beethoven's attitude toward freedom was expressed not only in his music but also in his life. He would not sit at the servants' table in the house of a prince. When a countess requested him to play and he did not wish to, he refused. When the best-dressed men at court wore powdered wigs, he appeared with his unkempt hair. Although he was impatient and sometimes even boorish, he was never unkind in the thoughtless manner of some aristocrats.

As deafness approached he became more desperate. His whole career depended on his keenness of hearing. He could not allow even his friends to suspect his difficulty. In conversations, he pretended to understand what was said. People thought that he was going out of his mind.

He then became totally involved in his work. He would compose with great speed and his notebooks were always filled with new ideas. He wrote nine symphonies, the opera *Fidelio,* five piano concertos, thirty-two piano sonatas, and other works for solo instruments, voice, and orchestra.

Usually Beethoven could shut out all non-musical thoughts. Once when he could not stand to be alone any longer, he rushed out, forgetting what he was wearing. Walking through the countryside half dressed, he was arrested as a tramp. He was quickly freed when it was discovered who he was.

On other walks along the trails of the Vienna woods outside the city, he enjoyed breathing the scent of the pine trees. Seated by an elm tree, he would ask a friend, "Is there a yellow-hammer bird singing in the topmost branches? There must be the sound of the brook joining the chorus of the yellowhammer, the quails, the nightingales, and the cuckoos. I can almost hear the village band at the town inn. The men often play in their sleep, their instruments gradually dropping down on their chests, then falling silent. Suddenly they wake up, play one or two notes, usually in the right key, and then fall asleep once more."

This love of nature and of life inspired him to write the "Pastoral" Symphony and other works such as the "Moonlight" Sonata. In spite of his difficult life he had faith in a joyful and just world in the future.

Beethoven left his mark all over the city. He never stayed long in one place, for he always wished to be somewhere else. He moved from one lodging to the next, from city to suburbs and back again. It is unbelievable how many buildings have signs that read "Beethoven lived here." His landlords were never too pleased when he left scribbled notes on windowpanes and shutters instead of on paper. They were happy to see him leave, for he played the piano loudly at all hours because of his deafness.

Beethoven Memorial Rooms, Mölkerbastei 8. In the **Adalbert Stifter Museum.** Open daily 9 A.M. to 4 P.M., Saturday 9 A.M. to 1 P.M.; closed Monday.

A devoted music lover, Baron Pasqualati became Beethoven's close friend and protector. He provided him with lodgings from 1804 to 1815. It was exactly what the composer had been seeking. His corner apartment allowed him to see far over the city walls out to the lovely countryside.

Even with a restless spirit, Beethoven delighted in his surroundings. The period turned out to be his most productive. He wrote several of his most famous symphonies, the Fourth,

Fifth, and Seventh, here. But the urge to move on was too strong. Occasionally he would disappear to another part of the city. The thoughtful Baron always kept his rooms in readiness for his return.

These rooms have many reminders of his pleasant life here. A typical morning in his routine might be something like this. Rising at seven o'clock, he quickly finishes cleaning himself with a fast splash here and there. Dashing from the water basin, he forgets to brush his hair, which remains unkempt. At the last moment he remembers to put on some clothes. He does not know that during the night friends have replaced his soiled garments with clean ones. Had they not attended to this chore, Beethoven would continue wearing the same clothes forever.

Peeking around the door of his study, he examines his piles of papers. Everything is in the disorderly state it was in the previous night, he thinks. The servants have been told no one may enter his room. All "tidying" and dusting is done before he awakens. The room serves as a study and sitting room. The largest piece of furniture in the room is his grand piano. The writing table nearby is piled high with manuscripts. Some of the compositions have fallen to the floor. They will remain there until dust completely covers them.

Suddenly he decides to go to the cupboard, take out a tin of coffee, and extract exactly seventeen beans from the can to serve as his breakfast. Carefully carrying the beans to the door, he beckons the servants to prepare his coffee. The servants are quite used to the daily activity. When they return Beethoven is completely involved in his work and doesn't notice the servants.

Today Beethoven is busy on the Seventh Symphony. On his table lies a pile of little dirty, thumb-worn notebooks. Some notebooks have covers; others are tiny bits and pieces of paper loosely stitched together; still others are backs of envelopes folded into bunches. Each bundle has its own date. Some go back ten years. And each unit is connected, with scarcely a month left out. He looks at one pile and then another until he feels he has arranged everything in a new order. Out of all this mishmash a creative genius will compose a masterpiece that will give hours of listening pleasure to millions.

In the first room see Beethoven's favorite piano. It starts on the key of C and ends on the key of F and is equipped with five pedals. There is also an almost perfect bust of the composer. The artist made a mold of Beethoven's face so all of his features would be exact, even scars from smallpox.

When you leave the building notice the house nearby. It is called **Drei Mäderl Haus** (The Three Maidens' House). Franz Schubert, another famous composer, wanted to court three sisters here at the same time. The story was made into an operetta. You'll read about Schubert in the next section.

In the center of the city you can find the beautiful Beethoven monument by Von Zumbusch, the sculptor who designed the Empress Maria Theresa monument near the main gates of the Hofburg Palace.

A little outside the city in the section of Döbling you'll locate the sections known as GRINZING and Heiligenstadt, which has several Beethoven homes.

Döblinger Hauptstrasse 92 is where Beethoven wrote the well-known "Eroica" Symphony in 1803.

In **Grinzinger Strasse 64** he occupied a suite of two rooms. In the back portion his friend Franz Grillparzer, the Austrian poet and playwright, lived with his family. Across the way is a tiny inn where the two friends talked for hours. Today over the entrance is a Beethoven portrait. A sign reads "Zum Beethoven."

Pfarrplatz 2 is where he lived in 1817. It has a delightful rustic atmosphere. From mid-May to mid-June it is the setting for a beautiful Beethoven serenade in the courtyard of the house.

From here take side trips to the hills of the Vienna woods.

Walk along the same path Beethoven strolled in his search for peace in nature. These quiet walks gave him his greatest inspiration. Visit the HEILIGENSTÄDTER PARK for a look at a statue of Beethoven. His flashing eyes and defiant glare give you the idea he could step off the pedestal and start his daily stroll.

Another favorite is along the DÖBLINGER HAUPTSTRASSE past the "Eroica" house, then to the left up a winding, shaded path known as BEETHOVEN WEG (path). Here pass the brook, birds, and perhaps the site of the thunderstorm that became part of the "Pastoral" Symphony. Near the upper end of the path is a tiny park and a bronze bust of the master.

FRANZ SCHUBERT (1797–1828) Schubert's whole personality, sunny yet shy, outgoing but romantic, was a mirror of the Vienna of the nineteenth century. As a young man he decided to give up teaching and wander about aimlessly. He had no regular income, no set meals, and no home of his own. His friends, many of them from his days as an imperial choir boy, offered him different places to stay.

The lives of Mozart, Haydn, and Beethoven had nothing of value to offer him. His circle of friends was not the nobility but young people whose aim was to assist the composer in any way they could. These young people enjoyed meeting in lively cafés and going to parties, theater, and opera.

Unlike Beethoven, whom he adored, Schubert did not ponder days or years about the form or type of music he would compose. A bubbly melody entered his head and he simply wrote it down. One evening at his favorite café, a friend recited the Shakespeare poem "Hark, Hark, the Lark." Quickly Schubert drew some lines on the back of the menu and in a short time a complete song was born.

During his early career he never wrote music with the thought of being paid. His friends recognized his talent and introduced him to the famous singer Johann Michael Vogl, who sang Schubert's melodies on every possible occasion. Despite himself, Schubert was beginning to be known as a talented person.

And then there were the Schubert musical evenings held at a friend's house. With plenty of sparkling wine, Vogl sang Schubert's latest lovely melody with the composer himself at the piano, his short, fat fingers trying to keep up with his inspired imagination. His friends had nicknamed him "Schwammerl" (Tubby) because he had grown quite stout and would much rather compose dances than do them. At the evening's end, he would be urged to play a lilting tune, one of the three hundred minuets, waltzes, or galops he might very well have composed for gatherings such as these.

His irregular life was hard on his health. By 1822 he had become seriously ill. Depressed and bothered constantly by debts and poverty, he died six years later at the age of thirty-one.

At first it seemed as if Schubert's music died with him. Then suddenly, almost like a windstorm, from musty attics, old, dirty trunks, locked cupboards, and other storage places, manuscripts appeared by the hundreds. Some compositions may still be tucked away somewhere under cover and left to rot from old age.

Now we know of more than six hundred songs, nine symphonies, piano compositions, and beautiful chamber music, splendid melodies that will stay with us forever.

Schubert Museum, Nussdorfer Strasse 54. Open daily 9 A.M. to 4 P.M., Sunday 9 A.M. to 1 P.M.; closed Monday.

Through the back door of the house where Schubert was born you enter a courtyard. Before going inside notice the fountain statue of the lovely maiden. It's called "Die Forelle" (The Trout) and was inspired by one of Schubert's songs.

On display within the house are pictures, letters, certificates, manuscripts, and other mementos left by Schubert. Look closely at his piano, the porcelain stove, and his easy chair. Find the picture of the composer at sixteen, his devoted singing friend Vogl, and all of the happy group that met for musical evenings. You'll also see his iron-framed spectacles and a lock of his red-brown hair. Among the manuscripts seek out the score to "Hark, Hark the Lark."

Before leaving, enjoy the garden. Its flowers are the ones that bloomed when Schubert was alive. This portion of Vienna where the house stands is almost as it was 150 years ago. There are scores of quaint two-story houses with low tiled roofs and tiny windows which show you today the same scenes as in Schubert's time.

JOHANN STRAUSS, JR.: THE WALTZ KING (1825–99) "Shocking! Wild! Young people will be ruined by it." Everyone was gossiping about a wicked new dance, the waltz. All agreed it was the dance of the future.

It started in Upper Austria as a peasant dance with mad hopping, stamping, and gliding. Finally the male partner with two hands on his girl's waist would lift her up in the air with a loud "yah!" The songs were originally composed to accompany people working in the field, sowing, reaping, gathering crops.

As the dance moved from the country to the city and onto smoothly polished dance floors, the hopping and skipping disappeared and became mainly gliding. By the nineteenth century the dance took on a different quality. Couples began by swaying back and forth, ever so gently. Then with nimble steps they began to make small circles, slowly, slowly. Soon the music became more vigorous, the dancers' circles became larger. The dancers became one with the music as they gracefully circled the entire ballroom almost as if floating on air.

Johann Strauss, Jr., and his father before him wrote music which was not just a fad of the day. It proved to be as lasting as a classic symphony or opera. For Johann Jr., lovingly called "Schani," his talent was almost stopped before it could flower.

When he was sure his father was sound asleep, five-year-old Johann Jr. would steal into the workroom to look at the wonderful instruments the men in the orchestra played. There they were—the cello, the clarinet, the flute, the violin. No, that was not a violin. It was a contrabass, a huge violinlike instrument that is played with a bow in a standing position. The tone that came out was the deepest sound he had ever heard.

Johann Jr. loved everything about music and wanted desperately to learn all he could. One evening he was allowed to watch his father conduct in one of Vienna's lovely ballrooms. When he was forced to leave he pledged that he would duplicate his father's success and be a part of this exciting musical world. His father would hear nothing of it. Perhaps he feared the competition or maybe he was protecting his son from the difficult life he would live. Strauss's mother understood her son's desire to play and compose music. When her husband was away on one of his longer tours she engaged a teacher for the boy.

At the age of nineteen, Johann Jr. felt he was ready to conduct his own orchestra. He arranged all the necessary city permits and organized a group of musicians. They rehearsed endless hours getting ready for the opening night.

When his father found out, he was in a rage. He told a close friend to have a large number of people jeer and boo at the first performance. When the gala evening came, all of Vienna was excited. The great Strauss's son was making his debut. Could he possibly be as good as his father?

It was late in the afternoon and not very warm. Yet the crowds in the Great Hall of Domeyers Restaurant kept coming in until five thousand people had arrived and the heat was impossible. At the appointed hour of six, the door onstage opened and Johann Jr. made his appearance. A murmur and an occasional hiss came from the crowd. The young man took his violin, tilted the bow, looked at his musicians, and then let his bow fall on the strings. With a mighty chord the orchestra began; the overture opened like a thunderclap. Startled faces could be seen throughout the hall and at the conclusion of the overture there was thunderous applause. Next came the "Courtship Waltz," the conductor's own work. The appointed group tried hissing again but the applause drowned them out. The audience was enchanted.

The orchestra had to repeat the selection four times. Even the men who had been sent to jeer found themselves cheering. The enthusiasm increased after each piece. The last waltz had to be played seventeen times before the sound of "Bravo! Bravo!" would quiet down.

As the crowds were shouting hurrahs, young Strauss stood quietly at the very edge of the stage. Many thought he would repeat the last waltz. But no. There was something else on his mind. Gently he placed the bow to his violin and the crowd became perfectly still. Softly the melody of a different waltz was heard. He could play no further. Everyone recognized one of his father's own waltzes as thousands shouted together, "Hurrah for Johann Strauss!"

Just as the beginning of his career was difficult, so was the start of his most famous waltz, "Blue Danube." He had been asked to write a vocal piece for a change, a work for many voices. He came across a poem he liked which had a phrase repeated a number of times, "On the beautiful blue Danube." The magnificent river had castles, craggy hills, and charming towns, but it was not blue. This did not disturb him. He presented his new work before an excited audience. When the chorus was through the audience reacted politely. The composer was stunned. He was used to stormy applause. The reception of the waltz pained him. There was something in this selection that was special. He would rework it with new words and fuller orchestration, and present it again.

He chose the Paris World's Fair of 1867 to introduce the new version. This time the waltz was a hit. It exploded like a chain of Chinese firecrackers lighting up the sky. From Paris it traveled through the world. It was hummed, sung, whistled, and played as no other music had ever been.

Then Johann Jr. felt he wanted to try something bigger. He decided on the musical theater. Here his singable tunes would have colorful costumes and bright scenery. He would tell amusing stories with comic characters. As a format, he chose the operetta, the "little opera" which had been introduced in Paris by Jacques Offenbach. His first big success was *Die Fledermaus* (The Bat). It has all kinds of songs, marches, and dances. The high point in the show is when the entire cast, attending a masked ball, simply sweeps the audience into an unforgettable waltz tempo. His later operettas were also successful, but one more than the rest, *The Gypsy Baron*. The action is in Hungary and tells of Sandor Barinkay, who is returning to his ancestral home after leaving as a child. He finds it taken over by gypsies, who have made it their home. By the end he falls in love with one of them, Saffi.

Johann Jr. loved the life of his city with all his heart. He took pleasure in being close to the people who on warm summer nights would stroll aimlessly along the great avenues or drive into the country and wander among vineyards. How right it seemed for people to sing out at jolly dances where there was no end of laughter and merriment. This was why he wrote "Tales of the Vienna Woods," "Voices of Spring," "The Artist's Life," "The Emperor Waltz," and more than five hundred waltzes, so many he could not remember their titles.

Here are a few places to visit to help you understand more about this amazing man.

The Johann Strauss, Jr., monument is in the STADTPARK. The setting is almost from an operetta. Vivid flowers and greenery surround the area. The floating genii, which form an arch about the statue, seem to be moving to the strains of a Strauss melody. Perched on a stand with his violin in hand, Strauss seems ready to begin playing. What would you like to hear?

A second monument in the RATHAUSPARK (Town Hall Park) is of his father and Joseph Lanner, who first took the simple tunes of the farmers, vintners, and laborers and created the Viennese waltz. Strauss Sr. improved upon his work and became his partner for a while. The two statues are exact likenesses of the men. Behind the statues is a scene of people whirling around the dance floor. If you listen carefully you may even hear the orchestra in the background.

While you're here, take a few minutes and look around the park itself. It is the largest park in the center of the city and was laid out over a hundred years ago. Families of wild ducks nest here; in the summer storks, pelicans, and flocks of peacocks cross the paths. During Easter week white rabbits and curly lambs suddenly appear.

Before leaving this part of the city look over to the RATHAUS (Town Hall) building. The tower is over 321 feet high and is topped by a ten-foot figure, the iron Rathausmann, with his twenty-foot flag. He has become the symbol of the city.

The Historical Museum of the City of Vienna (Historisches Museum der Stadt Wien), Karlsplatz. Open Tuesday to Friday 9:15 A.M. to 6 P.M., Saturday and Sunday 9:15 A.M. to 1 P.M.; closed Monday.

Look for the Strauss Room. You'll find portraits of the family, manuscripts, an original writing desk, and an unusual upright piano, "Giraffen." The case goes clear to the floor. There are five foot pedals instead of the usual three. These were sometimes used for added sounds—drums, bells, triangles. The strange name may very well come from the odd shape of the piano.

The entire museum will give you an idea of Vienna's past history and life.

Learning about these great composers, seeing their memorial statues and homes may bring you closer to their music. But the music itself can express more than just the feeling of the composer. It can give you an image of a particular time, a certain place, or a group of people leaving their mark on history. Listening to Mozart's and Haydn's music, you are in a gleaming palace with exquisitely dressed people.

THE SETTING—BAROQUE

You'll hear the word "baroque" used quite often during your stay in Vienna. It refers to styles of architecture, painting, scultpure, and music. The best way to understand its meaning is to start with a visit to one of the most beautiful baroque buildings in Austria.

Karlskirche (St. Charles's Church) is a few blocks south of the Ringstrasse (Ring Street). The tall, Roman columns at either side of the entrance rise almost as high as the great round dome of the church. Designs have been carved on the stone columns to make them look as though they twist upward to the little towers on the top. The columns and the great dome differ from each other, yet they blend in a perfect harmony of form.

The word "baroque" comes from the French for "imperfect pearl" but has come to mean "irregular in form." An added explanation is that during the beginning of this period, around the 1500s, scientists had decided the earth actually leaned on its axis and did spin around. The sense of movement then became a part of all artists' creations. Looking at the curved and twisting surfaces of St. Charles's Church you can begin to understand the meaning of baroque architecture.

A story about the church relates that the columns were included in the design due to a sudden inspiration of Fischer von Erlach's, the architect. In Rome one evening he was sitting on a hill overlooking the city and caught a glimpse of both the dome of St. Peter's and the Trajan Column. He decided to combine these two beautiful forms into a single building.

All the streets surrounding the church seem to lead to the building. Most baroque buildings are in a lovely setting. The architects believed the sites of the buildings were almost as important as the buildings themselves.

Other Baroque Buildings

Baroque architecture was generally for princes. Before this time most people were poor and for that reason buildings were made of stone, something stable, mighty, and perfect. When money was plentiful princes wanted to see something for it. They built with brick and mortar. Instead of marble they used stucco, and rich, gilded churches and palaces arose in a short span of time.

Belvedere Palace, Prinz-Eugen Strasse 27. Open Tuesday to Saturday 10 A.M. to 4 P.M., Sunday 9 A.M. to 1 P.M., closed Monday. Fee: 5 schillings (20 cents), half price for children.

The palace is made up of two parts, the Lower and Upper Palace, separated by a long, narrow garden. The palace and the gardens were built from 1700 to 1725 as a summer residence for Prince Eugene as a gift to himself for winning the war against the Turks.

Lower Belvedere, at Rennweg 6A, was finished first as a temporary home for the Prince until the larger palace was completed. It now houses some remarkable baroque art. The statue "Apothéose des Prinzen Eugen" (Glory of Prince Eugene) by Balthasar Permoser shows the Prince's foot defiantly placed on a defeated Turk while several creatures clutch him tightly and move about cheering his victory. On the top, a small cupid sings of the hero's success. The subject is done on a grand scale with lots of movement. Both are important qualities to look for in baroque statues.

There are several paintings by Franz Anton Maulbertsch where men on white horses charge through the sky, angels float freely, and people show pain or happiness broadly. All of the ideas in the paintings are shown in bold manner. This is characteristic of baroque paintings.

On the crest of the hill is Upper Belvedere. Coachmen dressed in splendid finery drove carriages glittering with gold up to the palace entrance. Royal guests were ushered into rooms sparkling with chandeliers, mirrors, and gold, where fantastic banquets and receptions were held.

On the **Sala Terrena** (Ground Floor Room) notice the elaborate stucco ceilings curving in and out and held up by huge straining giants made of stone. Don't worry about the fairy castle crashing down. All of the superhuman strength and waving lines are part of the baroque "look." As you roam through the palace picture the brilliant receptions of Prince Eugene with hundreds of guests from all parts of the empire dressed in colorful uniforms and lovely gowns with glittering jewels. Inspect the royal art treasures carefully. Could you ever get to call this palace home?

Near the entrance to the Upper Belvedere Palace is a park for young people. Late in the afternoon everyone meets to have fun. You may have a chance to get acquainted with your first Austrian friend.

Schönbrunn Palace, Vienna 13. Guided tours from 9 A.M. to noon and 1 to 5 P.M. (until 4 P.M. October 1 to April 30). Fee: 10 schillings (40 cents), half price for children.

Before going inside the main palace go around to the back and look at one of the few horizontal clocks in existence. A gold eagle statue points out the time.

The palace was originally erected by Joseph I and Charles II but the Empress Maria Theresa is mainly responsible for what it looks like today. It has over fourteen hundred rooms, and the Empress had a difficult job of keeping track of everyone's living quarters. She had sixteen children. Court rules insisted that each member of the royal family have his own bedroom, drawing room, reception room, antechamber, and study even if he was still a babe in arms. Guests wishing to see everyone had to chase upstairs and downstairs and along endless halls so that everyone was in the right order beginning with the oldest son.

You can spend many hours exploring Schönbrunn, wandering through the forty rooms open to visitors. The Grand Gallery is a long hall with candelabras, glistening chandeliers, frescoed ceilings, and elaborate decorations. There are rooms where Napoleon lived on two occasions when he came to Vienna as a conqueror. In the Hall of Ceremonies Mozart gave concerts. A picture will show you exactly what these events looked like.

Best of all are the cozy living quarters of the Empress, her family, and her successors. The whole palace still breathes life. Perhaps it is because the Viennese love this palace and keep streaming back to be part of its past glories.

The Park

Schönbrunn Zoo. Maria Theresa opened this herself in 1752. Long before that time Emperor Maximilian II decided to produce a spectacle by driving in a carriage drawn by eight white horses followed by courtiers carrying parrots, a troop of monkeys, a camel, a dromedary, and then the not-to-be-forgotten elephant. The Viennese thought it was wonderful and from that moment on the elephant became the ruling favorite in the zoo.

You can see a new aquarium, rare tropical fish, and curious alpine animals, all in a baroque setting.

Wagenburg (Coach Room). Open every day 10 A.M. to 9 P.M. (to 4 P.M. October 1 to April 20). Fee: 5 schillings (20 cents).

A unique collection of coaches and carriages are housed in the Empress Elizabeth's former winter riding school. History seems to come alive here. Examine the royal coach of Charles VI, which he rode in on the day he became Emperor. It is 250 years old and is said to be the most beautiful coach in the world. The other, very different coronation coach belonged to Napoleon when he crowned himself King of Lombardy. Glancing out into the park, you can imagine his son, the little King of Rome, driving in his white and gold children's carriage pulled by white sheep.

THE CURTAIN RISES—SIGHTS AND SOUNDS OF THE CITY

Vienna in the twelfth century was a major market for traders en route between the Mediterranean world and the East. Young Duke Henry II, known as Henry Jasomirgott because of his often used phrase "Ja so mir Gott helfe" (With God's help), built a castle in the center of the city. He made it strong and safe by building a moat, the "Graben," around it. Beyond the Roman city walls he made a "tiefer Graben" (lower moat).

Merchants stopped their long caravans outside the gate and traded silks, spices, velvets, and ivory. Soon the city inside became overcrowded with narrow alleys leading to tiny houses built as high as possible. Down below, the street ran to the Danube, where boats unloaded precious cargo.

The streets and lanes were named after the tradesmen to whose homes and shops they led, a tradition in the Middle Ages. Today many still have the same names. The butcher's shop and home was a "Fleischmarkt" (meat market). The goldsmith's street became "Goldschmiedgasse" and the cloth dealer's "Tuchlauben."

In 1857 by order of Emperor Francis Joseph the Roman city walls were ripped down. The hopping, croaking frogs lost their homes when the moats were completely filled in. The area was smoothed out and formed a large horseshoe with the two ends going to the Danube Canal. This became a grand tree-lined boulevard, the Ringstrasse.

Directions

Vienna is an easy town to find your way around in. It is shaped roughly like a gigantic wheel with a double rim. The oldest part of the town, the "Inner City," forms the center, with the Ringstrasse surrounding it. Farther out, the outer rim is the "Gürtel," another wide highway that runs around the built-up area. The main streets run out like spokes of a wheel. To find your way you follow the house numbers on one of these spokes. The numbers get lower as you get closer to the center.

In the heart of the Inner City, at the very center of the town, towers a single steeple of the city's greatest and most easily identified landmark.

Stephansdom (St. Stephen's Cathedral), Stephansplatz. The cathedral was first built in 1147. At that time it was outside the city. As the town grew it became the center and the watchful guardian. Although wars, fires, and other disasters have struck Vienna, St. Stephen's has always been the first building to be rebuilt.

Walking around the outside of the cathedral, you see old figures which have been completely restored just as they were originally. Some of these are statues of the princes who helped support the construction of the first building. Notice the prayer benches for those who do not have enough time to enter the cathedral. Also there is the half-length figure "Christ on the Cross," showing him with a painful expression. The Viennese say it is "Christ with a Toothache."

Inside there are many details to enjoy, but two oddities are Viennese favorites. They have to do with Anton Pilgram, one of the stone carvers who fashioned the cathedral. He wanted to leave a personal testament to his greatness. So at the base of the pulpit, looking out of a half-opened window, and again at the foot of the organ support, he sculptured portraits of himself. He peeks out, cool, confident, and a little amused at his cleverness.

The pulpit itself is a wonderful piece of carving. Heads of popes and bishops give it a lively touch. The staircase winding its way upward has on the banisters frogs and lizards scurrying up and down in fear and amazement. There are many explanations about these funny creatures being here. The most likely is that the frog was the symbol of evil during this period and is being attacked by the lizard, who always seeks light or knowledge.

Get a bird's-eye view of Vienna from the "Alter Steffl" (Old Steve), the cathedral tower which you can reach by tackling the 533 steps. From here you will see the huge twenty-two-ton bell, the "Pummerin" (the Boomer), cast centuries ago from the cannons taken from the Turks when the second siege of Vienna had been broken.

Near St. Stephen's is the "Stock im Eisen," a strange relic of a tree stump. It is attached to the corner of a large building. During the fourteenth century traveling journeymen used to drive a nail into the stump to protect themselves from evil. Now, over five hundred years later, you see the trunk covered with nails.

Clock with Moving Figures. Each day at noon on the Hoher Markt, history parades in front of you as you watch lovely figurines march across the face of a colorful clock. The clock itself serves as a bridge between two office buildings. The figurines, one for each hour of the day, represent such famous people as Marcus Aurelius, the Roman emperor; Walther von der Vogelweide, the minnesinger; "Papa" Haydn, the composer;

and Empress Maria Theresa and her husband. As each figurine makes an entrance, its own special tune is played on an organ.

Hofburg Palace, (Imperial Castle) between Ballhausplatz and Josefsplatz. You further explore the Inner City here, the imperial palace and the favorite home of the Habsburgs, a German royal family whose name is taken from Habsburg Castle in Switzerland. This family ruled Austria from about 1278 until 1918. These groups of buildings are almost like a town within a town.

The man in charge is the Castle Captain, a title which goes back four hundred years. His job today is to be alert for fires day and night and to take care of all activities inside the palace grounds.

To assist him, he has a small army of workers. The Castle Captain's office can be reached through the "Swiss Gate." Climb the steep stairway past the gables and attic of the palace. You'll get a view of the palace chimneys where small boy apprentice sweepers used to have to get inside to clear the flue. The chimneys are so tiny the boys really had to wiggle their way through.

After a chat with the Castle Captain, continue your royal inspection.

Spanische Hofreitschule (Spanish Riding School). Training every day September 1 to June 30, 10 A.M. to noon weekdays except Monday. Fee: 10 schillings (40 cents). Two-hour performance Sunday at 10:45 A.M. September to mid-December and mid-March to end of June.

A different sound of music! Anyone for dancing? Your partners, eight at one time, are stunning white horses, the Lipizzaners. Watching these horses perform is like watching a lovely ballet.

Start with the Winter School itself, a pure white oblong hall. The only touch of color is the yellow sand of the arena and the painting of Emperor Charles VI in the royal box on the first balcony. The Emperor was the founder of the school.

The hall recalls the happy days of the eighteenth century when one festivity followed another. Tournaments known as carrousels were held here. Competitions in races or tilting at the ring would be climaxed by a parade of stately carriages. Then like magic the Riding Hall would be changed into a fancy-dress hall. Another switch and Beethoven is conducting a mammoth concert in 1814 with more than one thousand musicians.

Today it is used strictly as the Riding School for the horses. Each weekday, fall through spring, you can attend a rehearsal performance. It is well worth a visit although you do not get a fixed seat. The lower gallery fills up quickly. Go up the narrow, winding staircase to the upper gallery where you'll have a good view of the prancing, superbly controlled horses.

The history of these unique, world-renowned animals goes back to 1580. Archduke Charles bought a farm for mating horses in Lipizza, a town which was part of the Austrian Empire in what is now Yugoslavia. The horses are from a proud race of Spanish horses that have been famous from Roman times. For three hundred years the briny sea winds bred sturdy animals. The finest horses were taken to Vienna for training in the Winter Riding School and the best were brought back to the farms to father equally fine sons and daughters.

There is a conducted tour of the school during July and August that takes you through the stable. Don't be surprised to find pure white mares nuzzling coal-black ponies. They are born dark and at three to four years turn white. The Lipizzaner horses are late in starting their training, about eight years old. They reach the height of their career at about fourteen.

The dance steps have remained unchanged for centuries. The "passage," the first basic step, is when the horse takes small steps, always on the same spot. Sitting back on the haunches, as if begging, is a "levade." This is followed by many exacting figures until the climax, the most difficult step of all, the "capriole." For this the horse must leap into the air with all four feet at the same moment and then lunge out as if to kick.

All of the dance steps are based on natural movements of the horse. Originally the movements were part of training a horse for tournaments and battle.

Throughout the hall there are many pictures of dance positions, as well as pictures of how the hall looked when it was used for fancy-dress balls and carrousels.

For more detailed information and tickets write to: Spanische Hofreitschule, I, Hofburg, Reitschulgasse I, Vienna, Austria.

Die Wiener Sängerknaben (Vienna Boys' Choir). At the Castle Chapel (Burgkapelle). High mass on Sunday and holy days 9:30 A.M., with Philharmonic orchestra and singers. Tickets on sale Friday 5 to 7 P.M.

The Boys' Choir, with its angelic-looking choirboys, serious and dressed in sailor suits, started back in the old, narrow streets of Vienna in 1498, when boys were selected for the court orchestra of Emperor Maximilian I. Some famous men, among them Mozart, Schubert, and Haydn have been members of the group. There are about eighty boys in the choir today, forming three different groups. Two remain in Vienna, alternating singing in the Castle Chapel, while the other choir tours.

It is considered an honor to be selected a member. Twice each year an advertisement is placed in the newspapers inviting parents of vocally talented young boys to bring them for an audition. About thirty boys are chosen to come to the Augarten Palace twice a week to study seriously and take vocal lessons. Choirboys must be able to read music on sight by the time they begin performing.

After two years of study (at about ages eight to twelve), if the boy is successful, he enters the organization. From then on he lives in the palace dormitory with his particular choir. For six or seven months of the year the day begins at 7:50 A.M. with four and a half hours of academic studies and musical training.

There are about thirty teachers. After lunch and free time for sports, the boys have a three-hour rehearsal.

Three months of the year the choir tours all parts of the world. Their programs include religious music, scenes from opera and light opera (Mozart), or entire operas sung and acted in full costumes.

The choirboys receive no pay, nor do their parents pay any fees. Once selected, their training is free and all of their other living expenses are taken care of.

When a boy can no longer sing with the choir because his voice has changed, he can still live on the palace grounds free. Here he continues his education and training for his future job.

Even after the boys become men and leave the palace, music continues to be a part of their lives. The Vienna State Opera right now has ten former choirboys. Others go on to various careers, a little richer for having shared beautiful musical experiences with thousands of people around the world.

A tour of the palace where they live can be arranged by writing Dr. Walter Tautschnig, Director, The Vienna Boys' Choir, Augarten Palace, Vienna, Austria.

Be sure to see the special room which helps the boys keep a suntan all year round.

Schatzkammer (Imperial Treasury). Open 9:30 A.M. to 3 P.M. Monday, Wednesday, and Saturday; 2 to 7 P.M. Tuesday and Thursday; 9 A.M. to 1 P.M. Sunday; closed Friday. Fee: 5 schillings (20 cents).

Strike up a royal march! Make way for the King and Queen. Here you will be fascinated to find the Habsburg crown jewels, especially the crown of the Holy Roman Empire, set with precious stones, each one standing for a special idea. The crown is believed to be nearly a thousand years old. Other rare exhibits include crusaders' robes and Napoleon's silver cradle.

A GHOST STORY. Making your way from the old castle of the palace to the National Library, you pass apartments that Emperor Francis Joseph I used for honored guests. The Crown Prince of Saxony, Frederick August, nicknamed "August the Strong," was such a visitor. The story goes that once there was a sudden outbreak of ghosts roaming the palace and terrifying everyone. Prince August, who was not only strong physically but also had strong nerves, met a ghost and tossed him out the window. The next day a poor castle servant was found lying in the moat with his legs broken. From that day on the ghosts disappeared.

Nationalbibliothek (National Library), Josefsplatz 1. Open 11 A.M. to noon, except Sunday. Fee: 2 schillings (8 cents).

The Great Hall, made of cool marble, is decorated in gold. Everything in the room seems to have a sense of movement—the walls curve in and out, the scenes in the paintings (frescoes) have floating figures, the statues are ready to spring forward. These are perfect examples of baroque style.

The building is a storehouse of treasures and facts. It contains over 1,500,000 books used for research. One collection has 100,-000 letters and documents on paper, wood, and leather written in Egyptian hieroglyphics or Greek and Arabic script. Locate the original score of the national anthem written by Haydn and other manuscripts by Mozart and Beethoven. The map collection has 120,000 maps from early times. From the theater section there are over 300,000 programs and thousands of models.

The Neue (New) Hofburg Collection, Heldenplatz. Open 10 A.M. to 1 P.M. Monday, Tuesday, and Saturday; 2 to 7 P.M. Friday; 9 A.M. to 1 P.M. Sunday. Fee: 5 schillings (20 cents).

On the first floor are medieval weapons and armor—sabers, helmets, crossbows, breastplates, and much more—still one of the finest collections in the world. The armor shown was not only for princes and knights but also for horses and for children only seven years old.

Nearby is a room with ancient musical instruments—harps, lyres, zithers, and others. These go back to before the 1500s.

One particularly rare instrument is a table-top "Hausorgel" (house organ). It looks like a combination accordion and piano.

Cross the Burgring to the square with the statue of Empress Maria Theresa seated on the imperial throne. Here are two more museums. The **Naturhistorisches Museum** (Natural History Museum) has a large skull and skeleton collection, thousands of rebuilt prehistoric men. The **Kunsthistorisches Museum** (History of Art Museum) has masterpieces from all periods and countries and more works by the Belgian artist Pieter Brueghel than any other collection in the world. His painting "Kinderspiele" (Children's Games) in Room X gives you a picture of young people's play activities two hundred years ago. The games will look familiar—hoops, tug of war, leapfrog, Johnny-on-a-pony, and blindman's buff.

SPECIAL MUSEUMS

Uhrenmuseum der Stadt Wien (Clock Museum of the City of Vienna), I, Schulhof. Open Tuesday, Friday, and Saturday 9 A.M. to 1 P.M.; Wednesday and Thursday 2 to 6 P.M.; every first Sunday in the month 9 A.M. to 1 P.M. and 2 to 4 P.M. Fee: 5 schillings (20 cents).

An old house contains thousands of old watches and clocks dating back to the sixteenth century, all in excellent working order. Mr. Lunardi will give you a personal tour to show you how the clocks run. You can't find a more delightful host.

Technisches Museum (Museum of Technology), XIV, Mariahilferstrasse 212. Open Tuesday to Friday 9 A.M. to 1 P.M., Saturday and Sunday 9 A.M. to 2 P.M.; closed on Monday. Fee: 5 schillings (20 cents).

Push a button! Turn a knob! Discover many inventions introduced by Austrians. The first gas-driven car was made by Siegfried Marcus. It stands terrifyingly massive in the museum.

The same goes for the sewing machine made by Josef Mader-sperger in 1815, the first typewriter by Peter Mitterhofer, and the first supersonic rocket. Only a few years ago an old Viennese scientist, Guido Perquet, who still enjoys wandering through the charming streets, was internationally honored for originating the first plans for a space station.

Climb aboard the actual antique trains and get a firsthand demonstration of how they work. Go to the lower depths of a coal mine and have a guide show you step by step the removal of the valuable ore.

THE SHOW—LIVING TYPICALLY VIENNESE

Living Viennese is staying in buildings rich in history and tradition. It's buying in shops which take pride in selling care-fully made products for hundreds of years. It's eating a meal pampered to perfection and topped off with a splendid, dreamy dessert.

Living Viennese is looking forward to an operetta, a concert, or an opera. It's taking an old-fashioned ride in a boat or a carriage to marvel at the wonders of the city and the Danube River. It is not denying the new and modern but rather appre-ciating the old because it is comfortable and familiar like a warm friend deciding to stay for a long visit.

When the world-famous Beatles performed in Austria, a small handful of teen-agers welcomed them at the airport. During an interview one of the Beatles was asked, "What do you think of Mozart?" The reply was, "Who is he?" In their minds, the Aus-trians thought, "Who are you? We'll see in two hundred years."

Here are some suggestions on how to live typically Viennese.

OPERA, CONCERTS, AND THEATER

Staatsoper (State Opera), Opernring 2. During a bombing of the city in World War II, the building was burned. Only the front lobby, the grand staircase, and the side walls remained. The Austrians decided it must be rebuilt almost as it was and as soon as possible, no matter what had to be sacrificed. Their reputation as the home of music was at stake.

It was quite an occasion on that day ten years later when a distinguished group of artists and dignitaries arrived for the opening. It was a national holiday and everyone felt he personally helped to make it happen.

Attending a performance here, you are part of an audience which knows and appreciates opera. When the lights dim, no one dares to utter a sound. You can hear each note in the orchestra, every voice in the chorus, and all the tones of the soloist.

Find out what opera is playing from the concierge at your hotel or go to the opera house and see its beauty and elegance. The red, gold, and ivory colors are retained from the days of emperors. The stage is modern, with a floor divided into six parts which can be raised or lowered. The opening of the stage itself can be made wider or narrower. You can go into the stars' dressing rooms and through an underground tunnel to see workshops and the costume and prop rooms. During July and August guided tours are given daily, every hour 9 to 11 A.M. and 1 to 3 P.M.; from September to the end of June at varying times. Call 53356 for exact information.

Theater an der Wien, Linke Wienzeile 6. Lavish productions of operettas are presented here. You'll find yourself caught up in the spirit of the waltz.

Vienna has a world-famous orchestra, the Wiener Philharmoniker (Vienna Philharmonic). It was established more than

100 years ago and has approximately 150 members. The word "philharmonic" comes from Greek words meaning "love of music." All the men are trained in Vienna and most were born there. The orchestra performs in concert halls not only in Vienna, but throughout the world.

Wiener Urania Puppenspiele (Vienna Puppet Theater) Urania I, Ringstrasse. Shows are usually on Saturday and Sunday, 2:30 and 4 P.M. Tickets: 6 and 7 schillings (24 and 28 cents). May to September the performances are held at the Strandbad Gänsehäufel at the Danube beach.

The two-and-one-half-foot puppets tell familiar fairy tales but specialize in the adventures of Kasperl. He is usually shown as the comic tramp who always gets into trouble helping someone with a problem. The stories are told with amazing stage effects —the puppets climb trees, fly rockets—and interesting sound and lighting effects. For backstage visits, write ahead to the director, Hans Kraus.

Pleasure Park—the Prater. The Prater is a delightful six-and-one-half-mile natural park. In the sixteenth century it was the scene of royal festivities usually ushering in the spring season. The rest of the year it was home for deer who would roam around freely. By 1766 Emperor Joseph II opened it to the public and it has been a Viennese favorite ever since.

The park has many activities: A ride in a horse-drawn carriage, the "Fiaker"; boating on the lake; or a puppet show. You can bring a picnic lunch or eat at one of several cafés.

The VOLKSPRATER (Fun Fair) is crammed with booths and rides. Go way up in the RIESENRAD (Great Wheel) 219 feet where you get a spectacular view of the city. Try the charming carrousels, cave grottoes, or switchback railways. Take the LILI-PUTBAHN (Miniature Railway) to the stadium to attend a sports event, or have a swim in the huge pool. But before you take the train stop for a while to visit a unique museum.

The Prater Museum (near the Great Wheel). Open Tuesday

4 to 8 P.M., Wednesday and Friday 4 to 7 P.M., Thursday 9 A.M. to noon, Saturday and Sunday 2 to 8 P.M. Closed Monday. Fee: 3 schillings (12 cents).

One of the rarest collections in the world, the Prater Museum has over six thousand items used in this amusement park through its history.

Just by the door stands the "Watschenmann" (the Slapping Man). He is made of strong leather. Viennese boys would impress their sweethearts by slapping his face very hard, their strength being measured on a sort of clockface. The hardest slaps of all made the "Watschenmann" groan.

Prints and photographs of old rides are there by the score, including horse-drawn carrousels and the "Grottenbahn," a forerunner of the ghost train. There are also posters of circuses featuring giants, bearded ladies, and a host of other novelties from a waxwork chamber of horrors; the mechanical dolls of "Swindler's Automatic Theater"; the favorite ventriloquist dummies Maxi and Amanda; antique peep shows; and still more.

SPECIAL WAYS TO TRAVEL

The Fiaker. Vienna's first means of public transportation was the sedan chair, an enclosed seat placed on props and carried by two runners, forerunners of the fiaker, a horse-drawn carriage and driver.

In the past there had been two kinds of carriages, those with numbers and those without. The numbered fiaker-driven coaches could be used by anyone who had the price of the ride: the unnumbered coach would take only certain private customers.

The fiaker himself is called by many nicknames, anything from his favorite dish "Bratfisch" (fried fish) to "Kepfelsch-marrn" (stand-up-collar milkman). On May Day and for flower festivals, the coaches and horses are literally blanketed with flowers. They stand in front of the State Opera and alongside St. Stephen's Cathedral.

Inspect several before you make your choice. You are allowed to sit up with the driver and for an extra tip he will even let you hold the reins to guide the horse. The price is about 40 to 80 schillings ($1.60 to $3.20) for a short ride.

Boating on the Danube. If time permits, a trip on a paddle boat steamer is exciting. They operate from May 13 to September 16. You can sail from Vienna to Linz, stay and see the sights, and return the next day; or you can sleep aboard the boat. Information and tickets can be arranged through DDSG, Kärntnerstrasse 19. The best cabin costs about 125 schillings ($5) one way.

The ship sails the same route that slow-moving royal courts used when the emperors wished to visit their cousins and other relatives. In the Middle Ages, the imperial group would take several days to complete the journey, stopping at a castle or a monastery on the way. Although the Danube is not blue, the scenery along the way is beautiful.

BLEIBEN: TO STAY IN HOTELS OR CASTLES

Ambassador, Neuer Markt 5. This hotel is near the center of town in a square that once was a fruit market. Now it contains the famous Donner Fountain by the baroque sculptor of the same name. Across the way is the Imperial Crypt of the Capuchin Church, where the tombs of almost all the emperors, empresses, and archdukes of the House of Habsburg can be seen.

The large rooms are a happy combination of old and new. Each gives the appearance of a rich living room decorated in red velvet. Walls, draperies, and antique furniture match. Hidden behind a brocade-covered door is a modern bathroom.

Kings and queens have stayed here and well-known personalities like Theodore Roosevelt; Samuel Clemens, whose pen name was Mark Twain; and Haile Selassie, Emperor of Ethiopia. Franz Lehar, the composer best known for his operetta *The Merry Widow,* was a close friend of the owner. To earn extra money he played piano every Friday night in the hotel's main salon. Original score sheets of his music are framed in the lobby off the main entrance. A double room with bath is about 550 schillings ($22).

Palais Schwarzenberg, Schwarzenbergplatz 9. The hotel is right around the corner from the Belvedere Palace, where you can explore the formal gardens for hours.

A charming, quiet place to stay, the hotel is the right wing of the Schwarzenberg Palace, one of the most beautiful baroque palaces in Vienna. You get the feeling that you are living in a country mansion surrounded by rose gardens and terraces overlooking your neighbor's house, another palace. Double rooms with bath are about 450 schillings ($18).

Parkhotel Schönbrunn, Hietzinger Hauptstrasse 12. Since this hotel is next to the Schönbrunn Palace, you can take another look at the zoo, aquarium, carriage houses, or palace. The hotel was used in olden times by monarchs who were the Emperor's guests. A double room with bath is approximately 400 schillings ($16).

Schloss Laudon, Mauerbachstrasse 43. Situated among the hills of the Vienna woods, the castle was built as a fort in the twelfth century. The victorious Field Marshal Gideon von Laudon received it as a reward from Empress Maria Theresa.

You can combine castle living with having fun in a private park setting; you can swim, bowl, play tennis, ride a saddle horse, or take a gondola ride on the lake. For a change of pace, visit the castle's botanical garden, hothouses, and farm. Double room with bath starts at 500 schillings ($20).

ESSEN: TO EAT A ROYAL FEAST OR A SNACK FOR A KING

Next to music, the most enjoyable part of life for the Viennese is having good food. The day begins with a simple breakfast of milk or cocoa with rolls, butter, and marmalade.

A mid-morning snack known as "Gabelfrühstück" (fork breakfast) is an old Viennese custom. At this time you can try some delicious open sandwiches with beef, or veal "Beuschel" and dumplings, or a frankfurter sausage.

Lunch is usually eaten between noon and 2 P.M. The mid-afternoon snack called "Jause" (a little something) takes place about 3 to 5 P.M. and includes a beverage and a pastry. The favorite is Strudel prepared according to one of the old recipes used for generations. Apple is the most popular. "Topfen" is a Strudel filled with cream cheese and is another favorite. Dinner is served about eight o'clock and is very simple.

Two types of places satisfy appetites during snack time.

There are many **Konditorei** throughout the city. They are pastry or bakery shops which sell the most fantastic cakes, tarts, and miniature sandwiches. The "Kuchen" (plain cakes) and "Torten" (fancy cakes) are very typically Viennese. These are cakes topped with slices of fruit; Strudels with apple, cherry, or cream filling; delicious little pastry boats filled with wild strawberries. Best of all is the Viennese chocolate layer cake called "Sachertorte."

Demel, Kohlmarkt 14, is a place where people have been stuffing themselves for over 150 years. The shop resembles an old-fashioned ice cream parlor. The display windows are a show in themselves. Recently they featured a puppet theater made from cookies, showing scenes of Vienna.

The inside also has a lot of character. Polished counters of heavy dark wood are loaded with good things for you to sample. Elderly waitresses bustle their way among marble-topped tables, greeting customers by name. If a new waitress is hired everyone in town knows about it.

Point out your selection to the counter girl and in a little while she'll bring your plate to the tiny table. You don't have to stick to sweets. Just as good are the mushrooms stuffed with cheese, fruit salad, and delightful tidbits of liver. Ask for English-speaking Frau Gretl to help you. The prices are about 5 to 10 schillings (20 to 40 cents) for each pastry.

Other comparable places are: **Heiner,** Kärntnerstrasse 21; **Lehmann,** Graben 12; and **Sacher,** Philharmonikerstrasse 4.

Coffeehouses began in Vienna and have a lengthy history. When Turkish invaders were driven out of Vienna in 1683 they left behind some mysterious green beans. An enterprising young Polish man who had acted as an Austrian spy against the Turks discovered what they were and how to prepare them. From Vienna, coffee as a drink and the café, the place to enjoy it, spread through the world.

Today artists, composers, and little groups of friends meet in coffeehouses. Tired shoppers, businessmen, and theatergoers find them a convenient place to be refreshed.

After you find a seat, the waiter brings one or two newspapers and a glass of water, and takes the order for any one of the more than fifty different coffees. Note the various combinations —coffee and whipped cream ("Kaffee mit Schlag"), hot or cold; more whipped cream than coffee ("Doppelschlag"); and black coffee in a glass with one blob of whipped cream ("Einspänner"—one-horse coach).

You may wish to order "Schokolade" (chocolate with a saucer of whipped cream) or "Gefrorenes" (mixed ice cream with wafers).

As you look around you'll notice some people have brought a chess game, letters to write, or books to read. This is a relaxed place to spend some leisure time.

Landtmann, Dr. Karl Lueger Ring 4, right by the Burgtheater, is both a restaurant and café. You'll find many famous people meeting here for a dessert. Juliana, Queen of the Netherlands, and Sophia Loren, Italian movie star, stop in when they are in Vienna. Ask about the "Marmorgugelhupf" (chocolate and vanilla cake) or "Nusskipfepl" (nut crescent).

Kursalon Stadtpark, Johannesgasse 33, is a concert café. At 4 P.M. a full orchestra strikes up a delightful Viennese tune while you sit back and relax.

Cafe Harwelka, Dorotheergasse 6, is rather dark, a place where poets, painters, and bearded students have excited conversations. It is very informal and often the owner introduces you to the person next to you.

Some other typically old-fashioned coffeehouses are: the one-hundred-year-old **Schwarzenberg** on the Ring corner at Schwarzenberg Square: **Walter,** at Mariahilferstrasse 127A, with Viennese music in the evenings; and **Wambacher,** at Lainzerstrasse 123 beyond Schönbrunn, with a beautiful garden and Viennese music on summer Sundays.

Do go to some of the great **Restaurants.** Viennese cooking is like a waltz in the frying pan, peppered with charm, sprinkled with zest. It did not actually originate in Vienna but is a mixture of Italian, Hungarian, and Czech.

Soup is particularly good. The "Leberknödelsuppe" is a clear meat broth with liver dumplings. Veal is the king, with various types of schnitzel, usually prepared by frying thin slices of veal cutlets which have been rolled in flour, beaten egg, and bread crumbs. Another dish is the "Cordon bleu," cheese and ham rolled together, dipped, and fried. "Tafelspitz (boiled beef) is a special Austrian favorite served with a delicious sauce.

Sausages are excellent. Order a plate with a sampling of each. Note the one you really like so you'll be ready to re-order. "Backhuhn" or "Backhendl" is like fried chicken and "Stierisches Brathuhn" is roast chicken turned on a spit.

The Knödel dumpling tops the list on every Austrian menu. It is usually served with the main dish, but the "damson" dumpling, made with potato flour filled with plums and rolled in bread crumbs dusted with sugar, is also served for dessert.

And now the moment you've anticipated—those heavenly desserts. Here's a small sampling: "Palatschinken," pancakes filled with almonds and chocolate, coated with melted butter, and covered with whipped cream; "Sachertorte," layer cake covered with apricot jam and iced with chocolate; and "Krapfen," the fluffy jelly roll, a carnival season specialty.

Here is a brief list of restaurants:

Zur Linde, Rotenturmstrasse 12, is an old-timer built about five hundred years ago near the original Roman wall. Here's your chance to try the veal "Cordon bleu" while listening to lovely music, played after 6 P.M. In the summer, dine in the garden. Cost: 50 to 60 schillings ($2 to $2.40).

Gösser Bierklinik, Steindlgasse 4, is in a narrow street in the oldest part of the city. It started as the city's first tavern in 1566. Dumplings are the specialty here. Also inexpensive, with prices similar to those of Zur Linde.

Balkan Grill, Brunnengasse 13. A little outside the center, this restaurant can bring out the gypsy in you. Listen to the violins, bass fiddle, and timbal as the colorful musicians play lively melodies. Watch the waiter in his bright gypsy costume create "Shish kebab a la Gendris's Flaming Sword" as it is served with a musical flourish. Cost: very inexpensive, 30 schillings ($1.20) for a single portion. Evenings only from 6:30 P.M. Closed on Monday.

Other places to bear in mind are: **Liesinger Stadtkeller,** Führichgasse 1, near the opera in a cellar atmosphere with music in the evenings; **Smutny,** at Elisabethstrasse 8; and **Barry,** Schwarzenbergplatz 17, where you get a fast, cheap lunch, 7 to 20 schillings (28 to 80 cents). Young people eat and meet here a great deal between noon and 2 P.M. weekdays.

Vienna is famous for the "Heuriger," (new wine). Enjoyment of wine led to the development of outdoor wine gardens named for the wine in the districts of **Grinzing** and **Heiligenstadt.** Visitors know when new wine is in by the bunch of pine twigs or little bundle of hay hung over doorways. You get the feeling of being at a picnic as balloons and toys are sold and some people bring their own cold food. You can, if you wish, buy sausage, cheese, and other cold treats.

What is particularly interesting is the playing of "Schrammel music." The originator, Johann Schrammel, was born in Vienna in 1850. The tunes are performed by a small group of musicians playing on two violins, an accordion, and an unusual guitar or the long forty-stringed instrument, the zither. The songs are always folk tunes handed down from one generation to the next.

Among some of the best of these wine gardens are: **Altes Haus,** Himmelstrasse 35, and **Poldi Kurtz,** Cobenzlgasse 20. Both are in Grinzing.

WHAT YOUR GELD (MONEY) BUYS

The basic unit is the schilling. Currently it takes about 25 schillings to make $1, enough to have three or four snacks at the Konditorei. One schilling is worth about 4 cents, which will allow you to make a phone call.

EINKAUFEN: TO SHOP

TOYS

Hans Pfeiffer, Neubaugasse 57. This is a treat for doll collectors. Dolls are about 100 schillings ($4).

Walter Bucherl, Liliput Spielwarenfabrikanten 29. Special model railroads and doll's houses are about 150 schillings ($6) and up.

CLOTHES

Lanz, Kärntnerstrasse 10. Austrian native dress can be worn in the city or country. Dirndl dresses are about 400 to 600 schillings ($16 to $24). Boys' jackets and lederhosen are about the same. Sweaters are around 250 schillings ($10).

ANTIQUES

Geschenktruhe, Friedrichstrasse 10. For a different gift you might consider antique toy pots or heating irons for 70 schillings ($2.80), or charming doors from old beehives with quaint scenes painted on them, 80 schillings ($3.20). The streets all around this area are filled with stores with amazing antiques, including old horses from carrousels.

Steffl's Department Store, Kärntnerstrasse 19, has inexpensive items for you to buy.

THE FINALE—FREUNDE (FRIENDS) TO MEET

Although most young people in Vienna dress very much like Americans, in the colder months some boys still wear leather shorts called lederhosen. All year round dirndl dresses are commonly worn by girls. These are full-skirted, made of cotton, linen, or silk, often worn with a bodice and always with an apron.

School begins in September and lasts until June. The day starts at 8 A.M. and continues until lunch at noon, when students go home for a light meal. Classes begin again at 1 P.M. and last until 3 P.M. Teachers assign large amounts of homework.

The first four years are spent in the primary school ("Volksschule"). The next eight years are those of the upper elementary grades and high school, including what the Viennese call "Gymnasium." From here students go on to a trade or enter the university if they pass the entrance examinations.

Evenings are family time at home, with homework in order for school children. The night may very well be topped off with music played by members of the family on the violin, accordion, and zither, or with a leisurely hour listening to folk music, opera, or popular tunes. Good music is always the most rewarding way to end the day in Vienna.

Holidays are eagerly anticipated and are usually spent enjoying the outdoors. Skiing is the most popular sport. The season is from December through late spring. The slopes are covered with people of all ages making graceful, sweeping turns. Young children begin taking lessons at an early age. Because skiing is so popular it is not uncommon to see many people hobbling around with casts on their legs even through the summer months.

Ice skating and curling are also popular winter sports. Curling is a game played on ice in which each team has four members. Each player slides two large, smooth stones toward a target at one end of the rink. After one side scores, the players slide the stones toward the target at the other end of the rink. In other places the game is played like ice hockey, but brooms are used instead of sticks.

Summers are spent mountain climbing, camping, or vacationing at the lake. More and more young people are visiting other European countries and returning home more knowledgeable about the world around them.

STARTING FRIENDSHIPS BEFOREHAND

Bundesjugendring, Friedrich-Schmidtplatz A-1080, Vienna. This organization represents several youth groups, both educational and recreational. Be sure to write clearly in your letter what your particular interests are.

AUF WIEDERSEHEN—I'LL BE SEEING YOU

Wonderful music, delicious food, and gracious living are some of the experiences you have had during your visit. Best of all, you have met charming people who have gone out of their way to be perfect hosts. They would even avoid telling you the truth if they thought it would hurt your feelings. The Viennese with their warm, happy moods, singing and enjoying life, make you become part of the spirit of "Gemütlichkeit," cozy and close.

SPRECHEN: TO SPEAK

ENGLISH	GERMAN	PRONUNCIATION
Good morning	Guten Morgen	Goo-ten more-gen
Good day	Guten Tag	Goo-ten tahg
Good evening	Guten Abend	Goo-ten ah-bend
What is your name?	Wie heissen Sie?	Vee hi-sen zee
My name is	Ich heisse	Isch hi-sah
How are you?	Wie geht es Ihnen?	Vee gate s ee-nen
I am fine	Es geht mir gut	S gate meer goot
Thank you very much	Danke sehr	Dunk-a sehr
Speak slowly, please	Sprechen Sie bitte langsam	Sprech-ken zee bit-a lahng-sam
You speak too fast	Sie sprechen zu schnell	Zee sprech-ken tsoo schnell
You're welcome	Bitte sehr	Bit-a zehr
Please	Bitte	Bit-a
Goodbye	Wiedersehen	Vee-dehr-zehn
Pardon me, please	Verzeihen Sie, bitte	Fehr-tsi-en zee, bit-a
What is that?	Was ist das?	Vas ist das?

ENGLISH	GERMAN	PRONUNCIATION
Where is	Wo ist	Vo ist
How do I get to	Wie komme ich zu	Vee Kom-a isch tsoo
Right	Rechts	Reschts
Left	Links	Links
Right around the corner	Gleich um die Ecke	Gleisch uhm dee ek-ka
Straight ahead	Geradeaus	Ger-ad-a-aus
Can you tell me where	Konnen sie mir sagen wo	Kur-nen zee meer sa-gen vo
Do you speak English?	Sprechen Sie Englisch?	Sprech-ken zee ehng-lisch?
Will you help me, please?	Wollen Sie mir helfen, bitte?	vol-len zee meer hel-fen, bit-a?
I am looking for the hotel	Ich suche das Hotel	Isch soo-ka das ho-tel
Excuse me, please	Entschuldigen Sie, bitte	Ehn-schul-dee-gen zee, bit-a
How do you say	Wie sagt man	Vee sockt mahn
How much does it cost?	Wieviel kostet das?	Vee-ful cost-a das
What time is it?	Wieviel Uhr ist es?	Vee-feel oohr ist s
Men/Women	Männer/Frauen	Men-ner/Fraw-en
Entrance	Eingang	Eyn-gahng
Exit	Ausgang	Aus-gahng
Drugstore	Drogerie	Dru-ge-rie
Barbershop	Friseur (Herren)	Frah-seur
Toilet	Toiletten	Toil-let-ten
1	eins	eynz
2	zwei	tswhy
3	drei	dry
4	vier	fear
5	fünf	fuhnf
6	sechs	sex
7	sieben	seeb-en
8	acht	acht
9	neun	nawyn
10	zehn	tsehn

ENGLISH	GERMAN	PRONUNCIATION
11	elf	elf
12	zwölf	tswolf
13	dreizehn	dry-tsehn
14	vierzehn	fear-tsehn
15	fünfzehn	fuhnf-tsehn
16	sechzehn	sex-tsehn
17	siebzehn	seeb-tsehn
18	achtzehn	acht-tsehn
19	neunzehn	nawyn-tsehn
20	zwanzig	tswan-such
50	fünfzig	fuhnf-sich
100	hundert	hoon-dert

FEIERTAGE: HOLIDAYS

January 6	**Celebration of Epiphany.** On the eve young carolers (street singers) dress in costume and go from house to house lighted by torches and lanterns. Next day men and boys wear strange masks in custom called "Perchten," a centuries-old tradition to scare winter away.
Thursday Following the eighth Sunday after Easter	**Corpus Christi.** Parade of flower floats. Battle of flowers in Prater Park.
June–September	**Sound and Light.** Belvedere Palace Park at 8:30 P.M.
Early July–early September	**Strauss Concerts.** Theater an der Wien, in the arcades of City Hall, and in parks.
Mid-September	**International Fall Fair.**
September–October	**Harvest Festivals.** In Grinzing, a parade of floats in mid-October.
December 6	**St. Nikolas Day.** Festivities throughout city. Austrian Santa Claus (St. Nikolas) and devilish assistant (Krampus) visit good children with sweets and bad children with pretended punishment.

EUROPEAN NATIONAL
TOURIST OFFICES
IN THE UNITED STATES

Austrian National Tourist Office
545 Fifth Avenue
New York, New York 10017

Suite 1401
332 South Michigan Avenue
Chicago, Illinois 60604

3440 Wilshire Boulevard
Los Angeles, California 90017

2433 North West Lovejoy Street
Portland, Oregon 97210

British Travel Association
680 Fifth Avenue
New York, New York 10019

39 South LaSalle Street
Chicago, Illinois 60603

612 South Flower Street
Los Angeles, California 90017

Danish National Travel Office
505 Fifth Avenue
New York, New York 10017

612 South Flower Street
Los Angeles, California 90017

French Government Tourist Office
610 Fifth Avenue
New York, New York 10020

18 South Michigan Avenue
Chicago, Illinois 60603

9418 Wilshire Boulevard
Beverly Hills, California 90212

323 Geary Street
San Francisco, California 94102

German National Tourist Office
500 Fifth Avenue
New York, New York 10036

11 South LaSalle Street
Chicago, Illinois 60603

323 Geary Street
San Francisco, California 94102

Irish Tourist Board
590 Fifth Avenue
New York, New York 10036

135 South LaSalle Street
Chicago, Illinois 60603

681 Market Street
San Francisco, California 94105

Italian Government Travel Office
626 Fifth Avenue
New York, New York 10020

203 North Michigan Avenue
Chicago, Illinois 60601

St. Francis Hotel
Post Street
San Francisco, California 94119

Netherlands National Travel Office
605 Fifth Avenue
New York, New York 10017

681 Market Street
San Francisco, California 94105

Swiss National Tourist Office
608 Fifth Avenue
New York, New York 10020

661 Market Street
San Francisco, California 94105

Stan Raiff is an experienced educator and knowledgeable about the field of travel. His professional career began as the Children's Theater Director at Syracuse University and as a special teacher for the Arlington, Virginia, County School System. His association with travel includes working for the Western Pacific Railroad Company on educational projects, the European Travel Commission, a non-profit organization of the twenty-one nations of Western Europe and Alitalia Airlines. Currently Mr. Raiff is director of Youth Market Counsel, a division of the National Student Marketing Corporation in New York City.